"In this collection of essays, the mature wisdom of Maxwell Johnson and new insights from the fresh eyes of his doctoral students combine to provide a rich feast for liturgical scholars and students alike. These studies will inspire further reflections on the eucharistic prayer, East and West, past and present."

—Bryan D. Spinks, Bishop F. Percy Goddard Professor Emeritus of Liturgical Studies and Pastoral Theology, Yale Divinity School

"This is a wide-ranging collection of impressive studies of eucharistic prayers, not only classic ones from the East and West, but of some only just beginning to be studied of Ethiopian and Maronite origins. It stands in a series of like collections edited by Paul F. Bradshaw and Maxwell Johnson. The sheer diversity of anaphoras examined and provocative issues analyzed makes this a remarkable, rewarding volume for students of the liturgy."

—The Rev. Michael Plekon, PhD, Professor Emeritus: Sociology, Religion & Culture, The City University of New York—Baruch College

"In every generation the Eucharist, the central activity of Christian worship, attracts some of the sharpest theological minds. The Eucharist is a corporate action, a locus of theological debate, a ritual of belonging and identity, and a mystery. In this collection of ten papers, we see that Christians are still seeking understanding. This collection opens up some of the most pressing questions facing us as liturgists, theologians, and worshippers; and provides us with a valuable 'state of the question' in eucharistic theology today."

—Thomas O'Loughlin, Professor Emeritus of Historical Theology, The University of Nottingham

Further Issues in Eucharistic Praying in East and West

Essays in Liturgical and Theological Analysis

Edited by Maxwell E. Johnson

LITURGICAL PRESS ACADEMIC

Collegeville, Minnesota
litpress.org

Cover design by David Manahan, OSB. Illustration by Frank Kacmarcik, OblSB.

Excerpts from the English translation of *The Roman Missal* (superseded) © 1973, International Commission on English in the Liturgy Corporation (ICEL); excerpts from the English translation of *The Roman Missal* © 2010, ICEL. All rights reserved.

© 2023 by Maxwell E. Johnson
Published by Liturgical Press, Collegeville, Minnesota. All rights reserved. No part of this book may be used or reproduced in any manner whatsoever, except brief quotations in reviews, without written permission of Liturgical Press, Saint John's Abbey, PO Box 7500, Collegeville, MN 56321-7500.

Library of Congress Cataloging-in-Publication Data

Names: Johnson, Maxwell E., 1952– editor.
Title: Further issues in Eucharistic praying in East and West : essays in liturgical and theological analysis / edited by Maxwell E. Johnson.
Description: Collegeville, MN : Liturgical Press Academic, [2023] | Includes index. | Summary: "Further Issues in Eucharistic Praying in East and West is a collection of essays concerned with the origins, development, and theologies of early Eucharistic praying"— Provided by publisher.
Identifiers: LCCN 2023024460 (print) | LCCN 2023024461 (ebook) | ISBN 9780814669372 (trade paperback) | ISBN 9780814669389 (epub) | ISBN 9780814669396 (pdf)
Subjects: LCSH: Eucharistic prayers—Catholic Church—History and criticism. | Catholic Church—Liturgy—Texts—History and criticism. | Eucharistic prayers—Eastern churches—History and criticism. | Eastern churches—Liturgy—Texts—History and criticism.
Classification: LCC BX2015.6 .F87 2023 (print) | LCC BX2015.6 (ebook) | DDC 264/.02036—dc23/eng/20230825
LC record available at https://lccn.loc.gov/2023024460
LC ebook record available at https://lccn.loc.gov/2023024461

In Memoriam

Father Allan R. Bouley, OSB (+ April 22, 2023)

Scholar, Colleague, Friend

Contents

Introduction   ix
    Maxwell E. Johnson

  I. Balancing Eucharistic Origins in the Work of Gordon Lathrop and Thomas O'Loughlin   1
    Megan Effron

 II. Shaping the Classical Anaphoras of the Fourth through Sixth Centuries   23
    Nathan P. Chase

III. The Εἷς Θεός Acclamations in the *Barcelona Papyrus*: A Eucharistic Liturgy without the Opening Line of the Christian Anaphoral Dialogue   61
    Arsany Paul

IV. The Making of the Maronite *Sharar*: A Reception History for the Anaphora of Addai and Mari   85
    Paul J. Elhallal

 V. The Egyptian Origins of the Anaphora in *Mystagogical Catechesis V* ascribed to Cyril of Jerusalem   131
    Maxwell E. Johnson

VI. The Deifying Sacrifice: *Thysia* in the Eucharistic Prayers of Byzantine Basil   153
    Lucas Lynn Christensen

VII. Authority and Confluence of Traditions in Aksum:
The Heritage of the Anaphora of the *Apostolic Tradition*
in the Ethiopian *Anaphora of the Apostles*   171
Andrij Hlabse, SJ

VIII. English Vernacular Translation of the Roman Canon   217
Julia Canonico

IX. Igbo Translations of the Roman Canon: Inculturation, the Battle
for the Soul of Latin, or . . . ?   255
Joachim Chukwuebuka Ozonze

X. Recent Thoughts on the Roman Anaphora: Sacrifice
in the *Canon Missae*   287
Maxwell E. Johnson

Acknowledgments   319

List of Contributors   321

Index   323

Introduction

This volume, like its predecessors, *Essays on Early Eastern Eucharistic Prayers* (edited by Paul F. Bradshaw),[1] and my own more recently edited collection, *Issues in Eucharistic Praying in East and West*,[2] is a collection of essays concerned with the origins, development, and theologies of especially early eucharistic praying. Like those two volumes, this one also owes its origins to original research papers in Notre Dame doctoral seminars focusing on the anaphora or eucharistic prayer, which I have now had the privilege of teaching over the past twenty-six years. Where it differs from the two predecessor collections is that it deals not only with some of the traditional eucharistic prayers within the wider Christian traditions of East and West (e.g., the anaphora in *Mystagogical Catechesis V*, attributed to Cyril of Jerusalem; the Barcelona Papyrus, a topic of wide scholarly interest today; Byzantine Basil; and the Roman Canon) but to prayers generating new scholarly interest today, namely, the Ethiopian Anaphora of the Apostles, in relationship to the so-called *Apostolic Tradition*; the Maronite prayer called from its first word in Syriac, *Sharar*, in relationship to that East Syrian anaphora known as Addai and Mari; and to new approaches in anaphoral development in general.

Again, like its immediate predecessor volume, *Issues in Eucharistic Praying, Further Issues* is organized thematically rather than chronologically, especially because the various anaphoras and other issues dealt with often come from within the same historical periods, although from differing churches and/or geographical areas. The first essay, however, Megan Effron's "Balancing Eucharistic Origins in the Work of Gordon Lathrop and Thomas O'Loughlin," does direct us back chronologically

---

1. *Essays on Early Eastern Eucharistic Prayers*, ed. Paul F. Bradshaw (Collegeville, MN: Liturgical Press, 1997).
2. *Issues in Eucharistic Praying in East and West: Essays in Liturgical and Theological Analysis*, ed. Maxwell E. Johnson (Collegeville, MN: Liturgical Press, 2010).

to New Testament and other early Christian documents with regard to the origins of the Eucharist. In my *Theology* review of Thomas O'Loughlin's 2015 study, *The Eucharist: Origins and Contemporary Understandings*,[3] I made the suggestion that it be read in tandem "with Gordon Lathrop's *The Four Gospels on Sunday: The New Testament and the Reform of Christian Worship*,[4] who argues unapologetically for a Christocentric Eucharistic focus. Indeed, these two books together would make for a lively seminar in Eucharistic origins."[5] This is precisely what Effron does in providing a critique and comparative analysis of Lathrop's christological model for early eucharistic meals, based on the theology of the institution narratives in the Gospels, together with Paul in 1 Corinthians 11, with O'Loughlin's more theocentric approach based on the *Didache* and the overall meal fellowship of early Christianity centered in its *eucharistia*, that is, its prayer of thanksgiving to the Father, especially in early Christian documents like the *Didache*, where there is no narrative of institution.

The second essay, Nathan Chase's "Shaping the Classical Anaphoras of the Fourth through Sixth Centuries," surveys both anaphoral texts and contemporary scholarship on those texts. He notes that, while scholars have long listed a number of influences that led to the development of the classical anaphoras, most of the influences on eucharistic praying that have been highlighted are post-Constantinian, or fourth and fifth century. Chase underscores that the possible presence of the *Sanctus* and epiclesis in third-century eucharistic texts necessitates also attending to pre-Constantinian influences as well, not only in texts but in social and cultural contexts as well. Chase's essay was well received in the Problems in the Early History of Liturgy Seminar at the 2022 meeting of the North American Academy of Liturgy.

Arsany Paul, in the third essay, "The Εἷς Θεός Acclamations in the Barcelona Papyrus: A Eucharistic Liturgy without the Opening Line of the Christian Anaphoral Dialogue,"[6] provides a detailed overview

---

3. Thomas O'Loughlin, *The Eucharist: Origins and Contemporary Understandings* (London and New York: Bloomsbury T&T Clark, 2015).

4. Gordon Lathrop, *The Four Gospels on Sunday: The New Testament and the Reform of Christian Worship* (Minneapolis: Fortress Press, 2010).

5. Book Reviews, *Theology* 118, no. 6 (2015): 445–46.

6. An expanded version of this article including multiple, colored images appeared in an online, open-access journal as "The Barcelona Papyrus and the Opening Dia-

of this unique feature in the anaphora, consisting of Εἷς Θεός, among others. While previous scholars (e.g., Michael Zheltov, Nathan Chase, and Alistair Stewart[7]) have argued that they represent a part of the liturgical formulary, generally replacing the staple opening of the anaphoral dialogue, Paul argues, through a detailed paleographical analysis of the phrase Εἷς Θεός with its various appendages in the liturgical portions of the manuscript (*P.Monts.Roca Inv.* 128–178, 292, and 338), and in comparison to other literary and material, visual cultural sources within Egyptian Christian customs, that these invocations are scribal practices rather than part of the pronounced prayers, and thus are "marginalia" that function externally to the liturgical formulary. Therefore, the anaphora in the *Barcelona Papyrus* is a eucharistic liturgy without the opening line of the staple Christian anaphoral dialogue. Like Chase's essay above, this one was also presented to and was well received in the Problems in the Early History of Liturgy Seminar at the 2022 meeting of the North American Academy of Liturgy.

Fourth, based on the methodology employed in an important 1993 *Studia Liturgica* article by Walter Ray on the East Syrian eucharistic prayer of Addai and Mari,[8] Paul Elhallal offers a new approach to *Sharar,* the famous anaphora of the Syriac Maronite Church, in his essay, "The Making of the Maronite *Sharar*: A Reception History for the Anaphora of Addai and Mari." In particular, he concludes that now with two anaphoras of the Syrian tradition viewed as being structured chiastically, the possibility is open to using the same methodology for the study of other Syrian anaphoras. Further, Elhallal argues that *Sharar* did not originate in West but in East Syria, and that the address to Christ in both Addai

---

logue of the Christian Anaphora: Resituating Egyptian Scribal Practices Amid Scholarly Anaphoral Reconstructions," in *Ex Fonte–Journal of Ecumenical Studies in Liturgy* 1 (2022): 129–68.

7. Michael Zheltov, "The Anaphora and the Thanksgiving Prayer from the Barcelona Papyrus: An Underestimated Testimony to the Anaphoral History in the Fourth Century," *Vigiliae Christiane* 62 (2008): 467–504; Nathan P. Chase, "Rethinking Anaphoral Development in Light of the Barcelona Papyrus" [unpubl. dissertation University of Notre Dame, Notre Dame, IN], 2020; Alistair C. Stewart, *Two Early Egyptian Liturgical Papyri: The Deir Balyzeh Papyrus and the Barcelona Papyrus with Appendices Containing Comparative Material* (Norwich, UK: Hymns Ancient and Modern, 2010).

8. Walter Ray, "The Chiastic Structure of the Anaphora of Addai and Mari," *Studia Liturgica* 23 (1993): 187–93.

and Mari and *Sharar* needs to be placed within an overall christological and polemical context, rather than necessarily reflecting a more primitive Christology as has often been assumed.

My first contribution, and the fifth essay in this collection, "The Egyptian Origins of the Anaphora in *Mystagogical Catechesis V* ascribed to Cyril of Jerusalem," was prepared originally for and presented at a conference on the Liturgy of St. James in Regensburg, Germany, in 2022.[9] This essay revisits several topics in the anaphora of *Mystagogical Catechesis V*, and argues, based on recent scholarship, that it represents not Syrian but Egyptian influence, that is, that Jerusalem and Egypt followed a similar eucharistic anaphoral pattern that scholarship would classify as "Egyptian," or "Alexandrian." Further, it challenges the use of *Mystagogical Catechesis V* as an undisputed source for the Liturgy of St. James, which represents, rather, an "Antiochenization" of Jerusalem liturgy.

In the sixth essay, "The Deifying Sacrifice: *Thysia* in the Eucharistic Prayers of Byzantine Basil," Lucas Christensen looks at the imagery of eucharistic sacrifice in this ancient Byzantine anaphora in the context of biblical and early Christian usage. He notes especially that this imagery considers the community to be Christ himself offering his eternal sacrifice in and through the assembly; it is this eucharistic oblation which continually realizes the community's identity as Christ.

Making critical use of Alessandro Bausi's text and commentary on the new Ethiopic version of the so-called *Apostolic Tradition*,[10] Emmanuel

---

9. An expanded version of this essay, "The Anaphora in *Mystagogical Catechesis V* attributed to St Cyril of Jerusalem and the Anaphora of St James," will appear in the *Acta* of that conference, published in the Studies in Eastern Christian Liturgies series (Münster: Aschendorff).

10. Alessandro Bausi, "La nuova versione Etiopica della Traditio Apostolica: edizione e traduzione preliminari," in *Christianity in Egypt: Literary Production and Intellectual Trends*, ed. Paolo Buzi and Alberto Camplani, 19–69 (Rome: Institutum patristicum Augustinianum, 2011); idem, "The 'So-called *Traditio apostolica*': Preliminary Observations on the New Ethiopic Evidence," in *Volksglaube im antiken Christentum*, ed. Heike Grieser and Andreas Merkt (Darmstadt: Wissenschaftliche Buchgesellschaft, 2009), 291–321; and idem, with Antonella Brita, Marco di Bella, Denis Nosnitsin, Nikolas Sarris, and Ira Rabin, "The *Aksumite Collection* or Codex Σ (*Sinodos of Qefreyā*, ms C_3-IV-71/C_3-IV-73, Ethio-SPaRe UM-039): Codicological and Palaeographical Observations; With a Note on Material Analysis of Inks," *COMSt Bulletin* 6, no. 2 (2020): 127–71.

Fritsch's work on the Ethiopic *Anaphora of the Apostles*,[11] and Paul Bradshaw's recent commentary on the so-called *Apostolic Tradition* itself,[12] Andrij Hlabse in the seventh essay, "Authority and Confluence of Traditions in Aksum: The Heritage of the Anaphora of the *Apostolic Tradition* in the Ethiopian *Anaphora of the Apostles*," explores the influence of the *Apostolic Tradition* anaphora on the earliest known redaction of the Ethiopian *Anaphora of the Apostles*. Central questions examined concern the extent of the influence of the Alexandrian tradition on the redaction of the *Anaphora of the Apostles* in comparison with that of the *Apostolic Tradition*, especially since Alexandrian practice is thought to have been typically dominant in early Aksum and the *Anaphora of Mark* is also found in the same manuscripts. Hlabse contends that a patient examination of the sources reveals the authority of the *Apostolic Tradition* and the theological concerns of this early Aksumite period.

The last three essays in this volume are all concerned with various issues regarding the Roman *canon missae*. First, in the eighth essay, "English Vernacular Translation of the Roman Canon," Julia Canonico provides a timely summary of the various translation and other issues involved in producing a text of the ancient Roman *canon missae* for English liturgical use today. Second, in an approach similar to that of Canonico in the previous essay, Joachim Chukwuebuka Ozonze, in the ninth essay in this collection, "Igbo Translations of the Roman Canon: Inculturation, the Battle for the Soul of Latin, or . . . ,?" analyzes the 1971 and 2017 translations of the Roman Canon into the Nigerian language of Igbo. Complete with the two Igbo translations in parallel columns, Ozonze provides a critical look at the process of translation, in light of new translation requirements stemming from *Liturgiam authenticam*. Together with a critique of that document as well, Ozonze argues that the

---

11. Emmanuel Fritsch, "New Reflections on the Image of Late Antique and Medieval Ethiopian Liturgy," in *Liturgy's Imagined Past/s: Methodologies and Materials in the Writing of Liturgical History Today*, edited by Teresa Berger and Bryan D. Spinks (Collegeville, MN: Liturgical Press, 2016), 39–62. "The Anaphoras of the Ge'ez Churches: A Challenging Orthodoxy," in *The Anaphoral Genesis of the Institution Narrative in Light of the Anaphora of Addai and Mari*, ed. Cesare Giraudo, OCA 295 (Rome: Edizioni Orientalia Christiana/Lilamé: Valore Italiano, 2013), 275–317.

12. Paul F. Bradshaw, *Apostolic Tradition: A New Commentary* (Collegeville, MN: Liturgical Press Academic, 2023).

1971 translation was far superior as an inculturated text in Nigeria and expresses hope, in light of Pope Francis's 2017 *motu proprio Magnum prinicipium*, wherein the pope highlights "the need for vernacular translations that are accessible to the people and expressive of their language while taking care that they be congruent with sound doctrine," for a truly inculturated text and not simply a text that reflects, in his words, "the soul of Latin."

The final essay, and my second contribution, "Recent Thoughts on the Roman Anaphora: Sacrifice in the *Canon Missae*," has its origins as a presentation in the "On the Way Seminar" of the North American Academy of Liturgy comprised of both Roman Catholic and Lutheran participants. Since the question of eucharistic sacrifice continues to be an issue that divides Roman Catholics and Lutherans, I revisit a number of the critical issues needing to be addressed. In particular I argue that the theology of sacrifice in the Roman Canon should be read as a Patristic theology akin to the theology of sacrifice in the "Greek canon" (i.e., the anaphoras of Chrysostom and Basil), which the Lutheran confessions actually find acceptable. Hence, the theology of sacrifice in the Roman *canon missae* should not constitute a stumbling block toward unity, although the recent English translation of the Canon makes the interpreter's task more difficult than it needs to be.

Let me underscore that again, like its predecessor volume, this collection introduces the reader to current doctoral students in and recent graduates of Notre Dame's doctoral program in liturgical studies. As such, it not only provides some cutting-edge research on the eucharistic prayer or anaphora in the liturgical traditions of East and West but also a beginning "who's who" to watch in the field of early liturgical scholarship in the future. As I move into retirement, I could not be more pleased to introduce these young scholars to a wider readership.

Finally, I want to acknowledge those people who have made this collection possible. Thanks go to the contributors themselves for trusting me to include their previously unpublished work here for the first time. My thanks go also to my student, Father Arsany Paul, for his assistance in proofreading and for preparation of the index. Finally, I wish to thank both Therese Ratliff and Hans Christoffersen of Liturgical Press in Collegeville, Minnesota, for their willingness to take on this project and see it through to publication under the Liturgical Press Academic imprint.

In addition, this book is dedicated to the memory of Allan Bouley, OSB (d. April 22, 2023), who taught liturgical studies at Saint John's School of Theology and Seminary in Collegeville from 1969 to 2008. Father Allan's *From Freedom to Formula: The Evolution of the Eucharistic Prayer from Oral Improvisation to Written Texts* (Washington, DC: Catholic University of America Press, 1981) remains a classic must-read in anaphoral development.

Maxwell E. Johnson
September 14, 2023
Feast of the Exaltation of the Holy Cross

Balancing Eucharistic Origins in the Work of Gordon Lathrop and Thomas O'Loughlin

Megan Effron

In his book, *Models of the Eucharist,* Kevin Irwin places ten different models for understanding the Eucharist side by side,[1] emphasizing that they are all "intrinsically interrelated, complementary, and mutually enriching."[2] Comparing the Eucharist to a jewel with many facets, Irwin believes "it is best appreciated when light is shed upon it from various directions and then it is viewed from various angles."[3] Such an approach enables him to uplift the great breadth of eucharistic theology from the Christian tradition without degenerating into polarizing rhetoric or emphasizing one single aspect against another in a mutually exclusive way. Irwin regards questions like "Is it a sacrifice or a meal?" as unhelpfully polemical, believing that "both of these helpful and traditional terms . . . deserve better than to be placed over against each other."[4] For Irwin,

---

1. The titles of his ten models are as follows: Cosmic Mass, The Church's Eucharist, The Effective Word of God, Memorial of the Paschal Mystery, Covenant Renewal, The Lord's Supper, Food for the Journey, Sacramental Sacrifice, Active Presence, and Work of the Holy Spirit.
2. Kevin Irwin, *Models of the Eucharist* (New York: Paulist Press, 2005), xiv.
3. Ibid.
4. Ibid., 4. Irwin specifically refers to polarization in the U.S. Catholic Church by drawing upon polling data.

juxtapositions lead not to competition but to complementarity. I seek to imitate his approach by placing the eucharistic theologies of Gordon Lathrop and Thomas O'Loughlin in conversation with one another, in the hope that their different angles might be mutually enriching. Both point to early Christian meal fellowship as a source of reform for modern eucharistic practice, but Lathrop's thesis is Christocentric, arguing that in the Eucharist we remember and encounter the crucified risen Christ, while O'Loughlin's thesis is theocentric, arguing that we bless and thank the Father (through Christ) for all God's gifts. My assessment is that we need not choose between the two; reading them side by side reveals that both of these eucharistic emphases were present early on in Christian practice, and both have something to say to our worship today. This study will proceed by comparing their methodologies, summarizing their main arguments, and examining the evidence for their respective claims. I will conclude by revealing the way in which they each offer constructive critiques of the other. Reading these studies together sheds light on their respective blind spots and better illuminates our understanding of the Eucharist.

Methodologies and Main Arguments

Lathrop's Methodology

As evidenced by his title, *The Four Gospels on Sunday: The New Testament and the Reform of Christian Worship*, Lathrop's exploration of early Christian meal fellowship is confined to an analysis of Scripture. The trajectory of the book follows three main questions: "What are the Gospels? What did they say about ancient Christian worship? What do they say to Christian liturgical assemblies today?"[5] As a self-described "liturgical theologian of the late twentieth and early twenty-first century," Lathrop sees this work as a "return to the place where [he] began . . . to explicit biblical studies."[6] While his trilogy of liturgical scholarship remains implicit in the background, Lathrop explicitly examines each of the four Gospels in detail—critically analyzing their respective literary

---

5. Gordon W. Lathrop, *The Four Gospels on Sunday: The New Testament and the Reform of Christian Worship* (Minneapolis: Fortress Press, 2012), xi.

6. Ibid., xiii–xiv. Lathrop completed his doctoral studies in New Testament with a dissertation on Mark.

structures and proposing the assembly as their intended audience and proper historical context.[7] He calls his methodology "biblical-liturgical thought—biblical studies aware of Christian worship, worship studies caring about the Bible," and recognizes that scholars engaging in this task may be "skating on thin ice."[8] Seeking to distance himself from the "panliturgism" of scholars who erroneously "find liturgy everywhere," Lathrop rejects the work of several scholars who claimed to discover a liturgical context behind New Testament writings,[9] but whose work has been debunked due to lack of evidence.[10] While Lathrop is wary of panliturgism, he also critiques overly apophatic tendencies in scholarship: "It has become common to argue in recent biblical studies that relatively little can be said about the worship of the communities that were addressed by these letters or that made use of the Gospel books."[11] Acknowledging that the texts are "not interested in any systematic report of communal worship, and the local situations were most likely quite diverse," Lathrop nevertheless claims that the four Gospels "all presume a community, an assembly, a meeting, as part of what they are, as part of their very genre," and that this should have consequences for the way we read them.[12]

Lathrop's Main Arguments

Conceding that we cannot lump references to Christian gatherings in the New Testament into one cohesive portrait and then refer to it as early Christian worship, Lathrop offers a tempered thesis that there is "a kind of mutual coherence between the four Gospels and the ancient Christian Sunday meetings."[13] This is not to say that the Gospels and assemblies were "co-extensive"; the Gospels do not constitute "direct

---

7. The titles of Lathrop's three major liturgical texts are as follows: *Holy Things: A Liturgical Theology* (Minneapolis: Fortress Press, 1993), *Holy People: A Liturgical Ecclesiology* (Minneapolis: Fortress Press, 1999), and *Holy Ground: A Liturgical Cosmology* (Minneapolis: Fortress Press, 2003).

8. Lathrop, *Four Gospels on Sunday*, 4.

9. Philip Carrington's *The Primitive Christian Calendar: A Study in the Making of the Marcan Gospel* and Aileen Guilding's *The Fourth Gospel and Jewish Worship*.

10. Lathrop, *Four Gospels on Sunday*, 4–5.

11. Ibid., 7.

12. Ibid., 9.

13. Ibid., 5.

scripts for the meetings," and they could also have been read outside of the meetings.[14] Nonetheless, Lathrop holds that they seem to have been intended for use in community; they "presume the Christian assembly and include it within their reference."[15] He argues that all four Gospels, like Paul, address assemblies and call for continuing reform of those assemblies in diverse ways. Furthermore, the assemblies being referenced and addressed were primarily meal fellowships and "part of the intention of each of the authors was likely to have been the reform of the meal practices of the churches . . . the most likely way in which the Christians met."[16] Lathrop believes the critique of early Christian meal practices in Paul and in the Gospels provides a glimpse into the origins of the Eucharist. While Christian meal practices in the first and second century were certainly diverse, Lathrop traces a common thread running through the New Testament words of reform to assemblies: "the heart of this reform must be the encounter with the crucified risen one,"[17] and this encounter must open up into ministry, particularly to the poor.[18] Christian meal fellowship must proclaim the death and resurrection of Christ; this is the meaning of the Eucharist that emerges from the reforming words of Paul and all four Gospels. Lathrop concludes by applying these reforms to our Eucharist today, maintaining that the Gospels were not only intended for ancient assemblies, but must "be read as having something to say about the meals of our meetings."[19]

O'Loughlin's Methodology

O'Loughlin describes his own methodology as "an exercise in historical theology."[20] As evidenced by his title, *The Eucharist: Origins and Contemporary Understandings*, O'Loughlin seeks to link past eucharistic practice (origins) with the present (contemporary understandings):

---

14. Ibid.
15. Ibid.
16. Ibid., 47.
17. Ibid., 200.
18. Ibid., 55.
19. Ibid., 156.
20. Thomas O'Loughlin, *The Eucharist: Origins and Contemporary Understandings* (London: T&T Clark, 2015), xv.

This book deliberately does not confine itself to the study of the past . . . such as might be found in a study of Christian origins (whether that study is carried out under the banner of 'NT studies', 'origins of the liturgy', 'early Christian studies' or 'patristics'), nor of the present such as might be found in a work of doctrinal theology or an attempt to form an ecumenical bridge between inherited bodies of doctrine.[21]

O'Loughlin believes that there has been "an amazing flowering of scholarship"[22] in the above-mentioned areas, but that links among them are still lacking, and "conversations cutting across disciplines are rare."[23] His book seeks to fill that gap by bringing modern sacramental theology into dialogue with history by analyzing how eucharistic practice arrived at the place where it is today. He critically examines our "view of our inheritance (the good, the bad and the simply confusing) from the past," characterizing shifts in eucharistic practice as a series of historical displacements.[24] Emphasizing that the Eucharist is first and foremost an activity, O'Loughlin "takes as [his] starting point the actual practices of Christians in their historical particularities."[25] Privileging praxis over formal reflection or doctrine, O'Loughlin asserts that the Eucharist "belongs to the domain of human 'doing' before that of 'believing,' "[26] and intends to look at "what Christians have done and have thought they were doing when they celebrated the Eucharist . . . not only as disciples but as human beings."[27] To that end, O'Loughlin brings historical studies of early Christian meal practice into dialogue with anthropology and sociology, emphasizing that

21. Ibid.
22. Ibid.
23. Ibid., 1.
24. Ibid., xvi.
25. Ibid., 1.
26. Ibid., 2. See O'Loughlin's more recent work, *Eating Together, Becoming One: Taking Up Pope Francis's Call to Theologians* (Collegeville, MN: Liturgical Press Academic, 2019), for an extended argument about why shared ecumenical and experiential eucharistic praxis should come before the articulation of doctrine about the Eucharist. This book is O'Loughlin's response to Pope Francis's call to theologians in November of 2015 to explore questions concerning eucharistic hospitality and intercommunion, specifically whether normal Catholic practice should be changed to allow Christians from other churches to share fully in the Eucharist.
27. Ibid., xvi.

we must "take the human as meal-sharer—*homo caenarius*—seriously" in our eucharistic theology.[28] O'Loughlin further explains,

> This book will argue that assuming there are some common traits in human activity in relation to food and the sharing of food—that indeed we are food-sharing animals—helps us to appreciate parts of our inheritance from the practice of Jesus and that of the early communities, while also being rich in potential for Christian renewal today.[29]

Two central questions orient the trajectory of the book: "First, what is specific about food sharing in the fashion of Jesus; and, second, because food sharing can build up different forms of human world, what sort of world should Christian food sharing bring into view?"[30]

O'Loughlin's Main Arguments

Examining the ways in which food has "been marginalized in our thinking about the Eucharist," O'Loughlin seeks to re-situate eucharistic theology within the context of the human ritual activities of preparing food and sharing meals.[31] O'Loughlin believes that understanding the Eucharist as meal has troubled churches "both practically and theologically,"[32] observing that "in the practice of most churches this 'meal' is both atrophied and desiccated," reduced to a mere token of bread and wine.[33] O'Loughlin argues that the Eucharist did not simply emerge from a meal but that the meal itself *was* and *is* the Eucharist: the activity of disciples gathering together to share food and offer thanks to the Father in Christ for all the gifts of creation.[34] O'Loughlin believes this is a foundational understanding of Eucharist that is in need of recovery, having been lost through a series of historical displacements. The first displacement was the separation of the Eucharist from the meal; it became a new "ritual which was reduced to, and so focused upon, the recognizably 'religious'

---

28. Ibid., 64. O'Loughlin also treats this topic in *Eating Together, Becoming One*, attending to the structure or "grammar" of all meals in the second chapter, "The Grammar of Meals," 21–32.
29. Ibid., xvi.
30. Ibid., xvii.
31. Ibid., 74.
32. Ibid., xvi.
33. Ibid., 65.
34. Ibid., 45.

elements of the symposium."[35] O'Loughlin admits that we do not know the cause of this first displacement, but the second displacement, a "shift in the theological and ritual focus of participants in the Eucharist," appears to have followed from the loss of the meal. The theocentric activity of "praising and thanking the Father for all his wonderful goodness" shifted to an "event at which Christ became present in a special way in the Church."[36] This Christocentric focus impacted the ritual in a number of ways: "the *anamnesis* aspect of the Eucharist became one of historical re-enactment in time; the *eucharistic* prayer—already long severed from being a table blessing—became a *consecrating* prayer."[37] The precise timeline of these first two shifts remains unclear, but O'Loughlin asserts that "by the fourth century both displacements had taken place."[38] The third displacement shifted "the agent of the eucharistic action" by distinguishing sacerdotal ministers as mediators; the Eucharist morphed "from being the action of the community" to "the action of those with the 'power of order' for the group."[39] The "collective activity" of sharing one loaf and one cup became "the business of a specialist group . . . performing a sacerdotal action—*in persona Christi*—on behalf of the church."[40] This displacement "ritually separated the Eucharist from other prayer," by relegating "all other thanksgiving into a secondary category."[41] Discontinuity between liturgy and daily life culminated in the fourth displacement, with a "chasm" having been "set up between our ritual activity of the Eucharist and the ethical demands of discipleship," cementing a divide between the sacred and profane.[42] O'Loughlin describes Eucharistic liturgies today as "functionally docetic," claiming they undermine the fundamental mystery of the incarnation because worship "does not take place from the midst of our world . . . but arises from a sacral event that is marked off in every way from life."[43] While these displacements reveal eucharistic emphases the church has forgotten,

35. Ibid., 192.
36. Ibid.
37. Ibid., 192–93.
38. Ibid.
39. Ibid., 193.
40. Ibid.
41. Ibid., 194.
42. Ibid., 196.
43. Ibid.

O'Loughlin believes we need not be "always forgetting" but may engage in "remembering afresh": recovering an understanding of the Eucharist as the activity of blessing the Father for all creation is a necessary corrective to a current emphasis upon encountering Christ's presence under the eucharistic species, a mode set apart from the rest of creation.[44]

Examining the Sources

It is worth noting from the outset that both Lathrop and O'Loughlin draw heavily upon Paul's First Letter to the Corinthians as a foundational source, citing many of the same passages to lay the groundwork for their ostensibly contradictory claims about whether early Christian meal fellowship was Christocentric or theocentric. For this reason, I will devote particular attention to their respective interpretations of Paul. O'Loughlin primarily complements his Pauline analysis with citations from the *Didache*, while Lathrop supplements his Pauline analysis with each of the four Gospels. Space does not permit me to rehearse all of the evidence here—particularly with regard to Lathrop's treatment of each Gospel—but some general patterns will be traced.

Lathrop's Evidence:
Accounts of the Last Supper in Paul and the Gospels

Lathrop's Christocentric thesis emerges from a scriptural study of Paul and the four Gospels. As mentioned above, the goal of his study is to define the genre of the Gospels ("What are the Gospels?") and to explore their relationship to early Christian meal fellowship ("What did they say about ancient Christian worship?").[45] As such, his project is not from the outset described as a history of eucharistic origins. However, he later puts forth this thesis:

> In reading the New Testament material, I propose that we have been observing the origins of the Eucharist. Those origins are not, therefore, hidden behind the texts we have, in some inaccessible period of history. Rather, the origins are being enacted before our eyes in these texts as we see the diverse meal practices of first- and second-century Christianity

---

44. Ibid., 197.
45. Lathrop, *Four Gospels on Sunday*, xi.

were being brought under the apostolic and evangelic critique which called for these meals to show forth the death of Jesus until he comes.[46]

Lathrop observes that "with the possible exception of the *Didache* . . . materials about meal practice before Paul, are inaccessible to us, capable of reconstruction only by conjecture."[47] While the *Didache* receives a passing reference,[48] it is not employed by Lathrop as a central text for understanding early Christian meal fellowship, and it does not provide further evidence for his claim that meal fellowship must proclaim the death of Christ. In fact, Lathrop acknowledges the "absence of reference to the crucifixion of Jesus in the prayers of *Didache* 9-10," and suggests that it is "one place in need of the reforming word of Paul and of the Gospels."[49] For Lathrop, New Testament critiques of meal practice are normative for understanding the meal's meaning.

Citations from Paul lay the foundation for Lathrop's argument that the Eucharist must proclaim the cross of Christ and be an encounter with the crucified risen one. 1 Corinthians 11 is particularly important in Lathrop's analysis: "Paul wanted to urge the Corinthians to know that 'as often as you eat of this bread and drink of the cup, you proclaim the Lord's death until he comes' (1 Cor 11:26)."[50] Paul's reforming words call for the "*anamnesis* of the Jesus who was killed and yet is still encountered at table," and also remind them of the "communal and ethical consequences that follow from this proclamation."[51] Lathrop observes that Christian meal fellowship likely "made some kind of use of the Greco-Roman meal pattern of *deipnon* and *symposion*," and that its banquet ideology concerning social identity "should be seen as having deeply influenced much material in the New Testament, including Paul's interest in meals and food."[52] Paul critiques preoccupations with social status that disrupt the unity and equality of the baptized, and rebukes Christians for the "economic disparity accentuated by the practice in

46. Ibid., 55.
47. Ibid.
48. Ibid., 55, 57–58.
49. Ibid., 57–58.
50. Ibid., 48–49.
51. Ibid.
52. Ibid., 41.

the Corinthian assembly: 'one goes hungry and another becomes drunk' (1 Cor 11:21)."[53] Lathrop suggests that Paul "wanted them to consider abolishing the full meal (11:22, 34; cf. 8:8), to be replaced instead both by the accented frame of the meal (the bread of the beginning of the *deipnon* and the cup of the concluding *symposion*, both seen to speak of Jesus' death) and, perhaps also, by the weekly collection for the poor (16:2)."[54] Lathrop proposes that the social ideology inherited from the Hellenistic "supper club" may have led Paul to "make an appeal to end the practice of full church suppers, with their inevitable exclusions and inequities."[55]

The reforming call begun by Paul is taken up by each of the evangelists; Lathrop builds upon this Pauline foundation by analyzing each of the four Gospels in turn, beginning with Mark. Pointing to the predominance of house references and meal scenes, Lathrop draws out the way in which Mark's literary composition continually invites his readers (or listeners) to see themselves within these assemblies; Mark "presents a series of meal accounts that can be read as intending a reinterpretation and reorientation of the meal practices of the assemblies that read the book."[56] While Lathrop attends to a diverse range of meal scenes in Mark—"the free distribution of food to the multitudes (6:30-44; 8:1-9), the eating with tax collectors and sinners (2:16), food for the once-dead daughter of Jairus (5:43)," and so on—his thesis about encountering the crucified risen Christ in the Eucharist relies most heavily upon the Last Supper accounts. Lathrop points to a chiastic ring structure in Mark's composition that highlights the way the passion predictions are interwoven with the meal, and reveals that "the content of this center of the book, once again, is the truth about the death and resurrection of Jesus and the concern that the life of the 'house' be formed by this truth."[57]

While the other Gospels do not share Mark's chiastic ring structure, Lathrop argues that "the Markan motif of Jesus telling his disciples, in assembly, in the house, of his death, resurrection and being seen again,

---

53. Ibid., 46.
54. Ibid., 49. This presents an interesting foil to O'Loughlin's interpretation of the loss of the full meal as a displacement.
55. Lathrop, *Four Gospels on Sunday*, 50.
56. Ibid., 52.
57. Ibid., 85.

is taken up" in their respective ways.[58] Though the evangelists differ in style and method, they share an interest in the assembly; they call their assemblies to reform; and they propose that the heart of such reform must be the "encounter with the crucified risen one."[59] The accounts of the passion and Last Supper (replaced by foot washing in John) are climactic moments in each Gospel, playing a central role in Lathrop's argument that meal fellowships proclaim the death and resurrection of Christ. While the oldest account of the Last Supper is the Pauline text, Lathrop recognizes that it is "unlikely that the narrative gives us any substantial historical information about the meal of the historical Jesus in the days in which he was being arrested, tortured, and killed."[60] The institutional narratives in both Paul and the Synoptics are not employed by Lathrop as historical evidence of what Jesus literally said and did, but are better understood as a theological interpretation of the meaning of the meal:

> The so-called institution narrative (or 'words of institution,' as this narrative is called in many traditions) is perhaps best understood as liturgical catechesis about the meaning of the central Christian meal, not as originally a ritual text or a set of ritual instructions. It has that role in Paul's letter to the Corinthians and in the Synoptic Gospels.[61]

Lathrop is more concerned with the meaning behind the meal fellowship than he is with the actual ritual structure of the practice. Applying a quotation from Augustine—"the word comes to the element and so there is a sacrament"—by way of analogy, he explains:

> The *element*, in this case, is the meal practice of early Christianity, in all of its diversity, in its many ways of using and of understanding the Hellenistic *deipnon-symposion* tradition . . . the *word* is then the call of Paul and of the evangelists—all of them, in this case, continuing this concern of Paul—speaking as in the name of the risen Lord, that this meal, in whatever form it took, must proclaim the death of Jesus Christ and thus be good news for the actually poor of the times.[62]

58. Ibid., 137.
59. Ibid., 199–200.
60. Ibid., 50.
61. Ibid., 170.
62. Ibid., 55.

Lathrop qualifies this explanation by noting that he does "not mean to suggest that all the meals of the churches after the execution of Jesus and before this apostolic and evangelical reform were *not* Eucharist. Rather, the question of whether they were Eucharist or not is anachronistic."[63] He prefers to conceive of this diverse meal fellowship as being "on the way to becoming Eucharistic; they were sometimes continuations of the meal practice and meal meanings of the Jesus movement and sometimes distortions or betrayals of that practice and those meanings."[64] This acknowledgement of distortions presents an interesting point of convergence with O'Loughlin's assessment of "displacements." However, Lathrop differs from O'Loughlin in that he would not regard a Christocentric emphasis as a distortion; rather, the Last Supper accounts bring the meal under an authoritative and authentic reform.

For Lathrop, the Last Supper accounts are by no means the only meals in the Gospels that contain a reforming word for the assemblies:

> The Christian assembly, in its practice of meal and baptismal bath, ought not forget the meal of the widow or the bath of the leper (4:14-30). The Christian meal is to be like the meal with Levi (5:27-38), with the sinful woman (7:36-50), with Mary and Martha (10:38-42), with the returned prodigal (15:1-2, 11-32), and with Zacchaeus (19:1-10), to name only a few Lukan stories.[65]

Nevertheless, the great diversity of meals (exhibited here by Luke) finds its climax in the passion: "All of these meals—in the travel narrative and in the first part of the Gospel—prepare us for the final meal accounts of the book: the Lukan version of the Last Supper (22:14-38) and the resurrection meal at Emmaus (24:28-33)."[66] The death and resurrection of Jesus functions as an interpretive key in Lathrop's assessment of all the New Testament meal scenes. The three Gospels after Mark "continue to lead their readers to the passion story, that remembrance of the crucified one which Mark had already proposed as the central concern of faithful

---

63. Ibid.
64. Ibid.
65. Ibid., 47.
66. Ibid., 116.

assemblies."[67] While early Christian meal practices vary, the New Testament meaning of the meal remains consistent: "Into the midst of this diverse practice, Paul and the evangelists urged the direct proclamation of the cross."[68]

O'Loughlin's Evidence: Paul and the Didache

In contrast to Lathrop, O'Loughlin views a Christocentric emphasis in meal fellowship as a later displacement. He believes undue weight attributed to the institution narratives has overshadowed the original meaning of the Eucharist as thanksgiving by shifting the "'direction' towards Jesus" and away from "the 'direction' towards the Father that is inherent in the early sources to which Christians constantly return."[69] These early sources to which O'Loughlin appeals are Paul's letters and the *Didache*; he observes that the "earliest securely datable reference to the religious significance of the meal gatherings of the followers of Jesus comes from Paul's first letter to the Corinthians written in AD 54."[70] Like Lathrop, O'Loughlin is also primarily concerned with the meaning of the meal rather than the precise ritual format in which it took place:

> The nature of that gathering need not concern us for the present, but simply Paul's view of that church's objective in celebrating their meal. . . . Paul, distressed about the implications of certain of the group's practices at their regular meals together, offers a theological reflection on what he sees as the significance of sharing a loaf and a cup.[71]

In contrast to Lathrop's interpretation, O'Loughlin argues that the primary significance for Paul is not the proclamation of Christ's death, but the offering of thanksgiving to the Father:

> Paul then underlines the theme of a right way of sharing within the whole meal by an appeal to an origin story, focused on the expression of thanking God, as the basis of the practice (11:23-9). Yet while explaining their

---

67. Ibid., 96.
68. Ibid., 56.
69. O'Loughlin, *Eucharist,* 28–29.
70. Ibid., 43.
71. Ibid.

fellowship (or the lack of it) in terms of their meal being a sharing in the body and blood of Christ (10:14), Paul is clear that the focus of the attention in uttering these blessings is the Father. They offer praise to God, the Father, and can do so because they are in Christ. This community in thanking the Father acts in contrast to those with many so-called gods: 'for us there is one God, the Father, from whom all things and for whom all things exist, and one Lord, Jesus Christ, through whom all things and through whom we exist' (8:6).[72]

In citing Paul's account of the Last Supper, O'Loughlin does acknowledge its memorial character—"gathering for the meal proclaims the Lord Jesus' death util he comes (11:26)"—but he emphasizes that "to be waiting on his return is to be waiting for him who 'delivers the kingdom to God the Father' (15:24)."[73] O'Loughlin's reading of Paul highlights that the "fundamental dynamic of the Eucharist—as with all Christ-based activity—is thanks directed to the Father by us 'in Christ.' "[74] Participation in Christ points us to the Father; it is this proper orientation of prayer that concerns Paul. He reminds the Corinthians that the Father is the one to whom their sacrifice of praise must be directed:

> In the act of properly sharing the cup and loaf of the Lord, they offer a sacrifice not to demons but to God (10:20) . . . Paul cannot imagine any true prayer—such as a meal's prayer of thanks—as being directed anywhere but to God—and for the followers of Jesus, this is a prayer placed before God, the Father, through Jesus.[75]

Thanking the Father is not only the "fundamental dynamic of the Eucharist" but it is in fact the central activity of all prayer, and of the life of discipleship in general: "In our prayers for you we always thank God, the Father of our Lord Jesus Christ" (Col 1:3).[76] O'Loughlin interprets Paul as situating the meal within the context of all Christian life, the culmination of all thanksgiving.

---

72. Ibid.
73. Ibid.
74. Ibid.
75. Ibid.
76. Ibid., 27.

O'Loughlin pairs citations from 1 Corinthians with Paul's letter to the Romans, recognizing that while their ecclesial context and date of composition may differ, Paul's understanding of the purpose of meal fellowship remains the same.[77] Like Corinth, Rome experienced "dissentions at the common meal."[78] Christians disagreed about what to eat or even whether to eat: "Some believe in eating anything, while the weak eat only vegetables. Those who eat must not despise those who abstain, and those who abstain must not pass judgment on those who eat; for God has welcomed them" (Rom 14:2-3). Paul is less concerned about the content of the meal here and more concerned with the reason for which they have come together. He resituates their disagreements within the shared purpose of thanksgiving:

> Those who observe the day, observe it in honour of the Lord. Also those who eat, eat in honour of the Lord, since they give thanks to God (*eucharistei gar tó theó*); while those who abstain, abstain in honour of the Lord and give thanks to God (*eucharistei tó theó*) (14:6).[79]

O'Loughlin sees Paul's willingness to relativize other concerns as particularly noteworthy. In an evaluation of 1 Corinthians and Romans together, he observes:

> What is perhaps most significant about these passages, written within a couple of years of one another, is that for Paul the very structures upon which he bases his teaching in one church, he is quite prepared to relativize in another, but what is not negotiable is the act of thanking God. This is the rationale for a properly conducted meal in Corinth, lest there be conduct that amounts to idolatry; this is the rationale for why the Romans should not be arguing over the details of eating together in special gatherings, for no matter what happens, as members of the church, they should be giving thanks to God. This alone is the purpose of the followers of Jesus having meals together.[80]

O'Loughlin proceeds from his analysis of Paul to an examination of the *Didache*, observing that while this text's precise date remains a topic of

---

77. 1 Corinthians was written in AD 54, whereas Romans was written in AD 56.
78. O'Loughlin, *Eucharist*, 43.
79. Ibid., 44.
80. Ibid.

debate among scholars, "one can hardly doubt that its traditions reflect usages that became well established in the first century, and with regard to its material on the Eucharist it reflects the situation before AD 70."[81] He believes the *Didache* contains "table prayers" that "reflect a clear Jewish context,"[82] and clearly highlight the importance of offering a sacrifice of praise to the Father:

> Now this is how you should engage in giving thanks (*tés eucharistias*), give thanks (*eucharistésate*) in this way. First, at the cup, say: We give thanks (*eucharistoumen*) to you, our Father, for the holy vine of David, your child (*tou paidos sou*), which you have made known to us. Through Jesus, your servant (*ou paidos sou*), to you be glory forever.[83]

The same pattern is then repeated with the bread: "Then when it comes to the broken loaf say: We give thanks to you, our Father; for the life and knowledge which you have made known to us."[84] O'Loughlin stresses that it is neither the cup nor the loaf that is blessed, but the Father Himself; the emphasis is not on the food itself, but their praise offered to God in gratitude. This gratitude is not restricted to the food on the table, but encompasses all God's gifts, particularly the gift of the covenant and God's revelation in Jesus. Jesus is the one who makes the Father known to us, but the prayers do not mention his crucifixion and death. The memorial character emphasized in the accounts of the Last Supper is not part of the *Didache*'s vision of Eucharist. O'Loughlin concludes:

> The structure of prayer in the *Didache* can be summarized thus: at the community's meal, there takes place their act of eucharist to the Father. God is blessed for the gift of the child/servant who has given them life and access to him, and so this blessing by the church is made in and through this son of David. This was to become, if it had not done so already, the paradigm for all liturgical prayer.[85]

---

81. Ibid.
82. Ibid.
83. Ibid., 44–45.
84. Ibid., 45.
85. Ibid., 46.

Conclusion: Illuminating One Another's Blind Spots

While Lathrop and O'Loughlin each seem eager to claim Paul as their exclusive ally, even this brief survey of evidence reveals that proclaiming the death of Christ and offering thanks to the Father are both important meanings of the meal for Paul. Both of these eucharistic emphases are well grounded in New Testament sources. Lathrop's study thus offers a critique of O'Loughlin's conception of history (as a series of displacements) by raising several questions: Does a Christocentric focus represent a later displacement, or was this dimension already present within the meal fellowship of some of our earliest sources? And if it is a later shift, does this change represent a problematic distortion or an authentic development?

O'Loughlin acknowledges 1 Corinthians to be the earliest datable reference to the significance of meal fellowship, and it is precisely there that Lathrop reveals a Christocentric focus. O'Loughlin's timeline of displacements appears overdrawn in light of this, particularly since he himself cannot ascribe a date to the Christocentric shift and merely observes that it is present by the fourth century. Lathrop's analysis of history contends that greater uniformity in eucharistic practice by this century may "be due not only to the fourth-century imperial interest in a unifying church but also and more profoundly to the common orthodox Christian heritage of the reforming word of the apostle and the Gospels."[86] If Lathrop were to concede that a Christocentric emphasis appeared later, he would nevertheless characterize it as an authentic, reforming development. O'Loughlin observes that eucharistic "practice and reflection can both improve and decay," and yet his own historical assessment fails to give due consideration to improvement in its focus on decaying displacements.[87] O'Loughlin is plainly reacting against the "misleading tacit assumption in many theologians' works to the effect that 'our now [perhaps with a little tweaking] is as it was intended to be'" and the "many desperate attempts to claim immunity from the ups and downs of history in the form of appeals to infallible traditions."[88] Counterbalancing such assumptions with historical contingence is laudable; O'Loughlin's willingness to admit that liturgical practice of "the now"

---

86. Lathrop, *Four Gospels on Sunday,* 57.
87. O'Loughlin, *Eucharist,* 6.
88. Ibid.

should "not simply be assumed as the ideal" is a strength of his study.[89] While his sketch of history may require greater nuance, O'Loughlin's assessment and critique of modern Christocentrism in practice remains quite persuasive:

> Go into virtually any church building when a celebration of the Eucharist is taking place, and there is a strange dissonance between, on one side, what the key liturgical actions and texts demand from their very nature and language, and, on the other, what long established prayers, customs and expectations stress as the kernel of the activity. At the heart of the celebration is the activity of thanksgiving—eucharist—and so the prayer of thanksgiving is addressed to the Father and concludes with the doxology: we make this prayer to the Father through, with and in the Christ. But the practical focus is upon the encounter with Jesus. This encounter may be presented as a recollection of his Last Supper and death, or as the coming of Jesus within the elements however this might be represented theologically, or with the fact that the prayer has as its 'product' that now there is the holy food which allows an encounter with Jesus.[90]

O'Loughlin's call for a renewed appreciation of the activity of Eucharist as thanksgiving addressed to the Father is a welcome pastoral corrective. However, Lathrop's exegesis reminds us that retrieving a theocentric emphasis need not be at the expense of a Christocentric one.

O'Loughlin offers a critique of Lathrop's study by questioning the normativity of the Last Supper accounts:

> The more we learn of the world of the first followers of Jesus, the more the notion of there being a single, original 'theology' recedes into the background. Indeed, the very notion that there is a 'firm' doctrinal datum, or a perfect causal moment such as 'the Last Supper' which institutes both the practice, the fundamental form, *and perhaps the core theological values*, appears as itself the product of the desire of later ages to resolve difficulties by an appeal to a pristine original moment whose description has all the characteristics of a supra-historical axiom.[91]

---

89. Ibid.
90. Ibid., 41.
91. Ibid., 7, emphasis added.

While Lathrop cannot be accused of interpreting the Last Supper as instituting either the practice or the fundamental ritual form,[92] he may be accused of deriving the core theological values from these accounts. Lathrop's concentration on the Last Supper is in keeping with his analysis of the literary structure of each of the Gospels; the passion accounts clearly function as the climax of the Gospels. However, one might question whether his analysis of meal fellowship relies unduly upon the Last Supper narratives, particularly considering that "the Last Supper version of the eucharistic sayings of Jesus may not have been as dominant in first-century Christianity as the existence of four accounts of it in the New Testament books may tempt us to suppose."[93]

Furthermore, Lathrop's emphasis on the Eucharist as proclaiming the death of Christ at times appears to be to the exclusion of other theological themes emerging from within Jesus's broader meal practice throughout the Gospels. O'Loughlin might ask Lathrop how the miracle accounts of feeding the multitudes fit into the framework of meal fellowship as the proclamation of the cross. O'Loughlin's exegesis of this scene in Mark's Gospel presents an alternative vision that does not make the Last Supper account or the passion his interpretive key:

> In the first feeding (6:35-44), we find this action: 'Taking the five loaves and the two fish, he looked up to heaven, and blessed, and broke the loaves, and gave them to his disciples to set before the people' (v. 41). Note the comma after 'blessed': we might think he 'blessed the loaves' but what it means is he took the loaves and blessed (*eulogésen*) the Father.[94]

Unsurprisingly, O'Loughlin highlights the eucharistic activity of blessing and thanking the Father in Mark—a dimension that goes unnoticed

---

92. "The so-called institution narrative (or 'words of institution,' as this narrative is called in many traditions) is perhaps best understood as liturgical catechesis about the meaning of the central Christian meal, not as originally a ritual text or a set of ritual instructions. It has that role in Paul's letter to the Corinthians and in the Synoptic Gospels" (Lathrop, *Four Gospels on Sunday,* 170).

93. Paul F. Bradshaw and Maxwell E. Johnson, *The Eucharistic Liturgies: Their Evolution and Interpretation* (Collegeville, MN: Liturgical Press, 2012), 23.

94. O'Loughlin, *Eucharist,* 50.

throughout Lathrop's Scriptural study. Placing O'Loughlin in conversation with Lathrop allows us to see that the proclamation of the crucified risen Christ is certainly not the *only* dimension of the Eucharist emphasized in the New Testament. As may be expected, O'Loughlin also identifies resonances between Gospel scenes like this and the *Didache*. The *Didache* itself, a text regarded by most scholars as contemporary with many of the New Testament writings, offers a critique of Lathrop's thesis by pointing to a greater diversity of meal meanings.[95] Lathrop's claim that the Eucharist proclaims the death of Christ must reckon with the historical data that "associating the bread that was eaten with the body of Christ may not have been made in every early Christian community."[96]

However, Lathrop might likewise offer a critique of O'Loughlin by raising a question about the normativity of the *Didache*: "The Didache provides no example of the golden age. Rather, it is a moving contact with one ancient Christian practice."[97] One might like to remind O'Loughlin of this. At various points throughout his study, he does seem to fall into the trap of wishful thinking or a nostalgic longing for a return to the first century, but Lathrop cautions, "The first century, even in its diversity, is not a candidate for what is sometimes called the 'golden age of liturgy.' The idea that there is such an age, always to be emulated by later generations, is a historical-theological-liturgical will-o'-the-wisp."[98] While the scope of Lathrop's study is transparently limited to an analysis of Scripture, the scope of O'Loughlin's historical investigation at times claims to be boundless:

> Although this book presumes a variety of practice and explanation as the normal situation among Christians, but because elements from that variety both in activity and teaching survived piecemeal into the later standard models, as we see them in their historical relics, it will not privilege any one strand or moment as a paradigm. . . . Treating any particular moment as normative would invoke the notion that the history of the church or its doctrine is somehow preserved from vicissitudes of time.[99]

---

95. Bradshaw and Johnson, *Eucharistic Liturgies*, 14.
96. Ibid., 24.
97. Lathrop, *Four Gospels on Sunday*, 58.
98. Ibid., 46.
99. O'Loughlin, *Eucharist*, 8.

O'Loughlin's overwhelming use of the *Didache* as the paradigm of early Christian fellowship certainly runs counter to his declaration to avoid "treating any particular moment as normative." He likewise claims to "deliberately subordinate formal reflection and doctrine to praxis," but one might wonder what is meant by "formal reflection" and how its subordination to "praxis" is possible given that our knowledge of "praxis" is only available to us through written accounts (which necessarily include some degree of reflection).[100] Both O'Loughlin and Lathrop recognize the Gospels to be formal theological reflection rather than a historical report of praxis; they both approach the Last Supper narratives as "liturgical catechesis"[101] or "explanation"[102] rather than paradigms for imitation, recognizing that "the question is not 'what did Jesus do at the last supper' but what view of discipleship did the evangelists wish to convey to an assembly about the significance of the meal their audiences were sharing as they listened to their accounts."[103] O'Loughlin, however, wants to distinguish the formal theological reflection of the Gospels from the praxis of the *Didache*:

> If we consider liturgy/community practice as 'theologia prima' which is followed by interpretation, then the actual prayers of the *Didache*, taken as typical, relate to the category of primary theology for the Eucharist, while the 'institution narratives' must be considered as secondary aetiological interpretations.[104]

Such an approach to the *Didache* is certainly open to debate. Moreover, in his treatment of the *Didache*, O'Loughlin observes that "debating the date of the *Didache* has become one of the sub-specializations within early Christian studies," but he does not engage with scholarly debates concerning dates and redactions.[105]

In sum, Lathrop uplifts the Last Supper accounts as normative, while O'Loughlin makes the *Didache* his paradigm regarding the true meaning of early Christian meal fellowship. Blind spots emerge with either

---

100. Ibid., 2.
101. Lathrop, *Four Gospels on Sunday,* 170.
102. O'Loughlin, *Eucharist,* 180.
103. Ibid., 182.
104. Ibid., 91.
105. Ibid., 44.

approach; placing these studies alongside one another allows each to serve as a counterweight, bringing their respective strengths and weaknesses into greater relief. To return to Irwin's framework of "intrinsically interrelated, complementary, and mutually enriching" models of the Eucharist, Lathrop and O'Loughlin taken together enrich our understanding of six of Irwin's models in particular: Lathrop enriches our understanding of Eucharist as the "Memorial of the Paschal Mystery," "The Lord's Supper," and Christ's "Active Presence," while O'Loughlin enriches our understanding of the Eucharist as "Cosmic Mass," "Covenant Renewal," and "Food for the Journey."[106] Both books have much to commend themselves, but they are best read side-by-side.

---

106. Irwin, *Models of the Eucharist*, vii–viii.

II

Shaping the Classical Anaphoras of the Fourth through Sixth Centuries

Nathan P. Chase

Scholars have long noted a number of influences that led to the emergence of the classical anaphoras, particularly in the fourth century, and their subsequent development. The most frequently cited factors include the influence of doctrinal controversies, the shift from oral to written texts, and the need for the liturgy to be more instructional.[1] These are thought to have led to the addition of a number of units—in particular the *Sanctus*, epiclesis, institution narrative with anamnesis, and wide-ranging intercessions—into less developed anaphoral prayers.[2] The later addition of these units into eucharistic praying is clear from the absence of these units across a number of early anaphoras:

---

1. For a summary, see Allan Bouley, *From Freedom to Formula: The Evolution of the Eucharistic Prayer from Oral Improvisation to Written Texts*, Studies in Christian Antiquity 21 (Washington, DC: Catholic University of America Press, 1981); Paul Bradshaw, "Introduction: The Evolution of Early Anaphoras," in *Essays on Early Eastern Eucharistic Prayers*, ed. Paul Bradshaw (Collegeville, MN: Liturgical Press, 1997), 1–18.

2. For a summary, see Paul Bradshaw and Maxwell Johnson, *The Eucharistic Liturgies: Their Evolution and Interpretation* (Collegeville, MN: Liturgical Press, 2012). For a recent treatment of the intercessions in particular, see Nathan Chase, "The Fruits of Communion in the Classical Anaphoras," *Orientalia Christiana Periodica* 87 (2021): 5–70.

- **No *Sanctus*:**[3] *The Apostolic Tradition* (ApTrad) chap. 4,[4] the anaphora in the various recensions of *Testamentum Domini* (TD),[5] the Anaphora of Epiphanius of Salamis,[6] the earliest (reconstructed)

---

3. Robert Taft provides a comprehensive list—see "The Interpolation of the Sanctus into the Anaphora: When and Where? A Review of the Dossier I," *Orientalia Christiana Periodica* 57 (1991): 305–6. See also Robert Taft, "The Interpolation of the Sanctus into the Anaphora: When and Where? A Review of the Dossier Part II," *Orientalia Christiana Periodica* 58 (1992): 83–121.

4. Paul Bradshaw, Maxwell E. Johnson, and L. Edward Phillips, *The Apostolic Tradition: A Commentary*, Hermeneia—A Critical and Historical Commentary on the Bible (Minneapolis: Fortress Press, 2002). For just the anaphora, see Paul Bradshaw and Maxwell Johnson, eds., *Prayers of the Eucharist: Early and Reformed*, 4th ed. (Collegeville, MN: Liturgical Press, 2019), 44–49 (hereafter cited as PEER[4e]).

5. The various recensions of the *Testamentum Domini*, hereafter TD, and their relationship is complex and needs further study. There are three main witnesses to this church order: the Syriac, Ethiopic, and Arabic, as well as fragmentary witnesses in Greek (the original language), Georgian, Coptic, and Latin. The Arabic is divided into four separate recensions: B, L, M, and D. For an overview of the sources, see Martin Lüstraeten, "Edition und Übersetzung der Euchologie der Eucharistiefeier der Redaktion 'M' des arabischen *Testamentum Domini* (I.23-I.28)," *Ex Fonte - Journal of Ecumenical Studies in Liturgy* 2 (2023): 65–179; Martin Lüstraeten, "The Eucharistic Prayer in the Arabic Tradition of the *Testamentum Domini*," forthcoming in proceedings from *The Eighth International Congress of the Society of Oriental Liturgy, 13–18 June 2022, Thessaloniki, Greece*. An English translation based on the current studies appears in R. C. D. Jasper and G. J. Cuming, eds., *Prayers of the Eucharist: Early and Reformed*, 3rd ed. (Collegeville, MN: Liturgical Press, 1990), 138–41 (hereafter cited as PEER[3e]). The abbreviations and sources of TD are:

Arb-TD.B = Arabic recension B—Anton Baumstark, "Eine ägyptische Mess- und Taufliturgie vermutlich des 6. Jahrhunderts," *Oriens Christianus* 1 (1901): 1–45.

Arb-TD.M = Arabic recension M—Gérard Troupeau, "Une version arabe de l'anaphore du *Testamentum Domini*," in *Christianisme oriental. Kérygme et histoire, mélanges offerts au père Michel Hayek*, ed. Šārl Šartūnī (Paris: Geuthner, 2007), 247–56; Martin Lüstraeten, "The Eucharistic Prayer in the Arabic Tradition of the *Testamentum Domini*."

Ethio-TD = Ethiopic version of TD—Robert Beylot, *Testamentum Domini éthiopien* (Louvain: Peeters, 1984), 167–71.

Syr-TD = Syriac version of TD—I.E. Rahmani, *Testamentum Domini nostri Iesu Christi* (Moguntiae: F. Kirchheim, 1899), 39–45.

Arb-TD.B is a conflation of BAS (see n. 134) with MARK (see n. 80). As a result, it is really its own tradition. Arb-TD.M Recension M is the only Arabic witness to the same anaphoral text that appears in Ethio-TD and Syr-TD.

6. PEER[3e], 141–42.

form of the Roman Canon (RC),[7] Klaus Gamber's reconstructed *Missale Gothicum*,[8] Mai Fragment VII,[9] an anaphora attributed to Theodore of Mopsuestia,[10] and the Ethiopian Anaphora of Our Lord Jesus Christ.[11]

- **No Institution Narrative:** Addai and Mari (AM),[12] Theodore of Mopsuestia's *Catecheses*,[13] Cyril of Jerusalem's *Mystagogical Catecheses* chap. 5 (MC 5),[14] the "Persian Anaphora,"[15] possibly the Ethiopian Mystagogical Catechesis (Ethio-MC),[16] and a variety of

---

7. PEER[4e], 200–210. For more on the interpolation of the *Sanctus* into the RC, see Bryan Spinks, *The Sanctus in the Eucharistic Prayer* (Cambridge: Cambridge University Press, 1991), 93–98. Here Spinks follows a number of earlier scholars who have noted (among other things) the absence of the *Sanctus* in Ambrose, the literary disconnect of the *Sanctus* and the parts of the RC when it does appear, and the absence of the *Sanctus* in the Mai fragments, which otherwise closely parallel the RC.

8. Klaus Gamber, "Älteste Eucharistiegebete der lateinischen Osterliturgie," in *Paschatis Sollemnia*, ed. Balthasar Fischer and Johannes Wagner (Wien: Herder, 1959), 166–68.

9. Anton Hänggi, *Prex Eucharistica: Textus e Variis Liturgiis Antiquioribus Selecti*, 2nd ed., Spicilegium Friburgense 12 (Fribourg: Éditions Universitaires Fribourg Suisse, 1968), 422.

10. W. F. Macomber, "An Anaphora Prayer Composed by Theodore of Mopsuestia," *Parole de l'Orient* 6–7 (1975/76): 341–47.

11. Taft, "Interpolation of the Sanctus I," 306n89. For the text, see Hänggi, *Prex*, 150–52.

12. PEER[4e], 64–69.

13. PEER[4e], 155–58.

14. PEER[4e], 133–39. This text has also been attributed by some to John, Cyril's successor. There is also a debate on the exact shape of the anaphora being described. For a helpful overview, see John Paul Abdelsayed, "Liturgical Exodus in Reverse: A Reevaluation of the Egyptian Elements in the Jerusalem Liturgy," in *Issues in Eucharistic Praying in East and West*, ed. Maxwell Johnson (Collegeville, MN: Liturgical Press, 2010), 149–51. See also Maxwell E. Johnson, "The Egyptian Origins of the Anaphora in *Mystagogical Catechesis V* ascribed to Cyril of Jerusalem," in this volume, 133–54 below.

15. R. H. Connolly, "Sixth-Century Fragments of an East-Syrian Anaphora," *Oriens Christianus* 12–14 (1925): 99–128.

16. Emmanuel Fritsch, "The *Order of the Mystery*: An Ancient Catechesis Preserved in BnF Ethiopic Ms d'Abbadie 66-66bis (Fifteenth Century) with a Liturgical Commentary," in *Studies in Oriental Liturgy: Proceedings of the Fifth International Congress of the Society of Oriental Liturgy New York, 10–14 June 2014*, ed. Bert Groen et al. (Louvain: Peeters, 2019), 195–263.

sources in which it is "lacking or unusual,"[17] like some recensions of TD.[18]

- **No Epiclesis:** The RC, and many texts in the Hispano-Mozarabic and Gallican traditions.[19]

- **No intercessions and/or diptychs:**[20] Hispano-Mozarabic and Gallican traditions, the East Syrian and Tikritan traditions of Mesopotamia (no diptychs),[21] ApTrad, and the anaphora in the "Barcelona Papyrus" (BARC).[22]

According to most scholars, the addition of the institution narrative and expanded intercessions into eucharistic prayers dates to the mid-fourth century at the earliest; however, studies of AM,[23] BARC,[24] and other

---

17. Enrico Mazza, "Didache 9–10: Elements of a Eucharistic Interpretation," in *The Didache in Modern Research*, ed. Jonathan Draper (New York: Brill, 1996), 291. See also Robert Taft, "Mass without the Consecration?: The Historic Agreement on the Eucharist between the Catholic Church and the Assyrian Church of the East Promulgated 26 October 2001," *Worship* 77 (2003): 491.

18. Ethio- and Syr-TD contain the words of institution over the bread, but not the cup; see Mazza, "Didache 9–10," 290n58. Arb-TD.M, however, contains these words. Arb-TD.B should be excluded from consideration here; see n. 5.

19. PEER[4e], 216–24.

20. Chase, "Fruits of Communion." See also Robert Taft, *The Diptychs*, Orientalia Christiana Analecta 238 (Rome: Pontificium Institutum Studiorum Orientalium, 1991), 24–25.

21. Taft, *Diptychs*, 71–74.

22. The anaphoral tradition best represented by the Greek Anaphora in the *Barcelona Papyrus* (P.Monts.Roca inv. 154b–155a)—Nathan Chase, "Rethinking Anaphoral Development in Light of the Barcelona Papyrus," PhD diss. (Notre Dame: University of Notre Dame, 2020). My dissertation has been revised and is in preparation as Nathan Chase, *The Anaphoral Tradition in the "Barcelona Papyrus,"* Studia Traditionis Theologiae (Turnhout: Brepols, forthcoming).

23. Bryan Spinks, *Do This in Remembrance of Me: The Eucharist from the Early Church to the Present Day*, SCM Studies in Worship and Liturgy (London: SCM Press, 2013), 52–58.

24. Michael Zheltov, "The Anaphora and the Thanksgiving Prayer from the Barcelona Papyrus: An Underestimated Testimony to the Anaphoral History in the Fourth Century," *Vigiliae Christianae* 62 (2008): 467–504; Chase, "Rethinking Anaphoral Development."

texts[25] have strongly suggested that in some cases the *Sanctus* and/or a non-pneumatic and non-consecratory epiclesis may have entered into eucharistic praying before the fourth century.[26] The fourth century did, however, see the homogenization of eucharistic prayers and the wide adoption of these units across anaphoral traditions.[27]

This chapter will provide a brief overview of the major changes in eucharistic praying in the first through third centuries, before then sketching the processes and influences that shaped the classical anaphoras of the fourth through sixth centuries. These and additional influences will be addressed in more detail in a forthcoming monograph,[28] though this chapter delves deeper than the forthcoming monograph into the endurance of eucharistic meals into the fifth century, the shift from oral to written texts, the use of model liturgical prayers, and authorial attribution.

Early Celebrations of the Eucharist and Greco-Roman Meal Practices

Beginning with the New Testament accounts of the Last Supper and carrying into early eucharistic texts like *Didache* chaps. 9–10, it is clear that the eucharistic celebration began as a substantial meal that included not only bread and wine, but also other food stuffs like cheese, olives, milk, honey, etc.[29] These eucharistic meals were not just for ritual

---

25. See, in particular, the epicleses in the Syrian apocryphal acts, especially the *Acts of Thomas*—Nathan Chase, "From *Logos* to Spirit Revisited: The Development of the Epiclesis in Syria and Egypt," *Ecclesia Orans* 39 (2022): 29–64.

26. Some scholars have also argued for an early date for the institution narrative in texts like ApTrad chap. 4; see Predrag Bukovec, "Der Einsetzungsbericht: Die Genese des Eucharistischen Hochgebets" PhD diss. (Vienna: Universität Wien, 2016).

27. Paul Bradshaw, "The Homogenization of Christian Liturgy—Ancient and Modern: Presidential Address," *Studia Liturgica* 26 (1996): 1–15.

28. For a more detailed study of the influences on eucharistic praying from the first to sixth centuries, see Nathan Chase, *Factors That Influenced the Development of Early Eucharistic Prayers*, Alcuin/GROW Joint Liturgical Studies (Norwich: Hymns Ancient and Modern, anticipated 2024).

29. For a helpful summary, see Andrew McGowan, *Ascetic Eucharists: Food and Drink in Early Christian Ritual Meals* (Oxford: Clarendon Press, 1999); Andrew McGowan, "'The Firstfruits of God's Creatures': Bread, Eucharist and the Ancient Economy," in *Full of Your Glory: Liturgy, Cosmos, Creation*, ed. Teresa Berger (Collegeville, MN:

purposes—they were also for provisioning, and were linked to food doles given to Christians by the Church.[30] These meals would have varied greatly in the early church. Some of them would likely have been lavish affairs, with relishes and many of the foodstuffs noted above. Others may have consisted of a substantial bit of bread and, in some cases, perhaps only water depending on socio-economic conditions and one's ascetical practices.[31] In each case, however, they were meals, i.e., meant for sustenance no matter how lavish or sparse they were.

These meals were also rooted in older Greco-Roman and Jewish meal practices, the latter of which were largely based on broader Greco-Roman models.[32] Of those practices, the most influential on early Christian eucharistic celebrations appear to have been *symposia, collegia* (meals of associations), morning *salutationes*, and *refrigeria*.

Liturgical Press, 2019), 69–86. For more on cheese, in particular, see more recently Elizabeth Klein, "Perpetua, Cheese, and Martyrdom as Public Liturgy in the *Passion of Perpetua and Felicity*," *Journal of Early Christian Studies* 28 (2020): 175–202.

30. Clemens Leonhard, "Morning *Salutationes* and the Decline of Sympotic Eucharists in the Third Century," *Zeitschrift Für Antikes Christentum/Journal of Ancient Christianity* 18 (2014): 420–42; McGowan, "Firstfruits."

31. Andrew McGowan, *Ancient Christian Worship: Early Church Practices in Social, Historical, and Theological Perspective* (Grand Rapids: Baker Academic, 2014); McGowan, "Firstfruits."

32. For a few studies, see Dennis Smith, *From Symposium to Eucharist: The Banquet in the Early Christian World* (Minneapolis: Fortress Press, 2003); Andrew McGowan, "Rethinking Agape and Eucharist in Early North African Christianity," *Studia Liturgica* 34 (2004): 165–76; McGowan, "Firstfruits"; Valeriy Alikin, "Eating the Bread and Drinking the Cup in Corinth: Defining and Expressing the Identity of the Earliest Christians," in *Mahl und Religiöse Identität im Frühen Christentum/Meals and Religious Identity in Early Christianity*, ed. Matthias Klinghardt and Hal Taussig (Tübingen: Francke, 2012), 119–30; Hal Taussig, *In the Beginning Was the Meal: Social Experimentation and Early Christian Identity* (Minneapolis: Fortress Press, 2009); Hal Taussig, "Introduction: The Study of Identity and Religion in Relationship to Early Christian Meals," in *Mahl und Religiöse Identität im Frühen Christentum/Meals and Religious Identity in Early Christianity*, ed. Matthias Klinghardt and Hal Taussig (Tübingen: Francke, 2012), 15–23; Paul Bradshaw, "Jewish Influence on Early Christian Liturgy: A Reappraisal," in *Liturgies in East and West: Ecumenical Relevance of Early Liturgical Development: Acts of the International Symposium Vindobonense I, Vienna, November 17–20, 2007*, ed. Hans-Jürgen Feulner (Zürich: Lit Verlag, 2013), 47–59. See also Alistair Stewart, *Breaking Bread: The Emergence of Eucharist and Agape in Early Christian Communities* (Eerdmans: Grand Rapids, forthcoming).

In the Greco-Roman world, a *symposium* was an afternoon or evening meal that consisted of "[1] a blessing of bread including wine in some cases [2] followed by its distribution and [3] which end[ed] with a blessing over wine [4] also followed by its distribution."[33] The *symposium*-style meals of the Greco-Romans bear a close resemblance to early Eucharists described in the New Testament, the *Didache*, and the writings of many of the early church fathers. While *symposium*-style meals have long been seen by scholars as possible forerunners to the Christian Eucharist, Clemens Leonhard notes issues with an uncritical acceptance of the *symposium*-style of meal as the predecessor to the eucharistic liturgies of the fourth century: "In sympotic celebrations, one would debate philosophical questions or affairs of one's group during the drinking party after the meal. A reconstruction of the early history of the Eucharist must account for what resembles a complete inversion of the sequence of the customary elements of *symposia*."[34] Thus, scholars must be cautious to not overemphasize the connection between early Christian eucharistic celebrations and *symposia*.

Other early Christian eucharistic practices bear a close relationship to the meals—known generally as *collegia*—of the Greco-Roman associations. These associations were established for a variety of reasons—religious, political, as funerary associations, or as guilds based on one's craft—and they periodically celebrated a common meal together.[35] The structure of these meals was usually a *symposium*, though at times particular adaptations were made for each association. These associations also provided material aid to their members. The distribution of food to poor members of the church could be explained by the church functioning as an association.[36]

33. Leonhard, "Morning *Salutationes*," 423.
34. Ibid.
35. Smith, *From Symposium to Eucharist*, chap. 5; John S. Kloppenborg and Richard S. Ascough, eds., *Greco-Roman Associations: Texts, Translations, and Commentary*, Beihefte Zur Zeitschrift Für Die Neutestamentliche Wissenschaft (Berlin: De Gruyter, 2011); Markus Öhler, "Mähler und Opferhandlungen in griechischrömischen Vereinigungen: Das frühchristliche Herrenmahl im Kontext," in *The Eucharist, Its Origins and Contexts: Sacred Meal, Communal Meal, Table Fellowship in Late Antiquity, Early Judaism, and Early Christianity*, ed. David Hellholm and Dieter Sänger, vol. 3, Wissenschaftliche Untersuchungen zum Neuen Testament 376 (Tübingen: Mohr Siebeck, 2017), 1413–39.
36. Smith, *From Symposium to Eucharist*, 106.

The morning *salutatio* was a Greco-Roman practice that occurred at the house of a patron, where "clients of wealthy and influential people used to assemble in the early morning. They were waiting there to be admitted into certain parts of their patron's house."[37] At the morning *salutatio,* clients would receive gifts (*sportulae*) that usually included food.[38] Beginning primarily in the third century, Christians began to assemble at the church rather than in patrons' homes and waited on the bishop as chief Christian patron. The focus on episcopal patronage in documents like ApTrad might be the result of tensions between older lay patronage practices and the emerging episcopate.[39]

Finally, *refrigeria* had a profound effect on early Christian eucharistic practices.[40] These were meals celebrated at graves or tombs during the funeral of the deceased, and at specific times of memorial throughout the year. There is ample archeological evidence for the *mensae* and benches in cemeteries on which these meals would have been celebrated.[41] These meals carried over into Christian practice and became celebrations of the Eucharist. We see this already in the *Didascalia* chap. 26 (third century,

---

37. Leonhard, "Morning *Salutationes*," 425–30, here at 425.

38. McGowan, "Firstfruits," 80–81.

39. See Charles Bobertz, "The Role of Patron in the *Cena Dominica* of Hippolytus' *Apostolic Tradition*," *Journal of Theological Studies* 44 (1993): 170–84. His study dates ApTrad to second-century Rome, though most scholars now date it to the fourth century and see it as a composite document from different regions. For more on the tension between lay and episcopal patronage, see Kimberly Diane Bowes, *Private Worship, Public Values, and Religious Change in Late Antiquity* (Cambridge: Cambridge University Press, 2011).

40. For an overview, see Robin Jensen, "Dining with the Dead: From the *Mensa* to the Altar in Christian Late Antiquity," in *Commemorating the Dead: Texts and Artifacts in Context*, ed. Laurie Brink and Deborah Green (New York: Walter de Gruyter, 2008), 107–43; Eliezer González, *The Fate of the Dead in Early Third Century North African Christianity: The Passion of Perpetua and Felicitas and Tertullian*, Studien Und Texte Zu Antike Und Christentum = Studies and Texts in Antiquity and Christianity 83 (Tübingen: Mohr Siebeck, 2014); Fred Klawiter, *Martyrdom, Sacrificial Libation, and the Eucharist of Ignatius of Antioch* (Lanham: Lexington Books/Fortress Academic, 2022).

41. Ulrich Volp, *Tod und Ritual in den christlichen Gemeinden der Antike* (Leiden: Brill, 2002). For examples from Egypt, see G. Cipriano, *El-Bagawat: Un cimitero paleocristiano nell'Alto Egitto* (Todi: Tau Editrice, 2008), 68–69 and 74–83.

Syria), which calls for the celebration of the Eucharist as part of the funeral liturgy, often at the gravesite.[42]

The influence of Greco-Roman meal practices—*symposia, collegia,* morning *salutationes,* and *refrigeria*—on the early Christian community were not mutually exclusive, and Christian eucharistic practices were undoubtedly influenced by all of these types of meals.

The Shift from a Eucharistic Meal to Token Food and Drink

Already by the second and third century, early Christians began to focus primarily on the bread and wine within their eucharistic meals.[43] This was a result of the increasing sacrality of the bread and wine apart from the eucharistic meal. While some scholars have argued that the sacrality of the eucharistic food in contrast to, or apart from, the whole eucharistic meal and the gathering of the assembly had begun already in the New Testament period, most scholars now locate this development in the second century.[44] However, the meal itself, and specifically the gathering of the whole assembly, was still a key part of early Christians' understanding of the presence of Christ.[45] Nevertheless, the sacrality of the bread and wine apart from the eucharistic meal likely accounts for the reservation of the Eucharist for distribution to the sick in the time of Justin Martyr and its reservation in homes already by the time of Tertullian.[46] According to Andrew McGowan, by Cyprian's time "the

---

42. Alistair Stewart-Sykes, ed., *The Didascalia Apostolorum: An English Version,* Studia Traditionis Theologiae 1 (Turnhout: Brepols, 2009), 255–56.

43. Bradshaw and Johnson, *Eucharistic Liturgies,* 44–50.

44. McGowan, "Rethinking Agape"; Bradshaw and Johnson, *Eucharistic Liturgies,* 44–50. See also Nathan Mitchell, *Cult and Controversy: The Worship of the Eucharist Outside Mass* (New York: Pueblo, 1982), chap. 1.

45. See, for instance, the writings of Ignatius of Antioch—Klawiter, *Martyrdom, Sacrificial Libation.*

46. See William Freestone, *The Sacrament Reserved* (London: Mowbrays, 1917), 40–50; Otto Nussbaum, *Die Aufbewahrung der Eucharistie* (Bonn: Hanstein, 1979), 266–84; Mitchell, *Cult and Controversy,* chap. 1; Robert Taft, "Reservation and Veneration of the Eucharist in the Orthodox Traditions," in *Inquiries into Eastern Christian Worship,* ed. Bert Groen, Steven Hawkes-Teeples, and Stefanos Alexopoulos, Eastern Christian Studies 12 (Leuven: Peeters, 2012), 99–120; Stefanos Alexopoulos, *The Presanctified Liturgy*

understanding of the sacrality of the eucharistic food had developed to the point that it was the food itself more than the banquet that was the attraction."[47] Even then, however, Cyprian stresses the importance of both the eucharistic food and the gathering of the whole assembly.

Nevertheless, a major shift was underway in the eucharistic celebrations of this period, mainly the shift from a meal to a token distribution of food and drink.[48] While some scholars again have tried to place this shift as early as the New Testament, Paul Bradshaw and Maxwell Johnson have noted that "the transition from full meal to symbolic rite appears to have been gradual, taking place before the middle of the second century in some places, after the middle of the third century in others."[49] This was the result of several factors: 1) the increased sacrality of the eucharistic food (noted above); 2) greater food security;[50] 3) the increasing size of many assemblies;[51] and 4) the shift from an evening to morning eucharistic celebration.[52] It is not clear whether the morning Eucharists that emerged as a result of this latter shift were complete celebrations of the Eucharist, or simply times for the reception of communion. Likely these morning (Sunday?) Eucharists began as a set time for the distribution of leftovers from the communal meal the night before (Saturday?).[53]

---

in the Byzantine Rite: A Comparative Analysis of Its Origins, Evolution, and Structural Components, Liturgia Condenda 21 (Leuven: Peeters, 2009), 8–34.

47. McGowan, "Rethinking Agape," 176.
48. Ibid.
49. Bradshaw and Johnson, *Eucharistic Liturgies*, 58; see also chaps. 1 and 2.
50. McGowan, "Firstfruits," 85.
51. The best evidence for this in the third century is Cyprian; see McGowan, "Rethinking Agape," 172–75; Valeriy A. Alikin, *The Earliest History of the Christian Gathering: Origin, Development and Content of the Christian Gathering in the First to Third Centuries*, Supplements to Vigiliae Christianae 102 (Leiden: Brill, 2010), 144. This was even more so the case in the fourth century, though we should not be too quick to buy into the traditional narrative that there was a sudden influx of people with the legalization of Christianity; see Maxwell Johnson, *The Rites of Christian Initiation: Their Evolution and Interpretation* (Collegeville, MN: Liturgical Press, 2007), 115–20; Bradshaw and Johnson, *Eucharistic Liturgies*, 61–63.
52. McGowan, "Rethinking Agape"; Leonhard, "Morning *Salutationes*"; Paul Bradshaw, "The Earliest Eucharist: Saturday or Sunday?," *Ecclesia Orans* 36 (2019): 225–40.
53. Leonhard appears to dispute this idea; see Leonhard, "Morning *Salutationes*," 427; Clemens Leonhard, "Establishing Short-Term Communities in Eucharistic Celebrations of Antiquity," *Religion in the Roman Empire* 3 (2017): 79.

The Endurance in Some Places of the Eucharistic Meal into the Fifth Century

Scholars have traditionally argued that the shift from a eucharistic meal to a token distribution of bread and wine—primarily on Sunday morning—was largely complete in most places by the fourth century. However, this seems to betray an urban, male, episcopal, and largely Nicene-Christian historical perspective. There is ample evidence for the continuation of eucharistic meals into the fifth century, as well as the continuation of practices that were rooted in Greco-Roman meal culture. These pieces of evidence have, however, often been overlooked.

The first set of evidence comes from the East Syrian tradition. Literary sources from fifth-century East Syria strongly suggest that the eucharistic liturgy may still have been a meal in that period.[54] Reinhard Meßner has noted prohibitions against domestic eucharistic celebrations in canon 13 of the Synod of Seleucia-Ctesiphon (410 CE)—"Und die Angelegenheit dieses alten Gedenkens soll von nun an nicht mehr unter uns geschehen: in den Häusern soll das Opfer nicht mehr dargebracht werden."[55] This mirrors an earlier canon from the Synod of Laodicea (canon 58). The Synod of Laodicea in canon 28 had also prohibited the setting up of couches in churches, a practice rooted in a Greco-Roman dining context.[56] But it is not just the prohibitions against domestic eucharistic celebrations in the Synod of Seleucia-Ctesiphon that suggest the continuation of eucharistic meals in fifth-century East Syria. Rather, Meßner has argued that the liturgy of the word was slow to be adopted into regular eucharistic practice in East Syria. This likely points to the continuation in this period of older meal practices linked to a *symposium*-style eucharistic celebration.

Second, it is clear from literary and archeological evidence that house-churches still existed in some places into the fourth and fifth centuries.

---

54. Reinhard Meßner, "Die Synode von Seleukeia-Ktesiphon 410 und die Geschichte der ostsyrischen Messe," in *"Haec sacrosancta synodus:" Konzils- und kirchengeschichtliche Beiträge*, ed. Reinhard Meßner and Rudolf Pranzl (Regensburg: Friedrich Pustet, 2006), 59–85.

55. Ibid., 84–85, here at 84. "And the tradition of this ancient commemoration should from now on no longer be among us: the sacrifice shall no longer be offered in houses."

56. Ibid., 85.

Bradshaw, for instance, notes that the *Passio SS. Dativi, Saturnini presb. et aliorum* "lists the names of the members of an African house-church arrested during the Diocletian persecution in February 304."[57] Other evidence points to the continuation of house-churches in Rome, Constantinople, and other locations for a variety of reasons: (1) due to resistance to imperially regulated Christianity; (2) as places for heretical *and* Nicene groups to gather when they did not have access to publicly controlled churches; (3) as the Church spread into rural locations; and (4) in places outside of the empire.[58] There are also several archeological examples of domestic structures that were converted into churches in the fourth century. The best examples come from Egypt,[59] as well as several villas on rural estates like Lullingston in modern-day England.[60]

While the continuation of house-churches does not always imply that the Eucharist was still being celebrated as a meal rather than a token distribution of bread and wine, the evidence from East Syria noted above,

---

57. Paul Bradshaw, "The Fourth Century: A Golden Age for Liturgy?," in *Liturgie und Ritual in der alten Kirche: patristische Beiträge zum Studium der gottesdienstlichen Quellen der alten Kirche*, ed. Wolfram Kinzig, Ulrich Volp, and Jochen Schmidt, Studien der Patristischen Arbeitsgemeinschaft 11 (Leuven: Peeters, 2011), 104n17.

58. Harry Maier, "Heresy, Households, and the Disciplining of Diversity," in *Late Ancient Christianity*, ed. Virginia Burrus, A People's History of Christianity 2 (Minneapolis: Fortress Press, 2005), 213–33; Meßner, "Die Synode von Seleukeia-Ktesiphon 410 und die Geschichte der ostsyrischen Messe"; Bowes, *Private Worship*; Bradshaw, "Fourth Century."

59. Possible examples from Egypt include the small east church at Kellis and the small church at Munisis, as well as the church at Kysis and maybe the church at 'Ain el-Gedida. Charles Bonnet, "L'église du village de Douch," in *Douch 3: Kysis, Fouilles de l'IFAO à Douch, Oasis de Kharga, 1985–1990*, edited by Michel Reddé et al, 75-86. (Le Caire: Institut français d'archéologie orientale, 2004); Nicola Aravecchia, *'Ain El-Gedida: 2006–2008 Excavations of a Late Antique Site in Egypt's Western Desert*, Amheida IV (New York: Institute for the Study of the Ancient World, New York University Press, 2018), 9–11 and 200–208, and chaps. 3 and 5. The west I house at Narmuthis may also be a *domus ecclesiae*; see Edda Bresciani, *Rapporto preliminare delle campagne di Scavo 1968 e 1969* (Milano: Istituto Editoriale Cisalpino, 1976), 25.

60. See Edward Adams, *The Earliest Christian Meeting Places: Almost Exclusively Houses?*, Library of New Testament Studies 450 (London: T&T Clark, 2016), 110–11; Jenn Cianca, *Sacred Ritual, Profane Space: The Roman House as Early Christian Meeting Place*, Studies in Christianity and Judaism Series 1 (Montreal: McGill-Queen's University Press, 2018), 104–10. For other examples of rural villa churches, see Bowes, *Private Worship*, chap. 3.

as well as some of the archeological evidence from Egypt, suggests that this was likely still the case. The fourth-century church complex at 'Ain el-Gedida in the Dakhla Oasis in Egypt, for instance, contains cooking spaces within (room B6)[61] and next to (room B10) the church complex.[62] Across the passageway (street B12) from the church complex there are also a series of ovens (B14–15).[63] It has even been suggested that the assembly room (A46) in the church complex may have served as a refectory.[64] Other examples of church complexes in Egypt that contained food preparation spaces include the east churches at Kellis.[65] These food preparation spaces seem to be too large for token distributions of bread and other foodstuffs. It is not clear whether these were part of a program for food distribution or for the preparation of a eucharistic or non-eucharistic meal for the Christian community; however, it is strongly suggestive of an enduring connection between Christian ritual and meal practices.

Third, in ApTrad's descriptions of Christian meal practices (chaps. 23, 27, and 29C), the text distinguishes between communal meals that are non-eucharistic and what it considers to be the "actual" Eucharist (chaps. 4; 21.25–29 and 31–37; 33). This distinction is specifically made in chaps. 23.4 and 29C. In both of these chapters, the communal meals are described as *not* being a Eucharist. Chap. 29C.16, for example, says: "And as those believers who are there are eating the supper, they are to take a little bread from the bishop's hand before they break their own bread, *because it is a blessing and not the Eucharist* like the body of our Lord" (emphasis mine). However, these and other meal practices in ApTrad were likely once Eucharists as well.[66] Coupled again with the prohibitions in the synods of Laodicea and Seleucia-Ctesiphon, this likely points to the continuation in

---

61. Aravecchia, *'Ain El-Gedida*, 116–31.

62. Ibid., 143–51.

63. Ibid., 174–86.

64. Nicola Aravecchia, "Catechumens, Women, and Agricultural Laborers: Who Used the Fourth-Century Hall at the Church of 'Ain El-Gedida, Egypt?," *Journal of Late Antiquity* 15 (2022): 193–230.

65. Gillian Bowen, "The Fourth-Century Churches at Ismant El-Kharab," in *Dakhleh Oasis Project: Preliminary Reports on the 1994–1995 to 1998–1999 Field Seasons*, ed. Colin A. Hope and Gillian E. Bowen, Dakhleh Oasis Project 11 (Oxford: Oxbow Books, 2002), 71.

66. For more on these meals in ApTrad, see Bradshaw, Johnson, and Phillips, *Apostolic Tradition*.

some places of older eucharistic meal practices—now rejected as eucharistic—alongside the more ritualized morning eucharistic celebrations that were becoming typical from the late third century onward.

Finally, there is evidence for the continuation of eucharistic practices in domestic settings into the fourth and fifth centuries.[67] One example of this is ApTrad chap. 36, which mentions a fast before receiving the Eucharist. This chapter is likely addressing daily or frequent reception of the Eucharist outside of the full eucharistic celebration and specifically within a domestic setting.[68] Another example is the eucharistic service of a female ascetic described by Pseudo-Athanasius in the fourth/fifth century treatise *De virginitate*.[69] In that text, the female ascetic "is to 'eucharistize' (εὐχαριστήσασα) the bread on her table" with a blessing and "is then instructed to sit down at table and to break the bread. After making the sign of the cross over the bread three times, she is to 'eucharistize' (εὐχαριστοῦσα) the bread."[70] These prayers, as Teresa Berger notes, parallel prayers used within a eucharistic context in other early liturgical sources.

As a result, it is increasingly clear that the shift from eucharistic meal to token distribution of bread and wine was much more uneven than previous scholarship has suggested. In some places, such as Carthage, it began already in the third century, as witnessed by Cyprian (*Ep.* 63.15.1 and 63.16.1–2),[71] while in other places, such as East Syria, it continued on into the fifth century.

The Transition from Oral to Written Prayer Traditions[72]

While the shift from eucharistic meals to token distributions of bread and wine was occurring in the third through fifth centuries, there was

---

67. For an overview of the evidence, see n. 46.

68. Bradshaw, Johnson, and Phillips, *Apostolic Tradition*, 180–81.

69. Teresa Berger, *Gender Differences and the Making of Liturgical History: Lifting a Veil on Liturgy's Past* (Burlington: Ashgate, 2020), 88–93.

70. Ibid., 88, 89.

71. See McGowan, "Rethinking Agape," 172–75; Alikin, *Earliest History*, 144; Bradshaw, "Earliest Eucharist," 235, 238.

72. For more on this shift from oral to written prayer traditions, and their application to anaphoral praying, see Chase, "Rethinking Anaphoral Development"; and also the revision to my dissertation, Chase, *Anaphoral Tradition in the "Barcelona Papyrus."* It is in my dissertation that I first developed the terminology used in this section based largely on the work of the scholars noted in n. 73.

Shaping the Classical Anaphoras of the Fourth through Sixth Centuries 37

a concurrent shift that saw a rapid transition from extempore praying toward codified oral traditions and finally written anaphoral prayers.[73] It is also in the late third and early fourth centuries that the earliest extant classical anaphoras appear, namely AM,[74] ApTrad chap. 4,[75] and BARC.[76]

Prior to the shift toward written texts, bishops and priests were allowed to extemporize eucharistic prayers.[77] Extemporization allowed for additional units and phrases to be incorporated into model ritual texts and patterns (more below).[78] But with the shift to written texts, beginning especially in the fourth century, anaphoral patterns would harden along with the phraseology of each anaphoral tradition. This shift was often due to the need for doctrinal precision;[79] however, by the fourth century, many priests and bishops were simply not skilled enough to continue to extemporize quality eucharistic prayers, and there was also a strong desire for regional uniformity.

---

73. Bouley, *From Freedom to Formula*; Juliette Day, *Reading the Liturgy: An Exploration of Texts in Christian Worship* (London: Bloomsbury, 2014); Achim Budde, "Improvisation im Eucharistiegebet," *Jahrbuch für Antike und Christentum* 44 (2001): 127–41; Achim Budde, *Die ägyptische Basilios-Anaphora: Text, Kommentar, Geschichte*, Jerusalemer theologisches Forum, Bd. 7 (Münster: Aschendorff, 2004); Achim Budde, "Editing Liturgy—Working with Texts Which Develop in Use," *Studia Patristica* 34 (2006): 3–8.

74. For a summary of scholarship, see Spinks, *Do This in Remembrance*, 52–58.

75. Enrico Mazza, *The Origins of the Eucharistic Prayer* (Collegeville, MN: Liturgical Press, 1995), chap. 4; Matthieu Smyth, "The Anaphora of the So-Called 'Apostolic Tradition' and the Roman Eucharistic Prayer," in *Issues in Eucharistic Praying in East and West*, ed. Maxwell Johnson (Collegeville, MN: Liturgical Press, 2010), 71–97; Bukovec, "Der Einsetzungsbericht," 16–72; Chase, *Anaphoral Tradition in the "Barcelona Papyrus."*

76. Zheltov, "Barcelona Papyrus"; Chase, "Rethinking Anaphoral Development."

77. R. P. C. Hanson, "The Liberty of the Bishop to Improvise Prayer in the Eucharist," *Vigiliae Christianae* 15 (1961): 173–76; Ulrich Volp, "Liturgical Authority Reconsidered: Remarks on the Bishop's Role in Pre-Constantinian Worship," in *Prayer and Spirituality in the Early Church: Liturgy and Life (Vol. 3)*, ed. Bronwen Neil, Geoffrey Dunn, and Lawrence Cross (Stathfield: St Paul's Publications, 2003), 189–209.

78. Paul Bradshaw, "Continuity and Change in Early Eucharistic Practice: Shifting Scholarly Perspectives," in *Continuity and Change in Christian Worship*, ed. R. N. Swanson (London: Boydell Press, 1999), 10–12.

79. Bouley, *From Freedom to Formula*; Edward Kilmartin, "Early African Legislation Concerning Liturgical Prayer," *Ephemerides Liturgicae* 99 (1985): 105–27; Paul Bradshaw, "The Effects of the Coming of Christendom on Early Christian Worship," in *The Origins of Christendom in the West*, ed. Alan Kreider (Edinburgh: T&T Clark, 2001), 282–85.

The earliest written anaphoral texts emerged from these extemporized prayers and oral narrative traditions. Roughly three stages of development can be noted in the shift from oral anaphoral traditions to written anaphoral texts. The first stage is the oral period, in which the narrative structure of the anaphoral tradition emerged. In this period, the narrative structure was passed on orally, like a story, through oral conventions. In the second phase, the narrative structure and key phrases of these anaphoral traditions were written down, often as a memory aid or a model on which one could improvise. At this stage, the text remained open to extensive emendations and change. In the third and final stage, a fully composed written text emerged. In this stage, themes and phrases in the two previous stages were further codified and standardized based on regional patterns.

Especially in the first and second stages, the anaphoral traditions were narrative structures that were determined by thematic units (e.g. *Sanctus*, epiclesis, etc.) signaled by "unit structuring phrases" (USPs). These narrative structures are like ladders, where each rung is a USP on which further improvisation can be hung. A good example of a USP is: "It is fitting and right" to start a preface; or "send onto them your Holy . . . Spirit" in the anaphoral epiclesis. Further improvisation was often done by inserting stock phrases around these USPs.

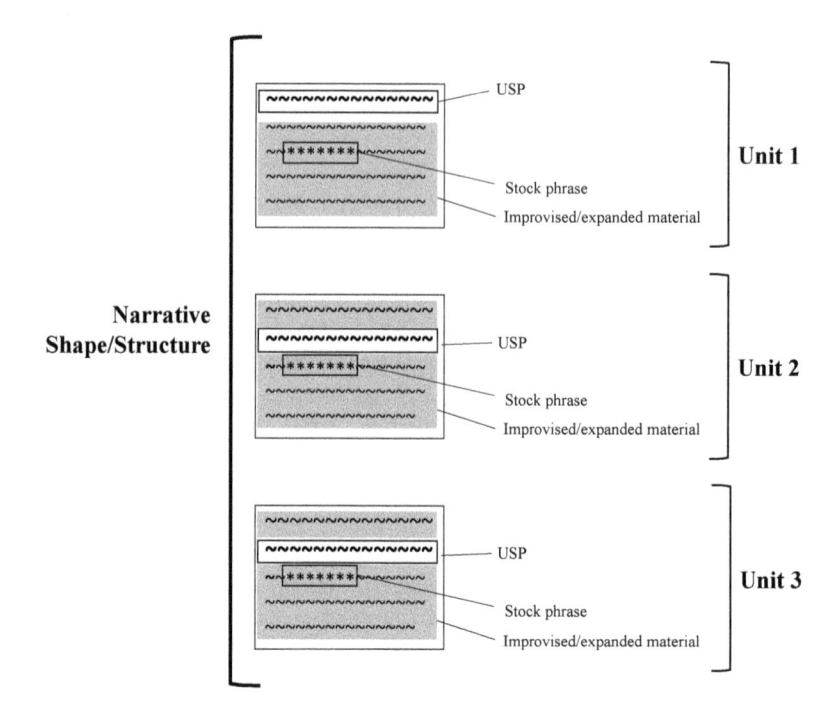

Shaping the Classical Anaphoras of the Fourth through Sixth Centuries 39

It should be noted, however, that USPs do not always occur at the beginning of a unit. An example of a USP that does not start an anaphoral unit is the USP of the epiclesis in BARC—"send onto them your holy and comforter Spirit from heaven," which follows after "we ask and beseech you." This latter phrase, while a common stock phrase in Egypt, is not a USP. Furthermore, USPs are sometimes different across and within regions. The different USPs of the anaphoral anamneses in Egypt and Syria can serve as a good example: (1) Egypt, as epitomized by the Anaphora of St. Mark (MARK)[80]—"Proclaiming . . . the death . . ."; or (2) Syria—"Remembering . . . his death . . ."[81]

As early as the second century, in the writings of Justin Martyr, it is clear that Christians prayed using structural patterns that relied on thematic units, USPs, and stock phrases.[82] The narrative shape of early anaphoral traditions becomes even more clear when looking at the writings of the fourth- and fifth-century mystagogues. MC 5, the mystagogical *Catecheses* of Theodore of Mopsuestia (fourth/fifth century), and the Ethio-MC from the fifth century,[83] give structural outlines, some of the USPs, and the thematic units of their anaphoras.

MC 5 is a perfect example (see table below). The pre-anaphoral dialogue in MC 5 begins with direct quotations of the anaphora: "Up with your hearts . . . we have them with the Lord" followed by "Let us give thanks to the Lord . . . it is fitting and right."[84] MC 5 then goes on to outline the thematic content of the preface and notes the transition to the *Sanctus* through the mention of the seraphim. This is followed by an

---

80. PEER[4e], 104–15.

81. Anne McGowan, "The Basilian Anaphoras: Rethinking the Question," in *Issues in Eucharistic Praying in East and West*, ed. Maxwell Johnson (Collegeville, MN: Liturgical Press, 2011), 256; Gohar Haroutiounian-Thomas, "L'anamnèse et l'histoire du salut dans les anaphores de la famille syrienne occidentale," in θυσία αἰνέσεως: *Mélanges liturgiques offerts à la mémoire de l'archevêque Georges Wagner (1930–1993)*, ed. J. Getcha and A. Lossky (Paris: Presses Saint-Serge—Institut de Théologie Orthodoxe, 2005), 114.

82. PEER[4e], 23–27; Bouley, *From Freedom to Formula*, 113. A structuralist approach containing formulaic phrases can likely be seen behind a number of early descriptions of the Eucharist, including those of Irenaeus, Cyprian, the Apocryphal Acts of the Apostles, the *Martyrdom of Polycarp*, and the *Martyrdom of Sts. Perpetua and Felicitas*.

83. Other examples include: the anaphoras described in Narsai's homilies, the anaphora described by Eusebius, and Ambrose's treatment of the RC.

84. PEER[4e], 137.

epiclesis which asks for the Holy Spirit to make the bread and cup the Body and Blood of Christ. Following this is an outline of the types of intercessions that are made.

USPs and Core Themes of MC 5	
Dialogue	Lift up your hearts
	We have them to the Lord
	Let us give thanks to the Lord
	It is right and just
Preface	- [It is truly right and just]
	- . . . heaven and earth and the sea, of the sun and the moon; of the stars and all creation . . .
Pre-*Sanctus*	Angels, archangels, dominions, principalities, powers, thrones, the cherubim
Sanctus	Holy, Holy, Holy . . .
Epiclesis	Send the holy spirit upon the offerings . . .
Offering	Bloodless worship
Intercessions	- For the . . .
	- We make memorial . . .
Doxology	[Not given][85]

Knowing the structure, the USPs, and the core themes of an anaphoral tradition, a presider could easily fill out and elaborate the structure during the performance of the ritual, or a redactor when writing down or copying the prayer. An example of how USPs and improvisation through stock phrases functioned within a particular anaphoral unit can even be seen in later written sources. The following is the epiclesis in the Ethiopian version of MARK in the Aksumite Collection (Ethio-MARK I)[86] circa fifth century, in comparison to a later form of MARK's epiclesis as seen

---

85. Though the doxology likely followed what is given in MC 5.23.

86. Emmanuel Fritsch, "New Reflections on the Image of Late Antique and Medieval Ethiopian Liturgy," in *Liturgy's Imagined Past/s: Methodologies and Materials in the Writing of Liturgical History Today*, ed. Teresa Berger (Collegeville, MN: Liturgical Press, 2016), 47–54.

in the Coptic version of MARK (CYRIL).[87] The USP is in bold, while the stock phrases that have been inserted to fill out the unit are underlined:

Ethio-MARK I	CYRIL
[A] <u>We pray and beseech you</u> **to send the Holy Spirit** and power **in this offering upon the bread and the cup** and [B] <u>to make the bread the body and the cup the blood of the new covenant of the Lord God, our King everywhere, Jesus Christ.</u>	[A] <u>We pray and beseech thy</u> goodness, [1] <u>O lover of man</u> . . . and **send down** [2] <u>from thine holy height and from heaven</u> . . . <u>the Paraclete thine</u> **Holy Spirit** . . . **send him** [**the Holy Spirit**] **down upon us** thy servants and upon [3] <u>these</u> thy precious **gifts** <u>which have been set before thee, upon</u> **this bread and** upon **this cup** that they may be hallowed and changed and [B] <u>that he may make this bread the holy body of Christ and this cup also his precious blood of the new testament even of our Lord and our God and our Saviour and the king of us all Jesus Christ.</u>

This unit (the epiclesis) is clearly structured around the sending down of the Holy Spirit upon the gifts. Phrase A appears as an early stock transitional phrase in the Egyptian tradition. Phrase B is a highly standardized way for requesting the transformation of the gifts in the Egypt anaphoras; it represents a later development in the Egyptian tradition, where it also became a stock phrase.[88] CYRIL's epiclesis has also included a number of other stock phrases in order to elaborate this unit: phrases 1, 2, and 3. These phrases appear in various epicleses in the Egyptian tradition.

It is worth noting that some anaphoral units provide more space for creativity and improvisation than others. This is especially the case in the preface, post-*Sanctus*, intercessions, and fruits of communion. Other units like the pre-anaphoral dialogue, institution narrative, anamnesis, and doxology tend to be very formulaic. While some of the technical language here may be new, in many ways anaphoral historians have long

---

87. F. E. Brightman and C. E. Hammond, *Liturgies, Eastern and Western: Being the Texts, Original or Translated, of the Principal Liturgies of the Church* (Oxford: Clarendon Press, 1896), 164–80. For more on this and the form and development of the epiclesis in the Egyptian tradition, see Chase, "From *Logos* to Spirit Revisited"; Chase, *Anaphoral Tradition in the "Barcelona Papyrus."*

88. Chase, "From *Logos* to Spirit Revisited."

noted the existence of these units and their formulas. Sebastian Brock, for instance, in his study of Syrian baptismal and eucharistic texts, drew attention to the use of formulaic building blocks in their construction.[89]

Further proof that early Christians thought in narrative units can be seen in the circulation of ritual units like the *Sanctus* and epiclesis across rituals in the Christian tradition.[90] Evidence suggests that these thematic units were circulating independently, even if some of the evidence comes from a later date. There is a great deal of evidence, for instance, pointing to the circulation of the *Sanctus*,[91] epiclesis,[92]

---

89. Sebastian Brock, "Invocations to/for the Holy Spirit in Syriac Liturgical Texts: Some Comparative Approaches," in *Comparative Liturgy Fifty Years After Anton Baumstark (1872–1948)*, ed. Robert Taft and Gabriele Winkler, Orientalia Christiana Analecta 265 (Rome: Pontificio Istituto Orientale, 2001), 398.

90. Brock, "Invocations to/for the Holy Spirit"; Sebastian Brock, "Studies in the Early History of the Syrian Orthodox Baptismal Liturgy," *Journal of Theological Studies* 23, no. 1 (1972): 16–64; Sebastian Brock, "An Archaic Syriac Prayer over Baptismal Oil," *Studia Patristica* 41 (2006): 3–12; Gabriele Winkler, "Further Observations in Connection with the Early Form of Epiklesis," in *Studies in Early Christian Liturgy and Its Context* (Aldershot: Ashgate, 1997), 66–80.

91. Theodore De Bruyn, "The Use of the Sanctus in Christian Greek Papyrus Amulets," *Studia Patristica* 40 (2006): 15–20; Theodore De Bruyn and Jitse Dijkstra, "Greek Amulets and Formularies from Egypt Containing Christian Elements: A Checklist of Papyri, Parchments, Ostraka, and Tablets," *Bulletin of the American Society of Papyrologists* 48 (2011): 163–216; Theodore De Bruyn, *Making Amulets Christian: Artefacts, Scribes, and Contexts*, Oxford Early Christian Studies (Oxford: Oxford University Press, 2017); Gabriele Winkler, "Nochmals zu den Anfängen der Epiklese und des Sanctus im Eucharistischen Hochgebet," *Theologische Quartalschrift* 174 (1994): 214–31; Gabriele Winkler, "The Appearance of the Light at the Baptism of Jesus and the Origins of Epiphany: An Investigation of Greek, Syriac, Armenian, and Latin Sources," in *Between Memory and Hope: Readings on the Liturgical Year*, ed. Maxwell Johnson (Collegeville, MN: Liturgical Press, 2000), 291–348. The use of the *Sanctus* in magical and other para-liturgical texts likely is due to the way in which the *Sanctus* functions as a high point in the ritual celebration, something that is also taken up by Winkler. But the way the *Sanctus* functions as a high point is also clear from "The Investiture of the Archangel Gabriel," a Sahidic apocryphon from the sixth/ seventh century; see Lance Jenott, "The Investiture of Archangel Gabriel," in *New Testament Apocrypha: More Noncanonical Scriptures*, ed. Tony Burke, vol. 2 (Grand Rapids: Eerdmans, 2020), 559–79. I thank Ágnes Mihálykó for the reference.

92. Cuthbert Atchley, *On the Epiclesis of the Eucharistic Liturgy and in the Consecration of the Font* (London: Oxford University Press, 1935); Sebastian Brock, "The Epiklesis in the Antiochene Baptismal Ordines," *Orientalia Christiana Periodica* 197 (1974): 183–218; Brock, "Invocations to/for the Holy Spirit"; Winkler, "Further Observations"; Winkler, "Nochmals"; Gabriele Winkler, "Weitere Beobachtungen zur frühen

anamnesis,[93] and intercessions.[94] Moreover, it has also long been noted that some anaphoras, like the RC, "[give] the impression of having been assembled from a number of independent prayer units, which suggest that it evolved slowly and perhaps in varying combinations to begin with."[95]

Looking at the structure and USPs within the classical anaphoras can help scholars determine the core of an anaphora and likely the oral tradition from which it emerged. However, it should be noted that some of the classical anaphoras, like BARC, lie closer to the oral traditions from which they derived. Later anaphoras are almost always the result of changes made to an anaphoral tradition that had already entered into a written form.[96] The Ethiopian Anaphora of the Apostles in the Aksumite Collection (Ethio-AA),[97] which is a conflation of two earlier written anaphoral traditions, is a perfect example of an anaphora that derives directly from a written rather than oral tradition.[98]

By studying the structure and USPs of an anaphora, scholars can uncover the narrative framework of that particular anaphoral tradition. Then they can investigate the anaphora further by analyzing the core theological themes and stock phrases used to fill out that structure. This gives the heart of the anaphoral tradition, which can allow scholars to deduce from fully extant anaphoras the general structure and hooks they had in their oral or early written stages. In cases where multiple forms of

---

Epiklese (den Doxologien und dem Sanctus): Über die Bedeutung der Apokryphen für die Erforschung der Entwicklung der Riten," *Oriens Christianus* 90 (1996): 177–200.

93. SM I 35 and SM I 23 in *Supplementum Magicum*; see Robert Daniel and Franco Maltomini, eds., *Supplementum Magicum*, Papyrologica Coloniensia, XVI.1 (Opladen: Westdeutscher Verlag, 1992).

94. John R. K. Fenwick, "The Significance of Similarities in the Anaphoral Intercession Sequence in the Coptic Anaphora of St. Basil and Other Ancient Liturgies," *Studia Patristica* 18, no. 2 (1989): 355–62; W. Jardine Grisbrooke, "Intercession at the Eucharist I.," *Studia Liturgica* 4 (1965): 129–55; W. Jardine Grisbrooke, "Intercession at the Eucharist II.1," *Studia Liturgica* 5 (1966): 20–44; W. Jardine Grisbrooke, "Intercession at the Eucharist II.2," *Studia Liturgica* 5 (1966): 87–103; Chase, "Fruits of Communion."

95. PEER[4e], 201.

96. See Chase, "Rethinking Anaphoral Development," 91–132.

97. Emmanuel Fritsch, "How the Antiochene Anaphora of the Apostolic Tradition Became the Ge'ez Anaphora of the Apostles," in *Holy Spirit University of Kaslik, Faculty of Religious and Oriental Sciences, Institute of Liturgy and Department of Syriac and Antiochian Sciences, International Conference "Anaphora in Syriac Rites" 26–28 April 2017* (Beirut: USEK, 2017), 115–58.

98. See n. 140.

an anaphora exist, or where two anaphoras have been brought together to create a new one through conflation (see the section "The 'Authorship' of the Classical Anaphoras" below), this process can help reveal shared themes and USPs that likely were part of an older written tradition, or which date back to an oral period.

This technique may also be able to uncover ancient connections between anaphoral traditions that appear quite divergent in their received texts. Again, this is a refinement of techniques that have long been deployed by anaphoral historians. Geoffrey Cuming, for instance, argued that the textual parallels between MARK, MC 5, and the Anaphora of St. James (JAS)[99] suggest that there was a "common ancestor" behind these anaphoral texts.[100] His intuition that MARK and JAS are related anaphoras has generated further reflection by Bryan Spinks,[101] John Paul Abdelsayed,[102] Maxwell Johnson,[103] and Anna Petrin.[104] By looking at the structure of these prayers and their USPs, as well as the core theological themes and stock phrases used to fill out that structure, I have recently argued that not only are MARK and JAS rooted in a common tradition, but so too is BARC.[105] The structural and textual parallels between

---

99. PEER[4e], 139–52.

100. Geoffrey Cuming, "The Shape of the Anaphora," *Studia Patristica* 20 (1989): 341. Here Cuming expands on the relationship between MARK and JAS articulated in Geoffrey Cuming, "The Anaphora of St. Mark: A Study in Development," *Le Muséon* 95 (1982): 115–29. Bryan Spinks remarked at the "Symposium on the Liturgy of Saint James" in June 2022 that Cuming later retracted his position at a conference, but never elaborated on why or put his retraction into print. I believe, however, that Cuming's initial instincts were right.

101. Bryan Spinks, "The Jerusalem Liturgy of the Catecheses Mystagogicae: Syrian or Egyptian?," *Studia Patristica* 18 (1989): 391–95.

102. Abdelsayed, "Liturgical Exodus."

103. Maxwell Johnson, "The Origins of the Anaphoral Sanctus and Epiclesis Revisited: The Contribution of Gabriele Winkler and Its Implications," in *Crossroad of Cultures: Studies in Liturgy and Patristics in Honor of Gabriele Winkler*, ed. Hans-Jürgen Feulner, Elena Velkovska, and Robert Taft, Orientalia Christiana Analecta 260 (Rome: Pontificio Istituto Orientale, 2000), 405–42.

104. Anna Adams Petrin, "The Egyptian Connection: Egyptian Elements in the Liturgy of Jerusalem," PhD diss. (Notre Dame: University of Notre Dame, 2018), especially chap. 4.

105. Nathan Chase, "The Anaphoras of the Barcelona Papyrus, St. Mark, and St. James: An Anaphoral Hydra?," forthcoming in proceedings from the *Symposium on the Liturgy of Saint James, Regensburg, Germany, June 2022*.

BARC, MARK, MC 5, and JAS suggest that there was a fairly standardized way of praying in the early fourth century that was shared between Egypt and Jerusalem. These texts all emerged from this shared—and at first oral—tradition.

As a result, a look at the structure, USPs, core themes, and stock phrases can shed light not only on the redactional history of a text, but also perhaps point to an oral tradition and, in some cases, a shared tradition from which several anaphoral texts emerged.

Model Anaphoral Texts

What has been said above about narrative structure, USPs, and stock phrases can shed further light on the important role anaphoral models played in the development and formalization of early eucharistic prayers. These models provided the basic narrative structure of a prayer with its USPs and core themes. These anaphoral models could be used as is, or could be elaborated on extemporaneously or in their written form by a redactor. The most influential anaphoral models were the liturgical prayers that were contained in the genre of texts known as the "church orders," which circulated broadly across the Christian world.[106]

One early model anaphora contained in the church orders is the eucharistic prayer in ApTrad chap. 4.[107] It is clear from ApTrad chap. 9 that this text could be used as is, or could serve as an example for the creation of another text or extemporized prayer.[108] As a model, ApTrad chap. 4 was one example of how various anaphoral units could be arranged to form a structural "ladder" that could be filled out in the ritual performance or in a prayer's written codification. This explains why ApTrad chap. 4 was expanded into a number of later anaphoras, e.g. Ethio-AA and TD.[109]

At the same time, model anaphoral texts like ApTrad chap. 4 were not always used as the base text for later anaphoral traditions. Oftentimes they were used as source texts for stock phrases that could be incorporated

---

106. Paul Bradshaw, *Ancient Church Orders*, Joint Liturgical Studies 80 (Norwich: Hymns Ancient and Modern, 2015).
107. Bouley, *From Freedom to Formula*, 123.
108. Bradshaw, Johnson, and Phillips, *Apostolic Tradition*, 68.
109. See n. 140 and n. 5 respectively.

into other very different anaphoral traditions. When the model text was well-known, the borrowing of a phrase from the model prayer into another anaphora also worked as an intertext. Intertextuality is the use of a text or formula from one source—oral or written—in another.[110] It generates meaning by bringing the worlds of multiple texts to bear in a single text. Intertextuality functions best when the model text is well-known.

The ancient reception of *Didache* chaps. 9 and 10 can serve as a helpful example of both the borrowing of stock phrases from a model text and intertextuality. Portions of the *Didache* were deployed in later anaphoral texts, particularly those in Egypt, and the text was cited by early Egyptian writers, though only the "Two Ways" section of the document may have been intended.[111] Whether or not early Egyptian writers were referencing just the "Two Ways" section of the text or both the "Two Ways" and the liturgical portions of the document, phrases from *Didache* chaps. 9 and 10—for example, "that the bread scattered on the mountains may be brought into one"—appear in early Egyptian prayers, such as the Anaphora of Sarapion of Thmuis (SAR),[112] and the anaphora in the *Deir Balyzeh Papyrus*,[113] as well as later texts like the anaphora preserved in several fragmentary ostraca (CO).[114] This and other evidence strongly suggests that the liturgical parts of the *Didache* were also cir-

---

110. Day, *Reading the Liturgy*, chap. 5.

111. Kurt Niederwimmer argues that the liturgical sections quoted in Egyptian prayers are simply rooted in a common tradition; see Kurt Niederwimmer and Harold W Attridge, *The Didache: A Commentary* (Minneapolis: Fortress Press, 1998), 4–17.

112. PEER[4e], 90–96.

113. PEER[4e], 100–102.

114. This is a single anaphora that is attested in three ostraca fragments: O.BM Nr. 32799; O.BM Nr. 33050; and O.Hermitage inv. 1133. W. E. Crum, *Coptic Ostraca* (London: Egypt Exploration Fund, 1902) Nr. 4 and 7; H. Quecke, "Das anaphorische Dankgebet auf den koptischen Ostraka B.M. Nr. 32 799 und 33 050," *Orientalia Christiana Periodica* 37 (1971): 391–405; H. Quecke, "Das anaphorische Dankgebet auf dem koptischen Ostrakon Nr 1133 der Leningrader Eremitage neu herausgegeben," *Orientalia Christiana Periodica* 40 (1974): 46–60. ET: Alistair Stewart, *Two Early Egyptian Liturgical Papyri: The Deir Balyzeh Papyrus and the Barcelona Papyrus with Appendices Containing Comparative Material*, Joint Liturgical Studies 70 (Norwich: Hymns Ancient and Modern, 2010), 52–54. See also Ágnes T. Mihálykó, *The Christian Liturgical Papyri: An Introduction*, Studien und Texte zu Antike und Christentum 114 (Tübingen: Mohr Siebeck, 2019), 306 and 312.

culating in Egypt at an early date.[115] While the text of chaps. 9 and 10 of the *Didache* did not serve as the base text for any of the extant anaphoral prayers from Egypt, these chapters likely functioned as a source for stock phrases. Given that the text seems to have been well known in Egypt, it would have even functioned as an intertext.

What facilitated the use of anaphoral models was the fact that early anaphoral forms were written on single sheets or on *libelli*[116] that were circulated for distribution. Ágnes Mihálykó has noted that these single sheets, as well as ostraca and other such things, likely were also used as memory aids.[117] While the term *libelli* is used primarily in a Western context, there is no reason why it could not apply to an Eastern context as well.[118] The prayers of Sarapion of Thmuis and those in the Euchologion of the Aksumite Collection are Eastern examples.[119] The prayer collection in the *Barcelona Papyrus* was also likely a *libelli* of sorts before it was incorporated into the larger mixed manuscript.[120] Achim Budde has also suggested that the sixth-century Greek fragment of BARC (Vienna, PVindob. G 41043) and some of the MARKan sources may have been circulated on single sheets or in *libelli*.[121]

---

115. See also Jonathan Schwiebert, *Knowledge and the Coming Kingdom: The Didache's Meal Ritual and Its Place in Early Christianity*, Library of New Testament Studies 373 (London: T&T Clark, 2008), chap. 8. A few other pieces of evidence suggest this, mainly the changes made to *Didache* chap. 10 in the Coptic fragment Br. Mus. Or. 9271 (Copt.) and the number of early Egyptian and Ethiopian sources; see Niederwimmer and Attridge, *Didache*, 21–27. While not known to Niederwimmer and Attridge, fragments of the *Didache* appear in the Aksumite collection; see Alessandro Bausi, "La *Collezione Aksumita* Canonico-Liturgica," *Adamantius* 12 (2006): 43–70.

116. For a helpful summary, see Eric Palazzo, *A History of Liturgical Books from the Beginning to the Thirteenth Century* (Collegeville, MN: Liturgical Press, 1998), 37–39.

117. Mihálykó, *Christian Liturgical Papyri*; see chap. 6, especially 210–19.

118. Bouley, *From Freedom to Formula*, 165, 168, 178, 179, 183, 185–86, 188, 194, 199, 210–11, 215, and 222n24.

119. Ibid., 222n24. This is affirmed by Heinzgerd Brakmann; see Heinzgerd Brakmann, "ⲂⲀⲠⲦⲒⲤⲘⲀ ⲀⲒⲚⲈⲤⲈⲰⲤ: Ordines und Orationen kirchlicher Eingliederung in Alexandrien und Ägypten," in *"Neugeboren aus Wasser und Heiligem Geist" Kölner Kolloquium zur Initiatio Christiana*, ed. Heinzgerd Brakmann, Tinatin Chronz, and Claudia Sode (Münster: Aschendorff Verlag, 2020), 90–104.

120. Mihálykó, *Christian Liturgical Papyri*, 236–38.

121. Budde, *Die ägyptische Basilios-Anaphora*, 561.

While it seems most likely that whole texts rather than units were circulated,[122] it is possible that this was not always the case. Individual parts of the anaphora may have circulated independently.[123] This is especially clear in the use of the *Sanctus* and epiclesis across Christian rituals,[124] but some texts may also be witnesses to the circulation of independent units, such as the early form of MARK preserved in the *Strasbourg Papyrus* (Strasbourg PGr 254),[125] which may have emerged first in a non-eucharistic setting;[126] Bonn 267;[127] CO;[128] and Vienna, Nationalbibliothek G 19937.[129] Even if a whole anaphoral text was circulated, particular units could have served as models without the whole anaphora needing to be adopted as a base text.

The circulation of model texts, in *libelli*, single sheets, or in other ways, would have allowed for the dissemination of these liturgical models.

The Emergence of New Anaphoral Construction Techniques

The shift to written texts and the creation of model anaphoras allowed for new anaphoral construction techniques to emerge, beginning possibly as early as the third century. As anaphoral traditions were shifting from oral traditions to written texts, the earliest written prayers were still open to emendation and change. This was especially the case in the fourth and fifth centuries. By the sixth century the anaphoras were much more codified.

Before the codification of the classical anaphoras in the sixth century, a variety of construction techniques were used in their expansion and development. As Cuming has remarked, "the process of assembling the

---

122. See Mihálykó, *Christian Liturgical Papyri*; see especially 227–29.

123. For a general discussion of this, see Budde, *Die ägyptische Basilios-Anaphora*, 560–61.

124. See nn. 91 and 92.

125. PEER[4e], 88–90.

126. Bradshaw, "Introduction," 6. Parallels can be seen in P.Oxy 3.407 and the Prayer in the Early Morning in the *Sinodos*; see George Horner, *The Statutes of the Apostles or Canones Ecclesiastici* (London: Williams & Norgate, 1904), 222.

127. Klaus Gamber, "Bemerkungen zu ägyptischen Anaphora-Fragmenten," *Ostkirchliche Studien* 22 (1973): 322.

128. For more, see n. 114.

129. For more, see Mihálykó, *Christian Liturgical Papyri*; see especially 227–29.

units varies from anaphora to anaphora."[130] But it is not just the process between anaphoras that varies. Evidence suggests that the process of assembling the units within an anaphora also varies from unit to unit. Between and within anaphoras, multiple processes of assembly—agglomeration, interpolation, and/or conflation—were at play.

Agglomeration/Addition: Agglomeration describes the addition of units to an anaphoral structure through the absorption of prayers around the central prayer. This implies a high degree of fluidity still in the anaphoral tradition/emerging textual form. As a result, this only applies to the early stages of anaphoral development, when anaphoras had yet to be viewed as a seamless whole. As a result, units were absorbed and melded together from the eucharistic liturgy in order to form a single prayer.[131]

Interpolation: The term "interpolation" should only be used to describe instances when a unit has been inserted into an already highly fixed anaphoral structure. AM and the RC are two helpful examples. The institution narrative was inserted into AM to form *Sharar*,[132] and the *Sanctus* appears to have been inserted into a pre-existing form of the RC to form the received text of the prayer.[133]

Conflation: Conflation is the process by which two distinct and relatively stable anaphoras (or anaphoral forms) are merged to create a new anaphora. Often, one anaphora serves as the base text and its structure and/or text is supplemented by a secondary anaphora or anaphoral form. Here we are talking about large-scale exchanges that usually involve some structural changes to the primary anaphora used as the base text. Examples of conflation include: a) the formation of JAS from MC 5 and the Anaphora of St. Basil (BAS);[134] b) the formation of the Anaphora of

---

130. Cuming, "Shape," 340.

131. Alistair Stewart has argued this with regard to the formation of MARK; see Stewart, *Two Early Egyptian Liturgical Papyri*, 5. Emmanuel Cutrone has suggested this with MC 5; see Emmanuel Cutrone, "The Liturgical Setting of the Institution Narrative in the Early Syrian Tradition," in *Time and Community*, ed. J. Neil Alexander (Washington, DC: Pastoral Press, 1990), 105–14.

132. PEER[4e], 69–76.

133. See n. 7.

134. For the text of BAS, see Egyptian version (E-BAS): PEER[4e], 115–23; Byzantine version (Byz-BAS): PEER[4e], 171–81. For more on the formation of JAS, see John R. K. Fenwick, *Fourth Century Anaphoral Construction Techniques*, Grove Liturgical Study

St. John Chrysostom (CHR)[135] from the hypothesized Anaphora of the Apostles (AP)[136] and BAS;[137] c) the formation of the (Syriac) Anaphora of the Twelve Apostles[138] from AP and a Syrian version of JAS;[139] and d) the formation of Ethio-AA from ApTrad chap. 4 and MARK.[140]

The "Authorship" of the Classical Anaphoras

In light of what has been said above about the shift from oral anaphoral traditions to written anaphoral texts, as well as the use of model anaphoras, it is worth briefly noting how this changes our understanding of the way in which the classical anaphoras were authored. Questions about authorship are largely foreign to an oral tradition, and the multi-redactional history of liturgical texts makes authorship difficult, if not impossible, to establish. Nevertheless, scholars have wrestled with ways to establish authorship. Cuming's work on CHR continues to be one of the most influential approaches to authorial attribution in anaphoral studies.[141] In that article, Cuming put forward three types of attribution:

1. Liturgies attributed to an apostle or other notable figure where the name is chosen to give authority to the text but none would consider them responsible for it: "pseudonymous attribution."

2. Liturgies attributed to a notable figure where the attribution is "in all probability correct," even though positive evidence may be lacking: "authentic attribution."

---

45 (Bramcote: Grove Books, 1986); John R. K. Fenwick, *The Anaphoras of St. Basil and St. James: An Investigation into Their Common Origin*, Orientalia Christiana Analecta 240 (Rome: Pontificium Institutum Orientale, 1992).

135. PEER[4e], 164–71.

136. For more, see John R. K. Fenwick, *"The Missing Oblation": The Contents of the Early Antiochene Anaphora*, Joint Liturgical Studies (Bramcote: Grove Books, 1989). No reconstruction has been posited.

137. Fenwick points to Byz-BAS, while Stefano Parenti points to BAS more generally; see ibid.; Stefano Parenti, *L'anafora Di Crisostomo*, Jerusalemer Theologisches Forum 36 (Münster: Aschendorff Verlag, 2020).

138. PEER[4e], 158–64.

139. Fenwick, *"Missing Oblation."*

140. Fritsch, "How the Antiochene Anaphora."

141. Geoffrey Cuming, "Pseudonymity and Authenticity, with Special Reference to the Liturgy of St John Chrysostom," *Studia Patristica* 15 (1984): 532–38.

Shaping the Classical Anaphoras of the Fourth through Sixth Centuries 51

3. And between these categories, attributions which may be pseudonymous or authentic. The named author may be sufficiently well known to attract attention to the text bearing his name (hence the risk of pseudonymity), but he flourished at the right time for the attribution (hence the possibility of authenticity).[142]

Furthermore, Cuming highlighted three ways to establish attribution:

1. Common words and phrases between a liturgy and an author's work;
2. The use of stock phrases;
3. Assessing stylistic similarities.[143]

Cuming's approach has been utilized by a number of scholars, but more recent scholarship has pointed out the limitations of this approach. Both Bradshaw and Juliette Day, for instance, have called for new understandings of authorship.[144] Writing about the church orders, Bradshaw explains why authorial attribution for early liturgical texts is problematic:

> Both the individual documents and the various composite collections of the material were subject to a process of emendation and "correction" by successive editors, copyists, and translators. Indeed, most of the church orders are not independent compositions at all, but themselves constitute a further stage of the rewriting of an earlier text in the series.[145]

Day has been even more critical of authorial attribution.[146] She uses SAR as her central example for how new understandings of authorial

---

142. Taken from Day, *Reading the Liturgy*, 28.
143. A longer summary appears in ibid., 29.
144. Paul Bradshaw, "Liturgy and 'Living Literature,'" in *Liturgy in Dialogue: Essays in Memory of Ronald Jasper*, ed. Paul Bradshaw and Bryan Spinks (London: SPCK, 1993), 138–53; Day, *Reading the Liturgy*. They are not alone; see Volp, "Liturgical Authority Reconsidered"; Budde, *Die ägyptische Basilios-Anaphora*; Bryan Spinks, "The Anaphora Attributed to Severus of Antioch: A Note on Its Character and Theology," in Θυσία Αἰνέσεως: *Mélanges Liturgiques Offerts à La Mémoire de l'archevêque Georges Wagner (1930–1993)*, ed. J. Getcha and A. Lossky (Paris: Presses Saint-Serge–Institut de Théologie Orthodoxe, 2005), 345–51; Bukovec, "Der Einsetzungsbericht," 562–63; Parenti, *L'anafora Di Crisostomo*, especially chap. 3.
145. Bradshaw, "Liturgy and 'Living Literature,'" 139.
146. Day, *Reading the Liturgy*, 21–40.

attribution can reshape our understanding of the text and its creation. While authorship is traditionally established through parallels between an anaphora and an author's other works, this leads to a number of methodological issues. In particular, it "risks a somewhat circular process whereby on the basis of a name appearing in a manuscript, a context and a relationship to other texts bearing the same name are presumed; that context and the other texts then serve to confirm the initial attribution."[147]

In an effort to further clarify our understanding of attribution and authorship, Day turns to the work of Harold Love,[148] who has noted four different kinds of authorship:

1. Precursory authorship, where a significant amount of material has been taken from previously existing sources, either by influence or direct borrowing.

2. Executive authorship, which closely resembles the traditional notion of "author"; she is the one who devises, orders, compiles, and makes a text ready for publication. This may be achieved by more than one person, although the sole executor carries greater esteem.

3. Declarative authorship consists of the process of a text's validation by a named individual whose involvement in its production may be severely limited or non-existent, but who nevertheless influences the contextualization and interpretation of the text. Love includes here the retrospective attribution of authorship to an anonymous text, as well as ghost-writing.

4. Revisionary authorship occurs after the creation of a text when it may be polished or corrected, edited or revised by a second author or editor.[149]

Day writes, "[A]uthorship in relation to texts which are based on a preceding oral tradition can only be envisaged as multiple, there cannot be a single creative origin, but instead a creative use of the traditions of structure and language in relation to the specific worshipping context."[150]

---

147. Ibid., 25.
148. Harold Love, *Attributing Authorship* (Cambridge: Cambridge University Press, 2002).
149. Taken from Day, *Reading the Liturgy*, 31.
150. Ibid., 35.

Since this applies to many of the classical anaphoras, this complicates our understanding of their authorship. In the age of oral improvisation, in which high numbers of stock phrases and the like were used in anaphoral construction, authorship is even more difficult to determine.[151] At the same time, Day is not willing to abandon the question of authorship, since "it forces us to consider how our texts are created; however, to retain it, 'author' cannot be assigned to an individual . . . it designates the processes which cause a text to come into being."[152]

An understanding of authorship as multiple and constrained by an oral and emerging written tradition necessitates new understandings of how these texts were formed. It also requires scholars to reevaluate their approach to authorial attribution, since behind these received texts are oral traditions and a chain of performers, redactors, and copyists.

The Legalization and Adoption of Christianity

Having looked at some of the processes that shaped the classical anaphoras of the third through sixth centuries, it is now worth looking at the factors that were especially influential in the formation and codification of the classical anaphoras from the fourth century onward. One of the larger contextual factors that shaped the classical anaphoras was the legalization of Christianity in 313 CE. The legalization and adoption of Christianity by Roman authorities led to the further incorporation of secular and imperial practices into the liturgy, as well as the expansion and dramatization of the liturgy and the anaphora.[153] At the same time, there was also some

---

151. Ibid., 33.
152. Ibid., 39.
153. See, for example, Margot Fassler and Peter Jeffery, "Christian Liturgical Music from the Bible to the Renaissance," in *Sacred Sound and Social Change: Liturgical Music in Jewish and Christian Experience.*, ed. Lawrence Hoffman and Janet Walton (Notre Dame: University of Notre Dame Press, 1993), 84–123; Bradshaw, "Homogenization"; Bradshaw, "Continuity and Change"; Bradshaw, "Coming of Christendom"; John Baldovin, "The Empire Baptized," in *The Oxford History of Christian Worship*, ed. Geoffrey Wainwright and Karen Westerfield Tucker (Oxford: Oxford University Press, 2006), 77–130; Kimberly Belcher, "Ritual Systems, Ritualized Bodies, and the Laws of Liturgical Development," *Studia Liturgica* 49 (2019): 103; Bradshaw and Johnson, *Eucharistic Liturgies*, 61–63; Nathan Chase, "Developments in Early Eucharistic Praying in Light of Changes in Early Christian Meeting Spaces," forthcoming in the *Journal of Early Christian Studies*.

resistance to this imperialization.¹⁵⁴ Nevertheless, the use of Greco-Roman meal practices as the ancient model for eucharistic celebrations allowed for the latter's quick imperialization after Christianity's legalization.¹⁵⁵

The legalization of Christianity and its subsequent growth resulted in the need for even larger worship spaces, as well as their proliferation.¹⁵⁶ It also necessitated changes to the eucharistic celebration in order to accommodate the increasingly large number of catechumens, since the catechumens could not (at least in theory) remain for the whole eucharistic liturgy.¹⁵⁷ But the legalization of Christianity also came with some less desirable consequences. The flood of catechumens meant the need to adopt new initiatory practices and establish more instructional rituals (see the sections below). It also often meant that places were filled with catechumens who could not receive the Eucharist. This ultimately contributed to the decline in the reception of communion, and an increasing perception of unworthiness among Christians.¹⁵⁸

Decline in Martyrdom

Martyrdom and its decline due to the legalization of Christianity had a significant impact on the early church, both in official and unofficial ways.¹⁵⁹ It necessitated changes in eucharistic practice as well as in the

---

154. See n. 58.

155. Leonhard, "Morning *Salutationes*," 439–41, here at 441.

156. For general summaries of developments in church architecture, see L. Michael White, *The Social Origins of Christian Architecture*, 2 vols., Harvard Theological Studies 42 (Valley Forge: Trinity Press International, 1990); Charles Anthony Stewart, "Churches," in *The Oxford Handbook of Early Christian Archaeology*, ed. David K. Pettegrew, William R. Caraher, and Thomas W. Davis (New York: Oxford University Press, 2019), 127–46. See also Chase, "Developments in Early Eucharistic Praying."

157. However, the *disciplina arcani* may have been more a fiction than a reality; see Craig Alan Satterlee, *Ambrose of Milan's Method of Mystagogical Preaching* (Collegeville, MN: Liturgical Press, 2002), 155–56.

158. Bradshaw, "Fourth Century," 113; Bradshaw and Johnson, *Eucharistic Liturgies*, 66–69.

159. Jensen, "Dining with the Dead"; Paul F. Bradshaw and Maxwell E. Johnson, *The Origins of Feasts, Fasts, and Seasons in Early Christianity*, Alcuin Club Collections 86 (Collegeville, MN: Liturgical Press, 2011), chap. 19; Albertus G. A. Horsting, "Transfiguration of Flesh: Literary and Theological Connections between Martyrdom Accounts and Eucharistic Prayers," in *Issues in Eucharistic Praying in East and West*,

eucharistic prayers themselves. As noted above, Christian eucharistic practice was shaped by Greco-Roman *refrigeria*, and this was especially true of the Eucharists (eucharistic-*refrigeria*) celebrated at the tombs of the martyrs. In fact, large shrines and *martyria* were constructed over the tombs of the martyrs to facilitate their cults. Christians would gather at these shrines for pilgrimages and commemorations, and they would celebrate the Eucharist in them. The celebration of these funerary and memorial meals, especially in the *martyria*, likely led to the proliferation of eucharistic celebrations, especially on weekdays in the West.[160]

It is also very likely that the decline of martyrdom was one of the factors that led to the introduction of the institution narrative into the anaphora. The addition of the institution narrative was one way to heighten the sacrificial dimensions of the Eucharist that were once apparent in the sacrifice of the martyrs.[161] Additionally, the celebration of the funerary/memorial Eucharists likely led to the introduction of intercessions for the dead—and other saints[162]—within the anaphora proper. In fact, intercessions for the dead were one of the first types of intercessions included in the classical anaphoras.[163]

Doctrinal Developments

Theologically the fourth century saw a flurry of doctrinal developments that influenced Christian liturgy, particularly the christological and trinitarian controversies. These developments led to the introduction of some new liturgical forms, like the use of trinitarian formulas in the doxology, but more importantly they spurred the widespread adoption

---

ed. Maxwell Johnson (Collegeville, MN: Liturgical Press, 2011), 307–26; Klawiter, *Martyrdom, Sacrificial Libation*.

160. Mitchell, *Cult and Controversy*, chap. 1; Bradshaw and Johnson, *Eucharistic Liturgies*, 68–69.

161. Maxwell Johnson, "Martyrs and the Mass: The Interpolation of the Narrative of Institution into the Anaphora," *Worship* 87 (2013): 2–22.

162. Maxwell Johnson, "*Sub Tuum Praesidium:* The *Theotokos* in Christian Life and Worship Before Ephesus," in *The Place of Christ in Liturgical Prayer: Trinity, Christology, and Liturgical Theology*, ed. Bryan Spinks (Collegeville, MN: Liturgical Press, 2008), 243–67.

163. Chase, "Fruits of Communion."

of liturgical practices, like the use of a *pneumatological* epiclesis.[164] In general, the need for doctrinal precision was one of the central driving forces that led to the codification of early anaphoras, as well as their elaboration.

However, the impact of doctrinal developments on eucharistic praying appears to have been much more limited than scholars have previously acknowledged. It was more or less confined to the epiclesis[165] and doxology[166]—those places where the distinct operations of the persons of the Trinity were outlined. Developments in other units within the anaphora, like the preface and christological post-*Sanctus*, cannot be *directly* attributed to doctrinal development, though their content likely was shaped by it. Creedal formulas, which emerged already by the second/third centuries,[167] provided a ready-made set of doctrinally acceptable stock phrases that could be incorporated into eucharistic prayers. They can often be seen in the post-*Sanctus*[168] and anamneses[169] of the classical anaphoras.

---

164. Bradshaw, "Introduction," 17. See also Paul Bradshaw, *The Search for the Origins of Christian Worship: Sources and Methods for the Study of Early Liturgy* (New York: Oxford University Press, 2002), 226–28; Chase, "From *Logos* to Spirit Revisited."

165. Anne McGowan, *Eucharistic Epicleses, Ancient and Modern: Speaking of the Spirit in Eucharistic Prayer* (Collegeville, MN: Liturgical Press, 2014), 92–96.

166. Larry W. Hurtado, "The Binitarian Pattern of Earliest Christian Devotion and Early Doctrinal Development," in *The Place of Christ in Liturgical Prayer: Trinity, Christology, and Liturgical Theology*, ed. Bryan Spinks (Collegeville, MN: Liturgical Press, 2008), 23–50; Larry W. Hurtado, *One God, One Lord: Early Christian Devotion and Ancient Jewish Monotheism* (London: T&T Clark, 2015); Paul Bradshaw, "God, Christ, and the Holy Spirit in Early Christian Praying," in *The Place of Christ in Liturgical Prayer: Trinity, Christology, and Liturgical Theology*, ed. Bryan Spinks (Collegeville, MN: Liturgical Press, 2008), 51–64; Maxwell Johnson, *Praying and Believing in Early Christianity: The Interplay Between Christian Worship and Doctrine* (Collegeville, MN: Liturgical Press, 2013), chap. 2.

167. Creedal language exists already in the New Testament, but semi-formal creeds first emerge with Justin Martyr in the mid-second century. The first proper creeds, however, do not appear until the third century; see J. N. D. Kelly, *Early Christian Creeds*, 3rd ed. (New York: Continuum, 2006).

168. Chase, "Rethinking Anaphoral Development," chap. 8.

169. See, for instance, Gabriele Winkler, "L'anamnèse dans les diverses versions de l'anaphore de St. Basile: Leurs liens avec le symbole d'Antioche et leur signification théologique," in *"Faire mémoire" L'anamnèse dans la liturgie*, ed. A. Lossky and Manlio Sodi (Vatican: Libreria Editrice Vaticana, 2011), 149–61; Gabriele Winkler, "Zur Erforschung orientalischer Anaphoren in liturgievergleichender Sicht II: Das Formelgut

The Liturgy as Increasingly Instructional

Alongside the importation of creedal formulae into the anaphora, Bradshaw has argued that the need for the liturgy to be more instructional in nature was a major factor in anaphoral developments in the fourth century.[170] The addition of the institution narrative into the anaphora is likely due, in part, to this instructional turn.[171] As the initiatory process broke down in the fourth century due to the growing number of initiates and the decline in their fervor, the liturgy increasingly had to take on the instructional role otherwise performed by mystagogy. This may also explain the insertion of creedal formulas into the classical anaphoras in this period.

Historicizing Tendencies

Finally, the tendency to historicize the liturgy also influenced the development of the classical anaphoras, particularly in the fourth century. Johannes Betz writes:

> After the reform of liturgical prayer at Caesarea and Antioch, the priestly action of Jesus as the here and now active mediator of our prayers and sacrifices—an action that had formerly been the object of keen Christian awareness—was increasingly obscured; the priestly activity of Jesus was increasingly located in his past work of redemption. In consequence, there was also an increasing emphasis on the Mass as a re-presentation, or making present, of the past saving act of Jesus.[172]

However, Robert Taft and others have shown that, before the fourth century, the liturgy was already being historicized, and that the historicization

---

der Oratio post Sanctus und Anamnese sowie Interzessionen und die Taufbekenntnisse," in *Comparative Liturgy Fifty Years After Anton Baumstark (1872–1948)*, ed. Robert Taft and Gabriele Winkler, Orientalia Christiana Analecta 265 (Rome: Pontificio Istituto Orientale, 2001), 469–75.

170. Bradshaw, *Search for the Origins*, 219–21.
171. Paul Bradshaw, *Eucharistic Origins* (Eugene: Wipf & Stock, 2012), 135.
172. Johannes Betz, *Die Eucharistie in der Zeit der griechischen Väter*, vol. I/1 (Freiburg: Herder, 1955), 128. Translation taken from Hans-Joachim Schulz, *The Byzantine Liturgy* (Collegeville, MN: Liturgical Press, 1986), 11.

of the liturgy in the fourth century should not be exaggerated.[173] Cyprian's insistence "that Christians must follow in their celebration exactly what Christ did at the Last Supper" is a case in point.[174]

At the same time, a look at the classical anaphoras does seem to point to an increase in the historization of the eucharistic liturgy in the fourth through sixth centuries. Two of the anaphoral units most shaped by historicizing tendencies were the institution narrative and anamnesis. For example, the form of MARK's institution narrative preserved in the *Rylands Papyrus* (P.Ryl 3.465) and the British Museum Tablet (BM EA 54036)[175]—dated to the sixth century, if not earlier—shows much more historicization than the earlier institution narrative in BARC:

BARC	Rylands Papyrus/British Museum Tablet
As he himself, when he was about to hand himself, having taken bread and given thanks, broke it and gave it to his disciples, saying: Take, eat, this is my body; Likewise after supper, having taken a cup and given thanks, he gave it to them, saying: Take, drink the blood, which is shed for remission of sins.	For our Lord and Savior and king of all, Jesus Christ, in the night when he was betrayed and willingly underwent death, took bread in his holy and undefiled [and] blessed hands, looked up to heaven to you, the Father of all, blessed, gave thanks over it, sanctified, broke [and] gave it to his disciples [and] apostles, saying, "Take and eat of this, all of you; this is my body, which is given for you for the forgiveness of your sins. Do this for my remembrance." Likewise, after supper, he took a cup, blessed, sanctified, [and] gave it to them, saying, "Take this and drink from it, all of you; this is my blood of the new covenant, which is shed for many for the forgiveness of their sins. Do this for my remembrance. For as often as you eat this bread and drink this cup, you proclaim my death [and] confess my resurrection."

---

173. John Baldovin, *The Urban Character of Christian Worship: The Origins, Development, and Meaning of Stational Liturgy*, Orientalia Christiana Analecta 228 (Rome: Pontificio Instituto Studiorum Orientalium, 1987), 87–90; Robert Taft, *Beyond East and West: Problems in Liturgical Understanding*, 2nd ed. (Rome: Ed. Orientalia Christiana, 2001), chap. 2.

174. Bradshaw and Johnson, *Eucharistic Liturgies*, 33.

175. PEER[4e], 102–4.

Conclusion

This essay has looked briefly at some of the key processes and influences that shaped the classical anaphoras of the fourth through sixth centuries. It began with an overview of the connection between Greco-Roman meal practices and the early celebration of the eucharist, before then turning to a number of developments and factors that lead to significant changes in the classical anaphoras:

1. *The shift from a eucharistic meal to the token distribution of bread and wine.* This shift occurred in most places in the third century but continued in some places into the fifth century. This resulted in the loss of a proper meal and the shift almost exclusively in focus to the bread and wine.

2. *Transition from oral to written prayer traditions.* The earliest anaphoras were oral narrative traditions. In a second stage of development, these oral narrative traditions began to be written down. In a final stage of development, a fully composed written text emerged. The transition of these anaphoral traditions to composed written texts was largely completed by the fifth century.

3. *The use of model anaphoral texts.* Possibly as early as the third century, but especially in the early fourth century, model anaphoral texts were composed. For presiders who could improvise eucharistic prayers well, these models would have served as inspiration. For other presiders, these texts might have been memorized and recited verbatim. These model texts were also used to construct new anaphoras in the fourth, fifth, and sixth centuries.

4. *New construction techniques.* The shift to written texts allowed for the development of new ways of constructing eucharistic prayers. This included agglomeration, interpolation, and conflation. The use of these techniques varied from anaphora to anaphora, but also from unit to unit within an anaphora.

5. *The authorship of the classical anaphoras.* An understanding of authorship as multiple necessitates new understandings of how these texts were formed. The classical anaphoras are the result of a chain of performers, redactors, and copyists. Rather than seeking

to pinpoint a single author, scholars should view the authorship of the classical anaphoras as a process.

6. *The legalization and adoption of Christianity.* The legalization and adoption of Christianity led to a variety of changes, including the imperialization of the eucharistic liturgy and the need for the liturgy to be more instructional.

7. *Decline in martyrdom.* The cult of the martyrs and its relationship to funerary meals shaped the early celebrations of the Eucharist. The decline of martyrdom by the fourth century also shaped eucharistic practice, and likely led to the introduction of the institution narrative into the anaphora.

8. *Doctrinal developments.* The trinitarian and christological doctrinal developments of the fourth and fifth century likely led to the codification and development of eucharistic prayers, particularly in the epiclesis and doxology. These doctrinal developments also led to the introduction of creedal formulae into the classical anaphoras.

9. *The liturgy as increasingly instructional.* With the legalization of Christianity, there was a need for new processes for instructing catechumens and recent converts. This resulted in the liturgy becoming more instructional in nature.

10. *Historicizing tendencies.* As a result of the decline of martyrdom and other practices, Christian liturgy increasingly became historicized, which particularly affected the institution narrative and anamnesis.

The Εἷς Θεός Acclamations in the *Barcelona Papyrus*

A Eucharistic Liturgy without the Opening Line of the Christian Anaphoral Dialogue*

Arsany Paul

Liturgical scholarship has established that, from around the fourth century, most Christian anaphoras were preceded by an opening dialogue between the celebrant and congregation, a practice that is omnipresent in liturgies of the Christian East.[1] However, the anaphora in the manuscript *P.Monts.Roca* inventory 128–178, 292, and 338 (*Montserrat Codex Miscellaneus*), now commonly known as the "Barcelona Papy-

---

* An expanded edition of this article, including colored images, appeared in an online, open-access journal as "The Barcelona Papyrus and the Opening Dialogue of the Christian Anaphora. Resituating Egyptian Scribal Practices Amid Scholarly Anaphoral Reconstructions," *Ex Fonte – Journal of Ecumenical Studies in Liturgy* 1 (2022): 129–68.

1. Paul F. Bradshaw and Maxwell E. Johnson, *The Eucharistic Liturgies: Their Evolution and Interpretation* (Collegeville, MN: Liturgical Press, 2012), 39. For more on the initial anaphoral dialogue in Eastern liturgy, see the following three publications by Robert F. Taft: "The Dialogue before the Anaphora in the Byzantine Eucharistic Liturgy I: The Opening Greeting," *Orientalia Christiana Periodica* 52 (1986): 299–324; "The Dialogue before the Anaphora in the Byzantine Eucharistic Liturgy II: The Sursum Corda," *Orientalia Christiana Periodica* 54 (1988): 47–77; and "The Dialogue before the Anaphora in the Byzantine Eucharistic Liturgy III: Let Us Give Thanks to the Lord—It Is Fitting and Right," *Orientalia Christiana Periodica* 55 (1989): 63–74.

rus," specifically the eucharistic text within MS *P.Monts.Roca*, fols. 154b–155b, lacks the typical first line of this staple introductory prelude. Copied in the fourth century in Middle Egypt, this anaphora represents one of the oldest extant manuscript examples of Christian eucharistic prayers.[2] While foundational and extensive studies on this anaphora have been set forth by the likes of Ramón Roca-Puig,[3] Mikhail Zheltov,[4]

---

2. Papyrological analyses have dated MS *P.Monts.Roca* to the fourth century. See R. C. D. Jasper and G. J. Cuming, *Prayers of the Eucharist: Early and Reformed*, 4th ed., ed. Paul F. Bradshaw and Maxwell E. Johnson, Alcuin Club Collections 94 (Collegeville, MN: Liturgical Press, 2019), 96. On the premise of a tripartite structure of praise, offering, and petition, as well as various correlations to the third-century church order known as the *Apostolic Tradition*, Bradshaw attempted to date the earliest recension of the anaphora in the Barcelona codex to the second century. Moreover, he proposes that, due to the usage of the word "child" (παιδός), which is a common expression in writings no later than the mid-second century, rather than "Son" (υἱός) in relation to Jesus in the preface (§1.4 below) and in the concluding doxology (§1.11 below), this anaphora reflects possible second-century origins. Paul F. Bradshaw, "The Barcelona Papyrus and the Development of Early Eucharistic Prayers," in *Issues in Eucharistic Praying in East and West*, ed. Maxwell E. Johnson (Collegeville, MN: Liturgical Press, 2010), 129–38, here at 136f.

3. His discovery of the *Barcelona Papyrus* in the 1950s and his 1966 publication of the first edition of its text opened the door to envisioning what a complete anaphora entails, since most now consider the eucharistic prayer in the *Barcelona Papyrus* as a complete anaphora. Although groundbreaking, his edition of the papyrus was criticized by Zheltov, who viewed it as undiplomatic, since Roca-Puig did not reproduce the manuscript verbatim, preserving the scribal hand. Moreover, Roca-Puig filled the lacuna in the second epiclesis (§1.10) with his own reconstruction that was dependent upon the Byzantine anaphoras of Basil and Chrysostom, though the Barcelona tradition should be considered Alexandrian in its ethos. See Ramón Roca-Puig, "Sui Papiri de Barcelona," *Aegyptus* 46 (1966): 91–92; Ramón Roca-Puig, *Anàfora de Barcelona I Alters Pregàries: Missa Del Segle IV* (Barcelona: n.p., 1999); Michael Zheltov, "The Anaphora and the Thanksgiving Prayer from the Barcelona Papyrus: An Underestimated Testimony to the Anaphoral History in the Fourth Century," *Vigiliae Christianae* 62 (2008): 467–504, here at 470.

4. Starting in 2002 but culminating in 2008, Zheltov provided a revised diplomatic text and an amended critical edition, which are now regarded as the textual standards for the Barcelona tradition. Michael Zheltov, "Греческая Литургия IV Века в Папирусе Barcelon. Papyr. 154b–157b," *Богословский Сборник* 9 (2002): 240–56; Zheltov, "Anaphora and the Thanksgiving Prayer," 471–94.

and Nathan P. Chase,[5] to name a few,[6] yet in the absence of the preanaphoral interchange, "The Lord be with you / And with your spirit," these scholars have attempted to reconstruct an analogous dialogue within

---

5. Nathan P. Chase, "The Antiochenization of the Egyptian Tradition: An Alternate Approach to the Barcelona Papyrus and Anaphoral Development," *Ecclesia Orans* 34 (2017): 319–67; Nathan P. Chase, "Rethinking Anaphoral Development in Light of the Barcelona Papyrus," PhD diss. (University of Notre Dame, 2020); Nathan P. Chase, "The Fruits of Communion Across the Classical Anaphoras," *Orientalia Christiana Periodica* 87, no. 1 (2021): 5–70. Many thanks to Nathan Chase for providing a copy of his final dissertation.

6. Among other scholarship is Paul Bradshaw, who once attempted to locate the prayers within the West Syrian tradition, though subsequent scholarship has not supported his view and has overwhelmingly placed the Barcelona tradition as Middle or Southern Egyptian. Still, Bradshaw's most grounded contribution to understanding the text remains his differentiation between what he identifies as the older nucleus of the prayer, that is, a "tripartite pattern of praise, offering, and petition," versus possible later supplements. Walter Ray also supports a tripartite structure. Like Bradshaw, Reinhard Meßner argues against the Egyptian origins of MS *P.Monts.Roca* since it lacks intercessory prayers and the verb "to fulfill," which typically connects the *Sanctus* prayer to the first epiclesis, that are common to other early Egyptian anaphoras. See also Alistair C. Stewart's treatment of the papyrus. Among other scholarship, looking at the material evidence, Tea Ghigo and Sofía Torallas-Tovar contributed to the material study of the papyrus through an archaeometric analysis performed upon the inks used within the codex to reaffirm that it was probably produced by a scribe over a period of time prior to the mid-fourth century. Bradshaw, "Barcelona Papyrus and the Development," 129–38; Walter Ray, "The Barcelona Papyrus and the Early Egyptian Eucharistic Prayer," *Studia Liturgica* 41 (2011): 211–29; Reinhard Meßner, "Das Eucharistische Hochgebet in den Traditionen und Kirchen des Ostens," *Österreichische Studien Zur Liturgiewissenschaft und Sakramententheologie* 13 (2020): 121–67; Alistair C. Stewart, *Two Early Egyptian Liturgical Papyri: The Deir Balyzeh Papyrus and the Barcelona Papyrus with Appendices Containing Comparative Material* (Norwich, UK: Hymns Ancient and Modern, 2010), 22–38; Tea Ghigo and Sofia Torallas-Tovar, "Between Literary and Documentary Practices: The Montserrat Codex Miscellaneus (Inv. Nos. 126–178, 292, 338) and the Material Investigation of Its Inks," in *Coptic Literature in Context (4th–13th Cent.): Cultural Landscape, Literary Production, and Manuscript Archaeology. Proceedings of the Third Conference of the ERC Project "Tracking Papyrus and Parchment Paths: An Archaeological Atlas of Coptic Literature. Literary Texts in Their Geographical Context ('PAThs')*," ed. Paola Buzi (Rome: Edizioni Quasar, 2020), 100–114.

the first line of the papyrus's anaphora, "Εἷς Θεὸς Ἰησοῦς ὁ Κύριος," or remained silent on the uniqueness of this commonly used expression.

Contrary to such arguments, however, I present that an attentive reading of the papyrus in its entirety, along with a comparison to similar literary, material, and visual culture evidence, reveal that this opening line is not part of the anaphoral formulary, and that an opening stanza containing anything close to "The Lord be with you / And with your spirit," is simply not found in the manuscript. Furthermore, the opening line of the papyrus's anaphora serves an entirely different function. In this chapter, I emphasize a new interpretation of the initial unit within the anaphora contained within the *Barcelona Papyrus*, namely, the opening dialogue, while relegating other discussions on colophons and other scribal practices to my published article.[7]

I open with an overview of the sources augmented with the various scholarly contributions, followed by an edition of the anaphora marking the said benedictions. After this, I outline the former studies and arguments on this opening line as part of the liturgical formulary. Then, I analyze the use of the Εἷς Θεός phrases throughout the entirety of the *Barcelona Papyrus*, followed by hypotheses on its intended usage with comparisons to similar literary works and material evidence. I conclude that the opening acclamation of Εἷς Θεός at the beginning of the anaphora and its variations prevalent within the codex are auxiliary "marginalia" that the celebrant does not pronounce as part of the formal prayer. Instead, these invocations are common forms of scribal practice attested in the manuscript and cultural traditions of Egypt.[8]

---

7. See opening note above. For direct access: https://doi.org/10.25365/exf-2022-1-5.

8. While my study emphasizes Christian sources, opening a text with a pious expression directed to God is not limited to Christian scribal traditions, but is also found in Islamic manuscripts; consult François Déroche et al., *Islamic Codicology. An Introduction to the Study of Manuscripts in Arabic Script*, Al-Furqān Publications 102 (London: Al-Furqān Islamic Heritage Foundation, 2005), 237f.

Sources

Manuscript *P.Monts.Roca inv.* 128–178, 292, and 338 is predominantly written in Greek, with some portions in Latin.[9] The anaphora under examination is found on fols. 154b–155a, with the remainder of the euchologion's prayers are attested on fols. 155b–157b.[10] In addition to this codex, two other primary sources have been identified as providing parallels to the content of the Barcelona tradition: (1) manuscript *PVindob.* G 41043 (MS *Vienna G 41043*), a subsequent Greek redaction considered a sixth-century source,[11] and, (2) manuscript *Louvain* 27 (MS *Louvain 27*), a Sahidic Coptic version of the prayers attributed to no later than the seventh century.[12] MS *P.Monts.Roca*, however, is the primary and sole textual witness to the pre-anaphoral dialogue debate in the Barcelona tradition, thus forming the exclusive textual reference of this study, since the latter two codices lack the section that would contain the anaphoral opening dialogue.[13]

---

9. A complete paleographical and codicological study is found in Sofía Torallas-Tovar and Klaas A. Worp, *To the Origins of Greek Stenography. P.Monts.Roca I*, Orientalia Montserratensia 4 (Barcelona: Publicacions de l'Abadia de Montserrat, 2006), 15–23.

10. Other prayers within the liturgical portion of this papyrus include (1) a prayer for the imposition of hands on the sick (fols. 155b–156a); (2) an exorcism of the oil for the sick (fols. 156a–b); and (3) an acrostic hymn on Abraham's offering of Isaac (fols. 157a–b).

11. For a critical edition and English translation consult, respectively: Kurt Treu and Johannes Diethart, *Griechische literarsiche Papyri christlichen Inhaltes II: Textband* (Wien: In Kommission Bei Verlag Brüder Hollinek, 1993), 68f.; Jasper and Cuming, *Prayers of the Eucharist*, 99f.

12. For a critical edition and an English translation consult, respectively: Louis-Théophile Lefort, "Coptica Lovanensia," *Le Muséon* 53 (1940): 22–24; Sebastià Janeras, "L'Original grec del fragment copte de Lovaina Núm. 27 en l'Anàfora de Barcelona," *Miscellània Litúrgica Catalana* 3 (1984): 13–25; Jasper and Cuming, *Prayers of the Eucharist*, 99.

13. The pre-anaphoral dialogue is omitted from both counterparts of MS *P.Monts. Roca*—the Sahidic Coptic text in MS *Louvain 27* and the later Greek edition in MS *Vienna G 41043*. This exclusion may simply be due to the fragmented nature of these two codices.

Edition

An edition of the anaphora and the thanksgiving prayer from the *Barcelona Papyrus* follows. Since Zheltov has already produced a revised critical and diplomatic edition, my own version does not differ much from his, beyond the fact that I have taken the liberty to structure and annotate my own rendering according to structural theories about this anaphora's development, as well as some minor adaptations to the English translation.[14] Thus, the text below should be read with the following in mind:

- The section column is added for clarity, and the corresponding section numbers and names are added to aid later discussions in the chapter.
- Adoption of the subsequent *sigla* appear throughout the text:
    - <…> Angled brackets indicate added text for clarification, not present in MS *P.Monts.Roca* but included within Zheltov's rendering that is also based upon the two other witnesses of the anaphora.
    - {…} Braces denote text that should be expunged.
    - (…) Letters within parentheses are supplied.
    - […] Square brackets represent a lacuna in the manuscript.
    - | A vertical bar indicates the start of a folio with the subsequent folio and side number written in superscript.

---

14. Zheltov's critical edition is bolstered through his philological decisions, which are based upon a conjectural reading of the sources and a detailed analysis of the texts using all three literary witnesses. Zheltov, "Anaphora and the Thanksgiving Prayer," 483–92.

Table 1: An Edition of the Anaphora according to MS P.Monts.Roca fols. 154b–155b.

Section	Greek Transcription	English Translation
1.1: Acclamation	¹⁵⁴ᵇ Εἷς Θεός Ἰησοῦς ὁ Κύριος	One God, Jesus the Lord
1.2: Prayer Title	Εὐχαριστία περὶ ἄρτου καὶ ποτηρίου	Thanksgiving for the bread and the cup
1.3: Introductory Dialogue	Ἄνω τὰς καρδίας ἡμῶν, εὔξωμεν πρὸς Κύριον. Ἔτι εὐχαριστήσομεν, ἄξιον καὶ δίκαιον.	Lift our hearts; we have to the Lord. Then, let us also give thanks; fitting and right.
1.4: Preface	Ἄξιόν ἐστιν καὶ δίκαιον· σὲ αἰνεῖν, σὲ εὐλογεῖν, σὲ ὑμνεῖν, σοὶ εὐχαριστεῖν, Δέσποτα Θ(ε)ὲ παντοκράτορ τοῦ Κ(υρίο)υ ἡμῶν Ἰ(ησο)ῦ Χ(ριστο)ῦ, ὁ ποιήσας τὰ πάντα ἐκ τοῦ μὴ ὄντος εἰς τὸ εἶναι· τὰ πάντα· οὐρανοὺς, γῆν, θάλασσαν καὶ πάντα τὰ ἐν αὐτοῖς, διὰ τοῦ ἠγαπημένου σου παιδὸς Ἰ(ησο)ῦ Χ(ριστο) ῦ τοῦ Κ(υρίο)υ ἡμῶν, δι' οὗ ἐκάλεσεν ἡμᾶς ἀπὸ σκότους εἰς φῶς, ἀπὸ ἀγνωσίας εἰς ἐπίγνωσιν δόξης ὀνόματος αὐτοῦ, ἀπὸ φθορᾶς θανάτου εἰς ἀφθαρσίαν, εἰς ζωὴν αἰώνιον·	It is fitting and right to praise you, to bless you, to hymn you, to give you thanks, O Master, God Almighty of our Lord Jesus Christ, who created all things from non-existence into being; all: heaven, earth, the sea, and all that is in them, through your beloved child Jesus Christ, our Lord, through whom you have called us from darkness into light, from ignorance to knowledge of the glory of his name, from decay of death into incorruption, into life eternal;
1.5.1: Pre-Sanctus	ὁ καθήμενος ἐπὶ ἅρματος, χερουβὶν καὶ σαραφὶν ἔμπροσθεν αὐτοῦ· ᾧ παριστᾶσιν χίλιαι χιλιάδες καὶ μύριαι μυριάδες ἀγγέλων, ἀρχαγγέλων, θρόνων καὶ κυριοτήτων, ὑμνούντων καὶ δοξολογούντων· μεθ' ὧν καὶ ἡμεῖς ὑμνοῦντες, λέγοντες,	Who sits on the chariot, cherubim and seraphim before it, who is attended by thousands and myriads of myriads of angels, archangels, thrones and dominions, hymning and glorifying, with whom we are also hymning, saying:

1.5.2: Sanctus	Ἅγιος, Ἅγιος, Ἅγιος, Κύριος Σαβαώθ· πλήρης {σου} ὁ οὐρανὸς <καὶ ἡ γῆ> τῆς δόξης σου·	Holy, Holy, Holy, Lord of Hosts! Heaven <and earth> are full of your glory,
1.5.3: Post-*Sanctus*	ἐν ᾗ ἐδόξασας ἡμᾶς διὰ τοῦ μονογενοῦς σου καὶ πρωτοτόκου πάσης κτίσεως Ἰ(ησο)ῦ Χ(ριστο)ῦ, τοῦ Κ(υρίο)υ ἡμῶν· ὁ καθήμενος ἐν δεξιᾷ τῆς μεγαλωσύνης σου ἐν τοῖς οὐρανίοις· ὃς ἔρχεται κρῖναι ζῶντας καὶ νεκρούς <οὗ τὴν θανάτου ἀνάμνησιν ποιοῦμεν·>	in which you have glorified us through your only-begotten, the firstborn of every creature, Jesus Christ, our Lord, who sits on the right hand of your greatness in heaven, who is coming to judge the living and the dead, <the remembrance of whose death we do>
1.6: Oblation	|[155a] δι᾽ οὗ προσφέρομέν σοι κτίσματά σου ταῦτα, ἄρτον τε καὶ ποτήριον·	through him we offer you these your creations, the bread and the cup:
1.7: Epiclesis I	αἰτούμεθα καὶ παρακαλοῦμέν σε ὅπως καταπέμψῃς ἐπ᾽ αὐτὰ τὸ ἅγιόν σου {τὸ ἅγιόν σου} καὶ παράκλητόν σου Πνεῦμα ἐκ τῶν οὐ(ρα)νῶν· εἰς τὸ σωματοποιῆσαι αὐτὰ καὶ πο(ι)ῆσαι τὸ(ν) μὲν ἄρτον σῶμα Χρ(ιστο)ῦ, τὸ δὲ ποτήριον αἷμα Χρ(ιστο)ῦ, τῆς καινῆς διαθήκης·	we ask and beseech you to send onto them your Holy and Comforter Spirit from heaven, to represent them materially and to make the bread the Body of Christ and the cup the Blood of Christ, of the New Covenant.
1.8: Institution Narrative	Καθὼς καὶ αὐτός, ἡνίκα ἔμελλεν παραδιδόναι <ἑαυτόν>, λαβὼν ἄρτον καὶ εὐχαριστήσας καὶ ἔκλασεν καὶ ἔδωκεν τοῖς μαθηταῖς αὐτοῦ λέγων· Λάβετε, φάγετε, τοῦτό μού ἐστιν τὸ σῶμα. Καὶ ὁμοίως, μετὰ τὸ δειπνῆσαι, λαβὼν ποτήριον, εὐχαριστήσας, ἔδωκεν αὐτοῖς λέγων· Λάβετε, πίετε τὸ αἷμα τὸ περὶ πολλῶν ἐκχυ(ν)όμενον εἰς ἄφεσιν ἁμαρτιῶν·	As he himself, when he was about to hand <himself> over, having taken bread and given thanks, broke, and gave to his disciples, saying, "Take, eat, this is my body;" likewise after supper, having taken a cup and given thanks, he gave to them, saying, 'take, drink the blood, which is being poured out for many for the forgiveness of sins.'

1.9: Anamnesis	Καὶ ἡμεῖς τὸ αὐτὸ ποιοῦμεν εἰς τὴν σὴν ἀνάμνησιν, ὡς ἐκεῖνοι ἂν συνέρχοντες, ποιοῦντές σου τὴν ἀνάμνησιν, τοῦ ἁγίου μυστηρίου διδασκάλου καὶ βασιλέως καὶ σωτῆρος ἡμῶν Ἰ(ησο)ῦ Χρ(ιστο)ῦ.	And we also do the same in your remembrance, like those whenever we meet together, we make the remembrance of you, of the holy mystery of our Teacher and King and Savior Jesus Christ.
1.10: Epiclesis II	Ναί, ἀξιοῦμέν σε, Δέσποτα, ὅπως εὐλογῶν εὐλογήσῃς καὶ ἁγίως ἁγιάσῃς [. . .] τοῖς πᾶσιν ἐξ αὐτῶν μεταλαμβάνουσιν εἰς πίστιν ἀδιάκριτον, εἰς μετοχὴν ἀφθαρσίας, εἰς κοινωνίαν Πνεύματος ἁγίου, εἰς καταρτισμὸν πίστεως καὶ ἀληθείας, εἰς συντελείωσιν παντὸς θελήματός σου,	Even so, we pray to you, Master, that in blessing you will bless and in sanctifying sanctify [. . .][15] for all communicating from them for undivided faith, for communion of incorruption, for communion of the Holy Spirit, for perfection of belief and truth, for fulfillment of all your will.
1.11: Doxology	ἵνα ἔτι καὶ ἐν τούτῳ δοξάζωμεν τὸ πανέντιμον καὶ πανάγιον ὄνομά σου, διὰ τοῦ ἡγιασμένου σου παιδὸς Ἰ(ησο)ῦ Χρ(ιστο)ῦ τοῦ Κ(υρίο)υ ἡμῶν, δι' οὗ σοὶ δόξα, κράτος εἰς τοὺς ἀκηράτους αἰῶνας τῶν αἰώνων· Ἀμήν.	So that in this and again we will glorify your all-revered and all-holy name, through your sanctified child, our Lord Jesus Christ, through whom glory [be] to you, power unto the unblended ages of ages. Amen.
1.12: Acclamation	[155b Εἷς Θεός	One God.

15. In his examination of the "Fruits of Communion" in various early Christian anaphoras, Chase filled this lacuna based on an extrapolation of the first epiclesis in CYRIL, completing the text as: "Ναί, ἀξιοῦμέν σε, Δέσποτα, ὅπως εὐλογῶν εὐλογήσῃς καὶ ἁγίως ἁγιάσῃς [ταῦτα τὰ πολύτιμα δῶρα σου ἐνώπιον τοῦ προσώπου σου τεθέντα, τὸν ἄρτον τοῦτον καὶ τὸ ποτήριον τοῦτο] τοῖς πᾶσιν ἐξ αὐτῶν μεταλαμβάνουσιν εἰς πίστιν ἀδιάκριτον, εἰς μετοχὴν ἀφθαρσίας, εἰς κοινωνίαν Πνεύματος ἁγίου, εἰς καταρτισμὸν πίστεως καὶ ἀληθείας, εἰς συντελείωσιν παντὸς θελήματός σου / Even so, we pray to you, Master, that in blessing you will bless and in sanctifying sanctify [these your precious gifts which have been set before your face, this bread and this cup] for all communicating from them for undivided faith, for communion of incorruption, for communion of the Holy Spirit, for perfection of belief and truth, for fulfillment of all your will . . ." Chase, "Fruits of Communion," 15–17.

1.13: Thanksgiving After Communion[16]	Ἔτι δεόμεθά σου, Δέσποτα Θ(ε)ὲ παντοκράτορ, καὶ εὐχαριστοῦμέν σοι ἐπὶ τῇ μεταλήμψει τοῦ ἄρτου τῆς ζωῆς καὶ τοῦ ποτηρίου, καὶ τοῦ ἁγιασμένου· καὶ παρακαλοῦμέν σε ὅπως ἁγιάσῃς ἡμᾶς πάντας τοὺς μετειληφότας ἀπ᾿ αὐτῶν· πρὸς τὸ μὴ γενέσθαι ἡμῖν εἰς κρίμα ἢ εἰς κατάκριμα, τοῖς μεταλαμβάνουσιν, ἀλλὰ μᾶλλον εἰς ὑγείαν σαρκὸς καὶ ψυχῆς, εἰς ἀνανέωσιν τοῦ πνεύματος ἡμῶν, εἰς πίστιν καὶ σωφροσύνην, εἰς ἰσχὺν καὶ δύναμιν, εἰς ἀγάπην καὶ φιλαλληλίαν, εἰς συντέλειαν παντὸς θελήματός σου, εἰς τέλειον σου ἄνθρωπον τὸν κατὰ Θεὸν κτισθέντα· ἵνα ὦμεν τέλειοι καὶ καθαροί, ἀμάχητοι, σεσωσμένοι ἀπὸ παντὸς ἀνομιῶν καὶ τελειωμένοι ἐν παντὶ θελήματι τοῦ Θ(εο)ῦ καὶ Π(ατ)ρὸς Κ(υρίο)υ Ἰ(ησο)ῦ Χρ(ιστο)ῦ· δι᾿ οὗ σοι δόξα, κράτος, αἰῶνος τιμή, μεγαλωσύνη· καὶ νῦν καὶ εἰς τοὺς σύμπαντας αἰῶνας τῶν αἰώνων· Ἀμήν.	Then, again, we pray to you, O Master, God Almighty, and give you thanks for the communion of the bread of life and the cup, and of the sanctified, and we beseech you, so that you will sanctify all of us who have partaken of them, so that they will be to us, the communicants, neither for judgment nor for condemnation, but rather for health of body and soul, for renovation of our spirit, for faith and chastity, for strength and force, for love and mutual love, for perfection of your will, for your perfect man, who is created after God, so that we will be perfect and clean, invincible, saved from each of crimes and being accomplished in every will of God and Father of our Lord Jesus Christ, through whom [be] to you glory, power, honor of aeon, greatness, now and unto all the ages of ages. Amen.
1.14: Acclamation	Εἷς Θεός	One God.

16. See Buchinger's treatment on the development of post-communion thanksgiving supplications, where he specifically discusses the anaphora in MS *P.Monts.Roca*: Harald Buchinger, "Die Postcommunio. Zu Frühgeschichte und Charakter eines eucharistischen Gebetes," *Ecclesia Orans* 38, no. 1 (2021): 45–94, here at 59–63. Also see Chase, "Fruits of Communion."

Discussion

Status quaestionis

The uncontracted (unabbreviated) forms of *nomina sacra*, that is, sacred names within religious texts, appear throughout MS *P.Monts. Roca* together with abbreviated forms. These unabbreviated forms also feature in those lines that I propose as auxiliary to the formulary texts. The four earliest Christian epithets commonly abbreviated are Θεός, Ἰησοῦς, Κύριος, and Χριστός, all of which are considered *nomina divina* titles. These form an earlier core to the practice and development of abbreviating *nomina sacra*, which later expanded to numerous other terms.[17] Within MS *P.Monts.Roca*'s liturgical portions, there are twelve witnesses for what comes to be later termed as *nomina sacra*, but most are given in an uncontracted form, which is typical for the papyrus's era.[18]

The introductory dialogue (§1.3) of the anaphora in MS *P.Monts. Roca* opens atypically without the ubiquitous presider's inaugural call of "The Lord be with you" and the subsequent congregational response of

---

17. For a comprehensive list of divine titles used as *nomina sacra* and for further details on this topic, consult Larry W. Hurtado, *The Earliest Christian Artifacts: Manuscripts and Christian Origins* (Grand Rapids: Eerdmans, 2006), 134. See his original treatment of this topic in Larry W. Hurtado, "The Origin of the *Nomina Sacra*: A Proposal," *Journal of Biblical Literature* 117, no. 4 (1998): 655–73. As an example, for its use specifically within Coptic practice, see the discussion below and Birger A. Pearson, "The Coptic Inscriptions in the Church of St. Antony," in *Monastic Visions: Wall Paintings in the Monastery of St. Antony at the Red Sea*, ed. Elizabeth S. Bolman (New Haven, CT: Yale University Press, 2002), 217–39, here at 219–20.

18. Paap's survey of early Christian Greek papyri concludes that the epithets Θεός, Ἰησούς, and Κύριος all remained unabbreviated through the first half of second century, while Χριστός in the first half of the third century. Anton H. R. E. Paap, *Nomina Sacra in the Greek Papyri of the First Five Centuries*, Papyrologica Lugduno-Batava 8 (Leiden: Brill, 1959), 119. Within the euchologion prayer text (§§1.4, 1.9. 1.11, and 1.13 above), the same "divine names" are contracted, which may represent an impersonation of Hebrew and Semitic consonantal writing systems where vowels are naturally omitted. Such a writing style, especially for nomenclature related to the divine, likely carried over into Christian practice. Ludwig Traube, *Nomina Sacra: Versuch einer Geschichte der christlichen Kürzung* (Munich: Beck, 1907), 36. A case in point is the contracted opening line, Εἷς θς, εἷς Χρς, of the circa fifth- to sixth-century Christian amulet prayer from the same genre. Sofía Torallas-Tovar and Klaas A. Worp, *Greek Papyri from Montserrat (P.Monts.Roca IV)*, Scripta Orientalia 1 (Barcelona: Publicacions de l'Abadia de Montserrat, 2014), 176.

"And with your spirit."[19] Instead, the folio containing the anaphora (fol. 154b) begins with "Εἷς Θεὸς Ἰησοῦς ὁ Κύριος."[20] Roca-Puig had previously postulated with hesitance that these phrases were likely outside the anaphoral prayer, yet he did not provide an argument or evidence for his statement.[21] On the contrary, Zheltov understood the first line in MS *P.Monts.Roca* fol. 154b, that is, the phrase "Εἷς Θεὸς Ἰησοῦς ὁ Κύριος," as part of the anaphoral prayer. Zheltov states that the "introductory dialogue" consists of lines 1–5, which begins with the phrase "Εἷς Θεός" and concludes with the words "Ἄξιον καὶ δίκαιον."[22] Then, in his commentary, he explains that the expression "Εἷς Θεός" serves as the initial greeting of the presider, arguing that the first line in MS *P.Monts. Roca* is a "brief form once popular in Egypt."[23] Zheltov, dependent on the work of Erik Peterson, is correct that the invocation of the name of God is a popular tradition in the early Christian church. At the same time, the popularity of declarations about God's oneness does not necessarily correlate to the usage of such as a form of anaphoral dialogue since no clear evidence can be cited to substantiate this claim.[24]

Chase followed and built upon Zheltov's argument in his 2020 dissertation dedicated to the anaphora in the *Barcelona Papyrus*. There, he drew connections between this phrase and affirmations of God's oneness

---

19. For treatment of the first stanza of the initial anaphoral dialogue in Eastern liturgies, see n. 1.

20. See figure 1 in Paul, "Barcelona Papyrus and the Opening Dialogue," 144.

21. Roca-Puig, *Anàfora de Barcelona*, 17. Janeras follows Roca-Puig in excluding this line from the anaphora. See Janeras, "Copte Lovaina Núm. 27," 16. Stewart seems to waffle on the question of whether or not such lines form part of the liturgical prayers of the papyrus. See discussion below.

22. Zheltov, "Anaphora and the Thanksgiving Prayer," 493.

23. Ibid., 494.

24. Peterson's study on the epigraphical usage of Εἷς Θεός does not illustrate it as a replacement for the commencing words of the anaphoral dialogue. Rather, his liturgical focus is primarily on the use of related phrases as a call to communion. Stewart, also extrapolating from Peterson, discusses the liturgical employment for such an acclamation. See Erik Peterson, Εἷς Θεός *Epigraphische, formgeschichtliche und religionsgeschichtliche Untersuchungen*, Forschungen zur Religion und Literatur des Alten und Neuen Testaments 41 (Göttingen: Vandenhoeck & Ruprecht, 1926), 130–40, 317. Zheltov's argument is found here, though his reference to Peterson is unclear: Zheltov, "Anaphora and the Thanksgiving Prayer," 486n61. Stewart, *Egyptian Liturgical Papyri*, 23n83.

as forms of early Christian acclamations stemming from various New Testament parallels, Stoic philosophy, and also within a Jewish milieu.[25] Based upon New Testament expressions, particularly 1 Corinthians 8:1–6, he puts forth the idea that "Jesus the Lord" (Ἰησοῦς ὁ Κύριος) is a congregational response to the initial celebrant's pronouncement of "One God" (Εἷς Θεός), essentially swapping these expressions in for a celebrant's typical opening line of "The Lord be with you" and the congregants' reply of "And with your spirit" found in other anaphoral sources.[26] Yet both Zheltov and Chase seem to have primarily analyzed the anaphora of the *Barcelona Papyrus* outside the context of the broader papyrus manuscript in which it is found, and without comparison to typical scribal customs in Egypt. Overlooked in their discussion of this phrase is the repeated use of this same line throughout other portions of the papyrus and the use of similar expressions in other manuscripts and visual sources of the same genre. When examined in its entirety and comparatively, the phrase employed at the beginning of this anaphora and throughout this codex serves an entirely different purpose, as discussed below.

I support Roca-Puig's initial suggestion, but wish to provide evidence as to *why* such acclamations are not part of the proper anaphora. To do so, a thorough analysis of this opening line's placement, its different uses, and derivations prevalent throughout MS *P.Monts.Roca*, as well as a comparison to other codicological and epigraphical practices attested within Christian Egypt, are needed. In doing so, I suggest that the use of "Εἷς Θεός" and its diverse adaptions are no more than auxiliary words used as invocational blessings, demarcations of a Christian text, and space fillers, especially when coupled with ornamentations, that are used throughout Egyptian Christian scribal practice.

Inscriptions of "Εἷς Θεός" in MS **P.Monts.Roca**

Upon inspecting digital, high-resolution colored images of the anaphora in MS *P.Monts.Roca*, the following observations are deduced about the invocation of God's name in this codex. The phrase "Εἷς Θεὸς Ἰησοὺς ὁ Κύριος" at the top of the first papyrus of the anaphora is written in a relatively large, majuscule script and enclosed in a rectangularly shaped

---

25. Chase, "Anaphoral Development," 228–31.
26. Ibid., 231.

structure formed by a repeated pattern (fol. 154b). This initial phrase occurs above the unanimously accepted title for the prayer, "Εὐχαριστία περὶ ἄρτου καὶ ποτηρίου" (Thanksgiving for the Bread and the Cup), which makes it challenging to consider the enclosed preceding line, "Εἷς Θεὸς Ἰησοὺς ὁ Κύριος," as part of the anaphora, since it is interjected with the prayer's header.

Neither Zheltov nor Alistair C. Stewart discusses the oddity of the prayer title's interpolation between what they consider liturgical phrases.[27] For his part, Chase acknowledged it as the prayer's title, but still concludes that "Εἷς Θεός" is the commencement of the anaphora, though it sits above the prayer's title.[28] It would be odd to have the beginning of the prayer interjected with a title, which suggests that the first line of "Εἷς Θεὸς Ἰησοὺς ὁ Κύριος" is outside the anaphora and could serve as a marker, or blessing, for initiating or concluding a prayer's text, as evident in the thanksgiving prayer (§§1.12–1.14).

Post-communion thanksgiving prayers are a well-attested practice in early eucharistic praying.[29] These supplications are typically an appendage to the anaphoral core, and thus are seen as a standalone petition. The anaphora in the *Barcelona Papyrus* concludes with a post-eucharistic thanksgiving prayer (fol. 155b, §§1.12–1.14).[30] Similar to the opening of the anaphora in *P.Monts.Roca*, the thanksgiving prayer not only commences with the phrase "Εἷς Θεός," but also concludes with the same acclamation (§§1.12 and 1.14). On the papyrus containing the thanksgiving prayer (fol. 155b), "Εἷς Θεός" is boxed off at the top center of the prayer on its own line, with the remainder of the space filled with various emblems, shapes, and *sigla*. Additionally, after the conclusion of the prayer's Ἀμήν, the exact phrase, "Εἷς Θεός," is repeated and flanked by a decorative line made up of several *diples* (>>>), a typical *siglum*

---

27. Zheltov, "Anaphora and the Thanksgiving Prayer," 486f., 493f.; Stewart, *Egyptian Liturgical Papyri*, 23.

28. Chase, "Anaphoral Development," 231. In an unpublished paper, John Paul Abdelsayed notes the idiosyncrasy of a supposedly recited text situated above a rubric or prayer title without elaboration or analysis in John Paul Abdelsayed, "The Barcelona Papyrus Reexamined," n.p./n.d.

29. See the analysis attesting to its early witness in Buchinger, "Die Postcommunio"; Chase, "Fruits of Communion."

30. See figure 2 in Paul, "Barcelona Papyrus and the Opening Dialogue," 147.

generally marking the conclusion or inception of a new section within late antique Greek papyri.[31] The termination of this prayer is further verified by the left-hand marginal *coronis*, the series of vertical *diples* common in Greek papyri, noting the terminus of a text or section.[32] I would therefore propose that, like the case before in the anaphora, the "Εἷς Θεός" phrases flanking either side of the post-communion prayer are not part of the recited prayer.

The theocentric invocations found around these eucharistic prayers are likewise written and expanded on fol. 156b after the conclusion of the prayer for the oil of exorcism and again on fol. 157b, after the acrostic hymn.[33] Both these folia have been considered as colophons pages, yet in my former article, I propose otherwise.[34] In these instances, "Εἷς Θεός" is written within a *tabula ansata*, a tablet design with dovetail handles flanking a rectangular box, with each *ansa* (dovetail) ornamented with *ansate* crosses.[35] This same

---

31. Ágnes T. Mihálykó, *The Christian Liturgical Papyri: An Introduction*, Studien und Texte zu Antike und Christentum 114 (Heidelberg: Mohr Siebeck, 2019), 175n100.

32. Compare the coronis marking the conclusion of fol. 155b to P.Oxy. X 1231 fol. 56 from the second century. For more on the use of a coronis reference Eric G. Turner, *Greek Manuscripts of the Ancient World* (Princeton, NJ: Princeton University Press, 1971), 14.

33. Stewart's edition of the exorcism prayer and the acrostic hymn in *P.Monts.Roca* includes the texts within and around the *tabula ansata* as part of the prayer formulary, though he specifically notes the ΙΧΘΥΣ on fol. 156b and the repeated Εἰς Θεὸς ἐν οὐρανῷ on fol. 157b as "scribal decorations." Stewart, *Egyptian Liturgical Papyri*, 28 and 30. The critical edition and English translation of an exorcism of the oil for the sick (fols. 156a–b) are respectively found in Wolfgang Luppe, "Christliche Weihung von Öl: Zum Papyrus Barc. 156a/b," *Zeitschrift für Papyrologie und Epigraphik* 95 (1993): 70; Stewart, *Egyptian Liturgical Papyri*, 27–28. A critical edition and corresponding English translation of the acrostic hymn are in A. Vinogradov, "Три Крещальных Гимна с Алфавитным Акростихом," *Вестник Древней Истории* 3 (2005): 91–114; Stewart, *Egyptian Liturgical Papyri*, 28–30. For images of these leaves, see figures 3 and 4 in Paul, "Barcelona Papyrus and the Opening Dialogue," 148f.

34. The following have titled these leaves as colophons: Puig, *Anàfora de Barcelona*, 113–15, 135; Chase, "Anaphoral Development," 163, 165; Mihálykó, *Christian Liturgical Papyri*, 208n84. On what qualifies as a colophon in Oriental manuscripts and my argument on these folia specifically see, respectively, Eugenia Sokolinski et al., eds., *Comparative Oriental Manuscript Studies: An Introduction* (Hamburg: COMSt, 2015), 85; Paul, "Barcelona Papyrus and the Opening Dialogue," 154–56.

35. On a history of *ansate* crosses as they relate to the ancient Egyptian *ankh*, and as distinct symbols from the staurogram, also employed by the scribe of the *Barcelona papyrus* (MS *P.Monts.Roca* fols. 154b and 156b, where the scribe makes a conscious

phrase is used at the opening of the anaphora (fol. 154b) examined above, though here, "ἐν οὐρανῷ" (in heaven) is added as an appendage, replacing "Ἰησοῦς ὁ Κύριος," to the main "Εἷς Θεός" inscription.

The phrase "Εἷς Θεὸς ἐν οὐρανῷ" is repeated a second time in a different box surrounded by various repeated patterns, crosses, staurograms, and asterisk shapes situated above the *tabula ansata* in fol. 156b and in a less decorative form below the table in fol. 157b. Above the *tabula* of fol. 156b, the vocative "Εὐλογεῖτε" (Bless!), flanked by two *crux ansata* symbols, are all exceptionally written upside down.[36] Within the geometric design, the abbreviation ΙΧΘΥΣ, which abbreviates "Ἰ(ησοῦς) Χ(ριστός) Θ(εοῦ) Υ(ἱός) Σ(ωτήρ)" (Jesus Christ the Son of God, Savior) is found, and represents a christological phrase similar to that used earlier by affirming Christ as God and Lord: "Εἷς Θεὸς Ἰησοὺς ὁ Κύριος." Although the acronym ΙΧΘΥΣ is in a contracted, abbreviated form, which typically represents post-third-century usage of the *nomina divina*, the scribe was likely utilizing the specific symbolism of the contraction ΙΧΘΥΣ, meaning "fish", which was already a well-established Christian symbol by the time the *Barcelona Papyrus* was written.[37] Outside, and below the *tabula ansata*, are the phrases "Ἐπ'ἀγαθῷ—Ἐν εἰρήνῃ" (for the good—in peace), flanked by *crux ansata*, though in this instance, this whole line of text and symbols are written traditionally in an upright manner.

---

distinction between the *ansate* and the staurogram), consult Gillian Spalding-Stracey, *The Cross in the Visual Culture of Late Antique Egypt*, Texts and Studies in Eastern Christianity 19 (Leiden: Brill, 2020), 93–94; Erika Dinkler-von Schubert "CTAYPOC: Vom 'Wort vom Kreuz' (1 Kor. 1,18) Zum Kreuz-Symbol," in *Byzantine East, Latin West: Art-Historical Studies in Honor of Kurt Weitzmann* (Princeton, NJ: Dept. of Art and Archaeology at Princeton University, 1995), 30–38; Larry W. Hurtado, "The Staurogram in Early Christian Manuscripts: The Earliest Visual Reference to the Crucified Christ?," in *New Testament Manuscripts: Their Text and Their World*, Texts and Editions for New Testament Study 2, ed. Thomas J. Kraus and Tobias Nicklas (Leiden: Brill, 2006), 207–26; Hurtado, *Earliest Christian Artifacts*, 135–54.

36. On theories of this line's magical, diaconal, and scribal practices, see Paul, "Barcelona Papyrus and the Opening Dialogue," 150–53.

37. On the Christian representation of abbreviation "ΙΧΘΥΣ," see Tuomas Rasimus, "Revisiting the Ichthys: A Suggestion Concerning the Origins of Christological Fish Symbolism," in *Mystery and Secrecy in the Nag Hammadi Collection and Other Ancient Literature: Ideas and Practices*, Nag Hammadi and Manichaean Studies 76, ed. Christian Bull et al. (Leiden: Brill, 2012), 327–48.

Commentary on Intended Usage

Having detailed the scribal witnesses and employment of the Εἷς Θεός acclamations and associated expressions within the codex, a discussion on their intended auxiliary usage outside the recited supplications is warranted. I first grant attention to the opening dialogue in response to the previous scholarship with which I opened this discussion. Then, I identify similar uses within later Egyptian Christian scribal and material cultural forms that testify to such uses within writings of the Medieval Copto-Arabic era and beyond.

The phrase "Εἷς Θεός," with its various appendages, presented in the whole of MS *P.Monts.Roca*, are not part of the prayers but are intended as a scribal profession and blessing for the work's commencement and completion. Employment of this acclamation occurs at the start or end of prayers, and typically occupies its own isolated space separate from the formulary prayers. These peripheral expressions are enclosed or written outside the body text in all cases within this codex, alluding to their external nature from the main corpus.[38] Moreover, the handwriting is often stylistically distinct, since it is generally larger and written in straight majuscule, distinguished from the smaller, more inclined style customarily followed for the prayer texts of the manuscript. In some instances, take the anaphora as an example (fol. 154b), this initial blessing for the written work appears *before* the title of the prayer, which allows us likewise to assert that the presider would not have pronounced this line as part of the supplication that follows.

These acclamations, aside from their benedictive application, specifically when ornamented with a *tabula ansata* or other emboxing methods, may also function as space fillers. If we were to look at the space occupying the formulaic prayers with the exclusion of these curious acclamations used throughout the papyrus, there would be a significant amount of dead or blank space within each papyrus. The papyrologist Ágnes T. Mihálykó suggests that various acclamations, theological statements, and/or hymns were used as "space fillers" throughout the making of

---

38. Hurtado discusses general principles of distinct writing styles that visually mark divine names in early Christian writing, which are also seen in this codex: Larry W. Hurtado, *At the Origins of Christian Worship: The Context and Character of Earliest Christian Devotion* (Grand Rapids: Eerdmans, 1999), 121.

Christian liturgical papyri.³⁹ When employed in the studied papyrus, the various theological acclamations and invocations could appear as space occupiers, possibly to prevent the opportunity for another hand to add further texts, similar to the modern-day signage in printed monographs: "This Page is Left Intentionally Blank." In this realm, it is most clearly seen on leaf 156b, where a prayer for the exorcism of oil concludes on the top first quarter of the page, and then detailed, ornate, and repetitive illustrations are used to fill the page inscribed with the various uses of the "Εἷς Θεός" invocation and its appendages as detailed earlier.⁴⁰ This is again employed on the last leaf of the liturgical section on folio 157b and other instances, such as the two texts on folia 149a and 165b.⁴¹

There is undoubtedly a strong possibility that these phrases and geometric designs are space fillers. Yet their use for filling space does not provide the best explanation for their utilization at the top of folia and, even if space filling is a motive in certain cases, this does not exclude other intentions, including blessing and distinguishing these texts as decisively Christian. With the eclectic blend of documents circulating in the early Christian period amid other literary and religious sources, the use of the *nomina sacra* emerged as a practice for signifying literature as distinctly Christian.⁴² In this tradition, the scribe would typically use the name of God or other distinctly theological titles in an abbreviated or complete form as an appendage throughout a document to signify its Christian authenticity.⁴³ As noted earlier, the four earliest attestations are the usage of Θεός, Ἰησοῦς, Κύριος, and Χριστός as *nomina sacra* within the corpus of Christian Greek papyri. Other words, such as οὐρανός and σωτήρ, also appear as later, mid-third to early-fourth century additions to the sacred name tradition, which also occur in the received texts of

---

39. Mihálykó, *Christian Liturgical Papyri*, 204, 210.

40. The critical edition and English translation of an exorcism of the oil for the sick (fols. 156a–b) are respectively found in Luppe, "Christliche Weihung von Öl," 70; Stewart, *Egyptian Liturgical Papyri*, 27–28.

41. For colored images of these folia, consult figures 5 and 6 in Paul, "Barcelona Papyrus and the Opening Dialogue," 153, 155.

42. Stewart, *Egyptian Liturgical Papyri*, 37.

43. For a detailed study on the *nomina sacra* within Greek manuscripts and within Egypt, see Paap, *Nomina Sacra in the Greek Papyri*.

MS *P.Monts.Roca*.⁴⁴ Simply, the scribe may be "consecrating" the text or invoking God's support by using these markers or sealers of the text's Christian identity while calling upon God to sanctify the work. The tradition of lucidly marking a text as belonging to a Christian genre may be more vital in the early centuries, as new anaphoras and prayers were still nascent and intermixed with a heterogeneous blend of pagan and Jewish sources. In a similar vein, the repeated use of these expressions, prominently abundant in folio 156b, which contains the conclusion of the exorcism prayer, could function in an apotropaic fashion. Nevertheless, regardless of which of these theories hold, of which they are not mutually exclusive, it is apparent that these phrases serve an auxiliary purpose in the papyrus and are not part of the recited prayer texts.

Invoking the Divine in Egyptian Christian Penmanship

The fragmentary nature of early liturgical papyri does not easily allow for drawing parallels within the same genre and era. Yet, it is safe to assume that the tradition of inserting acclamations invoking God before a prayer is typical, as Mihálykó and Arsenius Mikhail have noted in their study on a Coptic liturgical papyrus from the eleventh century.⁴⁵ Due to the paucity of surviving Egyptian Christian literary evidence in antiquity, I point forward to other sources to demonstrate how a similar tradition has carried over throughout medieval Coptic Egypt and into modernity.

Various benedictions invoking the name of God are written throughout Coptic, Copto-Arabic, and Arabic manuscripts, as well as material culture where these invocations are not part of the recited prayers or script. These opening phrases generally beseech God's blessing or mercy on the work undertaken. Within Egyptian Christian manuscripts, typically the name of God and Jesus Christ are usually written in Coptic or Greek in an abbreviated form within the headers, and are commonly associated with marking a quire, a grouping of a set number of leaves within

---

44. For a list of the four core *nomina sacra* and later additions, see Hurtado, *At the Origins of Christian Worship*, 97–98, and 134. On their development over time in Greek papyrology, consult Paap, *Nomina Sacra in the Greek Papyri*, 100–101, 104, 107, 109, and 119.

45. Ágnes T. Mihálykó and Arsenius Mikhail, "A Prayer for the Preparation of the Priest and the First Prayer of the Morning in Sahidic Coptic (P.Ilves Copt. 8)," *Orientalia Christiana Periodica* 87, no. 2 (2021): 353–70, here at 357.

a manuscript. Such traditions are common in Coptic and Copto-Arabic manuscripts known to date.[46] Take for instance MS *Suryān Liturgy 383* fol. 74r (1255 CE), from the Western Desert in Egypt, which contains a contracted form of the *nomina sacra* on the first page of each quire.[47] The abbreviations appear as ⲓ̅ⲩ̅ and ⲭ̅ⲩ̅ and flank an illuminated cross design, preserving a type of ornamental scheme as seen in the black and white decorations of MS *P.Monts.Roca*.

More profound, though, are unique inscriptions summoning God in a colorfully decorated, arched, geometric headpiece that demarks a new prayer section within codices. Surveying a selection of medieval manuscripts from the monastery known as Al-Muḥarraq, located in the middle of Egypt some 250 miles south of Cairo (in a similar geographical location where MS *P.Monts.Roca* is thought to have originated), proves the same scribal custom. Inscribed at the commencement of the prayers are various *nomina sacra*, which are not part of the pronounced petitions. For instance, MS *Al-Muḥarraq Ṭaqs Kanīsa 14K/4*, fol. 67r has a simple form of ⲥⲩⲛ ⲑⲉⲱ, "with God," and lacks an Arabic counterpart, whereas MS *Al-Muḥarraq Ṭaqs Kanīsa 14K/2*, fol. 71r contains an expanded form invoking God's powerful assistance in both Greek and Arabic—ⲥⲩⲛ ⲑⲉⲟⲥ ⲓⲥⲭⲩⲣⲟⲥ (بسم الله القوي), meaning "with God the powerful."[48]

---

46. Sokolinski, *Oriental Manuscript*, 145–46. See Zanetti's examination of this in Ugo Zanetti, "Les Manuscrits de Saint-Macaire: Observations codicologiques," in *Recherches de Codicologie Camparée. La Composition du Codex au Moyen Âge, En Orient et an Occident*, ed. Philippe Hoffmann (Paris: Presses de l'école normale supérieure, 1998), 171–82, here at 177.

47. For more on this manuscript's contents, including an edition and commentary of some of its prayers, as well as codicological and paleographical details, consult Arsany Paul, "Approaching the Ecclesia in Medieval Coptic Cairo: Church Entrance Petitions from the Thirteenth-Century Copto-Arabic Manuscript Suryān Liturgy 383 (Folia 190r–194r)," *Ecclesia Orans* 39, no. 1 (2022): 143–73. View the colored image (figure 7) in Paul, "Barcelona Papyrus and the Opening Dialogue," 159.

48. To view the colored plates, please refer to figures 8 and 9 in Paul, "Barcelona Papyrus and the Opening Dialogue," 159f. For a brief discussion on the use of this pious phrase in Byzantine Egyptian and Coptic literature, refer to: Philippe Luisier, SJ, "Σὺν Θεῷ: Signification et destin d'une formule d'invocation en Égypte." In *Κουράγιῳ ἀνδρί: Mélanges offerts à André Hurst*, ed. Antje Kolde, Alessandra Lukinovich, and André-Louis Rey (Genève: Librairie Droz S.A., 2005), 339–46, where he discusses such phrases as ancient relics adopted into scribal customs and as an indication of a work willed by God.

The Εἷς Θεός Acclamations in the Barcelona Papyrus   81

Such benedictions invoking God's divine assistance in undertaking the transcription extend beyond these brief entreaties. Often, new sections within a manuscript contain phrases such as "In the Name of God, God's hand before my hand" (بسم الله يد الله قبل يدي), calling upon God's hand to guide the scribe's hand. Suffice it to add one more witness to this scribal practice, where the copyist is emphatic about God's involvement in the work. Written above the prayer, scribes often express: "We begin with God's assistance and good fortune to transcribe" (نبتدي بعون الله تعالي وحسن توفيقه بنسخ). Each of these diverse acclamations is situated above the prayer in a decorated style, typically with distinct features, and commences a new section of the manuscript, all of which is like the scribal practice commencing or concluding the liturgical prayers in the *Barcelona Papyrus* presented earlier.

A similar tradition is also exhibited in the circa thirteenth-century iconographic campaign in the richly illuminated church at Saint Antony's Monastery in the Red Sea, Egypt.[49] In two instances, various epigraphic inscriptions begin with the same divine invocation as noted about MS *Al-Muḥarraq Ṭaqs Kanīsa 14K/4*, fol. 67r. In one illustration, before the master painter's prayerful inscription, Theodore begins by calling upon God with the phrase "ⲑ[ⲉⲟⲥ] ⲥⲩⲛ."[50] In another example, the same acclamation is employed at the top center of the scroll depicted in the hand of Arsenius the Great.[51] Moreover, visitors seeking intercessions at the monastery adopted the practice in their own "graffiti" etchings on the monastery walls, and would begin their appeals with similar phrases. For example, a lengthy supplication for remembrance opens with a similar benediction in Arabic: "In the name of God the benevolent and merciful" (بسم الله الرؤوف الرحيم).[52] The tradition of invoking God's assistance through

---

49. For high resolution, colored images of these inscriptions and icons at the Monastery of St. Antony, refer to the online version of this article: "Barcelona Papyrus and the Opening Dialogue," 162–63.

50. Reference the image (figure 11) in Paul, "Barcelona Papyrus and the Opening Dialogue," 162; Pearson, "Coptic Inscriptions," 217.

51. See figure 12 in Paul, "Barcelona Papyrus and the Opening Dialogue," 162.

52. For the image (figure 13), see Paul, "Barcelona Papyrus and the Opening Dialogue," 163. Sidney H. Griffith, "The Handwriting on the Wall: Graffiti in the Church of St. Antony," in *Monastic Visions: Wall Paintings in the Monastery of St. Antony at the Red Sea*, ed. Elizabeth S. Bolman (New Haven, CT: Yale University Press, 2002), 185–94, here at 187.

various inscriptions prior to commencing a task continues in current Coptic Orthodox practice, as demonstrated in modern liturgical publications and beyond.[53] Lastly, invoking God before undertaking a work appears as a customary scribal practice within the wider community of Egypt, with scribes of Islamic texts sharing the same writing practices.[54] These instances appeal to the strong affinity of the tradition in both professional and amateur scribal customs.

Such acclamations at the start of Egyptian Christian texts, iconographic works, and wall writings are typical scribal habits invoking God's divine assistance when undertaking the task to author or transcribe holy texts or in iconographic paintings. These lines mark a scribe's activity as being done with and in the service of God. MS *P.Monts.Roca* invites us to envision these later Coptic scribal practices in line with much earlier precedent.

Conclusion

Attention to visual presentations and scribal practices is indispensable for understanding liturgical texts not merely as disembodied edited texts, but as they occur *in situ* in their respective textual mediums. As demonstrated here, an attentive reading of the writings within its apparatus and comparatively with other literary and material evidence shows that the codicological acclamations and blessings, such as "Εἷς Θεὸς" with its various additional phrases, represent Egyptian Christian scribal annotations. In this study, I have demonstrated that these invocational blessings are not part of the pronounced prayer tradition within the *Barcelona Papyrus*, but rather fulfill other purposes, namely, to demarcate Christian texts, provide a blessing for the authorship, and as space fillers

---

53. The production of modern Coptic liturgical books typically preserves the inscription of various theological acclamations in the title page or before commencing prayer sections. See, for instance, the twentieth-century printed Copto-Arabic Liturgicon of Ṣalīb ʿAbd al-Masīḥ, ⲡⲓϫⲱⲙ ⲛ̀ⲧⲉ ⲡⲓⲉⲩⲭⲟⲗⲟⲅⲓⲟⲛ ⲉⲑⲟⲩⲁⲃ ⲉ̀ⲧⲉ ⲫⲁⲓ ⲡⲉ ⲡⲓϫⲱⲙ ⲛ̀ⲧⲉ ϯϣⲟⲙϯ ⲛ̀ⲁⲛⲁⲫⲟⲣⲁ ⲛ̀ⲧⲉ ⲡⲓⲁⲅⲓⲟⲥ ⲃⲁⲥⲓⲗⲓⲟⲥ ⲛⲉⲙ ⲡⲓⲁⲅⲓⲟⲥ ⲅⲣⲏⲅⲟⲣⲓⲟⲥ ⲛⲉⲙ ⲡⲓⲁⲅⲓⲟⲥ ⲕⲩⲣⲓⲗⲗⲟⲥ ⲛⲉⲙ ϩⲁⲛⲕⲉⲉⲩⲭⲏ ⲉⲩⲟⲩⲁⲃ [The Book of the Holy Euchologion, Which Is the Book of the Three Anaphoras of Saint Basil and Saint Gregory and Saint Cyril, and Other Holy Prayers] (Cairo: ʿAyn Shams, 1902), 17, 193, 451, 470, 555, 573, and 680.

54. See n. 8 above.

especially when combined with various ornamental sketches. Thus, in the case of the MS *P.Monts.Roca*, the opening benediction is not part of the anaphora, but merely an introductory scribal text typical of this area's manuscript tradition, which has carried over into medieval and modern Coptic practices. Therefore, concerning the opening dialogue in the anaphora of the *Barcelona Papyrus*, we should conclude that it contains no equivalent to "The Lord be with you / And with your Spirit," and if any such expressions were used in the original community to which this papyrus was destined, they were not recorded by this manuscript's scribe.

/ IV

The Making of the Maronite *Sharar*

A Reception History for the Anaphora of Addai and Mari

Paul J. Elhallal

Introduction

In the last several years, historical scholarship on the East Syrian anaphora attributed to Addai and Mari (hereafter AM) has largely come to a standstill. While the discovery of the Mar Esha'ya text by W.F. Macomber in 1966 (ca. tenth or eleventh century) resulted in a wave of studies that examined its implications on the redaction history of the anaphora, Anthony Gelston noted well in 1992 that "the most serious obstacle confronting the modern student of this ancient Eucharistic Prayer is the lack as yet of any MS text earlier than the tenth century."[1] Nevertheless, efforts to identify and reconstruct earlier strata of development or a purported 'original form' have abounded. Given the paucity of evidence, scholars have sought to contribute to the conversation by applying new methodological approaches to the same textual material. While several of these have made strides in identifying earlier strata in the development of AM, scholars have been unable to reach anything resembling a consensus on what constitutes the earliest or "original" form of AM.

---

1. W. F. Macomber, "The Oldest Known Text of the Anaphora of the Apostles Addai and Mari," *Orientalia Christiana Periodica* 32 (1966): 335–71; Anthony Gelston, *The Eucharistic Prayer of Addai and Mari* (Oxford: Clarendon Press, 1992), vi.

Many scholarly studies on AM have made use of the philological method, attempting to identify instances of logical rupture within the thought sequence of the text, and excising or rearranging the elements which were thought to have been the cause of such rupture.[2] Others have sought to identify what might be considered an "underlying structure," and then remove material which is thought to constitute a later interpolation.[3] Such methods run the risk of imposing *a priori* commitments on the material, or otherwise imposing subjective criteria for "antiquity" and "logical flow." Accordingly, the reconstructions of AM's earlier forms have been as numerous as the scholars who have attempted them.

Many have looked to Jewish liturgical practice as the basis for AM's original core. After Louis Bouyer identified the resemblance between AM and the *Birkat ha-Mazon*, the Jewish table prayer, several notable scholars have followed him in attempting to identify the underlying parallel structure in AM and reconstruct an original form on its account.[4] These have pointed out that AM contains three prayers of inclination, or *gehanatha* (sing. *gehanta*), that appear to parallel the three blessings in the *Birkat ha-Mazon* both structurally and thematically. While the idea gained much traction in the mid-twentieth century, Gelston, Spinks, and Bradshaw have demonstrated much caution in positing a direct succession between *Birkat ha-Mazon* and AM.[5] All of these, in turn, are indebted

---

2. See, for example: E. C. Ratcliff, "The Original Form of the Anaphora of Addai and Mari: A Suggestion," *Journal of Theological Studies* 30 (1928–29): 23–32; and Gregory Dix, *The Shape of the Liturgy* (London: Dacre Press, 1945).

3. Two notable studies in this school are J. Magne, "L'anaphore nestorienne dite d'Addée et Mari et l'anaphore maronite dite de Pierre III. Etude comparative," *Orientalia Christiana Periodica* 53 (1987): 107–58; and W. Marston, "A Solution to the Enigma of 'Addai and Mari,'" *Ephemerides Liturgicae* 103 (1989): 79–91.

4. Louis Bouyer, *Eucharist: Theology and Spirituality of the Eucharistic Prayer* (Notre Dame: Notre Dame University Press, 1968), 146–58. For studies following Bouyer on this point, see L. Ligier, "The Origins of the Eucharistic Prayer: From the Last Supper to the Eucharist," *Studia Liturgica* 9 (1973): 161–83; T. J. Talley, "From Berakah to Eucharistia: A Reopening Question," *Worship* 50 (1976): 115–37; S. Y. Jammo, "The Anaphora of the Apostles Addai and Mari: A Study of Structure and Historical Background," *Orientalia Christiana Periodica* 68 (2002): 5–35.

5. Gelston, *Addai and Mari*, 7–11; B. D. Spinks, "The Quest for the 'Original Form' of the Anaphora of the Apostles Addai and Mari," in idem, *Worship: Prayers from the East* (Washington, DC: Pastoral Press, 1993), 1–20; Paul Bradshaw, *The Search for*

to the great twentieth-century scholar Joseph Heinemann, who was the first to challenge longstanding narratives about Jewish prayer practices, emphasizing their oral nature and the relatively late date of their standardization.[6] Heinemann words it thus:

> We must not try to determine by philological methods the "original" text of any prayer without first determining whether or not such an "original" text ever existed. For we are dealing with materials which originated as part of an oral tradition and hence by their very nature were not phrased in any fixed uniform formulation—which at a later stage came to be "revised" and expanded—but rather were improvised on the spot; and, subsequently, "re-improvised" and reworded in many different formulations in an equally spontaneous fashion.[7]

This therefore precludes the possibility of a direct *textual* link between *Birkat ha-Mazon* and AM, though it does leave room for a possible structural or thematic connection. Gelston concedes as much, noting that "we can hardly go further than to say that there is evidence of the ultimate origin of Christian liturgical forms in Jewish forms, and some evidence of specific Jewish influence on Christian worship as late as the fourth century."[8] Robert Taft is a bit more optimistic, stating that "there is more or less consensus that the most primitive original eucharistic prayers were short, self-contained benedictions, without Sanctus, institution narrative, or epiclesis, comparable to the Jewish Birkat ha-mazon, *Didache* 10, and the papyrus Strasburg 254."[9]

The Maronite anaphora of Peter III, commonly called *Sharar*, has proven a helpful comparison piece in circumventing some of the major textual questions surrounding AM. *Sharar* shares much material in common with AM, and several scholars, following Rahmani (1899), have attempted to compare them in an attempt to reconstruct the "original

---

the Origins of Christian Worship: Sources and Methods for the Study of Early Liturgy (Oxford: SPCK, 2002), 21–46.

6. Joseph Heinemann, *Prayer in the Talmud* (Berlin: De Gruyter, 2012).
7. Ibid., 42; cited in Spinks, "Quest for the 'Original Form,' " 16.
8. Gelston, *Addai and Mari*, 8.
9. R. Taft, SJ, "The Interpolation of the Sanctus into the Anaphora," *Orientalia Christiana Periodica* 57 (1991): 290; cited in Jammo, "Anaphora of the Apostles," 14.

core" from which both anaphoras developed.[10] While comparison with *Sharar* has narrowed the field of possibilities for an "original core" and early redactions, it has also raised several more questions which are yet to be resolved, such as whether Sharar retains archaisms not found in AM, and why Sharar has no equivalent to AM's so-called "anamnesis." Despite the textual problems raised by this comparison, the structural similarity between the two is difficult to ignore. On this point, Sarhad Jammo's remarks on the relationship between AM and *Sharar* remain the most convincing:

> The fact remains that, this Anamnesis aside, every paragraph in A&M has a parallel in Peter III, but not *vice-versa*, i.e. not every paragraph in Peter III has a parallel in A&M. That should mean that the "Maronite" reviser had the text of A&M, basically as we find it in Mar 'Eshaya's Hudhra, in front of him, to be able to produce a parallel to every paragraph in it while redacting Peter III. This very fact eliminates the need for a phantom common core for both. A&M is the Urtext of Peter III.[11]

This does not mean that the common core between the two anaphoras was the "original form" of the anaphora, though it does provide an early point in the development of AM where we can point to a single redaction of AM. The question of an "original form" nevertheless remains vexed in spite of such comparisons.

There are two avenues of approach that appear promising in narrating a history of AM's development. First, the utility of *Sharar* has not been fully realized. Most of the studies that have made use of *Sharar* have treated it only as a comparative device for AM, and none of these com-

---

10. See H. Engberding, "Zum anaphorischen Fürbittgebet der Ostsyrischen Liturgie der Apostel Adda(j) und Mar(j)," *Oriens Christianus* 41 (1957): 102–24; Magne, "L'anaphore nestorienne," 107–58; J. M. Sanchez Caro, "La anafora de Addai y Mari y la anafora maronite Sarrar: Intento de reconstrucción de la fuente primitiva común," *Orientalia Christiana Periodica* 43 (1977): 41–69; W. F. Macomber, "The Maronite and Chaldean Versions of the Anaphora of the Apostles," *Orientalia Christiana Periodica* 37 (1971): 55–84; Spinks, "Quest for the 'Original Form,'" 1–20; Jammo, "Anaphora of the Apostles," 5–35.

11. Jammo, "Anaphora of the Apostles," 10.

parative studies have investigated *Sharar* on its own terms. J.-M. Sauget's 1973 critical edition of *Sharar* is the only such study of the anaphora, and his commentary on the text itself is limited to a brief prolegomena.[12] Only once *Sharar* has been studied in its own right can we make full use of its offerings as a comparative device for AM. Secondly, Walter Ray argued in a brief article in 1993 that AM is structured chiastically.[13] Ray was the first to propose this approach, but no one has pursued his line of inquiry or properly explored the implications of his findings since the publication of his article. Ray's analysis, though convincing, poses a problem to those who see the underlying structure as related to the *Birkat*

---

12. J.-M. Sauget, "XVIII Anaphora Syriaca Sancti Petri Apostoli Tertia," in *Anaphorae Syriacae: Quotquot in Codicibus Adhuc Repertae Sunt Cura Pontificii Instituti Studiorum Orientalium Editae Et Latine Versae* (Rome: Pontificio Istituto Orientale, 1973), 273–329.

13. Walter Ray, "The Chiastic Structure of the Anaphora of Addai and Mari," *Studia Liturgica* 23 (1993): 187–93. Some notable studies of chiasmus include Nils Lund, *Chiasmus in the New Testament: A Study in Formgeschichte* (Chapel Hill: University of North Carolina Press, 1942); John Breck, "Biblical Chiasmus: Exploring Structure for Meaning," *Biblical Theology Bulletin* 17 (1987): 70–74; and C. L. Blomberg, "The Structure of 2 Corinthians 1–7," *Criswell Theological Review* 4 (1989): 4–8. Blomberg lists a set of nine criteria for determining the presence of true chiasmus: (1) there must be a problem in perceiving the structure of the text in question, which more conventional outlines fail to resolve; (2) there must be clear examples of parallelism between the two 'halves' of the hypothesized chiasmus, to which commentators call attention even when they propose quite different outlines for the text overall; (3) verbal (or grammatical) parallelism as well as conceptual (or structural) parallelism should characterize most if not all of the corresponding pairs of subdivisions; (4) the verbal parallelism should involve central or dominant imagery or terminology, not peripheral or trivial language; (5) both verbal and conceptual parallelism should involve words and ideas not regularly found elsewhere within the proposed chiasmus; (6) multiple sets of correspondences between passages opposite each other in the chiasmus as well as multiple members of the chiasmus itself are desirable; (7) the outline should divide the text at natural breaks which would be agreed upon even by those proposing very different structures to account for the whole; (8) the center of the chiasmus, which forms its climax, should be a passage worthy of that position in light of its theological or ethical significance; (9) ruptures in the outline should be avoided if at all possible. Blomberg notes on page seven that "the more of these criteria which a given hypothesis fails to meet, the more sceptical [sic] a reception it deserves," but grants that even among true instances of chiasmus, few will pass all nine criteria.

ha-Mazon. A full treatment of the question of chiasmus in AM therefore must contend with the issue of justifying the underlying form as well as the possibility of its reception in *Sharar*, which was derived from it.

In light of the skeptical reception of Ray's article and the pertinent need to treat *Sharar* on its own, this study attempts to narrate the chronological development of *Sharar* through the lens of Ray's chiastic argument, beginning with the earliest stratum of AM and culminating in the completion of *Sharar*. Viewed through the lens of chiasmus, *Sharar* offers a sort of reception history for AM, shedding light on textual questions about AM from the perspective of a redactor/composer working just a few centuries after the composition of AM. In this way, we can address some of the still-pertinent textual and redactional questions pertaining to both anaphoras, and gain insight into *Sharar* as a unique anaphora in its own right. A methodologically robust comparison of the two anaphoras with an eye toward their mutual development can do much for our understanding of these texts by:

1. verifying the chiastic organization of AM proposed by Ray,

2. indicating the state of redaction or textual corruption in AM at the time of *Sharar*'s composition,

3. shedding light on textual questions in AM regarding the institution narrative and anamnesis,

4. demonstrating the manner in which *Sharar* was composed,

5. and illustrating the concerns of the community for which *Sharar* was written.

Accordingly, the next section outlines Ray's argument and findings, noting some more evidence in support of one of his hypotheses. Section three discusses the earliest recension of AM using a modified form of Ray's argument and comparing it with the *Birkat ha-Mazon* and *Didache* 10. Section four compares *Sharar* to AM in light of their shared chiasmus and analyzes the problematic materials. Section five summarizes the trajectory of development in four strata and offers brief concluding remarks on textual questions relevant to the two anaphoras.

Chiasmus in the Anaphora of Addai and Mari

Ray argues his case for chiasmus in AM with a presentation of the text, as follows:[14]

A A' = a major parallel pair

a a' = a minor parallel pair within a major block

X x = chiastic centers

boldface = parallel elements of a major parallel pair

italics = parallel elements of minor parallel pair

[ ] = material not found in the earliest manuscript (Mar Esha'ya)

// // = material found only in the earliest manuscript

A	a	Worthy of *praise* from every mouth, and of *confession* by every tongue, [and of *adoration and exaltation* from all creatures,] is the adorable and glorious name of [thy glorious Trinity,] Father and Son and Holy Spirit;
	b	Who didst create the world in *thy grace* and its inhabitants in thy pitifulness; who didst save mankind by thy compassion
	c	And *hast showed great grace unto mortals.*
	x	Thousand thousands of those on high bless and adore thy majesty, O my Lord; and ten thousand times ten thousand holy angels, and hosts of spiritual beings, ministers of fire and spirit, glorify thy name; with the holy cherubim and spiritual seraphim, [offering adoration to thy sovereignty] //glorifying thy name//, crying [and praising without ceasing, calling one to another and saying] //and singing//: Holy, holy, [holy, Lord God of hosts. Heaven and earth are full of thy praises and of the nature of thy being and of the

14. This chart retains the wording and notations from Ray, "Chiastic Structure," 188–90.

		excellency of thy glorious splendor. Hosanna in the highest. Hosanna to the son of David. Blessed be he who came and who cometh in the name of the Lord. Hosanna in the highest.] With those heavenly hosts **we give thanks to thee**, O my Lord, even we thy servants, weak and frail and miserable.
	c'	For *thou hast showed great grace unto us* which cannot be repaid
	b'	in that thou didst put on our humanity that thou mightest quicken us by thy divinity, and thou hast exalted our low estate and hast restored us from our fall, thou hast raised us out of a state of death and thou hast forgiven our debts and justified us from our guilt, thou hast enlightened our knowledge, and hast condemned, O our Lord and our God, our enemies, and hast granted victory to the weakness of our frail nature in the abundant mercies of *thy grace*.
	a'	//And because of this . . . // [For all thy aids and graces towards us, **let us lift up to thee** *praise and honor and confession and adoration,* now always and for ever and ever.] Amen.
B		Do thou, my Lord, in thy many and unspeakable mercies, make a good and acceptable memorial for all the just and righteous **fathers** who have been well pleasing before thee, **in the commemoration of the body and blood of thy Christ.**
C		which we offer to thee upon thy **pure and holy** altar, as thou has **taught us,**
X		And grant us thy safety and thy peace all the days of the world. //Amen. May// [Yea, our Lord and our God, grant us thy safety and thy peace all the days of the world, that] all the inhabitants of the earth know thee, that thou are God, the only true Father, and thou didst send our Lord Jesus Christ, thy Son and thy beloved,
C'		and he, our Lord and our God, [came and] in his life-giving gospel **taught us** all the **purity and holiness**

B'		of the prophets and apostles, of the martyrs and confessors, of the bishops and doctors, of the priests and deacons and of all the **children** of the holy catholic Church, even those who have been signed with **the living sign of holy baptism**.
		//And// we also, my Lord, thy weak, frail and miserable servants, who are assembled [in thy name] and stand before thee at this moment, having received by tradition the example from thee, rejoicing and glorifying and exalting and commemorating and celebrating [unto thee] this great and awful [and holy and life-giving and divine] mystery, of the passion and death and resurrection of our Lord and Savior Jesus Christ.
		And may thy Holy Spirit, O my Lord, come and rest upon this oblation of the servants, and may he bless it and hallow it and may it be to us, O my Lord, for the pardon of debts and for the forgiveness of sins and for the great hope of resurrection from the dead and new life in the kingdom of heaven, with all those who have been well-pleasing to thee.
A'		For all this great and wonderful dispensation towards us, **we give thee thanks** and glorify thee without ceasing, [with]//in// thy Church redeemed by the precious blood of thy Christ, with unclosed mouths and unveiled faces. [**Lifting up glory and honor and confession and adoration**, to thy living and holy and life-giving name, now always and for ever and ever.] Amen.

Ray finds the following parallels in AM:

A Praise and thanksgiving for God's work of grace

A' Praise and thanksgiving for the "great and wonderful dispensation towards us"

B fathers, eucharist

B' children, baptism

C God "taught us," "pure and holy"

C' Christ "taught us," "purity and holiness"

94 *Further Issues in Eucharistic Praying in East and West*

> X The central focus: a petition for peace and safety in this world for "us," and (based on the dependence of the text on John 17:3) eternal life for "all the inhabitants of the earth."

After his presentation of the text, Ray draws attention to a few points that are immediately evident: major block A is an embolism, a piece which is itself chiastically structured. At the center of the embolism in A, we find the *Sanctus*, which many scholars have dismissed as an interpolation. But because it fits so well into the center of the embolism, it cannot immediately be dismissed as secondary. It is nevertheless notable that the major parallel for block A ("we give thee thanks") comes outside of the *Sanctus*, which forces us to remain agnostic as to whether the *Sanctus* was part of the original chiastic structure of the whole anaphora.

Two major pieces do not fit into the chiastic structure, namely the anamnesis ("We also . . .") and epiclesis ("and may thy Holy Spirit . . ."), which come between B' and A'. The anamnesis section, in particular, is famously difficult material to account for because of its lack of a verb. He proposes three possible ways of dealing with this excess material. One could eliminate it from what could be considered the earliest stratum, which is what many scholars have done; one could find material elsewhere to balance it, which he argues an institution narrative would do reasonably well; or one could fit everything into the existing framework as much as possible. On this last point, he proposes an interesting arrangement regarding the anamnesis:

> Jean Magne, noting the close parallel between the subject of the anamnesis—"we . . . thy weak, frail and miserable servants"—and the subject of the thanksgiving in the center of the preface (Ax), has suggested that the missing main verb of the anamnesis is the "give thanks" of the concluding doxology. If we follow Magne's suggestion and link the anamnesis with the concluding doxology, either eliminating the epiclesis or moving it to "B" as suggested earlier, we produce an expanded doxology (A') which closely parallels the preface (A), and is itself chiastically structured.[15]

He therefore organizes this latter chiastic unit thus:[16]

---

15. Ibid., 192.
16. Ibid.

The Making of the Maronite Sharar 95

A'	a	**We** also, my Lord, **thy weak, frail and miserable servants**, who are assembled [in thy name] and stand before thee, having received by tradition the example from thee, rejoicing and *glorifying and exalting* and commemorating and celebrating [unto thee]
	b	this great and awful [and holy and life-giving and divine] mystery of the passion and death and burial and resurrection of our Lord and Savior Jesus *Christ*,
	x	for all this great and wonderful dispensation toward us, **give thee thanks** in thy Church
	b'	redeemed by the precious blood of thy *Christ*
	a'	with unclosed mouths and unveiled faces [**lifting up** *glory and honor and confession and adoration* to thy living and holy and life-giving name, now always and for ever and ever.] Amen.

The requirement of repositioning or excising the epiclesis is not particularly controversial, as most consider the epiclesis to be later anyway. Although connecting the anamnesis to the concluding doxology makes sense in a chiasmus, the grammar of this reconstructed A' block appears rather convoluted, with too much appositional material between the subject of the sentence ("we") and the verb ("give thee thanks") for it to make a naturally cohesive unit. Furthermore, it seems that the postpositive "also" after "we" indicates that the section is continuing an idea that was presented before. It is for this reason that Gelston, among others, has concluded that "[the anamnesis] is structurally an appendix to the intercessions of [sections B to B']."[17]

There is nevertheless reason to believe Magne was correct to see a connection between the anamnesis and the subsequent material. The East Syrian anaphora of Nestorius contains a similar "we also" prayer that provides a helpful counterpart to the anamnesis:

> We, therefore, my Lord, your lowly, weak and miserable servants [repeat] who were far off from you, and who because of your abundant mercy you

---

17. Gelston, *Addai and Mari*, 107.

have accounted worthy to stand and minister before you this dread and glorious service, and with one accord supplicate your glorious Divinity which renews all creatures.[18]

This prayer clearly parallels that in AM, but scholars are divided on whether its instance in AM is an interpolation from Nestorius, or whether Nestorius adapted it from AM. Like in AM, it appears at the end of a list of intercessions. It is likewise followed by an epiclesis and a concluding doxology which, by contrast, does not recapitulate the theme "we give thanks to you." Engberding notes that similar "we also" prayers are found commonly in the intercessions after a commemoration for the departed, and therefore concludes that this section in AM is connected to the previous material.[19] On the contrary, however, the structure of the Nestorius prayer gives substantial insight into how the compiler of the anaphora of Nestorius read AM. The subject "we" appears at the beginning, as in AM, and it is followed by a series of appositives that ultimately culminate in the verb "supplicate" at the end. This ordering would correspond well with Magne's and Ray's contention that the anamnesis is connected to the material that follows it. Although it does not end with a doxology like the reconstructed A' does, its conclusion does contain doxological language. The composer of Nestorius clearly understood this section to have the verb at the end of the prayer, and it is reasonable to presume that that is how he would have read AM, regardless of its context in the succession of intercessions, which certainly could have developed after the composition of AM. This seems to support the argument for the reconstructed A' section.

Ray ultimately concludes that, in light of the chiastic structure, we must remain agnostic about the originality of the *Sanctus*; it is unlikely that there was an original institution narrative; and the epiclesis is likely a later interpolation. But if one were to grant the existence of a reconstructed A' section, one may ask why the epiclesis was interpolated in that place in such a way that it severed the first part (the now anamnesis) from its verb. In my estimation, this is due to its proximity to the major theme in A'x, which would mirror the *Sanctus*'s proximity to the major theme in Ax. It is possible that as the East Syrians sought to adopt some

---

18. B. D. Spinks, *Mar Nestorius and Mar Theodore the Interpreter: The Forgotten Eucharistic Prayers of East Syria* (Cambridge, UK: Grove Books, 1999), 33.
19. Spinks, "Quest for the 'Original Form,'" 27.

of the elements characteristic of other liturgical traditions, such as the use of the *Sanctus* and epiclesis in the eucharistic liturgy, they attempted to retain the integrity of their prayer by fitting these new elements into the existing structure. To do so in spite of the syntactical rupture caused by the insertion of the epiclesis demonstrates a strong attachment and commitment to this organizational form. If true, this would suggest that the *Sanctus* entered AM before or at the same time as the epiclesis.[20]

Although Ray's article makes a rather straightforward argument with clear evidence, few scholars have engaged his work, and fewer still have been convinced by it. It is my impression that the reason for this has to do with the largely accepted notion that the basic underlying structure of AM is a meal prayer composed of three benedictions, a structure purported to be held in common with the *Birkat ha-Mazon* and *Didache* traditions. That an alternative basic structure could be proposed, ignoring what appear to be obvious parallels with the table prayer traditions, seems to be in tension with the general consensus on the archaic core of the anaphora. This tension is to some degree dependent upon the unresolved question of how AM is to be segmented into the three benedictions that make up the prayer, and how much of the received text of AM is included in those prayers. Stated otherwise, there is no clear sense of how the "table prayer" stratum of AM developed into the "classical anaphora" stratum as

---

20. That the Sanctus and epiclesis moved together as a single unit is not a novel idea. Nathan Chase, following Gabriele Winkler, was the most recent to argue this point in his dissertation, arguing from (a) Syrian initiatory and Egyptian anaphoral texts; (b) the use of common praise words and divine titles; and (c) the merkavah tradition. For his discussion of the relationship between these two liturgical units, see Nathan Chase, "Rethinking Anaphoral Development in Light of the Barcelona Papyrus," PhD diss. (Notre Dame: University of Notre Dame, 2020), 396f. Of particular interest to this study is the prayer for the consecration of the oil in the East Syrian rite of initiation. The consecration prayer is organized in a tripartite format, epiclesis-sanctus-epiclesis, which has no equivalent in any of the West Syrian rites of initiation. If the Maronite *Sharar* came from the East Syrian milieu, it is likely that such a connection would have been known. The Maronite ordo attributed to Jacob of Serugh is the only other rite to maintain a tripartite blessing of the oil, but it replaces the central *Sanctus* with the first of two prebaptismal anointings in accordance with West Syrian practices. For the East Syrian baptismal ordo, see E. C. Whitaker and Maxwell E. Johnson, *Documents of the Baptismal Liturgy*, rev. and exp. ed. (Collegeville, MN: Liturgical Press, 2003), 63–72. For the Maronite baptismal ordo, see Augustin Mouhanna, *Les rites de l'initiation dans l'église maronite* (Rome: Pontificium Institutum Orientalium Studiorum, 1980).

it appears in the earliest manuscripts, and the chiastic argument appears to ignore the evidence in support of structural and theological similarity between the Jewish table prayers and AM. This tension, however, can be resolved under close examination and need not undermine Ray's argument. The following section therefore seeks to establish the continuity of the chiastic argument with the consensus on the tripartite original core, but adding important caveats so as to be able to demonstrate both the origin of AM's chiastic structure and *Sharar*'s dependence on it.

The *Birkat ha-Mazon* and the *Didache*

Scholarly attempts to posit a direct connection between AM and the tripartite *Birkat ha-Mazon* loom large in the scholarly debate over the origins and redaction history of Christian eucharistic praying. However, in light of recent scholarship on the relationship between Jewish and Christian ritual meal prayers, one can no longer posit a linear succession between Jewish and Christian liturgical texts.[21] Moreover, even side-by-side comparisons between AM and Jewish prayer forms must necessarily be limited strictly to general observations about similar structures or themes if they are to be compared at all. But in the interest of reconciling the tripartite prayer form with the chiastic argument and bridging the gap between AM's "archaic core" and the "classical anaphora," it is helpful to examine a recent structural and thematic comparison between AM, the *Birkat ha-Mazon*, and *Didache* 10. This serves to clarify the similarities and differences between AM and the prayers to which it is purported to be related and allow us to identify the most basic shape of AM's original core.

Sarhad Jammo is perhaps the most recent scholar of AM to posit a succession between the *Birkat ha-Mazon* and AM.[22] In order to establish the tripartite structure of AM and its connection to the table blessing,

---

21. For a helpful overview of the scholarship on the inadmissibility of arguments premised on succession of Jewish liturgy, see Bryan D. Spinks, "A Tale of Two Anaphoras: Addai and Mari and Maronite Sharar," in *The Anaphoral Genesis of the Institution Narrative in Light of the Anaphora of Addai and Mari*, ed. Cesare Giraudo, OCA 295 (Rome: Edizioni Orientalia Christiana/Lilamé: Valore Italiano, 2013), 259–274, especially 263–267.

22. See Sarhad Y. Jammo, "The Mesopotamian Anaphora of Addai & Mari: The Organic Dialectic between its Apostolic Core and Euchological Growth," in The Anaphoral Genesis of the Institution Narrative in Light of the Anaphora of Addai and Mari, ed.

Jammo points to two early literary sources, the Babylonian Talmud and a letter from the Catholicos of the Church of the East Isho'yahb I (ca. 587). The Babylonian Talmud says:

> Our Teachers taught: the order of the blessing of food is the following: the first blessing is the one that is for "the One who nourishes," the second one the blessing for the land, the third is "for the One who will build Jerusalem." . . .
>
> Our Teachers taught: From where it results that the blessing for the food is contained in the Law? From where it says: "When you have eaten your fill, you shall bless" (Deut. 8, 10).[23]

For Jammo, the connection between AM and the three benedictions described here is obvious. While the first and second benedictions deal with the food and its origin, the third moves into the future, making a petition for the building and preservation of a quasi-eschatological reality. Three of the earliest eucharistic prayers from this region, *Didache* 10, *Apostolic Constitutions* VII, and AM, all make use of this tripartite structure, and it persists so markedly in the East Syrian tradition that even in the sixth century, Isho'yahb I could say:

> (The priest) at the end of each of the consecutive sections (*Yubal Pasoqe*), duly glorifying with his tongue, draws with his hand over the divine mysteries—according to the norm—the sign of the lordly cross. When he finishes the *three sections* (*Tlatheyhon Pasoqe*), he draws near to sign.[24]

Jammo therefore posits a succession from the Jewish meal prayer described in the Babylonian Talmud to the tripartite anaphora ultimately described by Isho'yahb I, saying that "the original euchological structure of A&M follows basically the pattern of the *Birkat ha-Mazon* in its Passover environment."[25] Cognizant of the methodological pitfalls in dealing

---

Cesare Giraudo, OCA 295 (Rome: Edizioni Orientalia Christiana/Lilamé: Valore Italiano, 2013), 387–242. See also Jammo, "Anaphora of the Apostles," 5–35.

23. Ibid., 12, quoting S. Cavalletti, *Il Trattato delle Benedizioni del Talmud babilonese* (Turin: 1968), 321–22.

24. Chabot, *Synodicon Orientale*, cited by Jammo, "Anaphora of the Apostles," 13.

25. Jammo, "The Mesopotamian Anaphora," 401.

with an orally-transmitted prayer like the *Birkat ha-Mazon* on a textual level, let us briefly examine his comparison in support of this claim:[26]

Birkat Ha-Mazon	The Anaphora of A&M
1) **Blessed are you, Lord our God, king of the universe**, for you nourish us and **the whole world with goodness, grace, kindness, and mercy** Blessed are you, Lord, for you nourish the universe.	1) **Glory to you the adorable and glorious Name** (of the Father and the Son and the Holy Spirit) **who created the world in his grace and its inhabitants in his compassion,** has redeemed men in his mercy and has effected great grace toward mortals.
2) **We give you thanks, Lord our God,** For you have given us for our inheritance a desirable land, good and wide, the covenant and the law, life and food **For all these things we give you thanks** and **bless your name** for ever and beyond.	2) **We give you thanks, Lord,** we your lowly, weak, and wretched servants, because you have brought about in us a great grace which cannot be repaid. For you put on our humanity to give us life through your divinity, you extalled [sic] our lowly state, you raised our fall, you restored our immortality, you forgave our debts, you justified our sinfulness, you enlightened our intelligence. You, our Lord and God, conquered our enemies, and made triumphant our weak nature through the abundant mercy of your grace.

26. Jammo's rendition of AM here is the result of his own reconstruction of the earliest material underlying AM and *Sharar* in the same article, "The Anaphora of the Apostles." Setting aside the anamnesis for later discussion, he concludes that AM is itself the common core between the two anaphoras, though a few purportedly original forms are preserved in *Sharar*. Then excising the three pieces that are considered later interpolations, namely the *Sanctus*, institution narrative, and epiclesis, he writes that "we should be able to extract a remnant formula parallel to Birkat Ha-Mazon in its structure and basic themes, and similar to Didache 10 and to the Mystic Eucharist of the Apostolic Constitutions VII. 25" (Jammo, "Anaphora of the Apostles," 14). The texts for the comparison itself can be found in Jammo, "Anaphora of the Apostles," 15, as well as in Jammo, "The Mesopotamian Anaphora," 399–400. All annotations to the text are his.

	And for all your help and graces toward us, we raise to you praise, honor, thanksgiving and adoration, now and for ever and ever. Amen.
3) **Have mercy, Lord our God, on us your people Israel**, and your city Jerusalem, on your sanctuary and your dwelling place on Zion the habitation of your glory, and the great and holy house over which your name is invoked. Restore the kingdom of the house of David to its place in our days, and speedily build Jerusalem.	3) **Lord through your many mercies which cannot be told, do make**, in the commemoration of your Christ, **a gracious remembrance for all the pious and righteous fathers** who were pleasing in your sight, the prophets, the apostles, the martyrs and confessors, the bishops, the priests and deacons, and all the sons who have been sealed with the living seal of holy baptism.
Blessed are you Lord for you build Jerusalem. Amen.	And for all your wonderful plan for us, **we give you thanks and glorify you unceasingly in your Church**, redeemed by the precious blood of your Christ, with open mouths and uncovered faces, as we offer up praise, honor, thanksgiving and adoration, now, and for ever and ever, Amen.

Most of Jammo's argument is made on the basis of comparable themes rather than direct textual links, which are limited largely to the incipits of the benedictions. But despite arguing for a thematic connection between the three themes of the *Birkat ha-Mazon* and those of AM, he himself identifies several thematic discrepancies. For one, he notes that the first section of AM does not give thanksgiving for the food as the *Birkat ha-Mazon* does, but rather gives thanks for creation and redemption.[27] He attributes this to the fact that the community dinner that preceded the eucharist had fallen out of common usage, as well as the idea that "the spiritual bread

---

27. Jammo, "The Mesopotamian Anaphora," 398.

and wine they were sharing were not part of the plan of creation but a climax of the redemptive economy."[28] Likewise, he says that the second benedictions are connected by a shared emphasis on the redemptive economy, but with AM bearing "clear Christological content."[29] Lastly, recognizing the difference between petition in the *Birkat ha-Mazon* and commemoration in AM, Jammo argues that the third benediction in the *Birkat ha-Mazon* is "formulated in the manner of a supplication, but its real content is a commemoration," noting that the insertion of the "memorial of the Lord" in this section in AM constitutes the establishment of a new pattern of the Lord's commemoration.[30]

Despite the shared tripartite structure and the focus on thanksgiving, I am inclined to see the connections Jammo sees between the three sections as rather forced. Jammo himself established that AM's rendition of the first prayer is wholly different from that of *Birkat ha-Mazon* in its thematic content. The second prayer in *Birkat ha-Mazon* stems directly from its logic in the first one—it acknowledges the good land from which the food in the first prayer came—while in AM it focuses directly on the redemptive economy in a way that the *Birkat ha-Mazon* does not. For the third, almost no thematic connection can be made without imputing AM's paradigm onto the *Birkat ha-Mazon*. The idea that the third benediction in the *Birkat ha-Mazon* is in fact a commemoration formulated as a petition extends the meaning of the prayer beyond what can plausibly be conceded on the basis of the text alone. It would seem that the connection in the third benediction can be made only on account of the word "mercy" in the incipits of the two prayers.

Jammo also sees this basic tripartite structure shared in common with the *Didache* 10, maintaining that "this basic original structure of A&M could be considered as a first stratum in the *Formgeschichte* of its final text in the manuscript."[31] He thus compares AM and the *Didache* in the same way:

---

28. Ibid., 398.
29. Ibid., 400.
30. Ibid., 400.
31. Jammo, "The Mesopotamian Anaphora," 401. Jammo only provides the incipits for this comparison. The specific references to the *Didache* and italic text of the prayer are my own additions to this comparison. The completed text of *Didache* 10 comes from R. C. D. Jasper and G. J. Cuming, *Prayers of the Eucharist: Early and Reformed*, ed.

The Making of the Maronite Sharar 103

Didache	A&M
(10.3) Almighty Lord, **you created all things for your Name's sake** . . . [*and gave food and drink to humans for enjoyment, that they might give thanks to you; but to us you have granted spiritual food and drink and eternal life through Jesus your servant. (10.4) Above all we give thanks to you because you are mighty; glory to you for evermore. Amen.*]	Glory to you, **the adorable Name** (of the Father and of the Son and of the Holy Spirit) **who created the world in his grace and its inhabitants in his compassion**, has redeemed mankind in his mercy, and has effected great grace toward mortals.
(10.2) **We thank you, holy Father,** for your holy name which you have made to dwell in our hearts . . . [*We give thanks to you, holy Father, for your holy name which you have enshrined in our hearts, and for the knowledge and faith and immortality which you have made known to us through Jesus your servant; glory to you for evermore.*]	**We give thanks to you, Lord** . . . , [*we your lowly, weak, and wretched servants, because you have brought about in us a great grace which cannot be repaid. For you put on our humanity to give us life through your divinity, you exalted our lowly state, you raised our fall, you restored our immortality, you forgave our debts, you justified our sinfulness, you enlightened our intelligence. You, our Lord and God, conquered our enemies, and made triumphant our weak nature through the abundant mercy of your grace. And for all your help and graces toward us, we raise to you praise, honor, thanksgiving and adoration, now and for ever and ever. Amen.*]

Paul F. Bradshaw and Maxwell E. Johnson (Collegeville, MN: Liturgical Press Academic, 2019), hereafter *PEER*.

(10.5) **Lord, remember your Church** . . . [*to deliver it from all evil and to perfect it in your love, and gather it together from the four winds, having been sanctified, into your kingdom which you have prepared for it; for yours is the power and the glory for evermore. Amen.*]	**Make, Lord, a gracious remembrance for all the fathers** . . . [*who were pleasing in our sight, the prophets, the apostles, the martyrs and confessors, the bishops, the priests and deacons, and all the sons who have been sealed with the living seal of holy baptism.* *And for all your wonderful plan for us, we give you thanks and glorify you unceasingly in your Church, redeemed by the precious blood of your Christ, with open mouths and uncovered faces, as we offer up praise, honor, thanksgiving and adoration, now, and for ever and ever, Amen.*]

While Jammo is careful to not to extend the similarities beyond structure and theme, there are nevertheless important discrepancies here which undermine even those. While the ordering of the prayers (or at least their incipits) was parallel between the *Birkat ha-Mazon* and AM, the incipits of the first two prayers in *Didache* 10 are switched in Jammo's comparison. The prayer beginning "We thank you" (10.2), listed second here, comes before the prayer beginning "Almighty Lord, you created all things" (10.3) in the *Didache* text. Moreover, the thematic content of the prayers in *Didache* 10 is likewise not equivalent to those in AM. *Didache* 10.2 is a thanksgiving for God's holy name and the communication of divine "knowledge and faith and immortality" through Jesus, whereas the purportedly equivalent section in AM gives thanks for the incarnation and the economy of salvation. Likewise, *Didache* 10.3 begins similarly to its equivalent paragraph in AM by addressing God as the creator of all things, but the content of the benedictions diverges significantly from there: *Didache* 10.3 deals with the spiritual food and drink and praises God for his might, whereas AM glorifies God for the act of creation and the gift of grace and redemption. One could argue here that the "spiritual food" of the eucharist is the communicator of redemption and the thing that effects "great grace toward mortals," but this cannot be established on the basis of the text alone. Lastly, *Didache* 10.5 is a petition for the sanctification and perfection of the Church in a future frame of reference, which it shares with the *Birkat ha-Mazon*, whereas AM has a commemoration for those who were pleasing to God in the past and present. The two share a quasi-eschatological theme, but differ nonetheless in that one is a petition for the future and the other is a retrospective commemoration of the past and present. So while Jammo acknowledges the differences in the developments of these formularies, he still maintains that "A&M in its first and earliest stratum still preserves the basic pattern of Eucharistic prayer similar to that of the *Didache*."[32] But the analysis above suggests that even this "basic pattern" does not match in the two anaphoras.

We can therefore note three important features of how these prayers relate to one another. First, the incipits of the benedictions bear the majority of the shared content between the texts, and even that is limited largely to individual words rather than formulas (e.g., "Have mercy . . . on us" vs. "Lord through your many mercies . . . do make"). The benedictions in AM and *Didache* 10 share much more content in common with one another than either of them does with the *Birkat ha-Mazon*, and most of the variances in the wording are much more minor, indicating the possibility of a developing formulaic style among the Christian texts. Second, similarity in the incipits does not translate to similarity in the benedictions' thematic content, which varies substantially between the *Birkat ha-Mazon*, *Didache* 10, and AM. The incipits to the benedictions therefore appear to serve an organizational and formulaic role for structuring the three sections, rather than functioning as a true introduction to the rest of the content in the benediction. And third, the actions done in each of the three benedictions vary in both kind and order. The apparent reordering of the first two benedictions in *Didache* 10 in particular appears to indicate a certain flexibility to the sequence of actions in this tradition. We can therefore see that almost every element of the benedictions in the *Birkat ha-Mazon*, *Didache* 10, and AM is subject to variation: the incipits, their wording, the action of the prayer, their

---

32. Ibid., 402.

ordering, and so on. The only elements underlying all three prayers are that they are tripartite, include thanks and praise or blessing to God, and are segmented by what appear to be quasi-formulaic incipits.

Most importantly, however, there is a significant structural discontinuity between Jammo's AM and the other two prayers examined here with regard to the internal organization of each of the benedictions. Each of the benedictions in the *Birkat ha-Mazon* and *Didache* 10 is organized with a kind of symmetry: the first line exposes the action of the benediction (praise/blessing, thanks, or petition), the second and following lines develop the theme, and the last line recapitulates the first line in its blessing or thanksgiving. In this way, each benediction is a discrete unit that opens and closes with a particular idea; it is therefore bounded not only at the beginning, but also at the end. On the other hand, the proposed early version of AM as presented by Jammo in the table above has only the last two prayers ending on a recapitulation of thanks or praise/ blessing. The first benediction reads much more like the introduction to a long prayer than a discrete and self-contained unit, on account of its lack of a concluding line. It cannot be considered a full benediction in this case, and the prayer cannot be considered tripartite according to Jammo's segmentation.

A Chiastic Resolution

We may resolve this issue, however, by taking seriously Ray's argument for chiasmus in AM and making yet another observation about the anaphora's structure. Granting that the A and A' sections each contain an internal chiasmus according to Ray's reconstruction above, we can note that the remaining material in the center, B C X C' B' also stands alone as an internally structured chiastic unit. This ultimately results in three internally-structured units that together form a larger chiasmus. The chart below lays out the parallels accordingly:[33]

---

33. Ray's analysis examined the English translation of the text for these parallels, but did not make use of Syriac, which helps clarify some slight ambiguities in the structure concerning which words do have a parallel and which do not. One such example is the minor parallel pair in the reconstructed A' section using the word "glory." The word rendered as "glorifying" in A'a is ܣܚܕܝ (root: *ḥdy*) in Syriac, whereas the word "glory" in A'a' is ܬܫܒܘܚܬܐ (root: *šbh*). While the parallel seems to work in translation, the word

A	a	Praise; confession	
	b	in his grace	
	c	showed great grace unto mortals	
	x	we give thanks to you	
	c'	showed great grace unto us	
	b'	in your grace	
	a'	praise and honor and confession and adoration	
B	a	just and righteous fathers; the commemoration of the body and blood of thy Christ	
	b	pure and holy altar	
	c	taught us	
	x	your safety and peace	
	c'	taught us	
	b'	purity and holiness	
	a'	children of the holy catholic church; the sign of holy baptism	
A'	a	We also, my Lord, thy weak, frail and miserable servants glorifying, exalting, commemorating and celebrating	
	b	Christ	
	x	give you thanks	
	b'	your Christ	
	a'	raising glory, honor, confession, and adoration	

stemming from *ḥdy* is better translated as "rejoicing." Moreover, it is not used anywhere else in the anaphora, and so cannot constitute part of the minor parallel pair. This, however, does not mean the chiasmus does not work, as the root *šbḥ* appears in both A'a and A'a', translated in its context as "exalting" and "glory" respectively, and so constitutes the minor parallel pair. Adjustments in light of the Syriac are included in the table below.

108 *Further Issues in Eucharistic Praying in East and West*

Such an arrangement of this new B block has precedent in the thought of Engberding, who noted the thematic parallels of "taught us" and "pure and holy" on either side of the petition for safety and peace, which he regards as a later interpolation splitting the text into two sections.[34] Following Engberding, Gelston proposes a reconstruction of the "primitive continuous text" with a beginning and ending corresponding exactly to those of the new B block proposed above, but without the chiastic center or any repetition of "taught us" or "pure and holy."[35] Such excisions do harm to the integrity of the text, removing pieces merely on account of repetition which would have served a rhetorical and organizational function. Nevertheless, their analysis supports the present proposal for the boundaries of this proposed B unit.

Were we to grant this, we would find that the entire anaphora is made up of three prayers, or benedictions, each containing a chiasmus, but also forming a chiasmus together. The first is a prayer of glory and thanks to God for his work of grace; the second, a prayer of commemoration and petition for peace; and the third, a prayer of praise and thanksgiving that recapitulates the first. The parallels between the A and A' blocks are obvious. The root for "give thanks," ܝܕܐ (*yda*), appears in both Ax and A'x, thus forming the centerpiece of their respective chiastic units and constituting a major pair in the overarching structure. Likewise, the final lines in Aa' and A'a', rendered as "glory, honor, confession, and adoration," share the roots of all four words and form a clear link between the A and A' sections.[36]

---

34. See Engberding, "Zum anaphorischen," 107f., cited in Gelston, *Addai and Mari*, 97.

35. Gelston, *Addai and Mari*, 98. Gelston even goes on to note that one of the difficulties of this reconstruction is the distance between the initial mention of the "fathers" and "the detailed list of categories into which they fall in the last four lines" (98). This, of course, is one of the major parallel pairs that Ray describes, and its organization makes sense in a chiastic structure, while seeming disjointed to the scholar that seeks to streamline the language.

36. On this latter point, however, we must remain cautious, because this line is not found at all in the Mar Esha'ya text. Something similar is true of ܫܡܐ, or "name" (root: šma), which appears in Aa and A'a: while it forms a very interesting major parallel between the A and A' blocks, the word ܒܫܡܟ ("in your name") is famously missing from A'a in the Mar Esha'ya text. It is therefore unclear whether these are later interpolations that became ubiquitous, or early features that fell out of the line of transmission of the Mar Esha'ya iteration.

Putting these prayers into the same format as the *Birkat ha-Mazon* and *Didache* above, we get the following:

Addai and Mari
Aa) Worthy of *praise* from every mouth, and of *confession* by every tongue . . . is the adorable and glorious name of . . . the Father and Son and Holy Spirit, who did create the world . . . Ax) . . . we give thanks to thee . . . Aa') . . . for all thy aids and graces towards us, let us lift up to thee *praise and honor and confession and adoration* now always and for ever and ever. Amen.
Ba) Do thou, my Lord, in thy many and unspeakable mercies, make a good and acceptable memorial for all the just and righteous *fathers* who have been well-pleasing before thee, in *the commemoration of the body and blood of thy Christ* . . . Bx) . . . grant us your safety and your peace . . . Ba') . . . of all the *children* of the holy catholic Church, even those who have been signed with *the living sign of holy baptism.*
A'a) We also, my Lord, thy weak, frail and miserable servants, who are assembled [in thy name] and stand before thee at this moment, having received by tradition the example from thee, rejoicing and *glorifying and exalting* and commemorating and celebrating . . . A'x) . . . [we] give thee thanks . . . A'a') . . . Lifting up *glory and honor and confession and adoration,* to thy living and holy and life-giving name, now always and forever and ever.

This arrangement solves the problems present in Jammo's segmentation of the text. The organization of each "benediction" is clear: it has a clearly delineated exposition, a development of the theme, and a recapitulation of the initial exposition. This has the benefit of incorporating the problematic anamnesis section, which Jammo considers to be a later addition. It is perhaps worth noting that the three benedictions together form the entire anaphora into this same ABA' structure. Moreover, it retains the three basic actions in *Didache* 10 of praise, thanks, and memorial or petition, though reordered to put the memorial in the center rather than at the end, thus indicating a uniquely Christian development. Every one of the liberties taken here by the author of AM finds its precedent in either the *Birkat ha-Mazon* or *Didache* 10, and not one of them is precluded by the analysis above. The fact of reordering of prayers finds precedent in the reversal of the first two benedictions in *Didache* 10, and the substitution of one incipit entirely for another likewise finds precedent between the *Birkat ha-Mazon* and the Christian texts. Such an arrangement of the texts preserves the rhetorical sequence of exposition, development, and recapitulation, which is perhaps the most consistent and identifiable current throughout *Birkat ha-Mazon* and *Didache* 10.

Three objections can be raised to this argument: (1) this segmentation of the text of AM ignores the apparently natural divisions of the text by the *qanone*[37]; (2) the second "benediction" does not contain a blessing in an exposition/recapitulation format; and (3) it appears to ignore the more obvious textual parallels for the incipits in the text. In response to the first objection, Anthony Gelston has argued that the segmentation of the text according to the *qanone* (the three *qanone* are the *Sanctus* and its introduction, the doxology in Aa', and the doxology in A'a') is misleading, noting that the similarity in subject matter between sections Aa and Aa', which are divided by the *Sanctus*, resists arbitrary division.[38] The segmentation of the text according to the above proposition solves this problem. If we were to presume, as many have, that the *Sanctus* was a later interpolation into AM, then the section would make sense as a cohesive unit organized around a single subject matter, here represented by the single A block. The other two *qanone* segmenting the text pose no issue to the current structure, for they function here as they otherwise would: the second *qanona*, thought to be the doxology of the second benediction, concludes the A block in this analysis; and the third *qanona*, the doxology at the very end of the anaphora, concludes the A' block.

Regarding the second objection, it must first be noted that the parallelism in the petition-benediction in *Didache* 10 and the *Birkat ha-Mazon* is more thematic than it is verbal. The *Birkat ha-Mazon* begins with the

---

37. A *qanona* is understood to be an audible conclusion to the *gehanta*, a prayer said by the priest in a low voice with an inclined head. *Qanone* is the plural form of *qanona*.
38. Gelston, *Addai and Mari*, 10.

theme of Jerusalem, petitions for restoration, and recapitulates the theme of Jerusalem as though the petition were granted. Likewise, *Didache* 10.5 begins with the theme of the Church, petitions for its salvation and gathering, and then concludes with the idea of the kingdom where the church will be gathered, "having been sanctified," as though the petition had been granted. However, there is little textual parallel between the exposition and recapitulation of these two petition-benedictions. In this sense, the B block in AM corresponds well with the thematic, rather than textual, organization of the equivalent units in the other prayers. Moreover, incorporating the whole B block, the prayer is able to take the logical progression from the beginning of the prayer to its conclusion, including not only the righteous and just who are departed, but also those who are living and signed "with the living sign of holy baptism," who would otherwise be left outside the prayer. The omission of an initial benediction from the B block does not itself constitute a radical departure from the form of the other two prayers, as the incipit of the third benediction in *Didache* 10.5 does the same. Neither does the lack of a concluding doxology to the B block cause greater difficulty than Jammo's proposal, for the first benediction in his own allocation lacks a doxological conclusion.

The response to the third objection stems from the other two. Having dealt with the other elements of the prayer, we must now recognize that this is the point at which the author of AM demonstrably and intentionally departs from the existing prayer form and inaugurates something new in the Syrian Christian tradition. The compiler of this first stratum of AM was clearly familiar with the prayer form of the *Didache* tradition, but decided to arrange the anaphora in an internally cohesive way that eschewed what might have been seen as a Judaizing prayer form in favor of a more uniquely Christian organization, putting at the center the memorial culminating in a petition for the preservation of the Church. This initial stratum of AM is therefore not simply a local variant of the *Birkat ha-Mazon* type, which likely did not have a stable form at the time; rather, it was an intentional, chiastically organized composition in the tripartite manner of Syrian Christians at the time.

The proposed A B A' organization therefore offers a more plausible allocation for AM's tripartite structure. Such an arrangement has several advantages. First, it provides a solid textual and structural basis for the presence of chiasmus in AM, bridging the theoretical gap between the "table prayer" stratum and the "classical anaphora" stratum in the scholarship. There is no need in this case to determine how much of the received text of AM was present in the earliest stratum: the chiasmus does the sorting. Second, this organization of AM provides a much more plausible analog to the three prayers described by Isho'yahb I in the sixth century than the usually accepted segmentation of the anaphora. Most importantly, however, these findings indicate that the first stratum of AM was through-composed as a single cohesive structure that could be memorized and reproduced with ease.

Accordingly, there is no longer need to see a tension between the chiastic argument and a tripartite archaic core. The continuity between the two is evident, though AM demonstrates a notable "Christianization" of the tripartite meal prayer form by its placement of the commemoration/petition in the middle, thereby constituting a departure from the tradition of the *Didache*. While these findings are certainly suggestive, perhaps the best argument in favor of the chiastic composition of AM is the recognition and appropriation of this chiasmus at a later date. In this way, *Sharar* provides an ideal comparison piece by functioning as a sort of 'reception history' for AM. Such a comparison can (1) help corroborate whether such a chiasmus existed in AM, (2) indicate what part of AM and the chiasmus was intact at the time of *Sharar's* composition, and (3) determine the nature of the relationship between AM and *Sharar*. Perhaps just as importantly, however, such an analysis also provides insight into the composition and redaction of *Sharar* as an anaphora in its own right. All of these are discussed in the next section.

Chiasmus in *Sharar*

Textual Comparison

In light of the discussion above, let us examine *Sharar* according to the parallel pairs identified in AM. I have included AM alongside *Sharar* for the sake of comparison:[39]

---

39. The text and annotations for Addai and Mari are reproduced from Ray's article and kept consistent throughout. The text of *Sharar* comes from Spinks' translation in *PEER*, 72–76, and the Syriac text for both comes from Gelston, *Addai and Mari*, 48–55, and MS Paris Syriac 71, respectively. The annotations, footnotes, and segmentation into chiastic units is mine. I have adjusted some things in the translations, noting them with footnotes and brackets.

The Making of the Maronite Sharar   113

	Chiasmus in Addai and Mari		Chiasmus in *Sharar*
1	Worthy of *praise*[1] from every mouth, and of *confession*[2] by every tongue, [and of *adoration and exaltation* from all creatures,] is the adorable and glorious name of [thy glorious Trinity,] Father and Son and Holy Spirit;	Aa	Priest: *Glory*[3] to you, the *adorable and glorious*[4] name of the Father and of the Son and of the Holy Spirit,
5	Who didst create the world in *thy grace*[5] and its inhabitants in thy pitifulness; who didst save mankind by thy compassion	b	who created the worlds by *[his] grace*[6] and its inhabitants in [his] mercy;
	And *hast showed great grace unto mortals.*[7]	c	and has *effected redemption for mortals by [his] grace.*[8]
8	Thousand thousands of those on high bless and adore thy majesty, O my Lord; and ten thousand times ten thousand holy angels, and hosts of spiritual beings, ministers of fire and spirit, glorify thy name; with the holy cherubim and spiritual seraphim, [offering adoration to thy sovereignty] //glorifying thy name//, crying [and praising without ceasing, calling one to another and saying] //and singing//: Holy, holy, [holy, Lord God of hosts. Heaven and earth are full of thy praises and of the nature of thy being and of the excellency of thy glorious splendor. Blessed be he who came and Hosanna to the son of David. Blessed be he who came and cometh in the name of the Lord. Hosanna in the highest.] With those	x	Your majesty, O Lord, a thousand thousand heavenly angels worship; and myriad myriads of hosts, ministers of fire and spirit, glorify in fear. With the cherubim and seraphim, who from one to another bless and sanctify and cry out and say, may we also, Lord, through your grace and your compassion be made worthy to say with them three times, Holy, Holy, Holy.
14			
19			

[1] ܬܘܕܝܬܐ
[2] ܬܘܕܝܬܐ; this word can also be translated as "thanksgiving", which would not be out of place here.
[3] ܬܘܕܝܬܐ
[4] ܫܡܐ ܣܓܝܕܐ
[5] ܒܛܝܒܘܬܟ; the Syriac here indicates a third-person possessive, which is retained in Spinks, Gelston, and Macomber. A more accurate translation here would be "in his grace". The text of Sharar in Paris Syr. 71 and Sauget's edition indicate the third-person Syriac reading, "by his grace". Spinks translates it in the second person ("by your grace") based on the notion that the entire anaphora was originally addressed to Christ.
[7] ܘܐܚܘܝܬ ܛܝܒܘܬܐ ܪܒܬܐ ܠܘܬ ܡܝܘܬܐ
[8] ܘܥܒܕ ܦܘܪܩܢܐ ܠܡܝܘܬܐ ܒܛܝܒܘܬܗ

	heavenly hosts **we give thanks to thee**,[9] O my Lord, even we thy servants, weak and frail and miserable.		**We give thanks to you**[10], Lord, we your sinful servants,
	For ***thou hast showed great grace unto us***[11] which cannot be repaid,	c'	because you have *effected in us your grace*[12] which cannot be repaid.
23	in that thou didst put on our humanity that thou mightest quicken us by thy divinity, and thou hast exalted our low estate and hast restored us from our fall, thou hast raised us out of a state of death and thou hast forgiven our debts and justified us from our guilt, thou hast enlightened our knowledge, and hast condemned, O our Lord and our God, our enemies, and hast granted victory to the weakness of our frail nature in the abundant mercies of *thy grace*.[13]	b'	You put on our humanity so as to quicken us by your divinity. You lifted up our poverty and righted our dejection. And you quickened our mortality, and you justified our sinfulness and you forgave our debts. And you enlightened our understanding, and vanquished our enemies, and made triumphant our lowliness. And for all *your grace towards us*,[14]
30	//And because of this...// [For all thy aids and graces towards us, **let us lift up to thee *praise and honor and confession and adoration*,**[15] now always and for ever and ever.] Amen.	a'	let us offer to you *glory and honor*[16], in your holy church before your propitiatory altar, now…
	Do thou, my Lord, in thy many and unspeakable mercies, make a good and acceptable memorial for all the just and righteous **fathers**[17] who have been well-pleasing before thee, in **the commemoration of the body and blood of thy Christ**[18]	**B**	You, O Lord, therefore in your many mercies, make a gracious **remembrance**[19] for all the upright and just **fathers**[20] in **the commemoration of your body and blood**,[21]

9 ܡܘܕܝܢ ܠܟ
10 ܡܘܕܝܢ ܠܟ
11 ܕܥܒܕܬ ܒܢ ܛܝܒܘܬܐ ܪܒܬܐ
12 ܕܥܒܕܬ ܒܢ ܛܝܒܘܬܟ
13 ܕܛܝܒܘܬܟ
14 ܘܥܠ ܐܦܝ ܗܠܝܢ ܟܠܗܝܢ ܛܝܒܘܬܟ ܕܠܘܬܢ
15 ܢܣܩ ܠܟ ܬܫܒܘܚܬܐ ܘܐܝܩܪܐ ܘܬܘܕܝܬܐ ܘܣܓܕܬܐ
16 ܬܫܒܘܚܬܐ ܘܐܝܩܪܐ ܢܣܩ ܠܟ
17 ܐܒܗܬܐ ܟܐܢܐ ܘܙܕܝܩܐ
18 ܒܥܘܗܕܢܐ ܕܦܓܪܗ ܘܕܡܗ ܕܡܫܝܚܟ
19 ܕܘܟܪܢܐ
20 ܐܒܗܬܐ
21 ܒܥܘܗܕܢܐ ܕܦܓܪܟ ܘܕܡܟ

The Making of the Maronite Sharar 115

37	C	which we **offer**[24] to you upon your **[living and] holy altar**[25], as you, our hope, have taught us[26] in your holy gospel and said, "I am the bread of **life**[27] which came down from heaven so that mortals may have life in me."
	which we offer to thee upon thy **pure and holy**[22] altar, as thou has **taught us**[23],	
41	Xa	We make, O Lord, the *memorial of your passion*[28] *as you have taught us*[29]: In the night when you were delivered up to the crucifiers, O Lord, you took bread in your *pure and holy hands*[30], and you looked to heaven to your glorious Father.
	And grant us thy safety and thy peace all the days of the world. //Amen. May// [Yea, our Lord and our God, grant us thy safety and thy peace all the days of the world, that] all the inhabitants of the earth [may] know thee, that thou are God, the only true Father, and thou didst send our Lord Jesus Christ, thy Son and thy beloved,	b	
46	x	You blessed, and signed, hallowed, O Lord, and broke and gave to your disciples, the blessed Apostles, and said to them, "This bread is my body, which is broken and given for the life of the world, and for those who take it, for the pardon of debts and forgiveness of sins; take, eat from it, and it will be to you for eternal life".
52	(x)	And likewise over the cup, you gave thanks and glorified and said, O Lord, "This cup is my blood of the New Testament, which is shed for many for the remission of sins. Take, drink from it all of you, and it

---

22 ܡܕܒܚܐ ܩܕܝܫܐ ܘܕܟܝܐ
23 ܐܠܦܬܢ
24 ܡܩܪܒܝܢܢ ܠܟ
25 ܡܕܒܚܐ ܩܕܝܫܐ ܘܚܝܐ
26 ܐܠܦܬܢ
27 ܚܝܐ
28 ܕܘܟܪܢܐ ܕܚܫܟ
29 ܐܠܦܬܢ
30 ܐܝܕܘܗܝ ܩܕܝܫܬܐ ܘܕܟܝܬܐ

			will be to you for the pardon of debts and forgiveness of sins; take, eat from it, and it will be to you for eternal life". Amen.
		b'	For whenever you eat from *this holy body*[31] and drink from this cup of life and salvation,
61		a'	you are *calling to remembrance the death and resurrection*[32] of your Lord, until the great day of his coming. People: *Your death, O Lord, we call to remembrance.*[33]
65 70	and he, our Lord and our God, [came and] in his life-giving gospel **taught us**[34] all the **purity and holiness**[35]	**C'**	Priest: We [adore][36] you, only begotten of the Father, first born of Being, spiritual lamb, who descended from on high to below to be a propitiatory sacrifice for all humankind to take away their sins voluntarily, and to pardon sinners through your blood and to sanctify the unclean through your sacrifice. Make us live, O Lord, through your true life, purify us through your spiritual expiation; and grant us that we may obtain **life**[37] by your life-giving death, and that we may stand before you in **purity**[38], and serve you in **holiness**[39] and **offer this oblation**[40] to your divinity, that the will of your majesty may be pleased by it, and your mercy flow out upon us all, Father…

31 ܦܓܪܐ ܗܢܐ ܩܕܝܫܐ

32 ܠܡܘܬܗ ܘܩܝܡܬܗ ܕܡܪܟܘܢ ܗܘܝܬܘܢ ܡܬܥܗܕܝܢ

33 ܠܡܘܬܟ ܡܪܢ ܡܬܥܗܕܝܢ

34 ܐܠܦ ܠܢ

35 ܕܟܝܘܬܐ ܘܩܕܝܫܘܬܐ

36 Spinks translates this as "We remember you", presumably picking up on the theme of the "commemoration of the body and blood". But the word used here, ܣܓܕܝܢ, is normally used to denote prostration, worship, or adoration, which is probably the more accurate translation.

37 ܚܝܐ

38 ܒܗܝܪܘܬܐ; a more obvious meaning for this word is "resplendence" or "excellency", though both appear to be admissible definitions.

39 ܩܕܝܫܘܬܐ

40 ܘܢܩܪܒ ܩܘܪܒܢܐ ܗܢܐ

76	Yes, we beg you, only-begotten of the Father, through whom peace has been proclaimed to us; Child of the Most High by whom the things above were reconciled with the things below, "the Good Shepherd, who laid himself down for his sheep and delivered them from ravening wolves", merciful Lord, who cried out on the cross and gathered us from the error of vanity:
85	El, God of spirits and of all flesh; may our prayers be lifted up to you and your mercy descend on our petitions, and may this oblation be acceptable before you; which we offer on your atoning altar in memory of your passion. May it please your divinity, and your will be fulfilled by it; and our debts pardoned by it, and our sins forgiven by it; and by it may our dead commemorated; and let us confess and worship and glorify you, and your Father who sent you for our salvation, and your living and Holy Spirit, now….
91	May the glorious Trinity be pleased by this incense and by this oblation and by this chalice; and may the souls be absolved by it and the spirits be sanctified by it for whom and on behalf of whom it was offered and sanctified. And upon me, feeble and sinful, who offered it, may the mercy of the glorious Trinity shine forth, Father…
97	Mother of our Lord Jesus Christ, pray for me to your only-begotten Son, who was born from you, that he will pardon my debts and sins from my lowly and sinful hands this oblation which my weakness offers upon this holy altar of Mar N…, through your intercession for us, Holy Mother.

102	of the prophets and apostles, of the martyrs and confessors, of the bishops and doctors, of the priests and deacons and of all the **children**[41] of the holy catholic Church, even those who have been signed with **the [living] sign of holy baptism**.[42]	B'	We offer before you, Lord, this oblation in **memory**[43] of all the upright and just **fathers**[44], prophets and apostles and martyrs and confessors; and of all our patriarchs, the Pope of the city of Rome and Metropolitan, bishops, chorepiscopoi, periodentai, priests, and deacons, and deaconesses, young men, celibates, virgins, and all the children of the holy Church who are marked with the mark of saving baptism and whom you have made to **participate in your holy body**.[45]
110			But especially and first of all we commemorate the holy and saintly and blessed Virgin Mary, the blessed Mother of God.

Deacon: Remember her, O Lord, God, and us through her pure prayers. |
| 114 | | | Priest: Remember, O Lord God, at this moment those far off, and those present, the dead and the living, the sick and the oppressed, the distressed and the afflicted, and those who are in various troubles.

Remember, O Lord God, at this moment our fathers and our brothers in spirit and flesh; and pardon their debts and their sins. |
| 121 | | | Remember, O Lord God, at this moment, those who offer oblations, vows, firstfruits and memorials. Grant to their petitions good things from your abundant treasure. |

41 ܕܚܬܡܝܢ ܒܪܘܫܡܐ ܚܝܐ ܕܡܥܡܘܕܝܬܐ

42 ܘܟܠܗܘܢ ܒܢܝܗ̈ ܕܥܕܬܐ ܩܕܝܫܬܐ. Ray's article includes the word "living" (ܚܝܐ) in this phrase, but Gelston's Syriac text and translation of AM does not. Spinks also omits it. Macomber's edition of the Mar Esha'ya text includes it, but adds a disclaimer that the word is added in the margins by a second hand and is not part of the original text (cf. Macomber, "The Oldest Text," 367). Its absence in Sharar would seem to indicate that its inclusion is a later development.

43 ܥܘܗܕܢܐ

44 ܐܒܗܬܐ

45 ܕܢܫܬܘܬܦܘܢ ܒܦܓܪܟ ܩܕܝܫܐ

The Making of the Maronite Sharar   119

131		Remember, O Lord God, at this moment, those who partake in commemorating your holy mother and your saints. Grant them recompense with a good reward. And for all who participated in this Eucharist which was offered upon this holy altar. Grant them, O Lord God, a good reward in your kingdom. And for all who have said to us, "remember us in your prayers because of our Lord", remember them, O God, and pardon their faults.
138		Remember O Lord God, at this moment, my miserableness, sinfulness, my importunity and my lowliness, I, who wittingly or unwittingly, freely or involuntarily, have sinned and committed evil before you. O Lord God, in your grace and mercy pardon and forgive me whatever I have sinned against you; and, O Lord, may this Eucharist be as a memorial of our dead and for the pardon of our souls. Remember, O Lord God, at this time, your weak and sinful servant George, who wrote (this). And pardon and forgive his debts and his sins, and pardon his fathers. Amen.
141	//And// we also, my Lord, thy weak, frail and miserable servants, who are assembled [in thy name] and stand before thee at this moment, having received by tradition the example from thee, rejoicing and glorifying and exalting and commemorating and celebrating [unto thee] this great and awful [and holy and life-giving and divine] mystery, of the passion and death and resurrection of our Lord and Savior Jesus Christ.	Ana
148	And may thy Holy Spirit, O my Lord, come and rest upon this oblation of the servants, and may he bless it and hallow it and may it be to us, O my Lord, for the pardon of debts and for the forgiveness of sins and for the great hope of resurrection from the dead and new life in the kingdom of heaven, with all those who have been well-pleasing to thee.	Epi	Hear me, O Lord. Hear me, O Lord. Hear me, O Lord. And may he come, O Lord, your living and holy Spirit, and dwell and rest upon this oblation of your servants. And may it be to those who partake for the pardon of debts and the forgiveness of sins and for a blessed resurrection from the dead, and a new life in the kingdom of heaven for ever.

120 *Further Issues in Eucharistic Praying in East and West*

| 154 | For all this great and wonderful dispensation towards us, **we give thee thanks**[46] and glorify thee without ceasing, [with]//in// thy Church redeemed by the precious blood of thy Christ, with unclosed mouths and unveiled faces. [**Lifting up glory and honor and confession and adoration**[47], to thy living and holy and life-giving name, now always and for ever and ever.] Amen. | A' | And for your glorious economy towards us **we give you thanks**[48], we your sinful servants, redeemed by your innocent blood, with open mouth which gives thanks in your holy church before your propitiatory altar, now.... |

46 ܣܘ̈ܕܝܢܢ
47 ܡܪܝܡܝܢܢ ܫܘܒܚܐ ܘܐܝܩܪܐ ܘܬܘܕܝܬܐ ܘܣܓܕܬܐ
48 ܡܘܕܝܢܢ

First, a few general observations are worth mentioning. Jammo, as I noted in the introduction, remarks that the only piece in AM not found in *Sharar* is the so-called anamnesis section in lines 141–147; but close examination indicates that *Sharar* also has no equivalent to lines 41–45 in AM, which falls directly at AM's chiastic center (X). Up until X, *Sharar* clearly mirrors AM very closely; but at line 38, *Sharar* quotes John 6:51 to introduce the institution narrative which immediately follows. This is the major point of departure between the two anaphoras, and they do not directly parallel each other again until the epiclesis in line 148, with two small exceptions in lines 65–66 and 102–105. But despite *Sharar*'s extensive interpolated prayers, the parallels in these two short sections are preserved in the order that they appear in AM; this is in contrast to the other East Syrian anaphoras of Nestorius and Theodore, which incorporate material from AM in small, decontextualized pieces. And lastly, all of the additional material in *Sharar* is localized in two groups: three prayers requesting the acceptance of the offering between C' and B', and a set of commemorations between B' and the epiclesis. This thematic and positional clustering appears to suggest that these were written into the anaphora with an eye toward the chiastic structure therein, rather than as a random accrual of liturgical units. Despite these additions, however, it is clear that *Sharar* retains all the pieces of the overarching chiasmus in AM identified by Ray, with the exception of "taught us," which does not appear at C' in *Sharar*. The difficulty, then, lies in ascertaining whether this is merely incidental, or if it is an intentional effort on the part of the composer of *Sharar* to retain this existing structure. There are several indications that the retention of the chiasmus in AM is deliberate, and these can be demonstrated by examining the chiasmus of *Sharar* on its own terms.

Chiasmus in **Sharar**

The major parallel pairs in *Sharar* are as follows:

A   =   We give thanks to you

A' =   We give you thanks

B   =   Remembrance; fathers; commemoration of the body and blood

B' =   Memory; fathers; participation in your holy body

C   =   offer; living and holy altar; life

122 *Further Issues in Eucharistic Praying in East and West*

    C' = offer; purity and holiness; life

    X   = Memorial of the passion, death and resurrection of Christ

    Turning now to examine the chiasmus in finer detail, we must recognize that Sharar preserves A, B, and C from AM in nearly pristine form. There are, of course, minor discrepancies, but these do not affect the meaning or organization of the text substantially. The entire A block, centered on the phrase "we give thanks to you" (ܡܘܕܝܢ ܠܟ) at Ax in line 20, is lifted from AM nearly verbatim with all its minor pairs. Section B, likewise comprised mostly of common material, retains chiastic themes of "fathers" and "the commemoration of the body and blood" from AM, but adds stronger parallels to both in B' with "fathers" (ܐܒܗܬܐ) in line 103 and "participate in your holy body" (ܢܫܬܘܬܦ ܒܦܓܪܟ ܩܕܝܫܐ) in line 109, rather than "children" and "sign of holy baptism" as in AM. Sharar also adds "remembrance" (ܕܘܟܪܢܐ) as a major parallel in this section, finding a recapitulation in B' (line 102) where there is no equivalent in AM. Section C, centered on the idea of the "living and holy altar" (ܡܕܒܚܐ ܚܝܐ ܘܩܕܝܫܐ) is also made up of mostly common material, but deviates from AM in line 38 with the addition of "in your holy Gospel," which introduces a quotation of John 6:51, "I am the bread of life." Sharar also drops "taught us" (ܐܠܦܬ) as a major pair from AM, but adds "we offer you" (ܡܩܪܒܝܢ ܠܟ) in line 37 and "life" (ܚܝܐ) in line 39 as two additional major parallel themes. All of these themes in C are recapitulated in the four-part request in C': the celebrant prays that we may "obtain life" (ܚܝܐ), "stand before you in purity" (ܕܟܝܘܬܐ)," serve you in holiness" (ܩܕܝܫܘܬܐ), and "offer this oblation" (ܢܩܪܒ ܩܘܪܒܢܐ ܗܢܐ) in lines 71–73.

    Unlike sections A through C, however, section X in *Sharar* departs radically from the content of the chiastic structure in AM. Instead of a petition for peace and tranquility, *Sharar* has in its place the memorial of the passion. Moreover, this section is itself chiastically structured, weaving together the themes from B and C and culminating in the bipartite institution narrative. Consider the following parallels:

    Xa   = memorial of the passion

    Xa' = remembrance of the death and resurrection

    Xb   = pure and holy hands

Xb' = this holy body

Xx = the two-part narrative of the memorial of the passion

The design of this section is clearly intentional and well considered. The first sentence announces the intention to make a memorial of the passion as Christ taught us, referencing the theme in B. The second sentence begins the first part of the narrative and emphasizes Jesus' "pure and holy hands," referencing the theme in C. The bipartite institution narrative indicates the way in which one is to make the memorial of the passion and then speaks of its effects: the pardon of debts, the forgiveness of sins, and eternal life. Following the bipartite narrative, the themes are brought to their fulfillment: "this holy body" (line 59) which we are to eat is the body of the same Christ whose "pure and holy hands" (lines 43–44) took bread. And when we do the same, we "call to remembrance the death and resurrection of the Lord" (lines 61–62).

As an important aside, the response of the people at the end of *Sharar*'s X section is a point of great interest: it is the only time in the entirety of the anaphora that the people are called to respond, and their only response is to repeat the central theme at the heart of the anaphora. While that alone is suggestive, many of the earliest manuscripts of AM likewise instruct the people to repeat the petition for peace, which sits at X in AM. It appears unlikely that such a parallel between the two anaphoras is merely coincidental. Cognizant of the centrality of the position X in the organization of both anaphoras, it is certainly not implausible that the people would be called upon to join in emphasizing the central and highest point of the prayer. Macomber notes the uniqueness of this repetition in AM, remarking that "the *lectio simplicior* [i.e., the omission of this repetition] . . . is no doubt to be preferred, but the repeating of this last phrase, found in all the older MSS., must have originated at a relatively early date."[40] While we must remain agnostic about whether or not this was an original or even an early feature of the text, I am inclined to think that this repetition in both anaphoras indicates a recognition of the chiastic center that was lost at some point in many communities, thus resulting in the discrepancy in AM's manuscript tradition noted by Macomber.

We see, then, that in most cases, *Sharar* preserved the pairs in AM, with the exception of "taught us" in C. In cases where the chiastic pairings

---

40. Macomber, "Oldest Known Text," 365n10.

in AM were not obvious, such as "fathers/children" and "body and blood/baptism" in B/B', the author of *Sharar* created more direct parallels in B' to match the content in B directly. The author of *Sharar* also replaced the center at X with a chiastically-structured institution narrative, and then added several more thematically related parallel pairs to the surrounding structure that introduce and frame the new material at X. It appears quite clear that the author of *Sharar* understood the chiastic structure in AM and adapted it according to his own purposes.

In light of this, we can note that the relationship between AM and *Sharar* changes markedly at X. Before X, the similarity between the two anaphoras is very close, with minimal additions in *Sharar*, preserving all of the parallel elements in AM and the thought sequence in which they are arranged. After X, the similarity of the thought-sequence between the two anaphoras breaks down entirely. Although many of the same word parallels from AM are reproduced *Sharar* after X, they are arranged in an entirely different sequence of thoughts and a new theological valence. In AM, the thought sequence continues in light of the petition articulated at X, asking in C' that all inhabitants of the earth know that the Lord "taught us the purity and holiness" (lines 65–66) in emulation of those who were pleasing to God, and extending that in B' to those "children" (line 104) who had been marked with the "sign of holy baptism" (line 105). By contrast, *Sharar*'s thought sequence continues in light of the central theme in X of the memorial of the Lord's passion. The C' themes of "purity and holiness" in line 73 relate to the injunction to "offer this oblation" (line 73), a new chiastic element in *Sharar*, and they come at the end of a longer prayer that picks up on the idea of the fruits of communion from Xx. The B' section follows, and it is framed in light of the new theme of "remembrance" in B that was added in *Sharar*. The oblation is made "in memory" (line 102) of those who were pleasing to God: the fathers, clergy, ascetics, and children of the church who bear the "mark of saving baptism" and who "participate in your holy body" (lines 108–109). The A' section functions as a thanksgiving rather than a concluding doxology as in AM, dropping the lines "lifting up glory and honor and confession and adoration" (lines 157–58) and a reference to the "name" of God (line 159) that are retained in AM.

Sharar also has interpolated material that does not fit into the chiastic structure, which warrants mention. The chiastic center X is immediately followed by C', which is in turn followed by a cluster of three prayers with no chiastic content or parallel in AM, asking that the oblation be acceptable to God. These three prayers, which separate C' from B' are closely related to the theme of the C' section and look to it for their justification. It is likely that these were added at some point after *Sharar* was composed, because the thought sequence begun in C' would otherwise flow very naturally into that of B' were it not interrupted by the intervening non-chiastic material. By contrast, the long list of commemorations between B' and the epiclesis is likely a feature of the original composition of *Sharar*, picking up on the main themes of B', but incorporating material from AM's anamnesis and epiclesis, and reusing some of the themes found throughout the chiasm. These commemorations culminate in the epiclesis, which mirrors that of AM very closely, and likewise does not contain any constitutive parts of the chiastic structure. This epiclesis is of the East Syrian "non-consecratory" type, which asks that the oblation be for the "pardon of debts and the forgiveness of sins and for a blessed resurrection from the dead, and a new life in the kingdom of heaven" (lines 150–53), making a distinct parallel with the fruits of communion in Xx.

We can see clearly that the elements of AM's chiastic structure are all preserved in *Sharar*, and that X is the point of linguistic and theological departure between the two anaphoras. In light of the different chiastic center at X in *Sharar*, the meaning of the themes held in common with AM differ radically in light of this different emphasis, which is framed by the addition of the themes in B and C. Moreover, all of the additional material in *Sharar* is directly related to the thematic elements in *Sharar*'s B' and C', each set of prayers following the relevant chiastic theme. Had the composer not intended to preserve the chiastic structure that was originally present in AM, the theological departure of *Sharar* from AM after X would have provided more than enough reason to excise or simply forget about that material.

Disputed Material: The Anamnesis and Institution Narrative

While it appears likely that the composer of *Sharar* understood and reworked the overarching chiasmus in AM, there is still material in AM left outside the chiasmus, as well as material in AM with no parallel in *Sharar*. The centerpiece of most of the questions surrounding AM, however, is the so-called anamnesis in AM (lines 141–47), which will be the basis of the following discussion. We have noted above that the lack of a verb has made this section and its relation to the surrounding material difficult to ascertain. In an earlier section, we examined Ray's reconstruction of the A' chiastic block following Magne, which relied on the idea that the epiclesis was interpolated at a later date, severing what is now called the anamnesis from the rest of the A' section and leaving it without a verb. The question must then be asked: how was this section understood by the composer of *Sharar*?

First, it is clear that the composer of *Sharar* did not see the anamnesis in AM as attached to the concluding doxology. He rather saw it as an orphan piece that contained material first for the intercessory commemorations, and second for the commemoration of the Lord's passion, death, and resurrection. With regard to the former, the composer of *Sharar* adds a lengthy list of commemorations after the B' section that builds upon the AM themes of "weak, frail and miserable servants" (line 141) and "at this moment" (lines 142–43), a phrase which occurs in all of *Sharar*'s commemorations. All of the commemorations, however, are on behalf of those who "stand before thee" (line 142), in the words of AM, and do what was exemplified by Christ and "received by tradition" (line 143).

But in light of *Sharar*'s verbose elaboration on the first part of AM's anamnesis, it is notable that the theme in the second part—"the mystery of the passion and death and resurrection of our Lord and Savior Jesus Christ" (lines 146–47)—does not feature at all in the commemorations or the subsequent material. This is also the line on account of which Botte and Bouyer thought the section uniquely hospitable to an institution narrative.[41] Spinks considers it to be a "primitive Syrian 'institution-anamnesis,' dating from a time when a reference to the institution or the Lord's example was regarded as quite adequate."[42] The only way to reasonably account for its disappearance is to conclude that the second part of the anamnesis was reworked into an institution narrative and placed elsewhere. Indeed, both Spinks and Jammo come to this conclusion. The epiclesis, which is nearly the same in both anaphoras, also plays a role in informing the construction of *Sharar*'s institution narrative with

---

41. See B. Botte, "L'Anaphore Chaldéenne des Apôtres," *Orientalia Christiana Periodica* 15 (1949): 270; and L. Bouyer, *Eucharist: Theology and Spirituality of the Eucharistic Prayer* (Notre Dame: Notre Dame University Press, 1968), 150–51.

42. Spinks, "Quest for the 'Original Form,'" 34.

its description of the fruits of communion: the pardon of debts, the forgiveness of sins, hope in the resurrection, and new life in heaven. The author of *Sharar* picks up on the theme and establishes it as a governing paradigm in the institution narrative, repeating it in the commemorations and capitalizing on its presence in the epiclesis.

Some have noted that the position of the institution narrative in the anaphora is strange. Spinks, for example, remarks that "the position of the narrative also suggests that it is a later addition" for "the writer knows of no other institution narrative that follows a commemoration of the dead."[43] The above analysis allows us to account for this strangeness simply by noting that the author of *Sharar* placed it at the center of the chiasmus, and its theological content inflects and permeates the rest of the anaphora. That it is itself chiastically structured and framed by additional chiastic themes only corroborates this explanation.

One further issue remains, which is the question of what happened to AM's chiastic center (lines 41–45)—petitioning for peace and security and asking that all the earth know God—in *Sharar*. Gelston considers it an intercession for the living, as do Engberding and Botte, suggesting that it might have been a "loose amalgam of short passages which were in the process of becoming traditional."[44] It would cause no problem if this were the case, as it could easily have been incorporated into one of *Sharar*'s intercessions, but it is at the center of AM's chiasmus and plays a central role in the framing of the anaphora. Cognizant of this, it is notable that this is the only piece of AM that entirely disappears in *Sharar*. I propose that its erasure and replacement by an institution narrative in *Sharar* is the final indication of the intentionality with which the author of *Sharar* composed the new anaphora. Were this simply incidental, the new institution narrative would have been inserted alongside the existing material from AM, as was the case with all of *Sharar*'s other insertions. That the material at the chiastic center was replaced, however, indicates the degree to which the author recognized the importance of this position in the structure of the anaphora.

---

43. Ibid., 33.
44. Gelston, *Addai and Mari*, 99; cf. Engberding, "Zum anaphorischen," 100–13, and B. Botte, "Problèmes de l'anaphore syrienne des Apôtres Addai et Mari," *L'Orient Syrien* 10 (1965): 89–106, here at 97f.

Conclusion: The Making of the Maronite *Sharar*

What, then, can we say about the relationship between *Sharar* and AM? It appears that the author of *Sharar* was intimately familiar with AM, able to identify and modify its elements with great facility. Nevertheless, the original tripartite structure of AM went unrecognized: the epiclesis had severed the original A' block, creating what became the anamnesis. Unlike in the anaphora of Nestorius, the author of *Sharar* did not recognize the connection between the anamnesis and the following material, as the anamnesis was repurposed and made into a set of commemorations and an institution narrative. The author almost certainly did not know AM to have an institution narrative for this reason, and this is corroborated by the fact that the new institution narrative replaced AM's chiastic center at X and became the governing principle for the new anaphora. The commemorations likewise appear to be a reworking by the author of *Sharar*, incorporating existing material from AM in the same way.

Overall, it appears that the author of *Sharar* was concerned with bringing the anaphora of his community into line with the standard liturgical practices within the Roman Empire at the time of its composition, while at the same time retaining those organizational and rhetorical features that were characteristic of the East Syrian anaphora. Therefore, the author sat down with the text of AM as he knew it, and reworked it according to these principles. He added an institution narrative and a list of commemorations and emphasized the commemoration of the life, death, and resurrection of Christ, most of which had largely been missing from the AM tradition.

Accordingly, we can now propose a general chronology of development for *Sharar* from the earliest form of AM to the oldest extant complete text of *Sharar* in the mid-fifteenth century. This chronology can be shown in four general strata:

Stratum 1:

> AM is composed in a Syrian tripartite chiastic structure according to the general style described by Catholicos Isho'yahb I and in the Babylonian Talmud. Each of the three parts is also organized chiastically according to the style of *Birkat ha-Mazon* and *Didache* 10. This structure and the themes within it function mnemonically,

helping the presider to pray entirely from memory. The prayer has no *Sanctus*, epiclesis, or institution narrative. What is now called the anamnesis is still a part of the A' block.

Stratum 2:

The *Sanctus* and epiclesis enter the anaphora and are arranged in chiastic parallel to one another. Because the *Sanctus* is inserted immediately before Ax, the epiclesis is forced into the corresponding spot before A'x, severing what is now called the 'anamnesis' from the rest of the original A' block. Perhaps it is assumed that the chiasmus was so obvious that people would remember that the 'anamnesis' was associated with the following material. (The equivalent paragraph in the anaphora of Nestorius corroborates the idea that such a thing could have happened.) At some point, the association between the "anamnesis" and the rest of the A' block is lost, perhaps as the epiclesis begins to play a more central role in eucharistic praying. The "anamnesis" is understood to be connected to the intercessions. Although the original tripartite structure is forgotten, people still recognize the overarching chiastic structure of the anaphora and use it to remember the order and words of the prayer.

Stratum 3:

The author of *Sharar*, in an attempt to rewrite the anaphora in light of liturgical practice within the Roman Empire, sits down with the text of AM. He does not see the original tripartite prayer, but recognizes the overarching chiasmus A B C X C' B' A' and a strange anamnesis lacking a verb. In light of the developing eucharistic emphasis within the empire, the author of *Sharar* takes the second part of the anamnesis and the final theme of the epiclesis and writes an institution narrative using its contents. He also structures it in the form of a chiasmus, and positions it at the center of the main chiasmus of the anaphora, replacing the existing petition for peace and conversion at X. He retains from AM all the chiastic themes that had been known to him for years. Before the new institution narrative (A, B, and C), they retain their meaning and context, but he adds to them 'oblation,' 'commemoration,' and 'life' in order to frame the new narrative, which is central to the new anaphora. After the narrative, the author recapitulates all of the themes from before, but repurposes them in service of the new paradigm of the institution narrative. The remaining portion of the anamnesis is used to construct a West Syrian-type set of intercessions and commemorations.

Stratum 4:

Three prayers appear in *Sharar* between C' and B' after the institution narrative, requesting the acceptance of the oblation. The anaphora is situated in a standardized eucharistic liturgy and eventually comes into the usage of the Maronite Church. In AM, the original tripartite structure is forgotten, and the anaphora is reorganized according to *gehanatha, kushape,* and *qanone,* which are delineated according to lines other than the chiastic ones.

This essay has attempted to show the manner and extent to which chiasmus was the guiding rhetorical and organizational principle of AM and *Sharar*. While the findings of this essay do not definitively solve all of the textual problems of AM or *Sharar*, they offer answers to several of the long-disputed questions on the original form of the anaphora and its relation to the Jewish table prayers, as well as redactional questions surrounding the anamnesis and institution narrative. Most importantly, however, these findings offer new avenues for investigation in the Syrian anaphoral traditions. We now know that there are two East Syrian-type anaphoras with recognizable chiastic structures. Further study is needed in order to identify whether this is a unique characteristic of East Syrian anaphoral prayers, a characteristic of Syrian praying in general, or whether this was simply an understudied characteristic of early Christian liturgy throughout the Mediterranean basin. Knowledge about the incidence and usage of such forms throughout the Late Antique Mediterranean world could give much-needed insight into the processes surrounding the composition of early anaphoras, and is an important topic for future research.

The Egyptian Origins of the Anaphora in *Mystagogical Catechesis V* ascribed to Cyril of Jerusalem

Maxwell E. Johnson

Introduction

Because of numerous verbal parallels between *Mystagogical Catechesis* (hereafter MC) V, ascribed to Cyril of Jerusalem,[1] and the later Anaphora of Jerusalem known as James (hereafter, JAS), MC V is generally assumed to be the earliest primary Jerusalem source for the Anaphora of JAS, along with some version of the Anaphora of St. Basil (hereafter, BAS)—whether Egyptian Sahidic Basil (EgSBAS), as argued by John R. K. Fenwick[2] or, as more recently demonstrated by Gabriele Winkler,[3] the first *Armenian* version of Basil (ArmBAS1).

---

1. Saint Cyril of Jerusalem, *Lectures on the Christian Sacraments: Greek Original and English Translation*, trans. Maxwell E. Johnson, Popular Patristics Series 57 (Yonkers: St Vladimir's Seminary Press, 2017), 135.

2. *The Anaphoras of St Basil and St James: An Investigation into Their Common Origin*, OCA 240 (Rome: Pontificio Istituto Orientale, 1992).

3. Gabriele Winkler, *Die Jakobus-Liturgie in ihren Überlieferungssträngen. Edition des Cod. arm 17 von Lyon, Übersetzung und Liturgievergeich*, Anaphorae Orientales 4, Anaphorae Armeniacae 4 (Rome: Pontificio Istituto Orientale, 2013); idem, "Preliminary

Preface and Introduction to the *Sanctus*

MC V

After this we make memorial of heaven and earth and the sea, of the sun and the moon; of stars and all creation, both rational and irrational, visible and invisible, of Angels, Archangels, Dominions, Principalities, Powers, Thrones, the Cherubim with many faces, saying with authority as in David, "magnify the Lord with me" [Ps 34:3]. We make memorial also of the Seraphim, whom by the Holy Spirit Isaiah saw encircling the throne of God, with two wings covering the face, with two the feet, and with two flying, and saying:

"Holy, holy, holy Lord of Sabaoth" [cf. Isa 6:3].

JAS

You are hymned by [the heavens and the heavens of heavens and all their powers; the sun and moon and all the choir of stars; earth, sea . . . angels, archangels, thrones, dominions, principalities and powers, and awesome virtues. The cherubim with many eyes and seraphim with six wings, which cover their own faces with two wings, and their feet with two, and fly with two, cry one to the other with unwearying mouths and never-silent hymns of praise, (*aloud*) [*singing*] with clear voice the triumphal hymn of your magnificent glory, proclaiming, praising, crying, and saying:

Holy, holy, holy, Lord of Sabaoth;

Epiclesis

MC V

. . . we call upon God, the lover of humanity, to send the Holy Spirit upon the offerings lying before him, that he may make the bread the body of Christ, and the wine the

JAS

. . . send down, Master, your all-Holy Spirit himself upon us and upon these holy gifts set before you,] (*aloud*) that he may descend upon them, [and by his holy and

---

Observations about the Relationship Between the Liturgies of St. Basil and St. James," *OCP* 76 (2010): 5–55.

Bloodless worship and sacrifice

MC V

Next, after the spiritual sacrifice has been perfected, the bloodless worship, we call upon God through that sacrifice of propitiation . . .

JAS

we offer you, [Master,] this awesome and bloodless sacrifice
. . .

Intercessions

MC V, 8-10

Next, after the spiritual sacrifice has been perfected, the bloodless worship, we call upon God through that sacrifice of propitiation, for the common peace of the church, for the well-being of the world, for kings, for armies and allies, for those in sickness, for those in affliction, and, in general, for all who are in need of help, we all pray and offer this sacrifice.

JAS

We offer to you, [Master,] for your holy places also, which you glorified by the theophany of your Christ [and the descent of your all-Holy Spirit;] principally for [holy and glorious] Zion, the mother of all the churches and for your holy, [catholic, and apostolic] church throughout the world; even now, Master, grant it richly the gifts of your [all-]Holy Spirit.

Remember, Lord, our most pious [and Christ-loving] emperor, his pious [and Christ-loving] empress, [all his court and his army, for their help from heaven and their victory:] lay hold upon weapon and

---

[left column top:] blood of Christ. For, truly, whatever the Holy Spirit has touched is sanctified and changed.

[right column top:] good and glorious coming may sanctify them,] and make this bread the holy body of Christ, (*People:* Amen) and this cup the precious blood of Christ. (*People:* Amen.)

buckler, and stand up to help him; subject to him all the warlike and barbarous nations that delight in war, [moderate his counsels,] that we may lead a quiet and peaceful life in all piety and gravity.

[Remember, Lord, those in old age and infirmity,] those who are sick, ill, or troubled by unclean spirits, [for their speedy healing and salvation by you, their God. Remember, Lord, every Christian soul in trials and afflictions, in need of your mercy and help, O God, and recovery of the lost.]

Next, we make memorial and commemoration those who have fallen asleep before us, first patriarchs, prophets, apostles, (and) martyrs, so that by their prayers and intercessions God might receive our petition. Next, for the holy fathers and bishops, who have fallen asleep before us, and, in general, for all who have fallen asleep before us, believing great profit will come to the souls for whom the petition is made as this holy and awe-filled sacrifice is being presented.	Vouchsafe yet to remember, Lord, of those who have been well pleasing to you from the beginning, [from generation to generation:] the holy fathers, patriarchs, prophets, apostles, [martyrs, confessors, holy teachers, and every righteous spirit perfected in the faith of your Christ.]

In the same way we also, offering our petitions to God for those who have fallen asleep, although they are sinners . . . we offer Christ slaughtered for our sins, propitiating God the lover of humanity both for them and ourselves.

Together with these parallels, scholarship on MC V has tended to focus on issues related to authorship and date, whether Cyril of Jerusalem himself in the 380s to his immediate successor, John II, or even, in light of Juliette Day's work,[4] to a date almost a century later (ca. AD 415). But with regard to the specific relationship between MC V and JAS, the question of authorship is somewhat tangential and peripheral, while, as we shall see, issues of anaphoral structure, including provenance and date, may be more important.

It was the great Anglican Benedictine scholar, Dom Gregory Dix, who first drew attention to parallels with and differences between the anaphoral outline in MC V and the Anaphora of JAS.[5] In particular, basing his approach on the frequently occurring use of ei\ta, "next," indicating sequence in the Anaphora of MC V, Dix noted that in comparison with JAS the anaphora has the following pattern or structure:

MC V. 4-10	JAS
Dialogue	Dialogue
Praise for Creation	Praise for Creation
Sanctus	*Sanctus*
	Post-*Sanctus* (Economy of Salvation)
	Words of Institution
	Anamnesis
Epiclesis	Epiclesis
Intercessions	Intercessions

According to Dix, this structure leaves no room for a narrative of institution and anamnesis before the epiclesis in MC V He wrote: "I find it hard to assume that in this one case by 'next' Cyril meant 'after a great deal of the prayer has been said.' And if he did mean that, why associate the

---

4. Juliette Day, *The Baptismal Liturgy of Jerusalem: Fourth- and Fifth-Century Evidence from Palestine, Syria and Egypt,* Liturgy, Worship and Society (Aldershot and Burmingham: Ashgate, 2007).

5. Gregory Dix, *The Shape of the Liturgy* (London: Dacre Press, 1945), 196–207. This section is dependent, in part, upon the summary of scholarship in Fenwick, *Anaphoras of St Basil and St James*, 36–45.

invocation so closely with the *Sanctus*: 'Next, having sanctified ourselves with these spiritual hymns, we call upon God, etc. . . .'?"[6]

It was also Dix who, along with Georg Kretschmar's work on early Egyptian eucharistic prayers,[7] drew attention to the fact that the text of the introduction to the *Sanctus*, unlike that of JAS, but like Origen of Alexandria, the Anaphora of Sarapion of Thmuis, and the Coptic version of the Anaphora of Mark (CYRIL), refers to the seraphim covering the "*Face*," presumably of God rather than their *faces*, which may well be related to the further development of trinitarian orthodoxy reflected in anaphoral praying.

With regard to the question of whether the institution narrative was present or not in Cyril's anaphora, Emmanuel Cutrone's compelling 1978 study, "Cyril's Mystagogical Catecheses and the Evolution of the Jerusalem Anaphora," argued against its inclusion based on Cyril's own theological εἰκῶν—μιμήσις interpretation of the liturgical-sacramental identification of the believer with Christ as a key characteristic of Cyril's catechetical approach.

> Since the anaphora does not make direct and pointed references to Christ, and since the Mystagogue feels that he is unable to introduce any new elements into the ritual, he must do the next best thing. He offers his interpretation of the Eucharist before he discusses the liturgy. In Mystagogical Catechesis IV, Cyril, using the framework of his εἰκῶν—μιμήσις methodology, naturally turns to the Last Supper and the Words of Institution as an interpretation of the Eucharistic meal. Thus the whole of his lecture explains how neophytes are made one with Christ in Communion. By contrast the commentaries found in Mystagogical Catechesis V are terse and without a great deal of perspective.[8]

And, further, against the suggestion by Georg Kretschmar that the narrative may have been there but recited silently, Cutrone states:

---

6. Dix, *Shape*, 198.
7. Dix, *Shape*, 165; and idem, "Primitive Consecration Prayers," *Theology* 37 (1938): 261–83.
8. Emmanuel J. Cutrone, "Cyril's Mystagogical Catecheses and the Evolution of the Jerusalem Anaphora," *OCP* 44 (1978): 52–64.

Everywhere else Cyril is at great pains to explain each thing that happened. He discusses each phrase of the dialogue, he enumerates all of the intercessions, he analyzes each section of the Our Father, and he describes each gesture used at Communion. This concern for detail is so great that it is hard to imagine that Cyril would not have mentioned a silent part of the anaphora. Since he does not mention either Silence or the Words of Institution it seems safe to conclude they were not there.[9]

If Cutrone built upon the work of Dix regarding the question of the institution narrative in Cyril's anaphora, it might surely be said that Geoffrey Cuming built upon Dix's initial insight regarding parallels in the introduction to the *Sanctus* in MC V with Egyptian or Alexandrian anaphoral sources. In his own work, however, Cuming went considerably beyond Dix in arguing that the core of the entire MC V anaphora was Egyptian. In his 1974 essay, "Egyptian Elements in the Jerusalem Liturgy," he confined himself to structural and linguistic parallels (e.g., the use of the singular "face" in the introduction to the *Sanctus*, what he considered to be the absence of *benedictus qui venit* from the *Sanctus*,[10] the position of the epiclesis immediately after the *Sanctus*, and the location of the intercessions at the end of the anaphora).[11] But in this same essay Cuming also argued that MC V would have contained a narrative of institution following the epiclesis. This he believed was demonstrated by the phrase Εἶτα μετὰ τὸ ἀπαρτισθῆναι τὴν πνευματικὴν θυίαν ("Next, after the spiritual sacrifice has been perfected,") since the Greek verb ἀπαρτισθῆναι (to perfect or complete) is used to refer to the narrative of institution by John Chrysostom. Bryan Spinks rightly challenged Cuming on his use of Chrysostom to interpret Cyril, especially since Theodore of Mopsuestia claims that it is the epiclesis itself which perfects the

---

9. Ibid.
10. On the possible later addition of the *Benedictus* to the *Sanctus* in Jerusalem, see Juliette Day, "The Origins of the Anaphoral *Benedictus*," *Journal of Theological Studies* 60, no. 1 (2009): 193–211. See also the critique of Day in John Paul Abdelsayed, "Liturgical Exodus in Reverse: A Reevaluation of the Egyptian Elements in the Jerusalem Liturgy," in *Issues in Eucharistic Praying in East and West: Essays in Liturgical and Theological Analysis*, ed. Maxwell E. Johnson (Collegeville, MN: Liturgical Press, 2010), 141–45.
11. See Geoffrey Cuming, "Egyptian Elements in the Jerusalem Liturgy," *Journal of Theology Studies* 25 *(1974):* 117–24.

sacrifice, which is exactly what Cyril seems to be saying.[12] In a later essay[13] and in his study of the Anaphora of St. Mark (MARK),[14] Cuming backed away from assuming the institution narrative was present in Cyril's anaphora and argued rather that the Egyptian connection in MC V was demonstrated by the tripartite structure of something like the *Strasbourg Papyrus* lying behind it, whether that prayer itself ever constituted a full anaphora or not. According to Cuming:

> If Sanctus and epiclesis are added to the Strasbourg anaphora, not at the end as in *St Mark*, but between the thanksgiving and the offering, the result is: thanksgiving—Sanctus—epiclesis—offering—intercessions; in fact, the exact sequence set out by Cyril. When the Jerusalem anaphora was merged with *St Basil* to produce *St James*, the first step would be the addition of institution narrative and anamnesis; then a christological section would take the place of the epiclesis, which would be moved to its Basilian position between the offering and the intercessions; the exact sequence of *St James*.[15]

While Cuming may have been correct in this approach, he did assume that the references in MC V to "bloodless worship" and the "sacrifice of propitiation" are indicative of a separate and distinct anaphoral element of oblation in the overall structure of the prayer. Although this is clear in JAS and other ancient anaphoras, it is not necessarily the case in MC V.

Other scholars have not been so quick to abandon the position that the anaphora reflected in MC V already contained the narrative of institution. Allan Bouley, for example, saw no compelling reason to assume that the narrative was absent from the eucharistic liturgy in fourth-century Jerusalem.[16] Edward Yarnold, in arguing for Cyrilline authorship of the

---

12. Bryan Spinks, "The Jerusalem Liturgy of the *Catecheses Mystagogicae*: Syrian or Egyptian?," *Studia Patristica* 18, no. 2 (1989): 391–96.

13. Geoffrey Cuming, "The Shape of the Anaphora," *Studia Patristica* 20 (1989).

14. Geoffrey Cuming, *The Liturgy of St. Mark: Edited from the Manuscripts with a Commentary*, Orientalia Christiana Analecta 234 (Rome: Pontificio Istituto Orientale, 1990).

15. Cuming, "Shape of the Anaphora," 341.

16. Allan Bouley, *From Freedom to Formula: The Evolution of the Eucharistic Prayer from Oral Improvisation to Written Texts* (Washington, DC: Catholic University of America Press, 1981), 233.

Mystagogical Catecheses as a whole and a date in the 370s or 380s, assumed the presence of the narrative in a late-fourth-century source such as this and thought it unthinkable that it would not be present.[17] And Yarnold's doctoral student Alexis Doval, in an important study on Cyrilline authorship of the *Mystagogical Catecheses*, has, as one of his primary concerns, establishing that the institution narrative was already part, or becoming part, of the Jerusalem anaphora in MC V. Nevertheless, Doval notes that the overall "simplicity of the anaphora" would tend to place it earlier rather than later. A later date, such as the end of the fourth or beginning of the fifth century, would have necessitated a more developed anaphoral structure, more akin to JAS, than to the simpler form appearing in MC V.[18]

It is precisely a later date that Juliette Day advocated in her 2007 study, *The Baptismal Liturgy of Jerusalem: Fourth- and Fifth-Century Evidence from Palestine, Syria and Egypt*.[19] While not dealing with the anaphora in MC V in any detailed manner, Day argues that the baptismal liturgy reflected in MC I–III can be no earlier than well *after* 397 (perhaps not yet even in Jerusalem until the end of the *fifth* century!), the year when Porphyrius, former senior presbyter at the Holy Sepulchre who, according to Day, did not know the baptismal rite of the *Mystagogical Catecheses*, left to become bishop of Gaza.[20] But, as I have noted elsewhere,[21] her conclusions about authorship and date with regard to the baptismal liturgy would either be strengthened or weakened by a similar analysis of the eucharistic liturgy and anaphora in MC V. Unless we are to assume that MC IV and

---

17. See Edward Yarnold, "Anaphoras Without Institution Narratives?," *Studia Patristica* 30 (1997): 395–410.

18. Alexis Doval, *Cyril of Jerusalem, Mystagogue: The Authorship of the Mystagogic Catecheses*, Patristic Monograph Series 17 (Washington, DC: Catholic University of America Press, 2001), 150–61.

19. *The Baptismal Liturgy of Jerusalem: Fourth- and Fifth-Century Evidence from Palestine, Syria and Egypt*, Liturgy, Worship and Society (Aldershot and Burmingham: Ashgate, 2007).

20. Day, *Baptismal Liturgy of Jerusalem*, 134.

21. Maxwell E. Johnson, "Baptismal Liturgy in Fourth-Century Jerusalem in Light of Recent Scholarship," in *Inquiries into Eastern Christian Worship: Selected Papers of the Second International Congress of the Society of Oriental Liturgy, Rome, 17–21 September 2008*, ed. Basilius J. Groen, Steven Hawkes Teeples, and Stefanos Alexopoulos, Eastern Christian Studies, vol. 12 (Leuven: Peeters, 2012), 81–98.

V belong to a different stratum of the document than I–III, then it would seem that the dating of the eucharistic liturgy would be of great importance in resolving the question. Does the eucharistic liturgy reflect a mid- to late fourth-century or a later fourth- and early fifth-century liturgical context? If later, then why does MC V not refer to an anaphoral text closer to that of JAS? If the eucharistic liturgy reflects the earlier context, which most scholars would assert, then why does the baptismal liturgy not reflect a similar overall context with the distinctions from the *Baptismal Catecheses* explained as being due simply to developments in the Jerusalem Rite in the time of Cyril, as at least Yarnold and Doval would assert?

At issue with regard to dating the anaphora in MC V, and, hence, the *Mystagogical Catecheses* as a whole, is this question of the institution narrative. And, here, with the exception of Yarnold, Baldovin, and Doval, most contemporary scholars would argue that there was no such narrative in the anaphora described in this text. Together with the recent conclusions of Gabriele Winkler on the "missing" or interpolated institution narrative in Ethiopic anaphoras,[22] most scholars today would tend to put *Didache* 9 and 10, the *Strasbourg Papyrus*, and the Anaphora of Addai and Mari together with the anaphora in MC V as witnesses to an anaphoral pattern that did not yet contain this narrative.[23] The one exception here has often been the anaphora in the so-called *Apostolic Tradition* 4. However, in our commentary on this document, we suggested that the institution narrative in the Latin and more recent Ethiopic versions was quite likely a fourth-century innovation made at the time when the institution narrative was beginning to be added to anaphoral texts, as witnessed to in the *Barcelona Papyrus* and the Anaphora of Sarapion of Thmuis.[24]

---

22. See Gabriele Winkler, "A New Witness to the Missing Institution Narrative," in *Studia Liturgica Diversa: Essays in Honor of Paul F. Bradshaw*, ed. Maxwell E. Johnson and L. Edward Phillips (Portland: Pastoral Press, 2004), 117–28.

23. Cf. Emmanuel J. Cutrone, "Cyril's Mystagogical Catecheses and the Evolution of the Jerusalem Anaphora," *OCP* 44 (1978): 52–64; Fenwick, *Anaphoras of St Basil and St James*, 36–45; and Kent Burreson, "The Anaphora of the Mystagogical Catecheses of Cyril of Jerusalem," in *Essays on Early Eastern Eucharistic Prayers*, ed. Paul F. Bradshaw (Collegeville, MN: Liturgical Press, 1997), 131–51.

24. See *The Apostolic Tradition*, Bradshaw, Johnson, and Phillips, 45–46. On Sarapion of Thmuis, see Maxwell E. Johnson, *The Prayers of Sarapion of Thmuis: A Literary, Liturgical, and Theological Analysis*, Orientalia Christiana Analecta 249 (Rome: Pontificio Istituto Orientale, 1995); and on Barcelona, see Paul F. Bradshaw, "The Barcelona Papyrus and the Development of Early Eucharistic Prayers," in *Issues in Eucharistic*

Neither the presence nor the absence of the institution narrative may be taken as absolute proof of the dating of the *Mystagogical Catecheses* in general. But it would seem that holding to a date *after* 397 would make the absence of such a narrative downright unthinkable, especially when the relatively complete JAS is itself dated to the end of the fourth century or beginning of the fifth century.[25] Even if Cyril himself is not the "author" of the *Mystagogical Catecheses*, it would seem that either with an institution narrative or not in the text, MC V would be inadequate as an exposition of a Jerusalem anaphoral shape *later* than the late fourth century—that is, quite possibly the later years of Cyril's episcopate.

While writing before the contributions of Doval, Day, and Winkler, it is important to take into account the work of John R. K. Fenwick with regard to MC V as a source for JAS. Like his *Doktoralvater*, Geoffrey Cuming, Fenwick is firmly convinced of the Egyptian connection of MC V, but follows both Dix and Cutrone on the absence of the institution narrative in the eucharistic liturgy:

> The best interpretation of the text of MC V *is simply that the anaphora being described contained no Institution Narrative nor any of the other 'Antiochene' material not referred to.* This conclusion is coming to be more widely accepted. As Stevenson has put it, '. . . it is no longer universally assumed that the Jerusalem liturgy at the time of Cyril was of the Antiochene type . . .'[26]

For another source of the Jerusalem anaphora, Fenwick directs our attention back to a famous 1963 essay of Massey H. Shepherd, "Eusebius and the Liturgy of St James,"[27] wherein Shepherd analyzed the concluding

---

Praying in East and West, ed. Johnson, 129–38; Michael Zheltov, "The Anaphora and the Thanksgiving Prayer from the Barcelona Papyrus: An Underestimated Testimony to the Anaphoral History in the Fourth Century," *Vigiliae Christiane* 62 (2008): 467–504; Nathan Chase, "The Antiochenization of the Egyptian Tradition: An Alternate Approach to the Barcelona Papyrus and Anaphoral Development," *Ecclesia Orans* 34 (2017): 319–67; And the essay by Arsany Paul, "The Εἷς Θεός Acclamations in the Barcelona Papyrus: A Eucharistic Liturgy without the Opening Line of the Christian Anaphoral Dialogue," above, 62–83.

25. See Burreson, "Anaphora of the Mystagogical Catecheses," 166–67.
26. Fenwick, *Anaphoras of St Basil and St James*, 38; emphasis in original.
27. Massey H. Shepherd, "Eusebius and the Liturgy of St James," *Yearbook of Liturgical Studies* 4 (1963): 109–25.

paragraphs of a sermon preached by Eusebius of Caesarea at Bishop Paulinus's cathedral at Tyre between 314 and 319. In those concluding paragraphs Shepherd noted liturgical parallels with both MC V and JAS, some elements of which are found in one and not in the other.[28] Nevertheless, because of verbal parallels in the pre-*Sanctus* and the reference to the unbloody sacrifice in what Shepherd calls the post-*Sanctus*, Fenwick notes that there appears "to be a reasonable probability that Eusebius is here an independent witness to the anaphora used in the area under the jurisdiction of Caesarea in Palestine, and therefore of Jerusalem."[29] As noted, the closest parallels between Eusebius and MC V appear in the pre-*Sanctus* and post-*Sanctus*, as reconstructed by Shepherd:

a) *Preface,* recounting the praise of God from His creation, visible and invisible: heaven and all their powers, the world beneath the sun, the earth, the heavenly Jerusalem, and choirs of angels, who offer their adoration through the seraphim in the *Sanctus*.

b) *Post-Sanctus*, reciting the blessings with which God has made us worthy, with an oblation of the unbloody sacrifice, and prayer for the remission of sins and participation in the life of the world to come.[30]

While it is impossible to know with any degree of certainty whether the so-called Anaphora of Eusebius contained an epiclesis, the institution narrative, or intercessions—which, like much of English anaphoral scholarship has held, entered the anaphora directly from the prayer of the faithful (a view that Taft strongly challenged)[31]—Fenwick assumed that

---

28. See ibid., 120, and Fenwick, *Anaphoras of St Basil and St James*, 39–42.
29. Fenwick, 40.
30. Shepherd, "Eusebius and the Liturgy of St James," 120, as quoted by Fenwick, 41.
31. Robert Taft states: "Were it not for *Ap.Trad.* 4 . . . no one would doubt that intercessions were part of the eastern anaphora from the start. . . . Intercessions are found in the Jewish prayer forms that constitute the putative parentage of the eucharistic anaphora, as well as in all other early anaphoral antecedents and sources: *Didache* 10:5; the *Euchology of Sarapion*, Cyril of Jerusalem, *Cat.* 5,8–9, Theodore of Mopsuestia, *Hom.* 16,14, *ApConst* VIII, 12:40–49, *TestDom* I, 23, the papyri *Strasbourg Gr.* 254 and *John Rylands* 465, the *Der-Balizeh Papyrus* . . . EgBAS, Addai and Mari, etc. So *ApTrad* 4 is far from normative, and liturgiologists are coming to realize how precarious is any hypothesis that takes

the reference to a post-*Sanctus* "oblation of the unbloody sacrifice" was a reference to a distinct anaphoral unit. Thus, Fenwick suggested further that the Jerusalem anaphora in MC V was derived in part from that cited by Eusebius with the addition of the epiclesis, following immediately the Eusebian "oblation with prayer for forgiveness," and the concluding intercessions transferred from the prayer of the faithful. According to Fenwick, then, "the original shape of the Jerusalem anaphora which was later conflated with 'Antiochene' material to produce JAS was:

Preface
Pre-Sanctus
Sanctus
Oblation with prayer for forgiveness
Epiclesis
Intercessions"[32]

With the addition of a Christologically oriented post-*Sanctus*, a narrative of institution, and an anamnesis connected to the oblation, all before the epiclesis, we are well on our way to JAS (or, for that matter, toward any anaphora of the Antiochene type).

The important thing to note here, of course, is that this anaphoral pattern is *not* what we have in MC V, which corresponds more closely to those Egyptian anaphoral structures that appear in texts like the Prayers of Sarapion of Thmuis, or both Greek and Coptic versions of MARK, as well as in other Egyptian eucharistic prayers. Indeed, the Egyptian connection must be analyzed more thoroughly here.

While, as we have seen, Juliette Day argued for a date later than the mid- or late fourth century for MC V, and did not deal with the anaphora, it also needs to be noted that she drew special attention to liturgical documents of Egyptian provenance that parallel MC V. She wrote:

> The author of *MC* was possibly influenced by a rite, which was more like that of *CH* [Canons of Hippolytus] and *Ser.* [Sarapion], than that of

---

this problematic, reconstructed text as its point of departure." Robert Taft, *The Diptychs*, Orientalia Christiana Analecta 238 (Rome: Pontificio Istituto Orientale, 1991), 25–26. The Barcelona Papyrus may be included here as well as an anaphora without intercessions.

32. Fenwick, *Anaphoras of St Basil and St James*, 42.

... Chrysostom, which is not to say that Jerusalem found a model for its rite in Egypt, but that *MC* may well have been subject to an influence from a source sharing similarities with *CH*.[33]

Day vindicated Cuming's "Egyptian connection" for the initiation rites in MC, building on a significant essay by John Paul (now Bishop Kyrillos) Abdelsayed,[34] Developing on Day, Anna Adams Petrin has recently done so for the Jerusalem anaphora in her 2018 Notre Dame doctoral dissertation, *The Egyptian Connection: Egyptian Elements in the Liturgy of Jerusalem*.[35] Petrin demonstrates the clear parallels that exist between the anaphoral elements of MC V with the *Strasbourg Papyrus*, the *Deir Balizeh Papyrus*, the *Barcelona Papyrus*,[36] and the Anaphora of St. Thomas, recently studied by Mary Farag.[37] In response to Spinks's argument against the Egyptian provenance of the post-*Sanctus* epiclesis, because Cyril does not clearly refer to the classic "*Plenum/pleni*" petition for the Spirit to fill the gifts, Petrin notes, following Abdelsayed, that this direct link to the *Sanctus* is also missing in the *Barcelona Papyrus*, to which could be added the somewhat later versions of *Barcelona* known as the *Louvain Coptic Parchment*, and the *Vienna Greek Papyrus*, although it must be noted that the "full" part of that link does appear. And, even without the "*Plenum/pleni*" link, there is no question but that the contents of the epiclesis in MC V are parallel in *Barcelona*, *Louvain*, and *Deir Balyzeh*, including the request that the Spirit "make" the bread and wine the Body and Blood of Christ.

Closely related to this is the question of offering the eucharistic sacrifice and the epiclesis. As noted above, both Cuming, because of the *Strasbourg Papyrus*, and Fenwick, because of Eusebius, in their presentations of the anaphoral pattern in MC V, suggest that some kind of

---

33. Day, *Baptismal Liturgy of Jerusalem*, 137–38.

34. Abdelsayed, "Liturgical Exodus in Reverse," see above, n. 21.

35. Anna Adams Petrin, *The Egyptian Connection: Egyptian Elements in the Liturgy of Jerusalem*, PhD diss. (Notre Dame: University of Notre Dame, 2018), 54–70, 182–204.

36. On the Barcelona Papyrus, see Nathan Chase, "Rethinking Anaphoral Development in Light of the Barcelona Papyrus," PhD diss. (Notre Dame: University of Notre Dame, 2020).

37. Mary Farag, "The Anaphora of St. Thomas the Apostle: Translation and Commentary," *Muséon* 123 (2010): 317–61.

"offering' or "oblation of the bloodless sacrifice" was also a constituent and independent element in the text. But there is no reason to assume this whatsoever. Again, the text in MC V is clear:

> Next, having sanctified ourselves with these spiritual hymns, we call upon God, the lover of humanity, to send the Holy Spirit upon the offerings lying before him, that he may make the bread the body of Christ, and the wine the blood of Christ. For, truly, whatever the Holy Spirit has touched is sanctified and changed. Next, after the spiritual sacrifice has been perfected, the bloodless worship, we call upon God through that sacrifice of propitiation.

The epiclesis is precisely that which perfects, changes, and sanctifies the "bloodless worship" which leads into the intercessions. That is, the epiclesis and the offering appear to be one unit, not separate units. This is also the case with the *Barcelona Papyrus*, the Anaphora of Sarapion of Thmuis, and Coptic MARK (CYRIL), as the following chart demonstrates:

Barcelona[38]	*Anaphora of Sarapion*[39]	*CYRIL*[40]
	Post-Sanctus	
Full is heaven and earth of Your holy glory. . . . Who is Coming to judge the living and the dead . . . Through him we offer you these your creations, the bread and the cup; we ask and beseech You to send onto them Your	Full is heaven and full also is the earth of your majestic glory, Lord of powers. Fill also this sacrifice with your power and with your participation. For to you we offered this living sacrifice, the unbloody offering. To you we offered this	Truly heaven and earth are full of thine holy glory through thine only-begotten Son our Lord and our God and our Saviour and the king of us all Jesus Christ. Fill this also thy sacrifice, O Lord, with the blessing that is from thee, through

---

38. ET from Chase, "Rethinking Anaphoral Development."
39. ET from Johnson, *Prayers of Sarapion*, 47, 49.
40. ET from F. E. Brightman, *Liturgies Eastern and Western*, vol. 1: Eastern Liturgies (Oxford: Clarendon Press, 1896), 176, 179.

| Holy and Comforter Spirit from Heaven, to represent them materially and to make the bread the Body of Christ and the cup the Blood of Christ, of the new covenant. | bread, the likeness of the body of the only-begotten . . . And we also offered the cup, the likeness of the blood. | the descent upon it of thine Holy Spirit, and in blessing bless [people: Amen] and in purifying purify [people: Amen] these thy precious gifts which have been set before thy face, this bread and this cup. |

Post-Narrative of Institution

| Even so we pray to you, Master, that in blessing you will bless and in sanctifying, sanctify . . . for all communicating from them for undivided faith, for communication of incorruption, for communion of the Holy Spirit. | God of truth, let your holy Word come upon this bread in order that the bread may become body of the Word, and upon this cup in order that the cup may become blood of truth . . . | Send down from thine holy height and from heaven thy dwelling . . . the Paraclete thine Holy Spirit . . . . send him down upon us thy servants and upon these thy precious gifts which have been set before thee, upon this bread and this cup that they may be hallowed and changed and that he may make this bread the holy body of Christ and this cup also his precious blood of the New Testament. |

Unlike *Barcelona*, where the explicit petition for the making of the Body and Blood of Christ appears in the first epiclesis (paralleled also in *Deir Balizeh*), both Sarapion and CYRIL place that emphasis in the second epiclesis after the institution narrative. Nevertheless, there is no question but that, like MC V, the language of the offering—most parallel in

Sarapion—is inseparably connected to the epiclesis. As Michael Zheltov has noted with regard to CYRIL:

> . . . the addition of the petition 'and in blessing bless and in purifying purify these thy precious gifts which have been set before thy face, this bread and this cup' in the very end of the first epiclesis . . . not only makes the first epiclesis more concrete, but also provides it with an idea of eucharistic offering.[41]

There is no need, therefore, to argue, as both Cuming and Fenwick do, that offering was a separate unit in the Jerusalem anaphora in the time of MC V. And, once again, the parallels are decidedly Egyptian.

Finally, what seems to be rather anomalous with regard to what has been seen as the normative structure of the Egyptian or Alexandrian anaphora—namely, the location of the intercessions near the end of the anaphora—is addressed by Petrin in reference to the work of Mary Farag. Petrin notes:

> In her analysis of the *Anaphora of St. Thomas* (*Thom.*), Mary Farag has proposed the existence of a "second" family of Egyptian prayers, basing her argument on the placement of the intercessions in *Barcel. P.* and *Thom.*, both of which she claims should be classified as part of the Egyptian liturgical tradition. Farag writes, 'Barcelona and Thomas, however, together witness to an Egyptian tradition of eucharistic prayers that do not infix petitionary prayers between the creation-centered preface and the Sanctus, as all other Egyptian anaphoras do. Barcelona and Thomas are Egyptian eucharistic prayers in which the Sanctus is couched in a larger praise context, thus obviating this second form critical argument's Egypt/Syria distinction.' She concludes, moreover, partially as a consequence of her recognition of this diversity of Egyptian anaphora patterns, that it may no longer be possible to classify anaphoras in liturgical "families" based on their structures.[42]

As I myself suggested several years ago, with regard to the so-called Antiochene location of the intercessions in the Anaphora of Sarapion of Thmuis, "the early Egyptian tradition knew more than one way to build

---

41. Zheltov, "Anaphora and the Thanksgiving Prayer," 467–504.
42. Petrin, *Egyptian Connection*, 207.

an anaphora."[43] And building upon this, Spinks[44] has argued that this is precisely demonstrated by the work of Farag on the Egyptian Anaphora of St. Thomas and by Zheltov on *Barcelona*,[45] to which I would add is a position further demonstrated and developed by Chase.[46]

With regard to the structure and contents of MC V, therefore, there is no reason to question its Egyptian provenance, a position hinted at by Gregory Dix in the 1930s and 1940s, and developed and expanded by Geoffrey Cuming in the 1970s, and generally accepted by a wide range of liturgical scholars today—including, with some nuance, Fenwick. The question remains, however, as to what significance this has for the further development of eucharistic praying in Jerusalem after the late fourth or early fifth century. Indeed, how does MC V become JAS? Or, does it?

Conclusion: An Alternative Hypothesis

As we have seen in the above, the approach of scholarship to the relationship of MC V to the Anaphora of JAS, from Gregory Dix to the present, might be summarized as having largely been the attempt to determine how it is that MC V became JAS by the addition of other anaphoral elements, usually from some version of BAS, attached to or interpolated into the core provided by MC V. This approach has necessitated in the conclusions of Geoffrey Cuming a complete renovation of MC V's structure of dialogue, preface, *Sanctus*, epiclesis, and intercessions, with the narrative of institution (according to Cuming originally between the epiclesis and intercessions) resulting in an anaphoral structure now consisting of dialogue, preface, *Sanctus*, christological post-*Sanctus*, narrative of institution, offering, epiclesis, and intercessions (i.e., the same structure as JAS). Fenwick is certainly correct here in noting that Cuming's approach "requires a rather haphazard process of re-arrangement, with sections of the prayer 'jumping' intermediate

---

43. Maxwell E. Johnson, *Liturgy in Early Christian Egypt*, Alcuin/GROW Liturgical Study 33, (Bramcote/Notts: Grove Books, 1995), 210.

44. Bryan Spinks, "Revisiting Egyptian Anaphoral Development," in David Pitt, Stefanos Alexopoulos, and Christian McConnell, *A Living Tradition: On the Intersection of Liturgical History and Pastoral Practice: Essays in Honor of Maxwell E. Johnson* (Collegeville, MN: Liturgical Press, 2012), 195–210, here at 210.

45. See Zheltov, "Anaphora and the Thanksgiving Prayer," 467–504.

46. Nathan Chase, "Rethinking Anaphoral Development."

portions to reach their final position."[47] But I am not convinced here either by Fenwick's appeal to the homily of Eusebius as the basis for MC V. While his placement of a hypothetical "oblation with prayer for forgiveness" before the epiclesis might be a logical place serving to attract a pre-oblation christological thanksgiving, narrative of institution, and anamnesis before the epiclesis and intercessions, we have seen that in MC V, as in other Egyptian anaphoras and fragments, offering and epiclesis go together as a single unit following the *Sanctus*. Fenwick's approach then also constitutes a bit of "jumping" and "re-arrangement" of anaphoral units, in this case the shifting separation of offering and epiclesis brought about by the addition of other units.

An alternative approach has been suggested by Nathan Chase.[48] Chase suggests that it was the narrative of institution that was interpolated into MC V between the *Sanctus* and epiclesis, with a christological post-*Sanctus* developing under some form of BAS. Further, since offering and epiclesis go together in other early Egyptian anaphoras after the *Sanctus* (e.g., the Anaphora of Sarapion of Thmuis, which includes "bloodless offering" language, the *Barcelona Papyrus*, and the *Louvain Coptic Papyrus*), it is important to note that this relationship remains in JAS now following the narrative of institution and anamnesis:

> . . . we offer you, [Master,] this awesome and bloodless sacrifice . . . .
>
> . . . [Have mercy on us, O God, according to your great mercy,] and send out upon us and upon these [holy] gifts set before you your [all-] Holy Spirit, (*he bows*) the Lord and giver of life . . . [send down, Master, your all-Holy Spirit himself upon us and upon these holy gifts set before you,] (*aloud*) that he may descend upon them, [and by his holy and good and glorious coming may sanctify them,] and make this bread the holy body of Christ, (*People:* Amen.) and this cup the precious blood of Christ. (*People:* Amen.)[49]

---

47. Fenwick, *Anaphoras of St Basil and St James*, 39.
48. Nathan Chase, "Rethinking Anaphoral Development," 628–30 and 716–17; and idem, "Antiochenization of the Egyptian Tradition," 349–62, here at 360–62. See also Chase's essay "Shaping the Classical Anaphoras of the Fourth through Sixth Centuries," above, 23–60.
49. PEER, 145–46.

Chase's approach suggests no real rearrangement of anaphoral units from MC V to approximate JAS, but depends rather only on the addition or interpolation of the narrative of institution alone before offering and epiclesis. I find his argument rather compelling, although even here it means abandoning what has been the "Egyptian" pattern of *Sanctus* and epiclesis.

Earlier, Kenneth Stevenson's comment was referred to—namely, that "it is no longer universally assumed that the Jerusalem liturgy at the time of Cyril was of the Antiochene type."[50] But even where this has not been assumed, the focus has been on how what we see in MC V relates to later anaphoral development in Jerusalem. And it is here, by way of conclusion, that I would like to present the following tentative hypothesis.

While it is certainly logical that MC V, as a clear and unmistakable witness to late fourth-century eucharistic liturgy in Jerusalem, would be of paramount importance for scholarly work on early liturgical sources for JAS, I would like to suggest that its explicit importance for JAS has been largely exaggerated. Yes, there are parallels, even close verbal parallels, between MC V and JAS in a few places (preface, epiclesis, the unbloody worship, and some of the intercessions), but these parallels are not always exact, and could also be explained by the use of common Jerusalem source materials rather than direct literary dependency of one upon the other. The fact that these parallels appear in Jerusalem, of course, is significant. But I wonder if there might be here a parallel to contemporary scholarship on the Syrian *Anaphora of the Twelve Apostles* and that of John Chrysostom (CHRYS). For a long time, scholars believed that *Twelve Apostles* was the Anaphora of Antioch that John Chrysostom himself brought to Constantinople and re-worked into the *Anaphora of CHRYS*. But thanks to the work of Taft and others, it is now commonly accepted that both *Twelve Apostles* and CHRYS are dependent upon an ur-source underlying both of them, and from which they are derived. Such could easily be the case for MC V and JAS as well. Where they are in agreement does not necessarily mean literary dependence, but rather demonstrates the use of common source materials.

In this case, then, perhaps we need not only to say with Stevenson that the Jerusalem liturgy at the time of Cyril was *not* of the "Antiochene"

---

50. Fenwick, *Anaphoras of St Basil and St James*, 38.

type, but that it was most definitely of the "Egyptian" type as that type is reflected in numerous anaphoral sources of different structures and patterns, including both *Barcelona* and *Sarapion*, as well as *Thomas* and the various other papyri and anaphoral fragments. It would mean also that at the time of MC V Jerusalem and Alexandria followed a very similar liturgical rite, pattern, and structure in both Christian initiation (with Syrian influence present in both Egypt and Jerusalem), and in the eucharistic liturgy, including the anaphora, whether that anaphora contained the words of institution after the epiclesis or not at all in Jerusalem.

We are all familiar with the recent excellent work of Daniel Galadza on the Byzantinization of the liturgy of Jerusalem, with the Anaphora of JAS ultimately abandoned by the Orthodox (i.e., Chalcedonian) Patriarch of Jerusalem in the twelfth century for the liturgies of BAS and CHRYS, leaving JAS as "the liturgy *par excellence* of the Syriac-praying non-Chalcedonian churches."[51] It seems to me, however, that an intermediate step between the Jerusalem eucharistic liturgy of MC V and the "Byzantinization" of the Jerusalem liturgy is precisely that of JAS, whether EgBAS, ArmBAS, or a combination of both. That is, what Nathan Chase has called "the Antiochenization of the Egyptian Tradition,"[52] with specific regard to *Barcelona*, seems particularly apt with regard to Jerusalem. That is, before any Byzantinization could take place, there was an Antiochenization of the Jerusalem liturgy reflected in JAS. But this is not simply an updating or revision of MC V by incorporating other anaphoral elements into its core. It is the replacement of one way of praying (Egyptian) with another (Antiochene). And, while some common early Jerusalem elements remain reflected in the new Antiochene Rite, the overall Rite of Jerusalem ceases being Egyptian in any recognizable form just as this new rite itself will be gradually replaced by that of the Byzantine, with essentially the same results.

While admittedly speculative and tentative, my hypothesis suggests that we abandon any further attempts to use MC V in order to discern or derive portions of JAS from its contents. Although, of course, the study of MC V remains important for its own sake and for early Jerusalem

---

51. Daniel Galadza, *Liturgy and Byzantinization of Jerusalem*, Oxford Christian Studies (Oxford and New York: Oxford University Press, 2018), 162ff.

52. See Chase, "Antiochenization of the Egyptian Tradition," 319–67. See also Chase's essay above, 23–60.

liturgy in general, the more fruitful approach to the study of Jerusalem liturgy, I would submit, is not simply the compilation of JAS as MC V's anaphoral replacement, but the reasons—theological, ecclesial, and otherwise—that made such a replacement, or, borrowing Chase's phrase, such "Antiochenization," desirable and/or necessary in the first place.

VI

The Deifying Sacrifice

Thysia *in the Eucharistic Prayers of Byzantine Basil**

Lucas Lynn Christensen

Introduction

In the liturgical tradition of Hagia Sophia, cathedral of Constantinople,[1] called the Great Church, the eucharistic prayers ascribed to Basil the Great, archbishop of Caesarea in Cappadocia (327–379), formed the normative Sunday liturgical prayer until the eleventh century, although in received practice the Byzantine Rite liturgy of Basil (ByzBAS) is now served only ten times a year.[2] The history of this anaphora's origins has been a matter of sustained inquiry and disagreement, with scholars

---

* I would like to offer thanks to Maxwell Johnson for his invaluable feedback on this project, and to the participants of his seminar on early anaphorae for their valuable input.

1. Modern day Istanbul, Türkiye.
2. On this shift, see Stefano Parenti, "La 'vittoria' nella chiesa di Costantinopoli della liturgia di Crisostomo sulla liturgia di Basilio," in *Comparative Liturgy Fifty Years after Anton Baumstark (1872–1948): Acts of the International Congress, Rome, 25–29 September 1998*, OCA 265, ed. Robert Taft and Gabriele Winkler (Rome: Pontifical Oriental Institute, 2001), 907–28; and Stefanos Alexopoulos, "The Influence of Iconoclasm on Byzantine Liturgy: A Case Study," in *Worship Traditions in Armenia and the Neighboring Christian East*, ed. Roberta Ervine (Crestwood: St. Vladimir's Seminary Press/St. Nersess Armenian Seminary, 2006), 127–37.

attributing its theoretical Urtext variously to Egypt, Syria, Cappadocia, Palestine, or even questioning the existence of an original altogether.[3] The nature of this contended origin speaks to the pan-Eastern presence of the Basilian anaphoral tradition. Further, the anaphora of Basil has entered into the prayers of Western churches via the liturgical movement of the twentieth century,[4] marking it as a peculiarly universal anaphoral tradition. Because of the near-ubiquity of Basilian anaphorae, and because of its prominence in the history of the Byzantine Rite in particular, it is fruitful to investigate ByzBAS to understand the development of eucharistic praying in Eastern Christianity, and to appreciate the nature of its continuing theological influence on anaphoral prayer throughout the Christian world.

ByzBAS contains numerous references to sacrifice and sacrificial themes, weaving them throughout, making reference to pre- and early Christian cult, as found in the Hebrew Bible and the New Testament. In order to understand sacrifice in ByzBAS, the present study begins by exploring the cultic context of its sacrificial language by briefly highlighting relevant aspects of second temple worship and its connections to cultic references in the New Testament. Second, I survey the specific instances of the word "sacrifice" in ByzBAS, considering each in light of the biblical context and the anaphora's own rhetorical framework. Finally, I synthesize the constellation of these references internal to the text of ByzBAS in light of the examined cultic context to appreciate how this anaphora communicates a vision of the community's eucharistic

---

3. For a thorough examination of the history of scholarship and the status quaestionis, see Anne McGowan, "The Basilian Anaphoras: Rethinking the Question," in *Issues in Eucharistic Praying in East and West: Essays in Liturgical and Theological Analysis*, ed. Maxwell E. Johnson (Collegeville, MN: Liturgical Press, 2010), 219–62.

4. The Egyptian recension of Basil "has served as the primary basis for Eucharistic Prayer IV in the *Roman Missal* of Paul VI (1969), Prayer D in Rite II of the American *Book of Common Prayer* (1979), and in several other Protestant liturgical resources, usually taken from Prayer D, which was itself the result of an ecumenical working group, including Roman Catholic, Episcopalian, Lutheran, and other collaborators." R. C. D. Jasper and G. J. Cuming, *Prayers of the Eucharist: Early and Reformed*, ed. Paul F. Bradshaw and Maxwell E. Johnson (Collegeville, MN: Liturgical Press Academic, 2019), 118.

sacrifice as corporately becoming Christ as an auto-oblation offered by and with Christ.

The texts I use in examining ByzBAS are the oldest extant manuscripts of the Great Church's recension (they are remarkably close to the received practice of the Byzantine Rite); preference is given to the older of the two, the Vatican Apostolic Library's Barberini gr. 336,[5] an incomplete eighth-century euchological manuscript. Supplementing the missing section is the tenth-century Grottaferrata Γ. B. VII.[6]

Sacrifice and the Second Temple

For first-century-CE Palestine, corporate ritual worship was identified with sacrifice offered at a temple. For worshipers of Yahweh this would have meant the system of sacrificial offerings made at the only authorized temple, that of Jerusalem. While the paradigm of this sacrificial system is still enshrined in the Hebrew Bible, by the time of the second temple the popular understanding was also reflected in, and informed by, literature that would come to be viewed as "extra-canonical," including the book of Jubilees and the Temple Scroll.

Alongside the temple ritual, prayer was offered privately, in the domestic context; the evidence suggests that there was not any fixed form to such prayer, although there may have been common threads.[7] Despite popular misconception, the ritual in the synagogue would not develop until much later; in the first century the assembly likely limited their corporate activity to the reading and exposition of Torah.[8] This is to say

---

5. From the edition of Stefano Parenti and Elena Velkovska, *Euchologion Barberini gr. 336* (Omsk: Golovanov, 2011).

6. From C. E. Hammond and F. E. Brightman, *Liturgies, Eastern and Western: Being the Texts, Original or Translated, of the Principal Liturgies of the Church* (Oxford: Clarendon Press, 1896).

7. Ruth Langer, "New Directions in Understanding Jewish Liturgy," in *Early Judaism*, ed. Frederick E. Greenspan (New York: New York University Press, 2018), 147–73.

8. Paul Bradshaw, *The Search for the Origins of Christian Worship Sources and Methods for the Study of Early Liturgy*, 2nd ed. (New York: Oxford University Press, 2002), 36; Andrew Brian McGowan, *Ancient Christian Worship: Early Church Practices in Social, Historical, and Theological Perspective* (Grand Rapids: Baker Academic, 2014), 71.

that what the various Judaisms of the first century considered corporate ritual worship to be, strictly speaking, was what happened at the temple, and it implied the offering of sacrifice which was typically a meal shared in communion with God, and which ensured that God would remember the offerer.

The temple in Jerusalem was the only authorized location for corporate ritual worship of Yahweh; its system of daily sacrifices, forming a rhythm of morning, midafternoon, and evening offerings, was enshrined in the book of Leviticus in the Hebrew Bible. There, regulations for worship, which is to say of sacrifices, were prescribed. The typical offering was food brought to the temple, whether an animal which was perfunctorily (i.e., not ritually) slaughtered,[9] or grain mixed with oil and incense, and a portion (the entirety, in the case of a whole-burnt offering) was immolated on the fire altar in the temple courtyard; in the case of animals, the blood was either deposited at the base of the altar or smeared or sprinkled on the altar itself; the portion that was immolated was referred to as the "memorial portion,"[10] because the offering caused the Lord to remember those making the offering.

Roland de Vaux, in his study of Israel's worship practices, identifies three functions of sacrificial worship: as a gift to God; as communion between God, the offerer, and the community; and as expiation for sin.[11] For the purposes of this examination, I would like to highlight two categories of sacrifice in particular—the memorial, and the sacrifice of praise—both of which emphasize de Vaux's three themes.

---

9. "The purpose of this destruction is not merely to destroy. In opposition to the theory that sacrifice consists in annihilation, and in opposition to a certain modern school of spirituality, we must maintain that God, who is Lord of life and of all being, cannot be honoured by the destruction either of being or of life. In this context we may recall that animals were normally killed by the man offering the sacrifice, not by the priest; the essence of sacrifice, then, does not lie in the immolation. Immolation is only a preparation for the sacrifice, like the laying-on of hands." Roland de Vaux, *Ancient Israel: Its Life and Institutions*, vol. 2 (New York: McGraw-Hill, 1997), 452.

10. אֶת־אַזְכָּרָתָהּ | τὸ μνημόσυνον αὐτῆς

11. De Vaux, *Ancient Israel*, 451–53.

Two Examples of Memorial Offerings

Leviticus 24:7–8

וְנָתַתָּ עַל־הַֽמַּעֲרֶ֖כֶת לְבֹנָ֣ה זַכָּ֑ה וְהָיְתָ֤ה לַלֶּ֙חֶם֙ לְאַזְכָּרָ֔ה אִשֶּׁ֖ה לַיהוָֽה׃ Lev. 24:8 בְּי֨וֹם הַשַּׁבָּ֜ת בְּי֣וֹם הַשַּׁבָּ֗ת יַֽעַרְכֶ֛נּוּ לִפְנֵ֥י יְהוָ֖ה תָּמִ֑יד מֵאֵ֥ת בְּנֵֽי־יִשְׂרָאֵ֖ל בְּרִ֥ית עוֹלָֽם	καὶ ἐπιθήσετε ἐπὶ τὸ θέμα λίβανον καθαρὸν καὶ ἅλα, καὶ ἔσονται εἰς ἄρτους εἰς ἀνάμνησιν προκείμενα τῷ κυρίῳ. τῇ ἡμέρᾳ τῶν σαββάτων προθήσεται ἔναντι Κυρίου διὰ παντὸς ἐνώπιον τῶν υἱῶν Ἰσραήλ, διαθήκην αἰώνιον.	You shall place on the pile [of loaves] pure frankincense and salt, and they shall be loaves for a memorial, set before the Lord. On the day of the sabbaths [Aaron] shall always place them before the Lord as an everlasting covenant with the children of Israel.
(HMT W4)	(Rahlfs LXX)	(Adapted from NETS)

Numbers 10:10

וּבְי֨וֹם שִׂמְחַתְכֶ֜ם וּֽבְמוֹעֲדֵיכֶם֮ וּבְרָאשֵׁ֣י חָדְשֵׁיכֶם֒ וּתְקַעְתֶּ֣ם בַּחֲצֹֽצְרֹ֗ת עַ֚ל עֹלֹ֣תֵיכֶ֔ם וְעַ֖ל זִבְחֵ֣י שַׁלְמֵיכֶ֑ם וְהָי֨וּ לָכֶ֤ם לְזִכָּרוֹן֙ לִפְנֵ֣י אֱלֹֽהֵיכֶ֔ם אֲנִ֖י יְהוָ֥ה אֱלֹהֵיכֶֽם	καὶ ἐν ταῖς ἡμέραις τῆς εὐφροσύνης ὑμῶν καὶ ἐν ταῖς ἑορταῖς ὑμῶν καὶ ἐν ταῖς νουμηνίαις ὑμῶν σαλπιεῖτε ταῖς σάλπιγξιν ἐπὶ τοῖς ὁλοκαυτώμασιν καὶ ἐπὶ ταῖς θυσίαις τῶν σωτηρίων ὑμῶν, καὶ ἔσται ὑμῖν ἀνάμνησις ἔναντι τοῦ θεοῦ ὑμῶν· ἐγὼ Κύριος ὁ θεὸς ὑμῶν.	And in the days of your joy and at your festivals and at your new moon celebrations, you shall sound with the trumpets over the whole burnt offerings and over your sacrifices of salvation, and it shall be a memorial before your God for you. I am the Lord your God.
(HMT W4)	(Rahlfs LXX)	(Adapted from NETS)

Compare these texts with the liturgical formula in Luke 22:19–20:

Καὶ λαβὼν ἄρτον εὐχαριστήσας ἔκλασεν καὶ ἔδωκεν αὐτοῖς λέγων· τοῦτό ἐστιν τὸ σῶμά μου τὸ ὑπὲρ ὑμῶν διδόμενον· τοῦτο ποιεῖτε εἰς τὴν ἐμὴν ἀνάμνησιν. καὶ τὸ ποτήριον ὡσαύτως μετὰ τὸ δειπνῆσαι, λέγων· τοῦτο τὸ ποτήριον ἡ καινὴ διαθήκη ἐν τῷ αἵματί μου τὸ ὑπὲρ ὑμῶν ἐκχυννόμενον.	And taking bread, he gave thanks, broke it, and gave it to them saying: "This is my body given for you, do this as my memorial." And likewise the cup after supper, saying: "This is the cup of the new covenant in my blood poured out for you."[12]
(NA28)	

In the Hebrew sacrifices it is God who remembers (ἀνάμνησις) the ones who offer the sacrifice to him. Francis Giordano Carpinelli argues that it is precisely this sense of "memorial" intended in Luke's Gospel: in this sacrifice of the new covenant it is *God* who is remembering the one who offers, not the offerer who is remembering Christ.[13] Although an indelible part of eucharistic praying as liturgical texts develop includes God's remembering of those offering (and those whom they commemorate), the community's remembering of Christ's saving economy forms a parallel. Perhaps there is a harmonization in the combined images of these sacrificial regulations, and the Passover sacrifice's mnemonic function as Israel is commanded to remember the saving work of God (Exod 12).[14] In such a harmonized understanding, it is God who remembers those offering, but the offerers also "proclaim his death" (1 Cor 11:26).

---

12. Translation mine; v.i. on the rendering of εἰς τὴν ἐμὴν ἀνάμνησιν.

13. "'Do This as My Memorial' (Luke 22:19): Lucan Soteriology of Atonement," *Catholic Biblical Quarterly* 61, no. 1 (January 1999): 74–91. For a similar treatment of 1 Cor 11:24–25 see Fritz Chenderlin, *"Do This as My Memorial": The Semantic and Conceptual Background and Value of Ἀνάμνησις in I Corinthians 11:24-25* (Rome: Biblical Institute Press, 1982).

14. See Stephen David Fahrig, "The Context of the Text: Reading Hebrews as a Eucharistic Homily," unpublished diss. (Boston College, 2014), 233.

The Sacrifice of Praise

Leviticus 7:2–5 (LXX) 12–15 (MT)

אִם עַל־תּוֹדָה יַקְרִיבֶנּוּ וְהִקְרִיב עַל־זֶבַח הַתּוֹדָה חַלּוֹת מַצּוֹת בְּלוּלֹת בַּשֶּׁמֶן וּרְקִיקֵי מַצּוֹת מְשֻׁחִים בַּשָּׁמֶן וְסֹלֶת מֻרְבֶּכֶת חַלֹּת בְּלוּלֹת בַּשָּׁמֶן: עַל־חַלֹּת לֶחֶם חָמֵץ יַקְרִיב קָרְבָּנוֹ עַל־זֶבַח תּוֹדַת שְׁלָמָיו: וְהִקְרִיב מִמֶּנּוּ אֶחָד מִכָּל־קָרְבָּן תְּרוּמָה לַיהוָה לַכֹּהֵן הַזֹּרֵק אֶת־דַּם הַשְּׁלָמִים לוֹ יִהְיֶה: וּבְשַׂר זֶבַח תּוֹדַת שְׁלָמָיו בְּיוֹם קָרְבָּנוֹ יֵאָכֵל לֹא־יַנִּיחַ מִמֶּנּוּ עַד־בֹּקֶר:	ἐὰν μὲν περὶ αἰνέσεως προσφέρῃ αὐτήν, καὶ προσοίσει ἐπὶ τῆς θυσίας τῆς αἰνέσεως ἄρτους ἐκ σεμιδάλεως ἀναπεποιημένους ἐν ἐλαίῳ, λάγανα ἄζυμα διακεχρισμένα ἐν ἐλαίῳ καὶ σεμίδαλιν πεφυραμένην ἐν ἐλαίῳ· ἐπ' ἄρτοις ζυμίταις προσοίσει τὰ δῶρα αὐτοῦ ἐπὶ θυσίᾳ αἰνέσεως σωτηρίου. καὶ προσάξει ἓν ἀπὸ πάντων τῶν δώρων αὐτοῦ ἀφαίρεμα κυρίῳ· τῷ ἱερεῖ τῷ προσχέοντι τὸ αἷμα τοῦ σωτηρίου, αὐτῷ ἔσται. καὶ τὰ κρέα θυσίας αἰνέσεως σωτηρίου αὐτῷ ἔσται καὶ ἐν ᾗ ἡμέρᾳ δωρεῖται, βρωθήσεται· οὐ καταλείψουσιν ἀπ' αὐτοῦ εἰς τὸ πρωί.	If he offers it for praise, then he shall bring for the sacrifice of praise cakes of fine flour made up with oil and unleavened wafers spread with oil and fine flour mixed with oil. In addition to leavened cakes he shall bring his gifts for a sacrifice of praise for salvation. And he shall present one out of all his gifts as an advance deduction for the Lord. It shall belong to the priest who pours out the blood of salvation. It shall be his. And the flesh of the sacrifice of praise for salvation shall belong to him, and on the day it is given it shall be eaten. They shall not leave any of it until the morning.
(HMT W4)	(Rahlfs LXX)	(Adapted from NETS)

The sacrifice of thanksgiving, or "sacrifice of praise" in the LXX text, is particularly noteworthy because the author of Hebrews uses this term, θυσίας τῆς αἰνέσεως (the parallel of the Hebrew זֶבַח הַתּוֹדָה), in chapter 13, which connects this sacrifice with the liturgical celebrations of the early Christians.[15] The sacrifice would first involve offering bread loaves ("of fine flour" in the LXX, "unleavened" in the MT) with oil as well as thin, unleavened cakes; with that sacrifice, one would also offer a meat sacrifice (species unspecified). The priest who poured out "the blood of salvation" (LXX; "peace" in the MT) received one of the loaves for himself. Of the meat offering, the portion belonging to the Lord was burned, as usual, but also a portion would be shared among those offering, forming a community meal, reflecting an understanding of sacrifice as the offering and partaking of a meal, creating networks of bonds simultaneously between the worshipers and God, and with one another.

It may be difficult for modern Westerners to appreciate how the sacrificial system built these bonds simultaneously, devoid of individualist piety, but perhaps a close approximation is the shared experience of civic entertainment, such as sport, wherein an event that ostensibly forms the purpose is the kernel of an epiphenomenon which can eclipse its cause. It is crucial to underline the understanding of sacrifice as shared meal, especially when examining later Christian debates around the Eucharist. For the first-century Jewish Christian, the question, "Is this a 'sacrifice,' or is it a 'meal'?" would have sounded as absurd as asking whether the structure in which they lived was a "building" or a "home."[16]

---

15. See Fahrig, "Context of the Text," 218ff. for a thorough examination of this passage as eucharistic and sacrificial. See also the fifth chapter of Matthew Olver's unpublished dissertation, "Three Central Uses of Hebrews in the Roman Canon: Melchizedek, *Sacrificium Laudis*, and Sacrificial Terminology," for a refutation of a purely metaphorical, immaterial interpretation of "sacrifice of praise" in the Hebrew bible, in the letter to the Hebrews, in early Christian commentary, and in the Roman canon, in "*Hoc Est Sacrificium Laudis*: The Influence of Hebrews on the Origin, Structure, and Theology of the Roman Canon Missae," PhD diss. (Marquette University, 2018), in particular 265–90. Robert Taft also notes the regular, early use of this phrase in connection with the Eucharist and its euchological deployment in the eucharistic rite rather than in the liturgy of the word in his review of *The Sacrifice of Praise: Studies on the Themes of Thanksgiving and Redemption in the Central Prayers of the Eucharistic and Baptismal Liturgies, in Honour of Arthur Hubert Couratin*, in *Worship* 56, no. 2 (March 1982): 176–79, cited in Olver, 270.

16. Later, in the medieval Germanic context, following the loss of the earlier understanding of sacrifice as shared meal, and the instrumentalization of the sacrament, this false division and the attendant confusion arises. See Mark R. Francis, "The Germanization

Terminology now familiar (to the point of cliché) to Christians surrounding the Eucharist was well established in the first century as part of the temple cult and the biblical descriptions of its practice. Later conventional understandings cannot be allowed anachronistically to dismiss such language as purely metaphorical, as this language is grounded in concrete ritual sacrifice. Having briefly considered this sacrificial context, I now turn to the pre-anaphoral and anaphoral text of ByzBAS in order to consider how it uses the term "sacrifice," in light of the examples it draws from earlier sacrificial worship.

The Use of "Sacrifice" in ByzBAS

I have briefly considered how the language used in the New Testament to describe worship is grounded in the concretely sacrificial worship of the tabernacle and the temple. In this section I will consider the catalogue of ByzBAS's use of the word "sacrifice" as the most obviously explicit example of a sacrificial theology, with reference to each instance's scriptural antecedents and its immediate rhetorical function.[17]

The word "sacrifice" itself, represented in Greek by θυσία, first appears in ByzBAS in the first "Prayer of the Faithful," after the opening of the εἰλητόν.[18] It reads:

---

of Christianity," in *Local Worship Global Church: Popular Religion and the Liturgy* (Collegeville, MN: Liturgical Press, 2014).

17. It is tempting to include references to poured blood, broken body, setting forth, offering, and the like, but without properly understanding the sacrificial *mise en scène* of ByzBAS, the purpose of this study, such inclusions would fairly be considered circular argumentation. For similar reasons, cataloguing related terms (altar, service, offering), which clearly have varying degrees of sacrificial meaning, becomes an endeavor secondary to establishing the meaning of "sacrifice" itself—that is to say, if sacrifice is meant in a purely metaphorical sense then these terms merely extend the metaphor. They only have significance if a concretely sacrificial understanding is reliably identified.

18. In received practice, the εἰλητόν is a silk cloth that enfolds and protects the antimension when the latter is not in use. An antimension is a square cloth with an icon of the deposition of Christ's body, which today serves as the hierarchical authorization for the local community to offer the Eucharist.

ἵνα ἀκατακρίτως στάντες ἐνώπιον τῆς ἁγίας δόξης σου, προσάγωμέν σοι θυσίαν αἰνέσεως[19]	so that, standing uncondemned before your holy glory, we may offer you sacrifice of praise[20]

As already mentioned, this text comes from Hebrews 13:15, which itself alludes to the sacrifice described in Leviticus 7:12ff. In this connection, the phrase should not be taken to denote sacrifice as a mere metaphor for singing doxological hymns (although hymns are *included* according to the liturgical context provided by Hebrews).[21] Rather, the image from Leviticus evokes the sacrificial offering of bread which, as conditioned by the passage in Hebrews, is then given to Christians to eat from their exclusive altar. The Levitical context is one of a sacrifice which is a shared meal between God and the community, and the corporate context of the sacrifice is underlined in Hebrews 13:16's use of κοινωνία, which the community is enjoined not to neglect.

Later in the same prayer, an earlier reference to Hebrews is repeated, this time explicitly connected with sacrifice:

δός, Κύριε, καὶ ὑπὲρ τῶν ἡμετέρων ἁμαρτημάτων καὶ τῶν τοῦ λαοῦ ἀγνοημάτων δεκτὴν γενέσθαι τὴν θυσίαν ἡμῶν καὶ εὐπρόσδεκτον ἐνώπιόν σου[22]	Lord, receive our sacrifice, grant it to be well pleasing before you, both for our sins and for the errors of the people

The reference to covering the clergy's sins and the people's errors is connected to the Day of Atonement sacrifice (Lev 16) by the author of Hebrews (9:7):

---

19. Parenti and Velkovska, *Barberini*, 271. This phrase has an analogue in the older of the two Armenian redactions of Basil (ArmBAS I), thought to predate ByzBAS: "to glorify you as the true God and to approach you as the 'sacrifice of praise' with a pure heart and humble spirit as our living and spiritual worship," Gabriele Winkler, *Die Basilius-Anaphora: Edition der beiden armenischen Redaktionen und der relevanten Fragmente, Übersetzung und Zusammenschau aller Versionen im Licht der orientalischen Überlieferungen* (Rome: Pontifical Oriental Institute, 2005), 140–41; my translation from Winkler's German.

20. Translations of ByzBAS are mine.

21. Fahrig, Context of the Text," 226–27; Olver, *"Hoc Est Sacrificium Laudis,"* 265ff.

22. Parenti and Velkovska, *Barberini*, 271.

εἰς δὲ τὴν δευτέραν ἅπαξ τοῦ
ἐνιαυτοῦ μόνος ὁ ἀρχιερεύς,
οὐ χωρὶς αἵματος ὃ προσφέρει
ὑπὲρ ἑαυτοῦ καὶ τῶν τοῦ λαοῦ
ἀγνοημάτων,

but into the second [section of
the temple] the high priest goes
by himself, only once a year, not
without blood, which he offers for
himself and for the errors of the
people

(NA28)

The adjective εὐπρόσδεκτος, used in the prayer to modify θυσία, is uncommon in the New Testament, appearing only five times. Two of its uses are sacrificial in nature: in conjunction with πνευματικὰς θυσίας in 1 Peter 2:5, which refers to the spiritual[23] sacrifices offered by the people of God, who constitute a holy priesthood and spiritual house; and with προσφορά in Romans 15:16, where Paul serves the nations as a priest (ἱερουργοῦντα) so that they may make an acceptable offering (προσφορὰ . . . εὐπρόσδεκτος). This sacrificial positioning of the nations evokes Malachi 1:11, with its promise of a pure sacrifice (θυσία καθαρά) from them specifically.

The celebrant's prayer during the Cherubic Hymn, the so-called *nemo dignus* (οὐδεὶς ἄξιος), is offered as the clergy prepare for the procession of the gifts of bread and wine through the assembly to the altar. This prayer's text places the sacrificial ministry firmly in the person of Christ, in connection with his incarnation:

γέγονας ἄνθρωπος,
καὶ ἀρχιερεὺς ἡμῶν ἐχρημάτισας,
καὶ τῆς λειτουργικῆς ταύτης καὶ
ἀναιμάκτου θυσίας τὴν ἱερουργίαν
παρέδωκας . . .
ἀξίωσον προσενεχθῆναι σοι τὰ
δῶρα ταῦτα καὶ ὑπ᾽ ἐμοῦ τοῦ
ταπεινοῦ καὶ ἁμαρτωλοῦ καὶ

having become human,
you became our high priest,
and you handed on the sacred
ministry of this liturgical and
bloodless sacrifice . . .
accept these gifts offered to you,
even by me, your humble and sinful
and unworthy servant.

---

23. "Spiritual" should not be mistaken for "non-material" or "purely metaphorical," cf. Olver, "*Hoc Est Sacrificium Laudis*," 268.

ἀναξίου δούλου σου.
Σὺ γὰρ εἶ ὁ προσφέρων καὶ
προσφερόμενος,
καὶ ἁγιάζων καὶ ἁγιαζόμενος,
Χριστὲ ὁ θεὸς ἡμῶν[24]

For you are the offerer and offering,
both sanctifier and sanctified,
Christ our God

This connection between incarnation and the high-priestly ministry of Christ is thoroughly (and exclusively, among the New Testament scriptures) of the book of Hebrews. The sacrificial offering which Christ hands on (παρέδωκας) is cast in terms of *self*-offering, one which the community is also enjoined to make.

Following the Great Entrance with the gifts, the celebrant offers the prayer of the *proskomidē*, after the people have completed the Cherubic hymn:

ἵνα γενώμεθα ἄξιοι τοῦ προσφέρειν
σοι τὴν λογικὴν ταύτην καὶ
ἀναίμακτον θυσίαν[25]

so that we may become worthy
to offer you this spiritual and
bloodless sacrifice

As I have just noted, Christ is offerer and offering, but this reference to λογική λατρεία which the prayer now makes evokes Paul's exhortation (Rom 12:1) that the very bodies of the faithful would be offered up as a living sacrifice (θυσίαν ζῶσαν) as their spiritual worship. This is to say, if Christ becomes human so that he might, as high priest, offer himself up as sacrifice (προσφέρων καὶ προσφερόμενος), then in order to realize the Christified humanity to which the Christian is called, the community must bear the sacrificial tradition which Christ handed on and offer themselves up to God in the same hieratic auto-oblation.

Later in the same prayer the celebrant asks:

Ἐπίβλεψον ἐφ᾽ ἡμᾶς, ὁ θεός,
καὶ ἔφιδε ἐπὶ τὴν λατρείαν ἡμῶν
ταύτην

Look upon us, God,
and look upon this our worship,
and accept it

---

24. Parenti and Velkovska, *Barberini*, 272.
25. Ibid., 273.

καὶ πρόσδεξαι αὐτὴν	as you accepted:
ὡς προσεδέξω	the gifts of Abel,
Ἄβελ τὰ δῶρα,	the sacrifices of Noah,
Νῶε τὰς θυσίας,	the whole-burnt offerings of
Ἀβραὰμ τὰς ὁλοκαρπώσεις,	Abraham,
Μωσέως καὶ Ἀαρὼν τὰς	the priestly services of Moses and
ἱερωσύνας,	Aaron,
Σαμουὴλ τὰς εἰρηνικάς·	the peace offerings of Samuel;
ὡς προσεδέξω ἐκ τῶν ἁγίων σου	as you accepted this true worship
ἀποστόλων τὴν ἀληθινὴν ταύτην	from your holy apostles,
λατρείαν,	even so, accept these gifts from the
οὕτως καὶ ἐκ τῶν χειρῶν ἡμῶν τῶν	hands of us sinners also
ἁμαρτωλῶν πρόσδεξαι τὰ δῶρα	
ταῦτα	

This prayer presents a panoply of explicit sacrificial images from both the Hebrew Bible (a list which parallels and condenses the survey of righteous figures given in Hebrews 11),[26] as well as a general reference to the post-New Testament church of the apostles, which includes the present celebration.

The examples from Hebrew worship come in two groups of three: the first are Abel, Noah, and Abraham, pre-Mosaic and therefore before the divinely instituted sacrificial system recorded in the Pentateuch. Abel, also mentioned first in the Hebrews list, is the first human recorded explicitly to offer sacrifice to God,[27] and his is a pure offering, pleasing to God (Gen 4:4). The death of Abel is compared to Christ's atoning death by the author of Hebrews, who uses the adjective "sprinkled" (ῥαντισμοῦ) to connect Christ's blood to that of the goat sacrificed on the day of atonement; while

---

26. Notably, ByzBAS includes Aaron, while Hebrews omits him, perhaps because of its project of distinguishing Christ's Melchizedekan priesthood from the Aaronic priesthood of the second temple. Cf. the Roman Canon's exclusion of Moses and Aaron in favor of pre-Mosaic examples of worship, as noted by Olver, "*Hoc est Sacrificium Laudis,*" 260.

27. I qualify with "explicitly" because the cosmology of Eden itself is cast in temple language, and so Adam and Eve inhabit a hieratic role, offering up all of creation to God, until they broke the sanctity of the paradisal precincts. For Eden as temple, see Gregory K. Beale, "Eden, the Temple, and the Church's Mission in the New Creation," *Journal of the Evangelical Theological Society* 48, no. 1 (2005): 5–31.

166   *Further Issues in Eucharistic Praying in East and West*

Abel's blood cried for vengeance, however, Christ's "speaks a better word" bringing forgiveness, peace, and reconciliation (12:24).[28]

Noah was the only faithful, righteous person on earth during his era, and for his sake God sent warning before wiping out everyone else in a cataclysmic flood. Immediately after Noah disembarked from the saving ark after a year afloat, he offered sacrifice to God who promised never to destroy the world in flood. At the same time, God also required two things: that Noah and his descendants never consume the blood of an animal (a prohibition so universal that it is further enshrined in the Mosaic covenant, e.g. Deut 12:23, Lev 7:26, and even persists into the new: Acts 15:20), nor shed that of another human. In a striking juxtaposition, it is Christ's blood, not that of an animal, which will be consumed. The language of the anaphora, following that of the New Testament (John 10:18), insists that it is self-offered: "he gave himself up for the life of the world" (παρεδίδου ἑαυτὸν ὑπὲρ τῆς τοῦ κόσμου ζωῆς[29]).

Abraham's sacrifices included an offering to God through Melchizedek (not mentioned in ByzBAS),[30] who is treated as a type of Christ-as-priest in the book of Hebrews and who famously offered to God the sacrifice of bread and wine; the sacrifice of Melchizedek appears combined with the sacrifice of Abel in mosaics of early presbyteria such as that of St. Vitale in Ravenna, where the altar of their oblation is dressed and accoutered in the same way as the physical altar in the apse below. At another time of Abraham's sacrifice he receives an ecstatic vision of God as a fiery furnace upon the latter's promise to make of his descendants a nation (Gen 15:17), but the most famous and artistically reproduced of Abraham's sacrificial scenes is his abortive sacrifice of his own son, Isaac (Gen 22),[31]

---

28. Harold W. Attridge, *The Epistle to the Hebrews: A Commentary on the Epistle to the Hebrews*, Hermeneia: A Critical and Historical Commentary on the Bible, Accordance ed. (Minneapolis: Fortress Press, 1989).

29. There is a lacuna in *Barberini gr. 336* at this point, so I have taken this from the slightly later Grottaferrata Γ.β. VII found in C. E. Hammond and F. E. Brightman, *Liturgies, Eastern and Western; Being the Texts, Original or Translated, of the Principal Liturgies of the Church* (Oxford: Clarendon Press, 1896), 327.

30. Olver refers to Willis's hypothesis that eastern anaphorae exclude Melchizedek due to bizarre legends that had developed; Willis, "Melchisedech," 280, cited in "*Sacrificium Laudis*," 264.

31. This is undoubtedly the specific referent as ByzBAS here lists Abraham's ὁλοκαρπώσεις, which the LXX only uses in conjunction with Abraham in the Aqedah narrative—presumably the plural refers both to Abraham's arrested offering of Isaac,

which the author of Hebrews not only mentions explicitly but exegetes as pointing to hope in the resurrection.

Moses, Aaron, and Samuel, the second triad, participate in the sacrificial ritual as prescribed in the law. Moses' life bears numerous typological antecedents to Christ's which the author of Hebrews briefly includes (11:23 ff.). Aaron is the first ritual priest, and Samuel is not only the child of a miraculous birth, but also one who inaugurated kingship over Israel through the offering of sacrifices for peace, alluded to in ByzBAS's mention of τὰς εἰρηνικάς (1 Sam 11:15).[32]

Finally, the list culminates in the apostles' "true worship" which is presented as the third and final phase of sacrificial worship in continuity with the pre-Torah period through the tabernacle/temple, to the new covenant. It is here that the community of ByzBAS finds itself, in that same apostolic continuity with the worship of the Hebrew bible. This relationship is indicated rhetorically by the parallel use of προσδέχομαι, "to receive," for the worship of the present congregation, for the pre-Christian exemplars *en bloc*, and for the apostles—a request that the accomplished fact for the latter two groups would be a present reality for the worshipping assembly here, now. Further, the worship of ByzBAS is identified as that very apostolic worship: the word λατρεία is used for both and only these two examples, and the true apostolic worship is identified as *this* true worship (τὴν ἀληθινὴν ταύτην λατρείαν). The prayer culminates with the celebrant asking God to count all present worthy to be able to stand together with such an illustrious retinue in presenting the gifts (τὰ δῶρα ταῦτα) which have just now been laid on the altar.

Conclusion: A Preliminary Sacrificial Theology of ByzBAS

In his essay on "Understanding the Byzantine Anaphoral Oblation," Robert Taft warned against looking for precise eucharistic theology in anaphoral prayers, as the project of the former is the province of the systematic theologian, but the genre of the latter is that of prayer.[33]

---

followed by his successful offering of the ram (provided, as he unwittingly predicted, by God): both intended as whole-burnt offerings.

32. Parenti and Velkovska, *Barberini*, 273, note k.

33. In *Rule of Prayer, Rule of Faith: Essays in Honor of Aidan Kavanagh, O.S.B.*, ed. Nathan Mitchell and John F. Baldovin (Collegeville, MN: Liturgical Press, 1996), 32–55, here at 36–37.

This synthesizing section takes Taft's own conclusions as its point of departure;[34] it is not an attempt to read a systematic theology of eucharistic sacrifice back into ByzBAS, but to note the thematic characteristics of its use of "sacrifice."

The sacrificial system of the second temple, as recorded in the Hebrew Bible, included memorial offerings intended to cause God to remember the one offering, and sacrifices of praise which included loaves and meat, a portion of which was burned on the altar, a portion of which was given to the priests, and a portion of which was given back to the one offering, and shared within that person's community. The New Testament assumes this context of sacrificial meal sharing when talking about worship.

The tradition of eucharistic praying that develops into ByzBAS enshrines the concept of sacrifice throughout its prayers, and it includes:

1. the sacrifice of praise, a literal oblation in second temple worship;

2. the atonement sacrifice "for our sins and for the errors of the people";

3. the understanding that this worship stands in continuity with the worship recorded in the Hebrew Bible, and is identified with the worship offered by the apostles;

4. acknowledgment that Christ is the one offering, it is his very self that he offers, and he sanctifies his offering; this he accomplishes through his assembled body.

---

34. They are:
"1. The Eucharistic memorial in its entirety is considered a sacrifice offered in memory of Jesus, and in obedience to his command, as recounted in the story told in the prayer.
"2. In the course of this ritual memorial, again following Jesus' command, the Church offers bread and wine, the antitypes ([Byz]BAS: τὰ ἀντίτυπα) of Christ's body and blood.
"3. The Church then prays that the Father's acceptance of these gifts be confirmed by the coming of the Holy Spirit on them, so that they be sanctified for our salvation.
"4. When the prayer is over, the Church believes in faith that this has been accomplished."
(Taft, "Byzantine Anaphoral Oblation," 53.)

In this vein the most obvious offering the community of ByzBAS makes is bread and wine, which is Christ's sacrifice, because these are *shown* (ἀναδεῖξαι) by the Holy Spirit to be the body and blood of Christ himself. And yet this is not the only sacrificial offering that these prayers present: the whole assembly is the abiding incarnation of his body, offered for the world. It is this community, as Christ's sacrificed body, who participate in his auto-oblation by offering their very selves, taking as their examples the righteous of the Hebrew Bible and the apostles. The gifts, the people, all become Christified, and the sacrificial movement is unitive in its character, *showing* them to be integrated into his eternal offering. This is to say, in the sacrificial understanding of ByzBAS (echoing Athanasius's soteriology of deification, and Paul's before him),[35] just as Christ becomes human in order to offer his high-priestly sacrifice for humanity, the whole church offers itself as his sacrifice in order to become Christ.

---

35. Cf. *De inc.* 54:3; PG 25, 192B; 2 Cor 8:9.

VII

Authority and Confluence of Traditions in Aksum

The Heritage of the Anaphora of the Apostolic Tradition *in the Ethiopian* Anaphora of the Apostles

Andrij Hlabse, SJ

There can be little doubt that the so-called *Apostolic Tradition* [AT] of Hippolytus holds a significant place in liturgical scholarship. Yet a re-dimensioning of just what its importance might be has also been a consistent part of its story—for example, in tracing its origin and influences from Egypt to Rome, and then to various parts of the Christian *ecumene*. Today, still another kind of coordination may be reason to reconsider AT's provenance and especially to deepen understanding of its value for the liturgical prayer of the early church. The Ethiopian *Anaphora of the Apostles* [EAA] bears witness to an Eastern tradition that makes significant use of the anaphora in AT 4 as a liturgical model, employing it in the church's life of prayer.[1] Avenues for research on the relationship between AT and EAA have only recently significantly broadened, on account of new manuscript evidence enriching the image of Christian prayer in the earliest centuries of the church. Jacques Mercier brought

---

1. Indeed, via the Ethiopian tradition, the AT could possibly be re-linked with the church in whose ambit the text was first discovered—the Coptic-Egyptian.

172   *Further Issues in Eucharistic Praying in East and West*

to scholarly attention and entrusted to Alessandro Bausi the study of a fifth- to seventh-century version of the EAA in the *Aksumite Collection*, far older than the fourteenth-century redaction that had previously been the basis of scholarship.[2]

A new phase in the study of AT has begun. In the words of Emmanuel Fritch, a collaborator of Bausi's,

> The *unicum* manuscript of the Aksumite Collection provides us with crucial late antique liturgical material that goes beyond even our wildest expectations in answering longstanding questions about the nature of the liturgy practiced in Aksumite Christianity. The eucharistic prayer of St. Mark and an actual liturgical edition of the anaphora found in the *Apostolic Tradition* and known as the Anaphora of the Apostles were indeed available in Ge'ez in the late antique polity of the Aksumites. Additionally, the Aksumite editing of the anaphora is relatively easy to detect.[3]

While this discovery opens up larger vistas for exploration, the present investigation will limit itself to the study of how this recently published Ethiopian redaction incorporated the text of AT 4 into the EAA. Obviously, the newly discovered fifth- to seventh-century text of EAA plays a significant role in witnessing to the Ethiopian tradition's earliest known appropriation of AT 4's anaphora, and offers a mediating stage to its Medieval redaction. Through better understanding the relationship of AT 4 and the EAA, valuable insights can be gleaned about both the value and authority of the AT and its influence on the Ethiopian tradition.

This essay will proceed first by placing new evidence in its historical and scholarly context before analyzing the prayers themselves. First, although contemporary scholarly debate on the anaphora of the AT will largely be left aside,[4] a few crucial elements are highlighted that prove useful for understanding the EAA redaction. Then, the EAA in its recently discovered fifth- to seventh-century version will be presented in

---

2. Alessandro Bausi, Antonella Brita, Marco di Bella, Denis Nosnitsin, Nikolas Sarris, and Ira Rabin, "The *Aksumite Collection* or Codex Σ (*Sinodos of Qefreyā*, MS C_3-IV-71/C_3-IV-73, Ethio-SPaRe UM-039): Codicological and Palaeographical Observations. With a Note on Material Analysis of Inks," *COMSt Bulletin* 6, no. 2 (2020): 159–62.

3. Ibid., 91–92.

4. For a concise very recent summary and analysis see Paul F. Bradshaw, *Apostolic Tradition: A New Commentary* (Collegeville, MN: Liturgical Press Academic, 2023).

historical and liturgical context, with references to the fourteenth-century recension, especially where this is useful to highlight a change in perspective or continuing evolution of the liturgical text. Then EAA will be studied according to its various anaphoral elements, with particular attention given to the parts of AT 4 retained in the Ethiopian tradition, while observing what is also borrowed from Mark. This will permit some conclusions about the authority of the AT and its influence on the shape of Ethiopian Christian prayer.

Relevant Aspects of the So-Called *Apostolic Tradition* of Hippolytus in Context

As Paul Bradshaw notes, since the discovery and first publication of the document in 1848, "attempts to trace the evolution of eucharistic prayers have always had to take into account the anaphora found in the ancient church order usually identified as the *Apostolic Tradition*."[5] This is the case in spite of the fact that the original Greek text of AT remains lost (except for a few fragments), and scholarship must therefore principally rely on a number of translations—including in Bohairic, Sahidic, and Arabic, as well as the two most significant texts, the Latin[6] and the earlier of two Ethiopic versions.[7] The importance of the text is tied in part to the very consolidated, developed, and unified anaphora it presents for such an early period,[8] as well as the influence it has had on other

---

5. Paul F. Bradshaw, "Introduction: The Evolution of Early Anaphoras," in *Essays on Early Eastern Eucharistic Prayers*, ed. idem (Collegeville, MN: Liturgical Press, 1997), 10. See also his brief summary on the progression of scholarship on AT in Bradshaw, *Apostolic Tradition: A New Commentary*, 1–11.

6. This Latin text is the oldest extant manuscript, copied in the late fifth century from a translation of the Greek original thought to be one hundred years older. See Paul F. Bradshaw, *The Apostolic Tradition Reconstructed: A Text for Students* (Norwich: Alcuin Club and the Group for the Renewal of Worship, 2021), 5; and Paul F. Bradshaw, Maxwell E. Johnson, and L. Edward Phillips, *The Apostolic Tradition: A Commentary*, ed. Harold W. Attridge (Minneapolis: Fortress Press, 2002), 7.

7. This earlier Ethiopic translation was only published in 2011 by Alessandro Bausi and seems to be from the period between the end of the fifth and seventh centuries. See Bradshaw, *Apostolic Tradition Reconstructed*, 6–7. The documents AT influenced can also be helpful in reconstructing the text. See below.

8. Bradshaw, "Introduction," 10–11.

church order documents like the *Apostolic Constitutions* and its *Epitome*, the *Canons of Hippolytus*, and the *Testamentum Domini*.[9] Given its proposed paternal position in the genealogy of these church order texts, as well as the ample use of it in the EAA, the AT is clearly a piece of living literature within a developing and diverse early Christian tradition.

AT's status as living literature is traceable not only by using it as a basis to look forward at subsequent texts, but also by interrogating its own possible composition. Following a line of research proposed by Marcel Metzger in the late 1980s and early 1990s that AT, through "its lack of unity or logical progression, its frequent incoherences, doublets, and contradictions . . . had all the characteristics of a composite work,"[10] Bradshaw, along with his colleagues Maxwell Johnson and L. Edward Phillips in their 2002 collaborative study on AT, reevaluate AT's provenance and take another route than attribution to Hippolytus. They argue that AT is "an aggregation of material from different sources, quite probably arising from different geographical regions and almost certainly from different historical periods, from perhaps as early as the middle of the second century to as late as the middle of the fourth."[11] Bradshaw posits North Africa, Rome, and Egypt as regions of possible *origin* for the base of AT's text, although in his view this is still inconclusive.[12] It is important to note that while this approach tends to exclude consideration of AT as representative of the consolidated tradition of any one Christian community, it does not eliminate the antiquity of the material. Indeed, through its criteria, material even older than the early third century (a traditional dating for AT) may be brought to light.

The eucharistic prayer in AT 4 is a unique witness to whatever of its material dates from before the mid-fourth century.[13] There are no

---

9. Paul F. Bradshaw, *The Search for the Origins of Christian Worship: Sources and Methods for the Study of Early Liturgy* (New York: Oxford University Press, 2002), 76.

10. Bradshaw, *Apostolic Tradition Reconstructed*, 5.

11. Bradshaw, *Search*, 83. Cf. Bradshaw, Johnson, and Phillips, *Apostolic Tradition: A Commentary*, 13–15.

12. Bradshaw, *Apostolic Tradition Reconstructed*, 9. See Alistair Stewart for an alternative approach favorable to Roman provenance and a certain link to Hippolytus. Alistair C. Stewart, *Hippolytus on the Apostolic Tradition: An English Version with Introduction and Commentary* (Yonkers: St. Vladimir's Seminary Press, 2015), 32–33.

13. Bradshaw, *Apostolic Tradition Reconstructed*, 14n6.

parallels with AT's anaphora in the ante-Nicene period, except for perhaps *Didache* 9–10; even the *Strasbourg Papyrus* and Addai and Mari show important differences.[14] Some scholars have also put forward a link with the *Birkat ha-Mazon* in AT's case, including Enrico Mazza, who held that AT 4 was a direct inheritor of the *Birkat ha-Mazon*'s tripartite structure, via the *Didache*;[15] but there are difficulties in general with this Jewish-source theory, on account of studies that highlight that first-century Jewish practice in this respect was not (contrary to previous ideas) highly homogeneous.[16] Parallels must be sought in other early Christian sources, like theological writings, and here interesting insights emerge. "Quite a number of words and phrases" bear resemblance to the extant writings of Justin, Irenaeus, and Hippolytus.[17] Of particular note is the likely Greek word behind the Latin *"puer,"* namely παῖς, meaning either servant or child, which was employed by early Christians in reference to Christ before eventually falling out of use.[18] The same can be said for the "angel Christology" that calls Jesus the "messenger of [God's] will," based upon the LXX's version of Isaiah 9:5 and witnessed also by Justin and Irenaeus.[19] A similar typical ancient interpretation is found in the phrase "stretched out [his] hands when he was suffering," an allusion to Isaiah 65:2 that is also found in Barnabas and Justin.[20] Mazza has gone so far as to argue for a kind of general dependence on second-century Easter homilies (like Melito of Sardis's Περὶ Πάσχα), and sees this especially evidenced in the first part of the anaphora, which in his view substituted the more general first thanksgiving for creation with a thanksgiving for the paschal work of Christ.[21] These more primitive

---

14. Bradshaw, Johnson, and Phillips, *Apostolic Tradition: A Commentary*, 44.

15. Enrico Mazza, "Omelie pasquali e *birkat ha-mazon*: fonti dell'anafora di Ippolito?," *Ephemerides Liturgicae* 97 (1983): 479–81.

16. Cf. Bradshaw, *Search*, 23–46.

17. Bradshaw, Johnson, and Phillips, *Apostolic Tradition: A Commentary*, 44.

18. Ibid., 37. Other sources with παῖς include *Didache, 1 Clement, Barnabas,* and the *Martyrdom of Polycarp.* Cf. Ivi., note 1. Cf. Bradshaw, *Apostolic Tradition: A New Commentary*, 8–9.

19. Ivi. Cf. Justin, *1 Apologia* 63; *Dialogus cum Trypho.* 56, 76, 126–28; Irenaeus, *Demonstratio* 55–56.

20. Ibid., 47, also n. 46. Cf. *Barnabas* 12.4; Justin, *1 Apologia* 35; *Dialogus cum Trypho* 97.

21. Mazza, "Fonti di Ippolito," 479–81.

theological expressions point to the second century as a source for some part of AT 4's text, and the Ethiopian redactor of the EAA will need to address each of them.

By way of anticipation, in comparison with EAA, a few other comments can be made. While AT 4 has received many elements considered to be consonant with a fourth-century development and has a consolidated final shape, it lacks the *Sanctus* which was being incorporated elsewhere into eucharistic prayers at this time.[22] This places it in contrast with the early version of EAA as well. Still, the clear structure and unity of AT 4's anaphora in its final form is striking. I contend that the Ethiopian redactor gives strong evidence of having recognized and respected this integrated structure through the nature of his edits and his borrowings from Mark in redacting EAA. Practically nothing from AT is omitted or even reordered, but only embellished or redeployed.

The Ethiopian *Anaphora of the Apostles* in Context

The *Aksumite Collection*, which is being published bit by bit, includes a significantly more ancient (fifth- to seventh-century) recension of EAA.[23] On the one hand, it makes robust use of the anaphora handed on in AT 4, thus bearing witness to this document's great authority and importance in the Christian East.[24] On the other hand, it shows the influence of the Alexandrine tradition in elements that have been incorporated into its anaphoral structure.[25] The text of the EAA found in the *Aksumite Collection*, as translated into English by Emmanuel Fritsch, can be found in the middle column of the comparative chart in Appendix 2.[26]

---

22. Bradshaw, *Apostolic Tradition Reconstructed*, 14n6.

23. Cf. Alessandro Bausi, "La nuova versione Etiopica della Traditio Apostolica: edizione e traduzione preliminare," in *Christianity in Egypt: Literary Production and Intellectual Trends*, ed. Paolo Buzi and Alberto Camplani (Rome: Institutum patristicum Augustinianum, 2011), 19–69.

24. R. C. D. Jasper and G. J. Cuming, *Prayers of the Eucharist: Early and Reformed*, ed. Paul F. Bradshaw and Maxwell E. Johnson (Collegeville, MN: Liturgical Press Academic, 2019), 125.

25. Ibid., 123–25.

26. For the full text in English see Emmanuel Fritsch, "New Reflections on the Image of Late Antique and Medieval Ethiopian Liturgy," in *Liturgy's Imagined Past/s: Methodologies and Materials in the Writing of Liturgical History Today*, ed. Teresa Berger and Bryan D. Spinks (Collegeville, MN: Liturgical Press, 2016), 47–52.

Authority and Confluence of Traditions in Aksum 177

The *Aksumite Collection* itself is "a specific canonical-liturgical collection of the late antique and early medieval Ethiopian Church," so far known only in a *codex unicus*,[27] that likely belonged for various centuries to the 'Ura Mäsqäl church located high on a rocky outcropping in territory near the border of modern-day Ethiopia and Eritrea.[28] According to Bausi, unlike the later *Sinodos* collection, most of which has been translated from an Arabic *Vorlage*,[29]

> the Aksumite Collection contains a set of translations from Greek to Ge'ez (Ethiopic) that on linguistic and philological evidence are datable to the Aksumite period, to a time range between the fifth and the sixth or at the latest the seventh century CE, while the codex is not precisely dated, but datable to the thirteenth century or earlier.[30]

Fritsch, who has collaborated with Bausi in the publication and study of the *Aksumite Collection*, specifies even further, arguing that, "composed in an Egyptian milieu, it was translated from Greek into Ge'ez between 477 and 686/687."[31]

A crucial question posed is the relationship between the version of the AT found in the *Aksumite Collection* and the others extant, especially the Latin text from the Verona Palimpsest, the earliest known. The version of AT in the *Aksumite Collection* strongly confirms the content of the Latin and gives evidence of their common dependence on a Greek original. The *Aksumite Collection*, as Bausi writes, "is definitely also a new *independent* witness to the archetype of the 'so-called *Traditio apostolica*': numerous agreements between [the] Latin and 'Ethiopic I' [AT in the *Aksumite Collection*] versions testify to its oldest so far retrievable textual phase and configure, at the same time, conjunctive errors (innovations) of all the other witnesses."[32] To find similar texts in such distant places and relatively mutually isolated communities as the

---

27. Bausi et al., "*Aksumite Collection*," 127.

28. Ibid., 130–34.

29. Alessandro Bausi, "The 'So-called *Traditio apostolica*': Preliminary Observations on the New Ethiopic Evidence," in *Volksglaube im antiken Christentum*, ed. Heike Grieser and Andreas Merkt (Darmstadt: Wissenschaftliche Buchgesellschaft, 2009), 296.

30. Bausi et al., "*Aksumite Collection*," 127. Cf. Bausi, "'So-called *Traditio apostolica*,'" 291.

31. Fritsch, "New Reflections," 42–43.

32. Bausi, "'So-called *Traditio apostolica*,'" 300.

178 *Further Issues in Eucharistic Praying in East and West*

Italian peninsula and the Aksumite Kingdom is a robust testimony to the authenticity of the underlying text.[33] Bausi also presents some evidence to suggest that the Ethiopian text is "a slavish *verbum de verbo* translation of a Greek lost text," through a comparison of the Ge'ez with the known Greek fragment on the reception of the Eucharist early in the day.[34] If the version of AT present in the *Aksumite Collection* does depend on the same Greek archetype as the Latin, it offers the translation of a text compiled "as late as the middle of the fourth [century]," according to Bradshaw,[35] or of a "common archetype, dating to the 4th century at the latest" according to Bausi.[36] Given that the Greek text at the base of the *Aksumite Collection* was almost certainly transmitted to the Ethiopian Church via Egypt, this latter location is strengthened as a hypothetical source for both the Latin and Ge'ez versions.

The *Aksumite Collection* does not, however, contain the anaphora of AT 4 in its usual place with the rest of AT, instead transferring it to the later "euchological section" of the collection.[37] While depending largely on AT 4, the anaphora presents additions and changes. Fritsch argues that it "is found already edited for the liturgy,"[38] a reality confirmed by the presence of liturgical rubrics that indicate roles for the priest, a deacon, and the people. He names it the "Anaphora of the Apostles," "identifying this text with the well-known anaphora of the same name, without prejudging ways of explaining that identity."[39] The dependence of this early version of EAA on AT 4 can easily be seen by comparing the texts in parallel. The continuities and discontinuities in this appropriation will constitute the center of this investigation.

Before proceeding, a brief word on the previously known, more recent redaction of EAA is useful. It is found in a larger collection called the *Sinodos*, largely translated from Arabic and datable to the fourteenth cen-

---

33. Ibid., 304–5.
34. Ibid., 305–6, 308.
35. Bradshaw, *Search*, 83. Cf. Bradshaw, Johnson, and Phillips, *Apostolic Tradition: A Commentary*, 13–15.
36. Bausi, "'So-called *Traditio apostolica*,'" 304.
37. Fritsch, "New Reflections," 45. For the complete structure of the collection as recomposed by Bausi, cf. Bausi et al., "*Aksumite Collection*," 136–42. Bausi considers the AT as part four (folia 16v–29v), and the "Euchologion" as part ten (folia 46r–62v).
38. Fritsch, "New Reflections," 45.
39. Ivi. and note 17 therein.

tury.[40] Its text in English translation is in the third column of the comparative chart in Appendix 2.[41] This later version of the EAA also conserves almost all of AT 4's anaphora, but is obviously much longer than even its Ethiopian antecedent on account of additions that are particularly visible in the regular interventions of the deacon and the responses of the people. Although this previously known version was relied upon in much scholarship, for our purposes it suffices to note this difference of recensions, and to stress that the recently discovered, older text bears witness not only to the early authority of the AT as a liturgical source in ancient Eastern Christianity,[42] but also to a considerably shorter anaphoral text that would seem to put some previous hypotheses based upon the later, longer *textus receptus* in jeopardy. While this study focuses primarily on the use of AT 4 by the earlier EAA, comparison with this more recent version can also occasionally be instructive.

Alexandrine Influence on the Ethiopian
Anaphora of the Apostles

Before embarking on the examination of elements taken over from AT, the Alexandrine influence on the overall anaphoral structure of the EAA should be considered. In both recensions of the EAA, the evidence of an Alexandrine influence seems clear, although the evidence they present is not the same. As mentioned above, a Ge'ez translation of the Alexandrian Anaphora of Mark is contained in the same "euchological section" of the *Aksumite Collection* as the EAA.[43] Evidence for this influence

---

40. Cf. Bausi, "'So-called *Traditio apostolica*,'" 292–93; and Bradshaw and Johnson, *Prayers of the Eucharist*, 123. Another Ethiopian version of the AT is part of the *Synodus Alexandrina*, in which there exists an Ethiopic version of the *Seventy-one Canons* or *Statues of the Apostles*, themselves a part of the much larger collection called the *Sinodos*. See Bausi, "Nuova versione etiopica della Traditio," 21.

41. The English translation is that found in Bradshaw and Johnson, *Prayers of the Eucharist*, 126–32, itself adapted from Marcos Daoud, trans., *The Liturgy of the Ethiopian Church*, rev. ed., rev. H. E. Blatta Marsie Hazen (Cairo: Egyptian Book Press, 1959; reprinted Kingston, Jamaica: Ethiopian Orthodox Church, 1991), 69–76.

42. Bradshaw and Johnson, *Prayers of the Eucharist*, 125. Bradshaw and Johnson depend on the previously known version of EAA for their assessment that does, however, remain valid for the new EAA. Information from the new text has been incorporated into their views.

43. Fritsch, "New Reflections," 45–54.

is thus structural, textual, and contextual. Bradshaw and Johnson note that elements characteristic of early Alexandrine anaphoras are present in the EAA, while they are absent from the fourth-century redaction of AT. These Alexandrine elements include

1. the intercessions in the preface;

2. the post-*Sanctus* transition being lexically and thematically linked to the *Sanctus* (without the *Benedictus*), "Truly the holiness of your glory fills heaven and earth . . ." (V–VII c.) / "Truly heaven and earth are full . . ." (XIV c.);

3. and the epiclesis, which, although also developed to be more explicitly consecratory, makes reference to both the "Holy Spirit" and "power," a possible echo of the language of the British Museum Tablet and the first epiclesis of the anaphora of Sarapion.[44]

Although these scholars base their comparison on the later version of EAA available at the time of their study, these observations hold also for the more ancient version of the EAA, with some specifications that follow.

First, the intercessions appear in the earliest recension only in very abbreviated rubrical form: "Let the names be read here." There is no clear evidence of what exactly this might have entailed, although the commemoration of the governing bishops or the saints attested in the later version present an attractive option. It would seem to be an error, however, to read the elaborate benedictions that are attached to the intercession element in the fourteenth-century redaction—including the blessing of the heavens, the earth, and the people—into this bare instruction. Thus, while evidence for "preface intercessions" exists in both recensions of EAA, these two anaphoras present radically different configurations of this element—moving from a sparse rubric to a developed listing of names and blessings. The second "Alexandrine" element given—the style of the post-*Sanctus* transition—retains great similarity between recensions, but again is not identical, with the verb being given in the active rather than passive voice in the older document, "Truly the holiness of your glory *fills* heaven and earth." This element is not merely typically Alexandrine, however; the entire *Sanctus* block would seem to be an

---

44. Bradshaw and Johnson, *Prayers of the Eucharist*, 124.

addition to AT. The third element, the epiclesis, is substantially shared by the two versions of EAA, although the texts are not a verbatim match with one another. Finally, although not noted by Bradshaw and Johnson, perhaps because all anaphoras have an opening dialogue in their structure, the EAA does add Mark's opening line to this first element.

In light of these interwoven, characteristically Alexandrine elements, the anaphoral traits shared by EAA in common with AT in its fourth-century redacted form would include the initial dialogue, the initial thanksgiving in a christological key, the institution narrative (present in AT's final form, even if Bradshaw argues it was an interpolation), anamnesis, epiclesis (also present in the final form of AT), and a concluding doxology. Elements that would represent additions in harmony with the Alexandrine tradition are the intercessions in the preface, the *Sanctus* block (pre-*Sanctus*, *Sanctus*, and post-*Sanctus* transition), and a more direct and elaborate epiclesis over the gifts.

Fritsch provides a useful comparative chart of the Alexandrian Anaphora of Mark found in the "euchological section" of the *Aksumite Collection* and the EAA, in which these borrowings can clearly be seen in parallel.[45] Taking his invitation for continued scholarship based on this new evidence, I will argue below that, despite Fritch's contention that "the structure of the rite [of EAA] is largely carried by Mark," upon closer examination there is strong evidence that AT plays a decisive role in the shape and theology of the anaphora, while accepting certain Markan elements.[46]

The Use of the *Apostolic Tradition* in the Ethiopian *Anaphora of the Apostles*

Before turning to examine directly the texts of AT and EAA in their various corresponding units, a few methodological notes must be made. First, on account of this author's lack of knowledge of Ge'ez, the texts will be dealt with in English translations. This means that philological and lexical points will have a secondary position because of their dependence on the translations, yet these translations are trusted not to obscure real additions to the text and to reflect faithfully their phraseology. In spite of

---

45. Fritsch, "New Reflections," 47–54.
46. Ibid., 54.

this limit, much can still come to light, especially structurally. Second, the analysis will focus on the relationship between AT and the earliest known version of the EAA, since this represents AT's entrance into Ethiopian liturgy as best as can currently be known. Finally, the study will proceed element by element, striving to draw out relevant liturgical and theological points. The reader is referred also to the comparative charts of the texts at the beginning of each subsection for convenient comparison. Below, EAA refers to the early version of the *Aksumite Collection*; reference to the previously known fourteenth-century redaction of EAA will be made explicit.

The Opening Dialogue

Mark[47]	AT[48]	EAA[49]
THE DEACON SAYS: Stand well in order to offer! Look to the east! We watch!		THE DEACON SAYS: Stand well in order to offer! Look to the east! We watch!
THE BISHOP SAYS: The Lord [be] with you all. PEOPLE: And with your spirit.	'The Lord [be] with you.' AND LET THEM ALL SAY, 'And with your spirit.'	THE POPE SAYS: The Lord [be] with you. PEOPLE: With your spirit.
Lift up your hearts! PEOPLE: We have them with the Lord.	'Up [with your] hearts.' 'We have [them] to the Lord.'	Lift up your hearts! PEOPLE: We pray to the Lord.
Let us give thanks to the Lord! PEOPLE: It is right and just.	'Let us give thanks to the Lord.' 'It is worthy and just.'	Let us give thanks to the Lord! PEOPLE: It is right and just, he is worthy.

The opening dialogue between priest and people already shows signs of the encounter between AT and the Alexandrian tradition. The basic

---

47. This and all subsequent sections cite Mark from Fritsch, "New Reflections," 47–54.

48. This and all subsequent sections cite AT from Bradshaw, *Apostolic Tradition Recons*tructed, 14–15.

49. This and all subsequent sections cite EAA from Fritsch, "New Reflections," 47–52.

structure is the same in AT and EAA; and in this case Mark also corresponds. In EAA the dialogue is preceded by the invocation of the deacon to the people to prepare for the anaphora evidently brought over from Mark, "Stand well in order to offer! Look to the east! We watch!" The eschatological dimension of the liturgy, looking east and watching (for Christ who comes), is clear in these diaconal commands. In this context even standing as the posture of offering might be taken to have an eschatological dimension, perhaps in light of its connection to the Lord's Day (and so the Resurrection) made at the Council of Nicea (canon 20), whose canons are also found in the *Aksumite Collection*.[50] The deacon commands or exhorts the congregation, as well as plays a role within it, evidenced by his use of the pronoun "we," which is taken up in the dialogue that follows.

The EAA also changes the people's second response to the priest's "Lift up your hearts," to "We *pray* to the Lord," as opposed to the reference in AT simply to the heart again (*Habemus ad Dominum*), also found in Mark.[51] Interestingly, the simple reference to the heart is restored in the fourteenth-century EAA, although in it the last two units of the dialogue have been inverted, with this one therefore coming last. The earlier EAA also adds a phrase to its final response that makes an explicit reference to God's worthiness of thanks, "It is right and just, *he is worthy*."

The Initial Christological Thanksgiving

AT	EAA
AND SO LET HIM THEN CONTINUE: 'We render thanks to you, God, through your beloved servant Jesus Christ, whom in the last times[52] you sent to us as savior and redeemer	We give you thanks, O Lord, through your beloved Son our Savior Jesus Christ whom in the last days you sent to us as savior

---

50. Bausi et al., "*Aksumite Collection*," 140.

51. This change is not in the Anaphora of Mark transmitted in the *Aksumite Collection*. Cf. Fritsch, "New Reflections," 47.

52. Borrowing from Bradshaw's evaluation in *The Apostolic Tradition Reconstructed*, 9, (cf. note 6 above), the underlined text is thought to be the latest material added to AT, dating mostly from the late third or early fourth century. The rest of the text of AT 4, apart from the opening rubric preceding the anaphora (which comes from the earliest layer, of the second century), is from the second layer, of the early-to-mid third century. This way of distinguishing the layers of redaction is used throughout this text.

and messenger of your will, <u>who is your inseparable word, through whom you made all things and it was well pleasing to you,</u> [whom] you sent from heaven into the virgin's womb, . . .	and redeemer and the angel of your counsel.[53] He is the Word while he is faithful, him through whom you made all things, you having decided, and you sent him from heaven into the womb of a virgin.
	LET THE NAMES BE READ HERE.
<u>. . . and who conceived in the womb was incarnate and manifested as your Son, born from the Holy Spirit and the virgin;</u>	He became flesh and was carried in the womb and your Son was known from the Holy Spirit.

The christological thanksgiving which occupies the first place in the anaphora is largely taken over from AT to EAA in terms of its overall content. EAA seems to prefer AT to Mark strongly at this juncture. (For this reason, Mark is not reproduced here.) Both versions of the EAA, however, break up the flow of the christological thanksgiving in various ways. They insert intercessions from the Alexandrian tradition: the earlier EAA between the first mention in AT of Christ's being sent into the Virgin's womb and the second (along the seam which Bradshaw takes to be the place of a later interpolation due to language about Christ's birth *ex Spiritu sancto et virgine*), the later EAA before *both* mentions of the Incarnation. In the earlier EAA, then, the two mentions of the Incarnation serve as "bookends" to the prayers of intercession, a creative solution to the unusual repetition in AT. In both versions of EAA, the second mention of Christ's Incarnation serves as the conclusion to the opening christological thanksgiving and leads to the subsequent *Sanctus*.

In the first part of the christological prayer certain vocabulary changes could indicate development in theological perspective. The AT's archaic christological titles come into focus first. EAA changes the phrase "your beloved servant [παῖς] Jesus Christ" to "your beloved *Son our Savior*

---

53. Fritsch in fact translates "angel of your council," but this would make little sense in context and does not correspond to the Greek βουλῆς in LXX Isa 9:5. Presuming an error in Fritsch's English spelling, I have rendered it with the correct homophone "counsel." See notes 54 and 73 below.

Jesus Christ," thus eliminating this archaism in preference for language that more clearly reflects theological development after the Arian controversy. Another archaic title, though, is maintained: "messenger of your will" (*angelum voluntatis tuae*) in AT is rendered in EAA as "angel of your counsel."[54] This continuity may have been facilitated by the clearer double significance of the Greek word ἄγγελος (from LXX Isa 9:5: μεγάλης βουλῆς ἄγγελος), which primarily means "messenger," and thus does not necessarily pose a problematic angel-ontology with reference to Christ. (Indeed, the original Ge'ez word in EAA and whether it shares both valences would seem to be especially relevant here.) "Word" Christology is maintained from AT to EAA, although the English of EAA makes it difficult to understand what the modifying phrase may intend, as AT describes the Word as "inseparable" but EAA as "faithful." After this, Christ's role in the creation and then the decision to work the Incarnation (its first mention) are also retained in the older EAA.

The Intercessions

At this point, the text of EAA has the bare rubric "Let the names be read here," which indicates the intercessions. Here the two versions of EAA further diverge. The more ancient version has only this rubric, presumably leaving the clergy free to commemorate the appropriate people, such flexibility typically corresponding to more ancient liturgical practice. It should be noted that while anaphoral formularies had already been consolidating into more stable forms with less improvisation elsewhere in the Christian *ecumene*, in the relatively remote Aksumite Kingdom this freedom may have had a longer life, as evidenced by this rubric from the fifth to seventh centuries. The early EAA text does not specify who makes the commemoration but, given that elsewhere in the text the deacon's role is explicitly clarified and the rubric follows immediately upon a priest's part, it would seem reasonable to think these intercessions are made by the priest himself. Contrariwise, in the later EAA the deacon is explicitly given the role of reading a lengthy list of intercessions that include the patriarch and archbishop; Sts. Stephen, Zacharias, and John the Baptist; the evangelists; Mary, the Mother of God; the apostles; and other figures of the apostolic age. The "three hundred and eighteen" fathers of Nicea

---

54. See note 53 above.

also receive explicit mention; in the final place are all the living ordained ministers of the church. An "assistant priest" then intervenes with "The Prayer of Benediction 1," which includes a change to address Jesus Christ directly. The priest blesses the heavens, the earth, and the people, interceding for these last in various categories including the scholars of the church, those who give gifts, those who suffer, and the deceased. After this prayer an "assistant deacon" repeats an intercession for all the Christian people according to rank, and the priest then continues with subsequent sections found also in the earlier EAA. Both the intercessions of the later EAA and perhaps even more so those of the contemporaneous version of Mark found in the *Aksumite Collection* could offer clues as to what the earlier EAA's rubric intended.

As discussed above, in the earlier EAA the second mention of the Incarnation in AT, displaced after the intercessions, concludes this anaphoral element by returning to a christological key. Yet, this christological phrase is not retained integrally from AT in either version of EAA. The earlier EAA divides two phrases that refer to the Incarnation. The Latin AT reads, "*misisti de caelo in matricem virginis*; [/intercessions in EAA/] *quique, in utero habitus, incarnatus est et Filius tibi ostensus est, ex Spiritu sancto et virgine natus.*"[55] The redactor goes further still, though, perhaps seeking to solve another difficulty in the AT text—the up to three seemingly repetitive mentions of the Virgin Mary in close proximity (*in matricem virginis, in utero habitus, ex . . . virgine natus*). He displaces the last reference to "the virgin" to a subsequent unit of the anaphora, the post-*Sanctus* transition to the institution narrative, as will be seen below, and concludes the intercessions simply with the phrase "and your Son was known from the Holy Spirit." Perhaps the redactor took the second reference to "the womb" to be enough to indicate Mary, preferring to avoid an ostensible redundancy, since the first mention of Mary earlier in the christological thanksgiving makes direct reference to "the womb of a virgin" (*matricem virginis*). Although the Latin clearly shows the last mention of "the virgin" to be part of the phrase "*Filius . . . natus*" and

---

55. Anton Hänggi and Irmhard Pahl, eds., *Prex Eucharistica: Textus e variis liturgiis antiquioribus selecti*, 2nd ed., Spicilegium Fribrugense 12 (Fribourg: Éditions Universitaires Fribourg Suisse, 1968), 81. For Bradshaw's analysis of this element in AT, including the possible more ancient integrity of its first phrase, see Bradshaw, *Apostolic Tradition: A New Commentary*, 28.

not the subsequent one that begins with "*qui*" and introduces a new theological idea, the redactor of EAA extracts it from its original placement. One could attribute a freer hand to the redactor here, who potentially did not respect the underlying grammar of the Greek text he received. Although the later EAA instead has both references to the Incarnation at the conclusion of the intercessions, it also omits the last reference to "the virgin," employing it in a way similar to the earlier EAA in the post-*Sanctus*.

The Sanctus and Post-Sanctus

Mark	EAA
AND THE DEACON SAYS: You who are seated, stand up! [Further petitions . . .] THE DEACON SAYS: Look to the east! It is you who are above every rank and authority and power and dominations and every name which is named; before you stand millions of millions and myriads of holy angels and archangels; before you stand your glorious living creatures, the seraphs with six wings and the cherubs. With two wings they cover their face, with two their feet, with two they fly and all of them always sanctify you. Accept our own sanctification as, together with all those who sanctify you, we say to you: THE PEOPLE SAYS TOGETHER WITH THE ONE WHO OFFERS:	AND THE DEACON SAYS: You who are seated, stand up! To you, whom sanctify the thousands and countless thousands of holy angels and archangels and your glorious animals, the seraphim and cherubim who have six wings, with two wings they cover the face, and with two they cover their feet, and with two of their wings they fly and all of them continuously sanctify you together with all those who sanctify you, accept our own sanctification as we say to you: Holy! AND THE PEOPLE TOGETHER WITH THE ONE WHO OFFERS:

Holy holy holy Lord Sabaoth! Perfect [is] the holiness of your glory in heaven and on earth! THE ONE WHO OFFERS SAYS: Perfect therefore is all the heaven and the earth by the holiness of your glory through the Lord our Savior Jesus Christ.	Holy, holy, holy Lord Sabaoth! Heaven and earth are filled with the holiness of your glory! Truly the holiness of your glory fills heaven and earth through our Lord and our Savior Jesus Christ. Your holy Son having been born of a virgin in order to fulfill your will and to make a people for you,

Since the *Sanctus* is perhaps the most notable absence from the otherwise quite developed AT anaphora, here the source must be sought in another tradition—for Ethiopian Christianity, the Alexandrian, best represented in the version of Mark in the *Aksumite Collection*. In EAA the pre-*Sanctus* again begins with an invocation from the deacon, "You who are seated, stand up!" The invocation seems to be taken directly from Mark, although it is noteworthy that EAA does not take over a further set of petitions found in Mark immediately after this invocation, but skips, as it were, directly to the mention of the heavenly hosts that immediately introduces the *Sanctus*. From here, EAA closely mirrors Mark in its account of the numerous angels. It does, however, adjust a few elements from the Alexandrian anaphora: "millions of millions and myriads" is changed to "thousands and countless thousands" of angels; while reference is kept to the living creatures (presumably from Ezekiel), the cherubim, and the seraphim; in EAA the description of having "six wings" is moved to after the mention of both ranks of angels, whereas in Mark it comes immediately after the seraphim only, more literally in accord with Isaiah 6:2.[56] Both Mark and EAA share the description of the activity of these wings also from Isaiah 6:2, although according to Fritsch's translation EAA retains "with two wings they cover *the* face," whereas Mark has "*their* face." This may be another indicator of a *verbum de verbo* translation of the Greek by the redactor of EAA, argued elsewhere by Fritsch, as the

---

56. Unfortunately, this author cannot work with the Ge'ez to see if the grammatical referent of the "six wings" in EAA is singular or plural, given that the translation and location in English are somewhat ambiguous.

LXX reads "καὶ ταῖς μὲν δυσὶν κατεκάλυπτον τὸ πρόσωπον," with the singular neuter article. The later EAA retains the same essential pattern, with invocation by a deacon punctuating the different sections.

Mark and the more ancient EAA then transition more directly to the *Sanctus* with a very similar petition to accept the praise of those in the liturgical assembly in union with the ceaseless praise of heaven. Both have an intervening rubric that says, "[T]he people says together with the one who offers"; and the *Sanctus*, without the *Benedictus*, follows. In Mark the *Sanctus* concludes, "*Perfect* [is] the holiness of your glory in heaven and on earth," and the post-*Sanctus* begins, "*Perfect* therefore is all the heaven and the earth by the holiness of your glory through the Lord our Savior Jesus Christ." EAA's *Sanctus* instead contains the phrase, "Heaven and earth are *filled* with the holiness of your glory," and transitions with "Truly the holiness of your glory *fills* heaven and earth through our Lord and our Savior Jesus Christ." The "perfect–perfect" combination of Mark is different from the more typical "filled–fills" found in EAA (as also in Sarapion), but both keep the traditional Alexandrian idea of a textual echo in the post-*Sanctus* transition.

Lastly, although the issue cannot be treated here thoroughly, it is worth noting that this *Sanctus* without a *Benedictus* contradicts Gabriele Winkler's hypothesis regarding the originality of the *Sanctus-Benedictus* unit to the EAA. Based on a study of Ethiopian Enoch and the later version of EAA—the only text available at the time of her study—Winkler had concluded that (1) the inclusion of the *Benedictus* is not always a later addition in anaphoras, being original in EAA;[57] (2) an older form of the EAA did not have the institution narrative;[58] and (3) this parallels the Syriac tradition in various important ways, which would have brought the *Sanctus* (without *Benedictus*) into anaphoral use from the baptismal liturgy.[59] Evidence only recently available now surely contradicts (1), and

---

57. Gabriele Winkler, "A New Witness to the Missing Institution Narrative," in *Studia Liturgica Diversa: Essays in Honor of Paul F. Bradshaw*, ed. Maxwell E. Johnson and L. Edward Phillips (Portland: Pastoral Press, 2004), 125.

58. Ibid., 128.

59. Cf. ibid., 127–28. Ethiopian Enoch was a translation of an Aramaic (Syriac) version of Enoch. Cf. Maxwell E. Johnson, "Recent Research on the Anaphoral Sanctus: An Update and Hypothesis," in *Issues in Eucharistic Praying in East and West: Essays in Liturgical and Theological Analysis*, ed. Maxwell E. Johnson (Collegeville, MN: Liturgical Press, 2010), 171–72.

the oldest extant available evidence of EAA in the *Aksumite Collection* also witnesses against (2). Although better textual evidence could still be found, the authoritative use made of AT, along with Mark—both of which have an institution narrative—in EAA would seem to mitigate against (2) overall, as will be seen. In fact, the more ancient EAA with only the *Sanctus* could lend still greater credence to the theory of Egyptian influence by positing another characteristic Alexandrine element in the earliest known version of EAA: the *Sanctus* without the *Benedictus*.

The Institution Narrative

Mark	AT	EAA
	. . . who fulfilling your will and gaining for you a holy people,	[Your holy Son having been born of a virgin in order to fulfill your will and to make a people for you,]
	stretched out [his] hands when he was suffering, that he might release from suffering those who believed in you; <u>who when he was being handed over to voluntary suffering, that he might destroy death and break the bonds of the devil, and tread down hell and illuminate the righteous, and fix a limit and manifest the resurrection,</u>	stretched his hand(s), suffering in order to set the sufferers free, those who rely on you, he was given to suffering by his will in order to overcome death and break the bounds {bonds?} of [the devil (Latin)/Satan] and tram[ple she]ol and lead the holy ones and establish a covenant, and make known the resurrection.
In the night when they handed him over he took bread with his holy and blessed hands	<u>taking bread [and]</u>	In the night in which they betrayed him he took bread on his holy [hand]

Authority and Confluence of Traditions in Aksum 191

and, having blessed and broken it,	giving thanks to you,	and looked up toward you, toward his Father, and blessed and broke
he gave (it) to his very disciples and to his apostles as he said:	he said:	and gave to them his own disciples and said to them:
"Take, eat from it all of you: This is my body which is given for you unto the remission of sins."	"Take, eat, this is my body that will be broken for you."	"Take, eat, all of you: This is my body. It is given to you, this by which sin is remitted."
Again, likewise for the chalice after they had supper, having taken (it), he gave thanks and gave as he said:	Likewise also the cup, saying,	And likewise the chalice, having given thanks he said:
"Take, drink from it all of you: this is my blood of the new covenant which is poured for you unto the forgiveness of sins."	"This is my blood that is shed for you.	"Take, drink all of you, this is my blood which will be poured for you, by which sin is remitted."
As often as you eat this bread and drink this cup then you announce this my death and you believe in my resurrection.	When you do this, you do my remembrance."	When you do this, you will do it for the commemoration of me.

After the traditional post-*Sanctus* transitional phrase, the EAA reconnects with AT. Although Mark has a petition for blessing the offering after this phrase, asking via another verbal echo, "*Perfect*, O Lord this sacrifice," EAA leaves Mark at this point, not making use of another form of "fill" and preferring to keep AT essentially intact. Here the previously omitted conclusion of the phrase at the end of the christological thanksgiving in AT regarding the Son's being "born from the Holy Spirit *and the virgin*" is used creatively as a transition to reintroduce speaking about Christ's economy, now with reference to the Passion. "*Your holy Son having been born of a virgin* in order to fulfill your will and to make a people for you . . ." The redactor of EAA has used one part of a previously unified phrase from AT to conclude the intercessions before the *Sanctus*, "known from the Holy Spirit," and the other part to conclude the post-*Sanctus* and lead to the institution narrative, "Your holy Son having been born of a virgin . . ." While omitting practically nothing from AT, its prayer has been creatively redeployed. This use may not only represent adaptation, but also a real continuity of theological insight between AT and EAA. Inserting the reference to the Incarnation here as a reintroduction to the economy leading into the institution narrative, rather than removing it entirely, would seem to indicate a desired connection among Incarnation, Passion, and institution narrative. This theological perspective is certainly conveyed by AT's concise prayer, and EAA's redactor retains this theological cohesion all while adapting and moving pieces of the prayer. The rest of the phraseology recounting Christ's willing suffering and victory over death and the devil is substantially the same in AT and EAA. Concluding the introduction to the Last Supper narration, the uncertain phrase in AT *et terminum figat*, rendered "fix a limit" by Bradshaw, is rendered by Fritsch from Ge'ez as "establish a covenant" (a translation also found in the later EAA). Whether this "covenant" might refer in some way to the Eucharist itself is an interesting question, and its connection with the strong emphasis in Ethiopian Christianity on certain practices tied to Old Testament covenants could also be explored.

The Last Supper narrative itself shows borrowings from Mark in EAA to expand AT, but an overall reticence to eliminate anything from AT. EAA seems to take the introductory phrase "In the night in which they betrayed him" from Mark, having previously omitted the temporal reference in AT, "*who when* he was being handed over," and transferring its purpose here. EAA also takes from Mark reference to Christ's hands, to his blessing and breaking the bread, and to the disciples. The phrase "giving thanks to you [God the Father]" in AT is replaced and embellished with an addition found in neither AT nor the version of Mark in the *Aksumite Collection*[60]—"and looked up toward you, toward his Father, and blessed and broke . . ." The formula of Christ's words in EAA reflects Mark almost exactly, first with its intensifier "Take, eat, *all of you*." Then, rather than refer to Christ's body as being "*broken* for you," as AT does, EAA follows Mark with the more neutral "*given* for (Mark)/to (EAA) you" and instead adds a concluding phrase highlighting the redemptive value of the sacrifice, "this by which sin is remitted." The transition to the cup seems to be a synthesis of the more laconic AT and the descriptive Mark, with the latter's reference to Christ's thanksgiving. The words over the cup themselves take over much from Mark, but omit a few phases, here shown in brackets. "Take, drink [from it] all of you, this is my blood [of the new covenant] which will be[/is] poured for you, by which sin is remitted." In this last phrase EAA prefers a literal repetition of its own more descriptive words over the bread, rather than Mark's phrase "unto the forgiveness of sins." Still, nothing from AT's simple "This is my blood that is shed for you" is omitted, only enriched.[61]

The final phrase put on the lips of Christ reconnects EAA very closely with AT, rather than Mark, which is more extensive. EAA has simply "When you do this, you will do it for the commemoration of me."[62] Another indication of the Ethiopian redaction's preference for maintaining a closer similarity with AT's somewhat simpler institution narrative, rather

---

60. It is, however, present in the much later version of Mark found in Bradshaw and Johnson, *Prayers of the Eucharist*, 113.

61. It should also be noted that this older version of EAA does *not* contain the controversial rendering of the Lord's words at the Last Supper, "This *bread* is my body . . . This *cup* is my blood," common in other Ethiopian anaphoras, including the later EAA. For one perspective on this topic, in spite of some now out-of-date speculations on the history of the EAA, see Emmanuel Fritsch, "The Anaphoras of the Ge'ez Churches: A Challenging Orthodoxy," in *The Anaphoral Genesis of the Institution Narrative in Light of the Anaphora of Addai and Mari*, ed. Cesare Giraudo, OCA 295 (Rome: Edizioni Orientalia Christiana/Lilamé: Valore Italiano, 2013), 275–317.

62. The later EAA's institution narrative preserves these same essential parts of the priest but is much more elaborate in terms of his ritual gestures and the various responses by the people during the Last Supper account itself. Also AT, EAA, and the later EAA are distinguished in this last element by the tense and mood of the second verb "do": present indicative, future indicative, and imperative respectively. This needs to be verified in the Ge'ez.

than entirely substituting Mark for it in spite of many borrowings, are the phrases of Mark that are omitted from EAA. In addition to those already seen in the words over the cup, "from it" and "of the new covenant," EAA does not use what is italicized: "to his very disciples *and to his apostles*," "likewise for the chalice *after they had supper*," "have gave thanks *and gave*," and "as often as you *eat this bread and drink this cup then* you announce." These omissions keep EAA shorter and simpler than Mark, perhaps preserving something of AT's directness, with EAA presenting itself overall as an enriched version of the latter.

Anamnesis and Epiclesis

Mark	AT	EAA
As we announce the death of my Lord almighty, your Only Son, the Lord and God, the king over all and our Savior Jesus Christ, as we believe in his resurrection, his ascension in the heavens, we have offered to you this your own gift from your own gift.	Remembering therefore his death and resurrection, we offer to you the bread and cup, giving thanks to you because you have held us worthy to stand before you and minister to you.	As we commemorate his death and resurrection, we offer to you this bread and cup as we thank you. Thereby you made . . . for us so that we may stand (before) you and serve you sacerdotally.
We pray and beseech you to send the Holy Spirit and power in this offering upon the bread and the cup and to make the bread the body and the cup the blood of the new covenant of the Lord God, our king everywhere, Jesus Christ.	And we ask that, you would send your Holy Spirit on the oblation of the holy church.	We pray and beseech you so that you may send the Holy Spirit and power to this bread and cup and (that) you may make it the body and the blood of the Lord our Savior Jesus Christ. Amen.

THE DEACON ONLY WHISTLES.		
So that it may be for all who take from it for faith, for understanding, for healing, for a renewal of soul, body and spirit, so that to you, in this as in all things, be glorified . . .	gathering [us] into one, you will give to all who partake of the holy things [to partake] in the fullness of the Holy Spirit, for the strengthening of faith in truth, that we may praise . . .	Having united, may you give to all those who take (of it) that they will be for holiness and the fullness of the Holy Spirit, [the strengthening] of the (true) faith so that they may glorify . . .

The anamnesis of EAA follows nearly verbatim AT rather than Mark. Their similarity can easily be observed in the parallel columns. Relying on Fritsch's translation "have offered" in the anamnesis of Mark to reflect accurately the verb tense in Ge'ez, we might see here the Egyptian aorist in the offering—but this characteristic element is not retained in EAA, which takes the present tense "offer" from AT.

At the epiclesis, however, the influence of the Alexandrian Mark is seen once again. Along with the very close phraseology in general, most notable in this respect is the request present in both prayers that God send "the Holy Spirit and power." Here there may be a Logos epiclesis in addition to a pneumatological one. Such a prayer pattern can already be found in Sarapion of Thmuis's anaphora from around the middle of the fourth century in Egypt.[63] Mary Farag contends that such δύναμις epicleses ought to be read as a reference to the Son in light of Athanasian modes of naming the Son and the Holy Spirit, especially relevant in the post-Nicene Egyptian context.[64] The redactor of EAA's ancient version removes AT's simpler request for God to send the "Holy Spirit on the oblation of the holy church" for a much more explicit consecratory formula with reference to the bread and cup being "made" the body and

63. Bradshaw and Johnson, *Prayers of the Eucharist*, 94–95.
64. Mary K. Farag, "Δύναμις Epicleses: An Athanasian Perspective," *Studia Liturgica* 39, no. 1 (2009): 63–79. Christ is called θεοῦ δύναμιν καὶ θεοῦ σοφίαν in 1 Cor 1:24, a key phrase in the Christology of Athanasius.

blood of Christ. The epiclesis of EAA reads, "We pray and beseech you so that you may send the Holy Spirit and power to this bread and cup and (that) you make it the body and the blood of the Lord our Savior Jesus Christ. Amen."

The epiclesis continues in both AT and EAA in a prayer over the people. Here, except for the final part, EAA follows AT quite precisely in petitions for the communicants that request unity, fullness of the Holy Spirit, and strengthening of faith in truth/the true faith in order to render God glory. The later EAA has these same features in both epicleses, although the first part of its epiclesis attributes the power to transform grammatically to the Holy Spirit, "May *he make* . . ." rather than "*you make* . . ." It also adds between the two parts of the epiclesis responses from the people and an exclamation by the deacon of the request for "the good communion of the Holy Spirit," which can be considered proleptic of the priest's second epicletic prayer that follows. It could be argued that here at the epiclesis EAA is least faithful to AT's sleeker form, by having structurally (although not theologically) added a "cesura" between the epiclesis over the gifts and that over the community via a more solemn and explicit consecratory formula and an "Amen."

Concluding Doxology

Mark	AT	EAA
. . . be glorified your holy and blessed name in everything, with Jesus Christ and the Holy Spirit.	. . . that we may praise and glorify you through your servant Jesus Christ, through whom [be] glory and honor to you, in your holy church,	. . . so that they may glorify and praise you and your Son our Savior Jesus Christ with the Holy Spirit.
THE PEOPLE SAY: As it was, is and shall be, and become for generations of generations for ever and ever. Amen.	both now and to the ages of ages. Amen.'	AND THE PEOPLE SAY: As it was, is, and shall be for ever and ever. Amen.

The concerns for trinitarian orthodoxy found in EAA's reformulations of some archaic christological expressions in the initial thanksgiving return in another form in the concluding doxology. Although EAA follows AT very closely in the second part of the epiclesis, at its end the redactor removes AT's more archaic "that we may praise and glorify you *through your servant (παῖς) Jesus Christ, through whom [be] glory and honor to you, in your holy church.*" Instead of references to Christ as παῖς and to the church, a full and grammatically coordinated trinitarian doxology is inserted. Theologically it shares more with Mark, although not strictly lexically. EAA reads "that they may glorify and praise you *and your Son our Savior Jesus Christ with the Holy Spirit.*" Notice should be given first to the more explicit titles "Son and Savior" given to Christ in place of παῖς as before, and to the mention of the Holy Spirit rather than the church. In addition, the Three Persons of the Trinity are equally made explicit recipients of the praise of the people—as God the Father is said to be praised not "through" Christ "in" the church [AT], but rather praise is given to God the Father "*and*" Jesus Christ "*with*" the Holy Spirit. These important changes reflect well not only the Arian controversy, which may underlie changes in the initial thanksgiving, but also the full trinitarian development of the First Council of Constantinople of 381. Finally, EAA, like Mark, places the conclusion of the doxology—"as it was, is, and shall be for ever and ever. Amen."—in the mouth of the people rather than of the priest [in AT]. In the later EAA the trinitarian invocations are expanded and intensified through various repetitions by the priest and the people.

Conclusion

The preceding analysis leads to several conclusions regarding the authority of AT and the Ethiopian redaction's strategies in negotiating the meeting of two distinct liturgical traditions. First, evidence shows AT had an authoritative role in the structuring of the EAA, contrary to Fritsch's earlier view that "the structure of the rite is largely carried by Mark."[65] While various elements of the Alexandrian liturgical tradition are synthesized with AT's form, practically nothing is *omitted* from AT—a striking

---

65. Fritsch, "New Reflections," 54.

fact. Conversely, the EAA redaction does permit omissions from Mark, not only of entire sections in preference to AT, but also while borrowing from Mark itself. Certainly the use of Mark speaks of the importance of certain Egyptian elements in Ethiopian worship; yet, it seems accurate to say that Mark was adapted into and enriched AT in forming EAA, not the inverse. Introduction of elements from Mark—like the intercessions and *Sanctus*—is associated with the progression of AT's prayers. Mark can also embellish AT, as in the institution narrative, but rarely does it simply substitute it where the two share anaphoral elements. This happens only when there are evident theological concerns and, relatedly, at the epiclesis. Textual changes to AT's basic meaning seem to come in two varieties: first, when theological concerns about christological or trinitarian orthodoxy require a change to archaisms and, second, when in certain very particular moments of the liturgy the authority of the Alexandrian tradition is preferred. There seems nonetheless to be an effort to maintain AT's integrity and to hold it as the authoritative structuring element of the anaphora. Those parts of the EAA which simply prefer AT directly over Mark's corresponding parts (including the "famous aorist" of the offering) express AT's governing position in this process succinctly.

Nonetheless, the EAA does creatively engage with AT's anaphora even when it does not change its words. This is seen especially in the way that EAA deals with the christological and Marian repetitions in the first part of the anaphora. The mentions of the Incarnation are separated, so as to serve as conclusions to the initial christological thanksgiving and the intercessions, respectively. Further, the EAA seems to be attentive to the various references to Mary in these phrases, and further divides them. This reveals a perception both stylistic and theological. After the *Sanctus* and post-*Sanctus*, the Marian and Incarnational reference is used to reintroduce the economy, now in respect to the Passion—a kind of theological introduction to the institution narrative in harmony with the anaphoral logic of AT and contrasting with Mark's lack of transition to it.[66] Such strategic (as opposed to casual) division of the text demonstrates both an attentive reading of AT and an attunement to how its text could be adapted for Ethiopian worship. All these facts would seem to mitigate against Bradshaw's recent hypothesis that "the reason for the omission

---

66. Cf. Matthieu Smyth, "The Anaphora of the So-called 'Apostolic Tradition,'" 83, in *Issues in Eucharistic Praying in East and West*, ed. Johnson, 71–98.

[of AT's anaphora in the *Aksumite Collection* from its usual place], therefore, is probably that it was so different from the prayer(s) known to its translator as to be of no practical use."[67] While it might be possible to surmise that an Alexandrian-structured anaphora like Mark was more familiar to the Ethiopian redactor than AT's West-Syrian structure, the redactor clearly found AT of enough authority and "use" to be adapted in a serious and attentive way to the Aksumite context.

Not only has the discovery of the fifth- to seventh-century version of EAA in the *Aksumite Collection* gone "beyond even our wildest expectations in answering longstanding questions about the nature of the liturgy practiced in Aksumite Christianity," as Fritsch has said.[68] A careful analysis has also revealed the living encounter of two liturgical traditions under the guidance of a (presumably) Ethiopian redactor, displaying something of this tradition's theological and liturgical sensibilities not just in one discrete eucharistic anaphora, but through its combination of two diverse traditions of prayer. The intelligent adaptations to what was presumably received from Egypt seen in EAA testify not only to AT's authority for liturgical practice even in the relatively remote Aksumite Kingdom, but also to the lively theological and liturgical awareness of the Ge'ez tradition within the period from the fifth to the seventh century.

Appendix 1

Traditio Apostolica 4 in Prex Eucharistica[69]

Qui cumque factus fuerit episcopus, omnes os offerant pacis, saluntantes eum quia dignus effectus est. Illi vero offerant diacones oblationem, quique imponens manus in eam, cum omni presbyterio, dicat gratias agens : Dominus vobiscum. Et omnes dicant : Et cum spiritu tuo. Sursum corda.—Habemus ad Dominum. Gratias agamus Domino.—Dignum et iustum est. Et sic iam prosequatur :

---

67. Bradshaw, *Apostolic Tradition: A New Commentary*, 22.
68. Fritsch, "New Reflections," 91.
69. The Latin text is reproduced from Hänggi and Pahl, *Prex Eucharistica*, 80–81, while reproducing visually Bradshaw's suggestions for the latter two redactional layers from *The Apostolic Tradition Reconstructed*. Cf. note 53.

Gratias tibi referimus, Deus, per dilectum puerum tuum Iesum Christum, quem

   in ultimis temporibus

misisti nobis salvatorem et redemptoerm et angelum voluntatis tuae,

   qui est Verbum tuum inseparabile, per quem omnia fecisti, et <cum> beneplacitum tibi fuit,

misisti de caelo in matricem verginis ;

   quique, in utero habitus, incarnatus est et Filius tibi ostensus est, ex Spiritu sancto et virgine natus.

Qui voluntatem tuam complens et populum sanctum tibi adquirens, extendit manus, cum pateretur, ut a passione liberaret eos qui in te crediderunt.

   Qui cumque traderetur voluntariae passioni, ut mortem solvat et vincula diaboli dirumpat, et infernum calcet et iustos illuminet, et terminum figat et resurrectionem manifestet, accipiens panem, gratias tibi agens dixit : Accipite, manducate, hoc est corpus meum quod pro vobis confringetur. Similiter et calicem dicens : Hic est sanguis meus, qui pro vobis effunditur. Quando hoc facitis, meam commemorationem facitis.

   Memores igitur mortis et resurrectionis eius,

offerimus tibi panem et calicem, gratias tibi agentes, quia nos dignos habuisti adstare coram te et tibi ministrare. Et petimus, ut

   mittas Spiritum tuum sanctum in oblationem sanctae Ecclesiae ;

in unum congregans, des omnibus qui percipiunt <de> sanctis in repletionem Spiritus sancti, ad confirmationem fidei in veritate, ut te laudemus et glorificemus per puerum tuum Iesum Christum : per quem tibi gloria et honor Patri et Filio cum sancto Spiritu in sancta Ecclesia tua et nunc et in saecula saeculorum. Amen.

Appendix 2

AT 4 with redactional layers[70] & EAA V-VII c. text[71] and XIV c. redaction[72]

	AT 4 (final redaction IV c.?)	Ethiopian Anaphora of the Apostles (V-VII c.)	Ethiopian Anaphora of the Apostles (XIV c. redaction)
	WHEN HE HAS BEEN MADE BISHOP, LET ALL OFFER THE MOUTH OF PEACE, GREETING HIM BECAUSE HE HAS BEEN MADE WORTHY. AND LET THE DEACONS BRING HIM THE OBLATION, AND LET HIM, LAYING HANDS ON IT WILL ALL THE PRESBYTERY, SAY, GIVING THANKS:		THE ANAPHORA OF OUR FATHERS THE APOSTLES, MAY THE BLESSING OF THEIR PRAYER BE WITH OUR RULERS AND PEOPLE, UNTO THE AGES OF AGES. AMEN.
DIALGOUE	'The Lord [be] with you.' AND LET THEM ALL SAY, 'And with your spirit.'	THE DEACON SAYS: Stand well in order to offer! Look to the east! We watch! THE POPE SAYS: The Lord [be] with you. PEOPLE: With your spirit.	PRIEST: The Lord be with all of you. PEOPLE: And with your spirit.
	'Up [with your] hearts.' 'We have [them] to the Lord.'	Lift up your hearts! PEOPLE: We pray to the Lord.	

70. The text of AT is taken from Bradshaw, *Apostolic Tradition Reconstructed*, 14–15.
71. The text of the earlier EAA is from Fritsch, "New Reflections," 47–52.
72. The text of the later EAA is that in Bradshaw and Johnson, *Prayers of the Eucharist*, 126–31.

INITIAL THANKSGIVING, XC-logical	'Let us give thanks to the Lord.' 'It is worthy and just.' AND SO LET HIM THEN CONTINUE: 'We render thanks to you, God, through your beloved servant Jesus Christ, whom <u>in the last times you sent to us as savior and redeemer and messenger of your will, who is your inseparable word, through whom you made all things and it was well pleasing to you,</u> [whom] you sent from heaven into the virgin's womb, . . .	Let us give thanks to the Lord! PEOPLE: It is right and just, he is worthy. We give you thanks, O Lord, through your beloved Son our Savior Jesus Christ whom in the last days you sent to us as savior and redeemer and the angel of your counsel[73]. He is the Word while he is faithful, him through whom you made all things, you having decided, and you sent him from heaven into the womb of a virgin.	PRIEST: Give thanks unto our God. PEOPLE: It is right, it is just. PRIEST: Lift up your hearts. PEOPLE: We have lifted them up unto the Lord our God. We give thanks to you, O Lord, through your beloved Son our Lord Jesus, who in the last days you sent to us, your Son, the Savior and Redeemer, the messenger of your counsel. The Word is he, who is from you, and through whom you made all things according to your will.
INTERCESSIONS		LET THE NAMES BE READ HERE.	DEACON: For the sake of the blessed and holy Patriarch Abba (__) and the blessed Archbishop

73. This word has been corrected from Fritsch's misspelled English "council." See n. 53 above.

Abba (__), while they yet give you thanks in their prayer and their supplications: Stephen, the first martyr, Zacharias the priest and John the Baptist. And for the sake of all the saints and martyrs who have gone to their rest in faith: Matthew and Mark, Luke, and John, the four Evangelists; Mary the mother of God, Simon Peter and Andrew, James and John, Philip and Bartholomew, Thomas and Matthew, Thaddaeus and Nathanael, James the son of Alphaeus and Matthias, the twelve apostles; and James the Apostle, brother of the Lord, Bishop of Jerusalem: Paul, Timothy, Silas, and Barnabas; Titus, Philemon, and Clement, the seventy-two disciples, the five hundred brethren, the three hundred and eighteen Orthodox; may the prayers of them all come unto us and visit us together with them.

And remember the peace of the universal apostolic church, which was made by Christ through His precious blood. Remember all the patriarchs, archbishops, bishops, priests, and deacons who keep straight the way of the true word.

THE ASSISTANT PRIEST SHALL SAY "THE PRAYER OF BENEDICTION (1)" OF ST. BASIL: O holy Trinity, Father, Son, and Holy Spirit, bless your people, beloved Christians, with heavenly and earthly blessings.

(1) BENEDICTION OVER THE PEOPLE. WHEN THE ASSISTANT PRIEST SAYS "BLESS," THE MINISTERING PRIEST SHALL BLESS IN THE APPOINTED DIRECTION.

And send upon us the grace of the Holy Spirit, and keep the doors of your holy church open unto us in mercy and in faith; and perfect unto us the faith of your holy Trinity unto our last breath. O my Lord Jesus Christ, visit the sick of your people; heal them; and guide our fathers and our brothers who have journeyed, becoming strangers: bring them back to their dwelling places in peace and in health.

Bless the airs of heaven (+ TOWARD HEAVEN), and the rains and the fruits of the earth of this year, in accordance with your grace, and make joy and gladness prevail perpetually on the face of the earth (+ TOWARD THE EARTH). And confirm for us your peace. Turn the hearts of mighty kings to deal kindly with us always.

Grant peace to the scholars of the church, who are continually gathered in Thy holy church; to all, to each by their several names, in the presence of powerful rulers, O our God, increase Thy peace.

Rest the souls of our ancestors, both our brothers and sisters who have fallen asleep and gained their rest in the right faith.

And bless those who give gifts of incense (+ OVER THE PEOPLE), bread and wine, ointment and oil, decorations and reading books, and vessels for the sanctuary, that Christ our God may give them their reward in the heavenly Jerusalem. And all of them that are assembled with us to entreat for mercy, Christ our God have mercy upon them: and all them that give alms before your awful and terrifying throne, receive.

And comfort every straitened soul, those who are in chains, and those who are in exile or captivity.

And those who are held in bitter servitude, our God, deliver them in your mercy. And all of them who have entrusted to us to remember them in our supplications to you O our Master Jesus Christ, remember them in your heavenly kingdom, and remember me, your sinful servant.

O Lord, save your people and bless your inheritance (+ OVER THE PEOPLE), feed them and lift them up forever.

ASST. DEACON: Lord pity and have mercy upon the patriarchs, archbishops, bishops, priests, deacons, and all the Christian people.

| SANCTUS | and who conceived in the womb was incarnate and manifested as your Son, born from the Holy Spirit. . . . | He became flesh and was carried in the womb and your Son was known from the Holy Spirit.

AND THE DEACON SAYS: You who are seated, stand up!

To you, whom sanctify the thousands and countless thousands of holy angels and archangels and your glorious animals, the seraphim and cherubim who have six wings,

with two wings they cover the face, and with two they cover their feet, and with two of their wings they fly | PRIEST: To these and to all grant rest to their souls, and have mercy upon them. Your Son whom you sent from heaven to the womb of a virgin, who was conceived in her womb, and was made flesh and your Son who became known by the Holy Spirit.

DEACON: You that are sitting, stand up.

PRIEST: There stand before you a thousand thousands and ten thousand times ten thousand, both the holy angles and archangels and your honorable beasts, each with six wings. (DEACON: Look to the east.) With two of their wings they cover their face, with two of their wings they cover their feet, and with two of their wings they fly from end to end of the world. |

Authority and Confluence of Traditions in Aksum 209

	and all of them continuously sanctify you together with all those who sanctify you, accept our own sanctification as we say to you: Holy!	(DEACON: Let us be attentive.) And they all constantly hallow and praise you, with all of those who hallow and praise you. Receive also our hallowing, which we utter to you: Holy, holy, holy, perfect Lord of hosts.
	AND THE PEOPLE TOGETHER WITH THE ONE WHO OFFERS: Holy, holy, holy Lord Sabaoth! Heaven and earth are filled with the holiness of your glory!	(DEACON: Answer you all.) PEOPLE: Holy holy holy, perfect Lord of hosts, heaven and earth are full of the holiness of your glory.
<u>ALEX.</u> <u>POST-SANTUS</u> ... and the virgin; who fulfilling your will and gaining for you a holy people,. . . .	Truly the holiness of your glory fills heaven and earth through our Lord and our Savior Jesus Christ. Your holy Son having been born of a virgin in order to fulfill your will and to make a people for you,	PRIEST: Truly heaven and earth are full of the holiness of your glory, through our Lord, God and Savior Jesus Christ, your holy Son. He came and was born of a virgin, so that he might fulfill your will and make a people for yourself. PEOPLE: Remember us all in your kingdom; remember us, Lord, Master, in your kingdom;

210   *Further Issues in Eucharistic Praying in East and West*

INSTIT. NARR.	. . . stretched out [his] hands when he was suffering, that he might release from suffering those who believed in you; who when he was being handed over to voluntary suffering, that he might destroy death and break the bonds of the devil, and tread down hell and illuminate the righteous, and fix a limit and manifest the resurrection.	stretched his hand(s), suffering in order to set the sufferers free, those who rely on you, he was given to suffering by his will in order to overcome death and break the bounds {bonds?} of [the devil (Latin)/Satan] and tramp[ple she]ol and lead the holy ones and establish a covenant, and make known the resurrection.	remember us, Lord, in your kingdom, as you remembered the thief on the right hand when you were on the tree of the holy cross. THEN THE ASSISTANT PRIEST SHALL PUT ON GRAINS OF INCENSE, AND PRESENT THE CENSER BOWL WITH LID TILTED BACK, TO THE CELEBRANT, WHO SHALL CROSS HIS TWO HANDS IN THE SMOKE OF THE INCENSE, THEN PASSING THEM OVER THE BREAD AND THE CUP THREE TIMES EACH. PRIEST: He stretched out his hands in the passion, suffering to save the sufferers that trust in him; he, who was delivered to the passion that he might destroy death, break the bonds of Satan, tread down hell, lead forth the saints, establish a covenant and make known his resurrection.

Authority and Confluence of Traditions in Aksum   211

Later incipit INSTIT. NARR.	taking bread [and]	In the night in which they betrayed him he took bread on his holy [hand]	In the same night that they betrayed him, he took bread in his holy, blessed, and spotless hands. (AT THIS TIME HE SHALL RAISE THE HOST.)
	giving thanks to you,	and looked up toward you, toward his Father, and blessed and broke	PEOPLE: We believe that this is he, truly we believe. PRIEST: He looked up to heaven toward you, his Father, gave thanks, blessed and broke (+ OVER THE BREAD THREE TIMES. THEN HE SHALL INDENT THE HOST LIGHTLY WITH HIS THUMB IN FIVE PLACES WITHOUT SEPARATION.) And He gave to His disciples and said unto them:
	he said:	and gave to them his own disciples and said to them:	
	"Take, eat, this is my body that will be broken for you."	"Take, eat, all of you: This is my body. It is given to you, this by which sin is remitted."	Take, eat, this (POINTING) bread is truly my body which will be broken on your behalf for the remission of sin.

212 *Further Issues in Eucharistic Praying in East and West*

Likewise also the cup, saying, "This is my blood that is shed for you."	And likewise the chalice, having given thanks he said: "Take, drink all of you, this is my blood which will be poured for you, by which sin is remitted."	PEOPLE: Amen. Amen. Amen. We believe and confess, we glorify you, O our Lord and our God; that this is He we truly believe. PRIEST: And likewise also the cup giving thanks, blessing it (+ OVER THE CUP THREE TIMES), and hallowing it, He gave it to His disciples, and said unto them: Take, drink, this (POINTING) cup is My blood which will be shed on your behalf as a propitiation for many. HE SHALL THEN MOVE THE CUP WITH HIS RIGHT HAND IN THE SIGN OF THE CROSS. PEOPLE: Amen. Amen. Amen. We believe and confess, we glorify you, O our Lord and God; that this is He we truly believe.

Authority and Confluence of Traditions in Aksum   213

	When you do this, you do my remembrance."	When you do this, you will do it for the commemoration of me.	PRIEST: And as often as you do this, do it in remembrance of me. PEOPLE: We proclaim your death, Lord, and your holy resurrection; we believe in your ascension and your second advent. We glorify you, and confess you, we offer our prayer to you and supplicate you our Lord and our God.
ANAMNESIS	Remembering therefore his death and resurrection, we offer to you the bread and cup, giving thanks to you because you have held us worthy to stand before you and minister to you.	As we commemorate his death and resurrection, we offer to you this bread and cup as we thank you. Thereby you made . . . for us so that we may stand (before) you and serve you sacerdotally.	PRIEST: Now, Lord, we remember your death and your resurrection. We confess you and we offer to you this bread and this cup, giving thanks to you; and thereby you have made us worthy of the joy of standing before you and ministering to you.
EPICLESIS (*CONSACR.*)	And we ask that, you would send your Holy Spirit on the oblation of the holy church.	We pray and beseech you so that you may send the Holy Spirit and power to this bread and cup and (that) you may make it the body	We pray and beseech you, O Lord, that you would send the Holy Spirit and power upon this bread and upon this cup. May he

		and the blood of the Lord our Savior Jesus Christ. Amen.	make them the body and blood of our Lord, God, and Savior Jesus Christ, unto the ages of ages. PEOPLE: Amen. Lord, pity us, Lord spare us, Lord have mercy on us. DEACON: With all our heart let us beseech the Lord our God that he may grant to us the good communion of the Holy Spirit. PEOPLE: As it was, is, and shall be unto generations of generations, world without end.
EPICLESIS OVER THE PEOPLE	gathering [us] into one, you will give to all who partake of the holy things [to partake] in the fullness of the Holy Spirit, for the strengthening of faith in truth, that we may praise and glorify you through your servant Jesus Christ,	Having united, may you give to all those who take (of it) that they will be for holiness and the fullness of the Holy Spirit, [the strengthening] of the (true) faith so that they may glorify and praise you and your Son our Savior Jesus Christ with the Holy Spirit.	PRIEST: Grant it together to all of them that partake of it, that it may be to them for sanctification and for filling with the Holy Spirit and for strengthening of the true faith, that they may hallow and praise you and your beloved Son, Jesus Christ with the Holy Spirit.
DOXOLOGY	through whom [be] glory and honor to you, in your holy church,		

Authority and Confluence of Traditions in Aksum

both now and to the ages of ages. Amen.'	AND THE PEOPLE SAYS: As it was, is, and shall be for ever and ever. Amen.	PEOPLE: Amen. PRIEST: Grant us to be united through your Holy Spirit, and heal us by this oblation, that we may live in you for ever. (THE PEOPLE REPEAT HIS WORDS.) Blessed be the Name of the Lord, and blessed be he that comes in the Name of the Lord, and let the Name of the Lord, and let the Name of his glory, be blessed. So be it. So be it blessed. (THE PEOPLE REPEAT HIS WORDS.) Send the grace of the Holy Spirit upon us. (THE PEOPLE REPEAT HIS WORDS.)

VIII

English Vernacular Translation of the Roman Canon

Julia Canonico

Sacrosanctum Concilium (SC), the Constitution on the Sacred Liturgy from the Second Vatican Council, explicitly calls for the reform and restoration of the liturgy in order that the faithful be led to "full, conscious, and active participation in liturgical celebration." Although the document itself does not specify the details of this reform, it does stipulate its general vision, mainly that

> the Liturgy is made up of immutable elements divinely instituted, and of elements subject to change. These [elements subject to change] not only may but ought to be changed with the passage of time if they have suffered from the intrusion of anything out of harmony with the inner nature of the Liturgy or have become unsuited to it. In this restoration, both texts and rites should be drawn up so that they express more clearly the holy things which they signify; the Christian people, so far as possible, should be enabled to understand them with ease and to take part in them fully, actively, and as befits a community.[1]

While the council documents did not call for the translation of all liturgical texts into the vernacular, especially the Eucharistic Prayer, this was the eventual result of the liturgical reforms that followed the council.

---

1. Vatican Council II, *Sacrosanctum Concilium* 14, 21 (December 4, 1963), Vatican.va.

This essay traces the reform and translation of one particular prayer in the Roman Catholic liturgy: the Roman Canon. This venerable anaphora acquired its definitive form between the fourth and seventh centuries, and has not been significantly changed since the time of Pope Gregory the Great.[2] Its tradition is notable because it displays a unique character among ancient anaphoras, not to mention the fact that it held near ubiquitous use in the Roman church throughout history (almost exclusively recited in Latin). The Canon is renowned for its abundance of moveable prefaces, a feature that allows for prayers that match specific feast days and highlight aspects of the unfolding of salvation history, while the Canon itself remains constant. Stylistically, the Roman Canon is known for its "theological precision and its sobriety of expression, [and] its comparative brevity."[3] In its current form, it appears as Eucharistic Prayer I in the Roman Missal of Paul VI, which can be prayed in Latin or in one of its many vernacular translations.[4] The widespread vernacularization of the Canon is a unique phenomenon in the twentieth century. It was both controversial and largely thought to be inconceivable prior to the council. This essay will follow the history of the translation of the Roman Canon into the English language and will seek to discern the principles that shaped its vernacular rendering.

Attitudes towards the Roman Canon Prior to Its Translation

After the promulgation of the Constitution on the Sacred Liturgy, Pope Paul VI formed the *Consilium ad exsequendam Constitutionem de Sacra Liturgia* in order to discern the specific liturgical reforms to be implemented based on the general principles established by the council documents. At this time, the Roman Canon was often understood to be one of the untouchable, immutable elements of the liturgy, a category

---

2. Enrico Mazza, *The Eucharistic Prayers of the Roman Rite*, trans. Matthew J. O'Connell (Collegeville, MN: Liturgical Press, 1986), 53.

3. Cipriano Vagaggini, *The Canon of the Mass and Liturgical Reform* (Staten Island: Alba House, 1967), 90.

4. The Roman Canon is also prayed in the extraordinary form of the Roman Rite. For further information regarding the state of the extraordinary form, see the following *motu proprio Traditionis Custodes* by Pope Francis (2021) and *Summorum Pontificum* by Pope Benedict XVI (2007).

designated by *SC*. In fact, the Council of Trent gave canonical validity to this attitude of reverence:

> Holy things must be treated in a holy way and this sacrifice is the most holy of all things. And so, that this sacrifice might be worthily and reverently offered and received, the Catholic Church many centuries ago instituted the sacred Canon. It is so free from all error that it contains nothing which does not savor strongly of holiness and piety and nothing which does not raise to God the minds of those who offer the Sacrifice. For it is made up of the words of our Lord Himself, of apostolic traditions, and of devout instructions of the holy pontiffs.[5]

The documents of Trent were not the sole instrument of the sacralization of the Canon—the ritual performance itself likely contributed to the general ambiance of mystery and inviolability. Enrico Mazza explains that

> [the Roman Canon] is venerable because of the impression its archaic and unusual language has made. It is full of words and phrases that are hard to understand and therefore evoke rather than communicate, suggest rather than say outright. It awakens a sense of the ineffable and undefinable or, in other words, a sense of mystery—but, be it noted, of mystery not in the biblical and patristic sense of the word, but in the sense of being mystifying and obscure. Once this sense of mystery is roused, the rationalizing unconscious forms the attitude, or, more accurately, the psychological mechanism which we call the "sense of the sacred." In fact, all the characteristics listed as making the Roman Canon venerable can be summed up in its sacredness.[6]

While the popular hand-missals of the early twentieth century provided the laity with side-by-side translations of the Latin Mass, even these devotional texts would sometimes omit the Canon from translation, fearing that its sacred mystery necessitated secrecy and silence.[7]

---

5. Council of Trent, Session XVII, Cap. 4, no. 1550. Trans. in Jacques Dupuis and Josef Neuner, *The Christian Faith in the Doctrinal Documents of the Catholic Church*, 6th rev. and enl. ed. (Staten Island, NY: Alba House, 1996), 589.

6. Mazza, *Eucharistic Prayers of the Roman Rite*, 53–54.

7. Kevin Magas, "Issues in Eucharistic Praying: Translating the Roman Canon," in *Worship* 89, no. 6 (2015): 484.

During this same period there were also many who had substantial critiques of the Roman Canon. Fr. Cipriano Vagaggini (influential in the drafting of *Sacrosanctum Concilium*) wrote about the difficult balance in recognizing the limits of the Roman Canon (1962 edition), while at the same time desiring to avoid changing it or replacing it with another anaphora. Like many, Vagaggini cherished the history and tradition of the Roman Canon, with its unique character and theology. He not only thought that the Church would be losing an irreplaceable treasure if it discarded the canon, but he also desired for this anaphora to remain the primary eucharistic text for the Roman Church. That aside, Vagaggini observed several issues in the Roman Canon that he hoped the reform could remedy, without changing the prayer in substance. His critique of the Roman Canon was leveled from the comparison of the prayer to other ancient anaphoras in the Christian tradition, primarily those of the Eastern churches. Constructing a composite formulation, seemingly based on *ressourcement* theology and an evaluation of the anaphoral tradition, Vagaggini explained that "[the] value of an anaphora depends not only on the ideas expressed, but also on the simplicity and clarity of its structure; on the natural and logical sequence of its ideas; on an absence of useless repetition and on its theology."[8] In his book *The Canon of the Mass and Liturgical Reform*, he laid out the perceived "defects" in the Roman Canon, according to this formulation:[9]

1. *Overall unity:* The Roman Canon appears to be an amalgamation of several prayers that have been placed together in succession. This fragmentary quality is accentuated by the termination of the different sections in *"Per Christum Dominum nostrum. Amen."* This construction gives the impression that each prayer stands alone rather than connects to the other prayers as a cohesive whole, a quality that Vagaggini found problematic.

2. *Lack of logical connection between prayers:* Following upon his previous critique, Vagaggini found that the separate prayers do not logically connect to each other in their order. For example, the *Te Igitur* begins with the phrase "Therefore . . . ," which implies a

---

8. Vagaggini, *Canon of the Mass*, 93.
9. Ibid., 93–106.

connection with the preceding idea, yet the *Sanctus* that comes directly before this prayer does not anticipate the *Te Igitur* by referencing the offering of the gifts or God blessing and sanctifying the offering.

3. *Arrangement of the prayers of intercession:* In several Eastern anaphoras, the prayers of intercession are grouped together. Vagaggini judged this to be the ideal construction for the intercessions and bemoaned the distribution of the intercessions among various prayers as found in the Roman Canon.

4. *An exaggerated emphasis on the idea of the offering and acceptance:* While Vagaggini held that the strong and persistent language of offering in the Roman Canon was one of its strengths, he also worried that its constant repetition overwhelmed the prayer and obscured the sense of *what* is being offered. For example, a prayer for the offering and its acceptance is present in the *Te Igitur (we ask you to accept and bless these gifts we offer you in sacrifice)*, the *Hanc Igitur (accept this offering)*, the *Quam Oblationem (Bless and approve our offering; make it acceptable to you, an offering in spirit and in truth)*, and the *Supra quae (Look with favor on these offerings and accept them as once you accepted the gifts)*. Vagaggini noted that this repetition does not serve to clarify what it is that we offer in the Mass—that is, "Christ our Lord himself, and ourselves with him"[10]—and thus, it is not a helpful or elucidating feature of the Canon.

5. *Presence of epicletic-type prayers that are disordered and incomplete:* Vagaggini noted three places in the Roman Canon that appear to reference an epiclesis;[11] the *Te Igitur*, *Quam Oblationem*, and the *Supplices*. Comparing these prayers with similar prayers in other anaphoras, he stated that the Roman Canon appears to contain parts of a proper epiclesis. Unfortunately, these prayers are incomplete and found in separate prayers of the Canon.

---

10. Ibid., 97.
11. It is unclear if Vagaggini thought that an epiclesis was previously present in these prayers and removed at some point in history. He seems to assume that these prayers were intended to be epileptic but now omit the crucial prayer for divine descent.

6. *Lack of theology of the Holy Spirit in the Eucharist:* While the Roman Canon appears to have traces of an epiclesis, Vagaggini noted that it does not contain a theology of the Holy Spirit's role in the Eucharist. This is especially problematic for him in light of the Second Vatican Council's interest in the economic Trinity. In this text, Vagaggini is frequently concerned with the presence and interpretation of contemporary theological currents within the Canon.[12]

7. *Issues in the Institution Narrative:* Vagaggini had several issues with the Institution Narrative in the Canon that were primarily theological in nature. First, he noted that, unlike other anaphoras, the Roman Canon only uses the dominical words *"Hoc est enim corpus meum"*—*"this is my body."* Without following these words with *"quud pro vobis datur"*—*"given for you"* or a similar biblical phrase, he held that the prayer's sacrificial character is weakened. The presence of Christ indicated in the phrase "this is my body" does not necessarily imply the sacrificial quality of the consecration and eucharistic prayer in general. Second, Vagaggini observed that the consecration of the wine does not mention Christ mixing the water with wine and blessing it, a feature common in the broader anaphoral tradition. He saw this action of pouring water and wine as an important sign of Christ's blood *poured out* for the remission of sins. Lastly, Vagaggini worried that the words *"mysterium fidei"* seem to be inserted into the words of the Institution Narrative during the consecration of the wine. It is unclear what these words refer to—is the consecrated wine the "mystery of faith" or, more fittingly, does the phrase refer to the whole of the consecratory action?

8. *Difficulties raised by the Supplices:* Two ideas are contained in this section of the anaphora: (a) "Lord, we pray that these gifts may be offered before your heavenly altar by your angel," and (b) "so that those who share in the body and blood of your Son may be filled with every heavenly grace." It is unclear how these two

---

12. Vagaggini was balanced in this concern, but I do find it quite interesting. "My own view is that the difficulty lies not in discovering the historical and literary origin of the various themes contained in the [prayer]; it lies rather in discovering the meaning that such a prayer can and ought to have today, as it stands and in its present context, always bearing in mind the origin and historical and literary meaning of these themes" (ibid., 104).

parts of the prayer are related to each other. Vagaggini felt that the incongruity could be alleviated by an intermediary prayer, perhaps "transform them, fill them with the Holy Spirit and make them into the body and blood of Christ." As it stands in the Roman Canon, the *Supplices* "can scarcely be called the ideal of clarity and liturgical simplicity."[13]

9. *List of the saints:* Vagaggini found the Roman Canon's list of the saints deficient in three ways: (a) its length, (b) the somewhat dubious history of the saints mentioned, and (c) the limited representation of Catholic life and holiness.

10. *The lack of an overall presentation of the history of salvation:* Finally, while Vagaggini recognized that one of the chief merits of the Roman Canon is the beauty of its moveable prefaces and its ability to depict and celebrate the events of salvation history over the course of a year, he saw a disadvantage in the Canon's inability to present the complete arch of salvation history culminating in the Eucharistic act. Vagaggini wondered if a solution could be found that would allow the Roman liturgy to have in its Canon at the same time both the riches of the movable prefaces that it had historically enjoyed, and the advantages of an overall expression of salvation history (like those found in Eastern anaphoras).

These examples of Vagaggini's reservations concerning the Roman Canon provide a general insight into concerns at the highest levels of the Roman Curia.[14] It should be noted that these perceived deficiencies were felt alongside the idea that nothing could be changed within the Canon, and thus a real tension manifested itself. In his own work, Vagaggini commented on the fact that these "defects" became more apparent when the text was read out loud—especially in the vernacular. In a sense, the problems were more hidden when the Latin was treated in a veiled manner. Vagaggini also noted that his concerns with the Roman Canon were mainly structural and linguistic, rather than dogmatic. These issues might inhibit pastors from encouraging the laity to fully comprehend, and thus participate in, the liturgy. It was felt

---

13. Ibid., 105.
14. Although Vagaggini held no exceptional position in the Curia, he directly aided in the drafting of *Sacrosanctum Concilium*.

that the language and composition rendered the Canon difficult to understand, yet the Church could not dispense with the Roman Canon.

Several options for reworking or changing the Canon were suggested to the Holy See, some being more drastic and others more conservative. Vagaggini's own recommendation was to slightly alter the Roman Canon (but not in any way that changed its substance) and also to introduce another anaphora into the Roman Rite which contained a fuller articulation of salvation history. Ultimately it was Vagaggini's proposal that Pope Paul VI selected. While the council was still in session, the Pope stated that "the present anaphora is to be left unchanged; two or three anaphoras for use at particular specified times are to be composed or looked for." This began the long process of reforming the venerable Roman Canon.

The Process of Vernacularization

Although *Sacrosanctum Concilium* did not envision the reform of the liturgy to include its complete vernacularization, the *Consilium*—the governing body that was charged with implementing the various revisions decreed by the Second Vatican Council—was overwhelmed with bishops' requests for this change. Amidst rumors of the possible authorization of the translation of the entire liturgy into the vernacular, a committee was formed by several of the English-speaking bishops' conferences to begin the process. This team, eventually called the Advisory Committee (AC), developed a set of principles of translation that would guide their work of reform. These principles were used from 1965 until formal principles for translation were released by the Vatican in 1969. The AC's principles were tenfold and primarily motivated by pastoral concerns. They are listed as follows:[15]

1. The task of the Advisory Committee and of its associates is limited to the provision of acceptable English translations from the liturgical books of the Latin rite. It does not extend to the composition of new (and in places possibly better) texts.

---

15. Taken directly from the appendix of J. M. Kemper, *Behind the Text: A Study of the Principles and Procedures of Translation, Adaptation, and Composition of Original Texts by the International Commission on English in the Liturgy*, PhD diss. (Notre Dame, IN: University of Notre Dame, 1992), 369.

2. Translators will therefore work from the latest typical editions of the Roman Missal, Ritual, and Pontifical.

3. To be acceptable in substance, a translation must faithfully express the meaning of the original texts. If the meaning of a passage is not certainly known, the translator may take some liberty of reasonable conjecture.

4. To be acceptable in style, translation must take account of (a) the sacral character of the original texts; (b) the tradition of devotional writing in the English language; (c) contemporary linguistic usage; (d) euphony; and (e) the practice of other Christian bodies.

5. Respect for the sacral character of the original texts and the demands of corporate public worship will prescribe a vocabulary and style not necessarily identical with those admissible in private and personal prayer.

6. Respect for contemporary linguistic usage will dictate the avoidance of words and phrases not in living use today.

7. Respect for euphony will involve the testing of all draft versions by reciting them aloud.

8. The word "acceptable" in the foregoing paragraphs is to be understood as requiring translators to work mainly with an eye to the middle range of church-goers rather than to the least or the most intelligent and literate.

9. Translators are entitled to assume that such words (e.g., grace, absolution, and salvation) will not be altogether foreign to their hearers.

10. Any question not covered by these norms is to be treated as an open question.

It should be noted that the first two principles articulate the limitations placed on any body of translators; they should be confined to the *translation* and not *free composition* of liturgical texts. These translations should express the meaning of the original text faithfully.[16] The following

16. Kemper, *Behind the Text*, 62.

principles (particularly four, five, and six) contain ambiguity as to the balance between the sacral character of the translation and contemporary forms of expression. The lack of clarity of these principles led to several debates within the process of translation about the best way to interpret the tenor of the liturgy in order for the faithful to participate in their fullest capacity.[17] This discussion about the vernacularization of the liturgy was widespread among lay and religious Catholics alike. The AC's principles of translation were published for public viewing in the English-speaking world, inviting both discussion and critique. One response caught the eye of the AC, which by this time had expanded its membership of exclusively clerics to include lay specialists within a larger structure called the International Commission on English in the Liturgy (ICEL). The response of interest was an essay composed by Edward Harold in *St. Joseph Magazine* that outlined a novel approach to translating the text of the canon.

Harold had an extensive background in classical and foreign languages, as well as fluency in the field of anthropology. He had also spent time living in Europe, North Africa, South Asia, and Latin America, giving him an air of cultural awareness. Additionally, Harold's work as the director of the Connecticut Child Welfare Association provided him with experience in public speaking and television production.[18] Harold's background and life experience lent itself well to the convincing nature of his argument. The article that he wrote articulated an appreciation for the liturgy and a desire for its full translation into the English language. However, Harold believed that this translation would only succeed at being fully comprehensible if it took seriously the English language as it is, rather than slavishly imitating the Latin text with all of its grammatical particularities, as could be seen in the multitude of popular hand missals. A vernacular liturgy would be best produced and understood if the Latin text was translated meaning for meaning, rather than word for word, a translation method called *dynamic equivalence*. Harold held that the central ideas of the Latin text should be stated "in a form native to those who were to use it. This entails a complete dismantling of the

---

17. Interestingly, this participation is understood almost exclusively as cognitive participation.

18. Kemper, *Behind the Text*, 110.

Latin. Afterwards the ideas can be reassembled along the lines of English structure. . . . The first rule for a good translation is that it should sound as though it were not a translation but an original."[19] This meant that the translation ought to be rooted in Anglo-Saxon vocabulary and grammatical structure—characteristically succinct and straightforward in its statements, with strong active verbs. "The limpid nature of the Latin, and its rich use of adjectival formulations simply would not translate into vigorous English; simplicity would have to replace polite formality."[20] ICEL found this novel approach to translation to be extremely interesting and uniquely promising. They asked Edward Harold to join their translation committee and to produce some textual interpretations according to his method, of course all the while adhering to the principles of translation already established.

Meanwhile, the *Consilium*, headed by Archbishop Annibale Bugnini, had granted permission to various bishops to translate parts of the Mass on an experimental basis. That being said, the members of the *Consilium* were fairly nervous about allowing for the translation of the Roman Canon itself. Some suggested that the Canon ought to be left in Latin while the rest of the Liturgy could be translated into the vernacular, and indeed for a time this was the common situation in some places following the first phase of experimental translations. In his book *The Reform of the Liturgy, 1948–1975*, Bugnini shared his thoughts on this partial-vernacular option:

> If the rest of the Mass were to be celebrated in the vernacular while the Canon remained in Latin, it would have been like opening all the doors of the house to a guest and then excluding him from its heart. It is in the heart that the life is to be found; it is in the Canon that the mystery resides. The Canon is a vital part of a living Liturgy. It did remain in Latin for over two years from the beginning of the reform, but pastoral experience showed that a situation in which the celebration was half in the vernacular and half in Latin was intolerable. This, then, is a classic example of a legitimate postconciliar development. It was a logical consequence of premises set down by the Council itself. In fact, even

---

19. Ibid., 110, quoting "The Canon in the Vernacular," *Saint Joseph's Magazine* 67, no. 9 (October 1966): 9–15.
20. Ibid., 113.

if the extension of the vernacular to the entire Liturgy can be called a broad interpretation . . . it cannot be said to contradict the Constitution on the Sacred Liturgy.[21]

For Bugnini, the very principle of total and fruitful lay participation in the mystery of the eucharistic celebration was called into question by this possibility. His testimony gives us a sense of both the reverence felt towards the Roman Canon and deep love of the Eucharist, as well as the real emphasis placed on lay participation in the ritual action of the eucharistic liturgy. Thus, the *Consilium* approved the vernacularization of the Roman Canon in 1967 and placed the onus for translations of the Canon on the individual bishops' conferences, although the Holy See retained the right to ratify the various translations upon completion. Following Pope Paul VI's directives to leave the Canon untouched, the *Consilium* instructed that the translations be accurate and faithful to the Latin Canon. "The texts should be taken as they are, without mutilation or simplifications of any kind. Adaptations to the character of the spoken tongue should be sober and prudent."[22]

The first comprehensive project that Edward Harold undertook for ICEL was the English translation of the Roman Canon. His draft was selected from among several translated options. The Advisory Committee required, however, that Harold make a few changes before the draft could be sent off for approval by the *Consilium*. The version that he submitted contained three substantive changes to the Canon: (1) the removal of the "*Per Christum Dominum*," which occurred at the end of most sections of the eucharistic prayer. Harold had dispensed with these recurring words based on the conviction that the repetition of this concluding phrase disrupted the unity of the prayer and created a segmented reading; (2) the elimination of the "two tongue-twisting lists of saints"; and (3) the removal of the *mysterium fidei*, which Harold (and many others) argued interrupted the consecration of the wine and thus confused the action of the prayer.[23] These substantive changes were eventually found to be

---

21. Annibale Bugnini, *The Reform of the Liturgy, 1948–1975* (Collegeville, MN: Liturgical Press, 1990), 110.
22. Kemper, *Behind the Text*, 108.
23. Ibid., 114.

problematic and required retranslation in a more direct manner.[24] Thus these three significant alterations did not make it to the final stage of the translation draft. Interestingly, each of these changes were eventually adopted in an amended form in later editions of the Roman Canon.

All of the other changes that Harold made to the Canon were found to be linguistic in nature, and therefore were considered translations rather than alterations. In the course of two appendices and an introduction included with the translated draft, Harold explained the interpretive choices that he made in translating certain words and phrases, and the difficulty posed by the task of translating words across cultural and historical dimensions. For example, he argued that the Latin word *famulus* was difficult to communicate in our present historical context because contemporary society has a different understanding of "servant" than that of Late Antiquity or even the early Middle Ages. Harold believed that earlier perspectives on servanthood involved a permanent relationship of almost familial bonding rather than a relationship of merely financial obligation. He wanted to stress both Christian freedom and the familial bond that we have with God through the Eucharist, thus he frequently omitted the word *famulus* and often replaced it with the phrase "your friends" or "your chosen people."[25]

Another conspicuous interpretive decision occurred in the *Te Igitur*. This section was heavily reformulated because Harold thought that the connection between the *Sanctus* and the beginning of the Canon did not logically flow together when they were connected by the word "therefore." In place of this awkward transition, he added the phrase "We come to you" in order to orient the whole of the eucharistic action communally toward God. In addition to this alteration, one of the most striking translation choices that Harold made was an extensive elimination of complimentary adjectives from the Canon. The Latin text uses an abundance of adjectives in its florid descriptions; however, it was particularly the non-limiting adjectives that Harold found most problematic. These are

---

24. The process of translation will be covered below. It should be noted that my description simplifies the process and highlights only a few key points in the many drafts that were produced. For the sake of readability, I have left out several influential figures who took part in the translation process. "Harold's translations" include the work of several other people. For greater detail see Kemper, *Behind the Text*, 105–84.

25. Ibid., 114.

words that do not serve to specify or limit the meaning of the modified noun, but rather function as an embellishment. For example, the adjective "holy" could be used in a limiting way to differentiate a noun, as in the case of "holy book" (this refers to a book that is specifically holy), or it could be used in a non-limiting way that adds no additional meaning to the noun, as in the case of "holy Mass" (since the Mass is always holy, the adjective does not give specific information).[26] Another example that became contentious was the translation of *accepit panem in sanctas ac venerabiles manus suas*—literally translated as *taking bread in his holy and venerable hands*. It was argued that the adjectives "holy" and "venerable" were embellishments rather than descriptive words, since Christ's hands are already known to be holy and venerable. Further, if it was stated that Christ "took bread," one could assume that he took bread in his hands, thus the extra description was not needed. The final translation simply read, "He took bread."

Harold found the Roman Canon's use of adjectives to be particularly troubling for translation into English. He argued that complementary adjectives added emotional color to the foundational words of the Canon—a particular flavor that worked well in the historical moment of its creation. However, Harold thought that this emotional, non-rational tenor would have a negative impact in the mind of the modern person. He claimed that, for many today, this florid tone would seem ingenuine, non-credible, and repulsive. Thus, he opted for the removal of several adjectival phrases, the absence of which were not felt to be a major departure from the substance of the Roman Canon, but a translation that communicates the eucharistic prayer to the contemporary mind. This is just one example of the important stylistic changes that Harold made to the Canon. He was also sensitive to what he found to be archaic in the Latin style, particularly the "sacral character" that he argued expressed medieval court manners and arose out of social custom. Harold sought to adjust this style so as to best convey meaning in a contemporary manner, one that would be understandable to the modern culture. At the same time, Harold was invested in translating the Latin style of the Canon into an authentically English style, thus formulating the best of *English* translation out of the best of *Latin*. There were two levels of difference that

---

26. These are Kemper's examples, 115.

needed to be translated: the historical and cultural level, which presented many stylistic and conceptual disparities; and the linguistic level, which held many grammatical differences. Harold held that linguistic beauty in modern English consists in simplicity of style and usage.[27]

The final note on stylistic considerations has to do with the way that ICEL envisioned *Sacrosanctum Concilium*'s aspirations for liturgical worship—that is, a liturgy that would be attentive to the participation of the whole ecclesial body. In translating the Canon, Harold took into account the conciliar understanding that the liturgy was intended to be prayed frequently by the community. As a public liturgical prayer, a style of private devotion was eschewed. Likewise, being a communal prayer, Harold thought that the language should be suitable for speaking aloud, and easily comprehensible for the congregation. And it needed to wear well with daily use. Harold consistently attempted to balance these many requirements of what constituted a worthy translation of the venerable Roman Canon.

1962 Canon Missae	Edward Harold's Draft of 1967[28] *Areas of significant change or disagreement italicized and bolded (original and translation indicated)
Te igitur, clementissime Pater, per Jesum Christum, Filium tuum, Dominum nostrum, supplices rogamus, ac petimus, uti accepta habeas, et benedicas haec dona, haec munera, haec sancta sacrificia illibata, in primis, quae	***We come to you in this spirit of thanksgiving***, Father. Through Jesus Christ, and with these gifts, [sic] We lay them before you as our sacrificial offering, a perfect offering. We ask you to accept them and give them your blessing.

---

27. While Harold was the translator of the Canon, ICEL approved his texts (making corrections and additions between drafts) and more or less backed his explanations. Their support was not unanimous at every stage of translation, but his work held majority approval. There were several more players in the development of the text; however, due to the constraints of space, I have limited my treatment to a focus on Harold's work. To read more on this complicated process, see chap. 3 in Jeffrey Michael Kemper's above noted dissertation.

28. Kemper, *Behind the Text*, 130–34. Areas of significant change or disagreement italicized and bolded (original and translation indicated).

tibi offerimus pro Ecclesia tua sancta catholica: quam pacificare, custodire, adunare, et regere digneris toto orbe terrarum: una cum famulo tuo Papa nostro N. et Antistite nostro N. et omnibus orthodoxis atque catholicae et apostolicae fidei cultoribus.	We offer you these gifts for the holy catholic Church. Keep it everywhere at peace; watch over it and guide it, and make it one. We offer these gifts for Paul, our pope, N., our bishop, and all bishops who hold and teach the catholic faith that comes to us through your apostles.
Memento, Domine, *famulorum, famularumque tuarum* N. et N. et omnium circumstantium, quorum tibi fides cognita est et nota devotio, pro quibus tibi offerimus: vel qui tibi offerunt hoc sacrificium laudis, pro se, suisque omnibus: pro redemptione animarum suarum, pro spe salutis et incolumitatis suae: tibique reddunt vota sua aeterno Deo, vivo et vero.	Remember, Lord, *your friends* N. and N, and all who are here. You know how firmly they believe in you, and dedicate themselves to you. They offer you this sacrifice of praise for themselves and all who are dear to them, for their own deliverance, and for the well-being they hope for. They stand before you in prayer, their true, their living, their eternal God.
Communicantes, et memoriam venerantes, in primis gloriosae semper Virginis Mariae, Genetricis Dei et Domini nostri Iesu Christi: sed et beati Ioseph, eiusdem Virginis Sponsi, et beatorum Apostolorum ac Martyrum tuorum, Petri et Pauli, Andreae, Iacobi, Ioannis, Ihomae, Iacobi, Philippi, Bartholomaei, Matthaei, Simonis et Thaddaei: **Lini, Cleti, Clementis, Xysti, Cornelii, Cypriani, Laurentii, Chrysogoni, Ioannis et Pauli, Cosmae et Damiani** et omnium Sanctorum tuorum; quorum meritis precibusque concedas, ut in omnibus protectionis tuae muniamur auxilio. **Per Christum Dominum nostrum. Amen.**	We are all together in one church with those whom we honor: Mary, forever virgin, mother of Jesus Christ, our Lord, Joseph, her husband, the apostles Peter and Paul, Andrew, James and John, Thomas, James, Philip, Bartholomew, Matthew, Simon and Thaddeus, **the martyrs, and all the saints.** May their prayers and good works move you to help and protect us.

Hanc igitur oblationem servitutis nostræ, sed et cunctæ familiæ tuæ, quæsumus, Domine, ut placatus accipias: diesque nostros in tua pace disponas, atque ab æterna damnatione nos eripi, et in electorum tuorum iubeas grege numerari. **Per Christum Dominum nostrum. Amen.**	Accept then, Father, this offering from your family, people and minister(s) together. Grant peace to our days; save us from damnation, and count us among the chosen.
Quam oblationem tu, Deus, in omnibus, quæsumus, benedictam, adscriptam, ratam, rationabilem, acceptabilemque facere digneris: ut nobis Corpus et Sanguis fiat dilectissimi Filii tui, Domini nostri Iesu Christi.	Bless these offerings, Lord; make them truly spiritual and acceptable. Let them become for us the body and blood of Jesus Christ, your only Son, our Lord.
Qui, pridie quam pateretur, accepit panem in sanctas ac venerabiles manus suas, et elevatis oculis in cælum ad te Deum Patrem suum omnipotentem, tibi gratias agens benedixit, fregit, deditque discipulis suis, dicens: Accipite, et manducate ex hoc omnes. Hoc est enim Corpus meum. Simili modo, postquam cenatum est, accipiens et hunc præclarumcalicem in sanctas ac venerabiles manus suas, item tibi gratias agens benedixit, deditque discipulis suis, dicens: Accipite et bibite ex eo omnes: Hic est enim Calix Sanguinis mei, novi et æterni testamenti:	The day before he suffered, he took bread, and raised his eyes to you, his all-powerful Father. He gave you thanks and praise, he broke bread, and gave it to his disciples, saying: take this and eat it, all of you; this is my body. At the end of the supper, he took this cup and once more he gave thanks and praise. Then, giving the cup to his disciples, he said: take this and drink from it, all of you; this is the cup of my blood, the blood of the covenant, the new and everlasting covenant—the mystery of faith. This blood is to be shed for you and all men to pardon sins.

mysterium fidei: qui pro vobis et pro multis effundetur in remissionem peccatorum. Haec quotiescumque feceritis, in mei memoriam facietis.	As often as you do this, do it in remembrance of me.
Unde et memores, Domine, nos servi tui, sed et plebs tua sancta, eiusdem Christi, Filii tui, Domini nostri, tam beatæ passionis, necnon et ab inferis resurrectionis, sed et in cælos gloriosæ ascensionis: offerimus præclaræ maiestati tuæ de tuis donis ac datis hostiam puram, hostiam sanctam, hostiam immaculatam, Panem sanctum vitæ æternæ et Calicem salutis perpetuæ.	And so, Lord, we your chosen people offer these gifts, recalling the passion of Christ, his resurrection from the dead, and his ascension into glory. From among the many gifts you have given us, we give back to you a holy sacrifice, perfect and without flaw: the bread of life, the cup of salvation.
Supra quæ propitio ac sereno vultu respicere digneris: et accepta habere, sicuti accepta habere dignatus es munera pueri tui iusti Abel, et sacrificium Patriarchæ nostri Abrahæ, et quod tibi obtulit summus sacerdos tuus Melchisedech, sanctum sacrificium, immaculatam hostiam.	Look with favor on these offerings as you did upon the gifts of Abel, the just man, the sacrifice of Abraham, our father in faith, and the bread and wine of your high priest, Melchisedech.
Supplices te rogamus, omnipotens Deus: iube hæc perferri per manus sancti Angeli tui in sublime altare tuum, in conspectu divinæ maiestatis tuæ: ut, quotquot ex hac altaris participatione sacrosanctum Filii tui Corpus et Sanguinem sumpserimus, omni benedictione cælesti et gratia repleamur. **Per eundem Christum Dominum nostrum. Amen.**	Let your angel now take them on high to your altar, Lord. Then, as we take the sacred body and blood of your son [sic] from this altar, fill us with your grace and your blessings.

English Vernacular Translation of the Roman Canon 235

Memento etiam, Domine, ***famulorum famularumque*** tuarum N. et N., qui nos præcesserunt cum signo fidei, et dormiunt in somno pacis. Ipsis, Domine, et omnibus in Christo quiescentibus, locum refrigerii, lucis et pacis, ut indulgeas, deprecamur. **Per eundem Christum Dominum nostrum. Amen.**	Remember Lord, ***your friends*** who have gone before us marked with the seal of faith, N. and N. They now sleep in peace. Lead them, and all who sleep in Christ, to a place of light and rest and peace.
Nobis quoque peccatoribus, famulis tuis, de multitudine miserationum tuarum sperantibus, partem aliquam et societatem donare digneris, cum tuis sanctis Apostolis et Martyribus: cum Ioanne, Stephano, Matthia, Barnaba, ***Ignatio, Alexandro, Marcellino, Petro, Felicitate, Perpetua, Agatha, Lucia, Agnete, Cæcilia, Anastasia*** et omnibus Sanctis tuis: intra quorum nos consortium, non æstimator meriti, sed veniae, quæsumus, largitor admitte. **Per Christum Dominum nostrum.**	For ourselves, we are all sinners, but we trust in your mercy. We hope for a place in the company of the apostles, John the Baptist, Stephen, Matthias, Barnabas, the martyrs, ***and all the saints.*** Grant us your forgiveness, Lord. Overlook what we deserve and admit us to their company.
Per quem hæc omnia, Domine, semper bona creas, sanctificas, vivificas, benedicis, et præstas nobis. Per ipsum, et cum ipso, et in ipso, est tibi Deo Patri omnipotenti, in unitate Spiritus Sancti, omnis honor et gloria per omnia sæcula sæculorum.	Through Christ out Lord you sustain all these things, make them holy, enliven them, bless them and give them to us. Through him, with him, in him all glory and honor come to you, Lord, the all-powerful Father, in the unity of the Holy Spirit, forever and ever through everlasting ages. Amen.

As a rule, ICEL's translations underwent a thorough review process. As such, Harold's Canon text was widely disseminated. Canon booklets were created and sent to all the bishops in the English-speaking conferences for evaluation. Comments on the translation ranged from vigorous approval to vehement criticism. Some critics argued that the Canon should remain in Latin, some believed that the whole Mass should remain untranslated, and another faction thought that this particular translation did not interpret the Roman Canon authentically. We will focus on this latter group, since the translation of the Canon into the vernacular had already been sanctioned by the Holy See.

Many believed that Harold's translation was problematic in its stylistic rendering. This critique was based on the way that the translation dispensed with sacred language, as well as Harold's selection of the style of "business English"—a perception no doubt informed by the simple and straightforward cadence of the translation. In terms of sacred language, some argued that eliminating this style ignored the living tradition of the Roman Canon, both as received from the Latin Canon and its translations used by the praying faithful in various missals. In the same vein, others held that the humble tone indigenous to the Roman Canon should be retained in the new translation, as well as the hierarchical language when referring to God (a theological argument, as opposed to a stylistic critique). While using sacred language could obscure the text to some degree, others argued that Harold's approach "left no room for technical terms which could be comprehended through mystagogy. [The pedestrian nature of the style] left the prayer univocal and lacking the layers of significance necessary for daily use."[29] At the same time, several also believed that the blunt and staccato style did not fully encapsulate modern eucharistic theology in general, nor was it a suitable tone for the Canon in particular. "[The] 'psychology of the prayer' [is] not discursive or instructive, but a proclamation of praise, with a controlled joy bordering on the ecstatic."[30]

While critiques were considerable, the English-speaking bishops' conferences approved ICEL's (Harold's) translation with a 6:1 margin. With the feedback from bishops, a few major edits were to be made to the text:[31] (a) the translation of *friend* for *famulus* was deemed inappro-

---

29. Ibid., 118.
30. Ibid.
31. There were several extra steps in this approval process, here shortened for the sake of readability. See ibid., 105–84.

priate. Replacing the translation with *your people* or simply removing the reference altogether was held to be a better option; (b) a "thou-form" translation had to be available for nations that desired that option; (c) the original list of saints was retained, as well as the "Through Christ our Lord," however a second version of the text was also submitted that omitted both items; and (d) the *Unde et memores* section needed to be reworked in order to better reflect the relationship between the anamnesis and offering. The first draft reads:

> And so, Lord, we your chosen people *offer these gifts, recalling the passion* of Christ, his resurrection from the dead, and his ascension into glory. From among the many gifts you have given us, *we give back to you a holy sacrifice*, perfect and without flaw: the bread of life, the cup of salvation.

Its revision emphasizes the memory of Christ's passion as primary to the eucharistic action, and connects this anamnesis to the offering of a holy sacrifice through the use of a conjunction that clearly unites the two actions:

> So now, Lord, we *celebrate the memory of Christ*, your Son. We, your people and your ministers, *recall his passion, his resurrection from the dead, and his ascension into glory; and* from the many gifts you have given us *we offer to you,* God of glory and majesty, *this holy and perfect sacrifice*: the bread of life and the cup of eternal salvation.

After these changes and a few others were made, the translation was sent to the Holy See in order to be ratified. Both the *Consilium* and the Congregation for the Doctrine of Faith examined ICEL's text.[32] Although it looked as if the *Consilium* favored the translation, it was not approved by the CDF for use as a definitive text. Since it was expected that the process of approving a final text would take a considerable amount of time, the *Consilium* issued a directive for the immediate use of an interim Canon at this point. It was up to the various bishops' conferences to approve a single translation (in any given nation) for their vernacular

---

32. This whole section also draws heavily on chapter three of Kemper's dissertation, 105–84.

worship, though it was also stipulated that this translation should be one that was already approved and in use, which caused confusion for several conferences.[33] ICEL immediately requested that all of the English-speaking nations use the translation that the CDF had just rejected. Some of the English conferences started using this text right away [1967 interim translation, as seen below on chart], while some held off due to a hesitancy over the CDF's rejection. ICEL requested that the CDF provide the reasoning for their denial of the translation, as well as their objections and suggestions for the text. ICEL and the CDF exchanged correspondence over the ensuing months about the translation. The CDF took issue with four items.[34] The first two were in reference to the address of Mary in the *Communicantes*. The CDF objected to the lack of mention of Mary's divine motherhood and to the omission of the reference to Mary's perpetual virginity. "*Semper* Virginis Mariae, Genetricis *Dei et Domini nostri Iesu Christi*" was translated as "Mary, the *virgin* mother of Jesus Christ *our Lord*" (missing a translation of the words *semper* and *Dei*). They proposed that the translation read "Mary the *ever-virgin* mother of Jesus Christ, our Lord *and God*." ICEL's Advisory Committee agreed to this alteration due to its dogmatic nature, although they felt that the original translation had been appropriate on an ecumenical level, as a gesture towards other Christians who held lower Marian doctrine.[35] The third objection involved the phrase "*accepit panem in sanctas ac venerabiles manus suas*" in the *Qui pridie* which had been translated "he took bread," omitting the phrase "in his sacred and venerable hands." The CDF and Advisory Committee argued back and forth about their respective positions on this translation. The AC held that the phrase "sacred and venerable hands" was foreign to the English language and also that it was not an issue of doctrinal accuracy, while the CDF insisted that at least part of the phrase ought to be retained. The AC settled on the phrase "sacred hands." The last matter that the CDF called into question was the translation of *enim, ex hoc, and ex eo* in the *Qui pridie* and *Simili modo*—words and phrases that were simply left out in the English

33. Ibid., 158–68.
34. Ibid., 167–76.
35. See the following chart for comparison between the interim text of 1967 and approved 1st edition of the Roman Missal of Paul VI, 1969.

translation. On this point, the Advisory Committee won the argument by insisting that these words were not necessary in the English interpretation because their essence was communicated by the sentence structure. The CDF acquiesced to their explanation. In the end, the Advisory Committee completed these revisions to the translation and resubmitted the new draft for ratification by the Holy See once again. Although the Congregation of the Doctrine of Faith had halted the approval of the translation of the Roman Canon, ICEL insisted that their translations were never found to be erring in doctrine.[36]

The final draft of the English translation was approved by Pope Paul VI in 1968. At this same time, the *Consilium* requested that the pope also approve additional changes to the Latin edition of the Roman Canon that would accompany the rest of the revisions of the Mass, which would include three additional eucharistic prayers. These requests resonate with the problem-spots that figures in this essay had already identified, particularly those recognized by Vagaggini and Harold. The first two requests included the making optional of the "*Per Christum Dominum nostrum*" phrase at the end of the *Communicantes*, *Supplices*, and the *Memento etiam*, as well as the optional omission of a portion of the two lists of saints. The third request was for the consecratory formula of the Roman Canon to identically match the other three eucharistic prayers. Practically speaking, this meant that the phrase "*quod pro vobis tradetur*" ("which will be given up for you") would be added to the consecration of the bread, and that the *mysterium fidei* would be extracted from the consecration of the wine.[37]

Changes in the consecratory formula for the bread:

Accipite et manducate ex hoc omnes:	Accipite et manducate ex hoc omnes:
Hoc est enim Corpus meum.	→ Hoc est enim Corpus meum, ***quod pro vobis tradetur.***

---

36. Kemper, *Behind the Text*, 176.
37. Ibid., 181–82.

Changes in the consecratory formula for the wine:

Accipite et bibite ex eo omnes:
Hic est enim Calix Sanguinis mei,
novi et æterni testament:
Mysterium fidei: qui pro vobis
et pro multis effundetur in
peccatorum.

Haec *quotiescumque feceritis, in
mei memoriam facietis.*

→

Accipite et bibite ex eo omnes:
Hic est enim Calix Sanguinis mei
novi et aeterni testament qui pro
vobis et pro multis effundetur in
remissionem peccatorum.

*Hoc facite in meam
commemorationem.*
Mysterium Fidei: Mortem tuam
annuntiamus, Domine, et tuam
resurrectionem confitemur, donec
venias. (or alternative)

These changes in the Latin version of the Roman Canon were reflected in the final approved translation of the English Canon as well (seen below bolded and italicized). Both prayers were approved by Pope Paul VI in 1968 and the entire Roman Missal was officially promulgated in 1969.

1967—interim text *Kemper Appendix 8	1969—approved text **Roman Missal 1st edition**	1998—approved text **Roman Missal 2nd edition**	2010—approved text **Roman Missal 3rd edition**
(*Te Igitur*)			
We come to you, Father, in this spirit of thanksgiving, through Jesus Christ your Son. Through him we ask you to accept and bless these gifts we offer you in sacrifice. We offer them for your holy catholic Church.	We come to you, Father, with praise and thanksgiving, through Jesus Christ your Son. Through him we ask you to accept and bless these gifts we offer you in sacrifice. We offer them for your holy catholic Church,	All-merciful Father, we come before you with praise and thanksgiving through Jesus Christ your Son. Through him we ask you to accept and bless these gifts we offer you in sacrifice. We offer them for your holy	To you, therefore, most merciful Father, we make humble prayer and petition through Jesus Christ, your Son, our Lord: that you accept and bless these gifts, these offerings, these holy and unblemished

English Vernacular Translation of the Roman Canon 241

Watch over it, Lord, and guide it; grant it peace and unity throughout the world. We offer them for N. our Pope, for N. our bishop, and for all who hold and teach the catholic faith that comes to us from the apostles.	watch over it, Lord, and guide it; grant it peace and unity throughout the world. We offer them for N. our Pope, for N. our bishop, and for all who hold and teach the catholic faith that comes to us from the apostles.	catholic Church, watch over it, Lord, and guide it; grant it peace and unity throughout the world. We offer them for N. our Pope, for N. our bishop, and for all who hold and teach the catholic faith that comes to us from the apostles.	sacrifices, which we offer you firstly for your holy catholic Church. Be pleased to grant her peace, to guard, unite and govern her throughout the whole world, together with your servant N. our Pope and N. our Bishop, and all those who, holding to the truth, hand on the catholic and apostolic faith.
(*Memento, Domine*)			
Remember, Lord, your people, especially those for whom we now pray, N. and N. Remember all of us gathered here before you. You know how firmly we believe in you and dedicate ourselves to you. We offer you this sacrifice of praise for ourselves and	Remember, Lord, your people, especially those for whom we now pray, N. and N. Remember all of us gathered here before you. You know how firmly we believe in you and dedicate ourselves to you. We offer you this sacrifice of praise for ourselves and	Remember, Lord, your people, especially those for whom we now pray, N. and N. Remember all of us gathered here before you. You know how firmly we believe in you and dedicate ourselves to you. We offer you this sacrifice of praise for ourselves and	Remember, Lord, your servants N. and N., and all gathered here, whose faith and devotion are known to you. For them we offer you this sacrifice of praise or they offer it for themselves and all who are dear to them: for the redemption of their souls, in

242 *Further Issues in Eucharistic Praying in East and West*

those who are dear to us. We pray to you, our living and true God, for our well-being and redemption.	those who are dear to us. We pray to you, our living and true God, for our well-being and redemption.	those who are dear to us; we pray to you, our living and true God, for our well-being and redemption.	hope of health and well-being, and paying their homage to you, the eternal God, living and true.
(*Communicantes*)			
In union with the whole Church we honor the memory of the saints. We honor Mary, **the virgin mother** of Jesus Christ **our Lord**. We honor Joseph, her husband, the apostles and martyrs Peter and Paul, Andrew, [James, John, Thomas, James, Philip, Bartholomew, Matthew, Simon and Jude; we honor Linus, Cletus, Clement, Sixtus, Cornelius, Cyprian, Lawrence, Chrysogonus, John and Paul, Cosmas and Damian;] and all the saints.	In union with the whole Church we honor Mary, **the ever-virgin** mother of Jesus Christ **our Lord and God**. We honor Joseph, her husband, the apostles and martyrs Peter and Paul, Andrew, [James, John, Thomas, James, Philip, Bartholomew, Matthew, Simon and Jude; we honor Linus, Cletus, Clement, Sixtus, Cornelius, Cyprian, Lawrence, Chrysogonus, John and Paul, Cosmas and Damian;] and all the saints. May their merits and prayers	We pray in communion with the whole Church, with those whose memory we now honor; especially with Mary, the glorious and ever-virgin mother of Jesus Christ, our Lord and God, with Joseph, her husband, the apostles and martyrs Peter and Paul, Andrew, [James, John, Thomas, James, Philip, Bartholomew, Matthew, Simon and Jude; we honor Linus, Cletus, Clement, Sixtus, Cornelius, Cyprian, Lawrence, Chrysogonus,	[I]n communion with those whose memory we venerate, especially the glorious ever-Virgin Mary, Mother of our God and Lord, Jesus Christ, and blessed † Joseph, her Spouse, your blessed Apostles and Martyrs, Peter and Paul, Andrew, (James, John, Thomas, James, Philip, Bartholomew, Matthew, Simon and Jude; Linus, Cletus, Clement, Sixtus, Cornelius, Cyprian, Lawrence, Chrysogonus, John and Paul, Cosmas and Damian) and all your Saints; we

May their merits and prayers gain us your constant help and protection. [Through Christ our Lord. Amen.]	gain us your constant help and protection. [Through Christ our Lord. Amen.]	John and Paul, Cosmas and Damian;] and all the saints. By their merits and prayers gain us your constant help and protection. [Through Christ our Lord. Amen.]	ask that through their merits and prayers, in all things we may be defended by your protecting help. (Through Christ our Lord. Amen.)
(*Hanc Igitur*)			
Father, accept this offering from your whole family. Grant us your peace in this life, save us from final damnation,	Father, accept this offering from your whole family. Grant us your peace in this life, save us from final damnation,	Lord, accept this offering from your whole family. Grant us your peace in this life, save us from final damnation,	Therefore, Lord, we pray: graciously accept this oblation of our service, that of your whole family, . . . order our days in
and count us among those you have chosen. [Through Christ our Lord. Amen.]	and count us among those you have chosen. [Through Christ our Lord. Amen.]	and count us among those you have chosen. [Through Christ our Lord. Amen.]	your peace, and command that we be delivered from eternal damnation and counted among the flock of those you have chosen. (Through Christ our Lord. Amen.)
(*Quam Oblationem*)			
Bless and approve our offering; make it truly spiritual and acceptable. Let it become for us the body and	Bless and approve our offering; make it acceptable to you, an offering in spirit and in truth. Let it	Bless and approve our offering; make it acceptable to you, an offering in spirit and in truth. Let it	Be pleased, O God, we pray, to bless, acknowledge, and approve this offering in every respect;

blood of Jesus Christ, your only Son, our Lord. [Through Christ our Lord. Amen.]	become for us the body and blood of Jesus Christ, your only Son, our Lord. [Through Christ our Lord. Amen.]	become for us the body and blood of Jesus Christ, your only Son, our Lord. [Through Christ our Lord. Amen.]	make it spiritual and acceptable, so that it may become for us the Body and Blood of your most beloved Son, our Lord Jesus Christ.
(*Qui pridie*)			
The day before he suffered **he took bread** and looking up to heaven, to you, his almighty Father, he gave you thanks and praise. He broke the bread, gave it to his disciples, and said: "Take this and eat it, all of you: this is my body." When supper was ended, he took the cup. Again he gave you thanks and praise, gave the cup to his disciples, and said: "Take this cup of my blood, the blood of the new and everlasting	The day before he suffered **he took bread in his sacred hands** and looking up to heaven, to you, his almighty Father, he gave you thanks and praise. He broke the bread, gave it to his disciples, and said: "Take this, all of you, and eat it: this is my body **which will be given up for you."** When supper was ended, he took the cup. Again he gave you thanks and praise, gave the cup to his disciples, and said:	The day before he suffered he took bread in his sacred hands and looking up to heaven, to you, his almighty Father, he gave you thanks and praise; he broke the bread, gave it to his disciples, and said: "Take this, all of you, and eat it: this is my body which will be given up for you." When supper was ended, he took the cup; again he gave you thanks and praise, gave the cup to his disciples, and said:	On the day before he was to suffer . . . , he took bread in his holy and venerable hands, and with eyes raised to heaven to you, O God, his almighty Father, giving you thanks, he said the blessing, broke the bread and gave it to his disciples, saying: "Take this, all of you, and eat of it, for this is my Body, which will be given up for you." In a similar way, when supper was ended, he took this precious chalice in his holy and

covenant—the mystery of faith. This blood is to be shed for you and for all men so that sins may be forgiven. Whenever you do this, you will do it in memory of me."	"Take this, all of you, and drink from it: this is the cup of my blood, the blood of the new and everlasting covenant. It will be shed for you and for all so that sins may be forgiven. ***Do this in memory of me.*** "	"Take this, all of you, and drink from it: this is the cup of my blood, the blood of the new and everlasting covenant. It will be shed for you and for all so that sins may be forgiven. Do this in memory of me."	venerable hands, and once more giving you thanks, he said the blessing and gave the chalice to his disciples, saying: "Take this, all of you, and drink from it, for this is the chalice of my Blood, the Blood of the new and eternal covenant, which will be poured out for you and for many for the forgiveness of sins. Do this in memory of me."
	Let us proclaim the mystery of faith: ***Christ has died,*** ***Christ is risen,*** ***Christ will come again.***	Great is the mystery of faith: Christ has died, Christ is risen, Christ will come again.	The mystery of faith. We proclaim your Death, O Lord, and profess your Resurrection until you come again.
(*Unde et memores*)			
So now, Lord, we celebrate the memory of Christ, your Son. We, your people and your	Father, we celebrate the memory of Christ, your Son. We, your people and your	And so, Lord God, we celebrate the memory of Christ, your Son: we, your	Therefore, O Lord, as we celebrate the memorial of the blessed Passion, the Resurrection

ministers, recall his passion, his resurrection from the dead, and his ascension into glory; and from the many gifts you have given us we offer to you, God of glory and majesty, this holy and perfect sacrifice: the bread of life and the cup of eternal salvation.	ministers, recall his passion, his resurrection from the dead, and his ascension into glory; and from the many gifts you have given us we offer to you, God of glory and majesty, this holy and perfect sacrifice: the bread of life and the cup of eternal salvation.	people and your ministers, call to mind his passion, his resurrection from the dead, and his ascension into glory; and from the many gifts you have given us we offer to you, God of glory and majesty, this holy and perfect sacrifice, the bread of life and the cup of eternal salvation.	from the dead, and the glorious Ascension into heaven of Christ, your Son, our Lord, we, your servants and your holy people, offer to your glorious majesty from the gifts that you have given us, this pure victim, this holy victim, this spotless victim, the holy Bread of eternal life and the Chalice of everlasting salvation.
(Supra quae)			
Look with favor on these offerings. Accept them as you did the gifts of your servant Abel, the sacrifice of Abraham, our father in faith, and the offering of your priest Melchizedek	Look with favor on these offerings and accept them as once you accepted the gifts of your servant Abel, the sacrifice of Abraham, our father in faith, and the bread and wine offered by your priest Melchizedek.	Look with favor on these offerings and accept them as once you accepted the gifts of your servant Abel, the sacrifice of Abraham, our father in faith, and the bread and wine offered by your priest Melchizedek.	Be pleased to look upon these offerings with a serene and kindly countenance, and to accept them, as once you were pleased to accept the gifts of your servant Abel the just, the sacrifice of Abraham, our father in faith, and the offering of your high priest Melchizedek, a

English Vernacular Translation of the Roman Canon 247

			holy sacrifice, a spotless victim.
(*Supplices te*)			
Almighty God, we pray that your angel may take this sacrifice to your altar in heaven. Then, as we receive from this altar the sacred body and blood of your Son, let us be filled with every grace and blessing. [Through Christ our Lord. Amen.]	Almighty God, we pray that your angel may take this sacrifice to your altar in heaven. Then, as we receive from this altar the sacred body and blood of your Son, let us be filled with every grace and blessing. [Through Christ our Lord. Amen.]	Almighty God, command that your angel carry this sacrifice to your altar in heaven. Then, as we receive from this altar the sacred body and blood of your Son, let us be filled with every grace and blessing. [Through Christ our Lord. Amen.]	In humble prayer we ask you, almighty God: command that these gifts be borne by the hands of your holy Angel to your altar on high in the sight of your divine majesty, so that all of us, who through this participation at the altar receive
			the most holy Body and Blood of your Son, may be filled with every grace and heavenly blessing. (Through Christ our Lord. Amen.)
(*Memento etiam*)			
Remember, Lord, those who have died, N. and N. They have gone before us marked with the sign of faith, and are now at rest. May these, and all who sleep in Christ, find in	Remember, Lord, those who have died and have gone before us marked with the sign of faith, especially those for whom we now pray, N. and N. May these, and all who sleep	Remember, Lord, your servants who have died and have gone before us marked with the sign of faith, especially those for whom we now pray, N. and N. Grant them and all	Remember also, Lord, your servants N. and N., who have gone before us with the sign of faith and rest in the sleep of peace. Grant them, O Lord, we pray, and

your presence light, happiness, and peace. [Through Christ our Lord. Amen.]	in Christ, find in your presence light, happiness, and peace. [Through Christ our Lord. Amen.]	who sleep in Christ a heavenly light and peace. [Through Christ our Lord. Amen.]	all who sleep in Christ, a place of refreshment, light and peace. (Through Christ our Lord. Amen.)
(*Nobis quoque*)			
For ourselves, too, we ask a place with your apostles and martyrs, with John the Baptist, Stephen, Matthias, Barnabas, [Ignatius, Alexander, Marcellinus, Peter, Felicity, Perpetua, Agatha, Lucy, Agnes, Cecilia, Anastasia,] and all the saints. Though we are sinners, we trust in your mercy and love. Do not consider what we truly deserve, but grant us your forgiveness, through Christ our Lord.	For ourselves, too, we ask some share in the fellowship of your apostles and martyrs, with John the Baptist, Stephen, Matthias, Barnabas, [Ignatius, Alexander, Marcellinus, Peter, Felicity, Perpetua, Agatha, Lucy, Agnes, Cecilia, Anastasia,] and all the saints. Though we are sinners, we trust in your mercy and love. Do not consider what we truly deserve, but grant us your forgiveness, through Christ our Lord.	For ourselves, too, sinners who trust in your mercy and love, we ask some share in the fellowship of your apostles and martyrs, with John the Baptist, Stephen, Matthias, Barnabas, [Ignatius, Alexander, Marcellinus, Peter, Felicity, Perpetua, Agatha, Lucy, Agnes, Cecilia, Anastasia,] and all your saints. Welcome us into their company, not considering what we deserve, but freely granting us your pardon.	To us, also, your servants, who, though sinners, hope in your abundant mercies, graciously grant some share and fellowship with your holy Apostles and Martyrs: with John the Baptist, Stephen, Matthias, Barnabas, (Ignatius, Alexander, Marcellinus, Peter, Felicity, Perpetua, Agatha, Lucy, Agnes, Cecilia, Anastasia) and all your Saints; admit us, we beseech you, into their company, not weighing our merits, but granting us your pardon, through Christ our Lord.

(*Per ipsum*)			
Through him you give us all these things. You fill them with life and goodness, you bless them and make them holy. Through him, with him, in him, in the unity of the Holy Spirit, all glory and honor is yours almighty Father, for ever and ever. Amen.	Through him you give us all these gifts. You fill them with life and goodness, you bless them and make them holy. Through him, with him, in him, in the unity of the Holy Spirit, all glory and honor is yours, almighty Father, for ever and ever. Amen.	Through Christ our Lord you give us all these gifts, you fill them with life and goodness, you bless them and make them holy. Through him, with him, in him, in the unity of the Holy Spirit, all glory and honor is yours, almighty Father, for ever and ever. Amen.	Through whom you continue to make all these good things, O Lord; you sanctify them, fill them with life, bless them, and bestow them upon us. Through him, and with him, and in him, O God, almighty Father, in the unity of the Holy Spirit, all glory and honor is yours, for ever and ever. Amen

1998 ICEL Translation

ICEL's English translation of the Roman Canon had lasting influence on the general translation style for liturgical texts. French and Spanish conferences followed a similar methodology in their translations, "neither [maintaining] a literal translation of the text, nor [shying] away from incorporating modern theological understandings and nuances."[38] Additionally, when the *Consilium* released its *Instruction on the Translation of Liturgical Texts* in 1969 (composed significantly in French and not Latin, *Comme le Prévoit*), they appear to have adopted, or at least sympathized with, ICEL's principles of translation, particularly on the theory of dynamic equivalence. The document states:

---

38. Magas, "Issues in Eucharistic Praying," 494.

> To achieve this end [of providing an authentic translation], it is not sufficient that a liturgical translation merely reproduce the expressions and ideas of the original text. Rather, it must faithfully communicate to a given people, and in their own language, that which the Church by means of this given text originally intended to communicate to another people in another time. A faithful translation, therefore cannot be judged on the basis of individual words: the total context of this specific act of communication must be kept in mind, as well as the literary form proper to the respective language.[39]

The years following the promulgation of the first edition of the Roman Missal of Paul VI in English translation saw a period of dialogue between ICEL, various consulters, and the Holy See. It was generally understood that the texts would need to be revised in response to the living reception of the translations by the faithful and their pastors. ICEL openly acknowledged that these texts had been produced in a rushed manner, and that they would require revision in the proceeding years. That process formally began in 1982 with the "Sacramentary project" and the following task for the revision of the Order of the Mass in 1984, the fruits of which can be seen in the 1998 translation of the Roman Missal.

In this round of translations ICEL adhered to their original principles; however, they "aimed for a fuller and richer rendering of the Latin vocabulary and syntax, resulting in a more nuanced theology and a denser literary style."[40] Kevin Magas notes that these translators appear less concerned with a strict principle of dynamic equivalence and were more open to an elevated and elegant style within their English translations. This approach struck a balance between formal and dynamic equivalence, what some have called "functional equivalence."[41] To this end, several adjectives that had been left out of the earlier translations were reintroduced to this new translation. "[The] adjective clementissimae is rendered as 'all-merciful' in the *Te igitur*, Abel now receives his proper

---

39. Consilium for Implementation of Sacrosanctum Concilium, "On the Translation of Liturgical Texts for Celebration with a Congregation" (issued January 25, 1969), 6.

40. Magas, "Issues in Eucharistic Praying," 495.

41. Keith Pecklers and Gilbert Ostdiek, "The History of Vernaculars and the Role of Translation," in *A Commentary on the Order of Mass of* The Roman Missal, ed. Edward Foley et al. (Collegeville, MN: Liturgical Press, 2011), 65.

title 'just' in *the Supra quae*, and 'your people' is expanded to 'your faithful people' in the *Memento domine*."[42] In addition, several phrases were expanded in the 1994 translation in order to more fully capture the theological depth of particular prayers in the Canon. The humble and supplicatory tone of the *Nobis quoque* was more fully realized by changing the beginning phrase from "For ourselves, too, we ask some share . . ." to "For ourselves, too, sinners who trust in your mercy and love . . ." The same essential words are present in both cases; however, the 1994 translation employed a more complex sentence structure in order to convey the balance of trust and supplication with an air of dignity and grace. While ICEL was hesitant to make any drastic changes to the text since the faithful had already become familiar with the words of the Canon, the main concern for this new translation was placed on the orality of the prayers and on the ability for the Church to participate in praying these words together. The intention was to alter the texts only minimally, but in doing so to improve the style, flow, and elegance of the translations. The final translation of the Roman Canon was finished in 1994 and approved by seventy-five percent of the English-speaking bishops' conferences, with the full Missal and Sacramentary appearing in 1998. It can be viewed in comparison with the prior translations in the chart above.

Liturgiam Authenticam and the 2010 Translation

While the English-speaking bishops' conferences approved the 1998 translation of the Roman Missal, it was not ratified by the Congregation for Divine Worship and the Discipline of the Sacraments (CDW). This move anticipated the CDW's promulgation of *Liturgiam Authenticam* (On the Use of Vernacular Language in the Books of the Roman Rite, hereafter referred to as *LA*) in 2001. The document conveys an anxiety over the authenticity of the previous liturgical translations and offers new guidelines for translation. Although some of *LA*'s guidelines correspond to the previous principles of translation, it is clear that the document intends a more literal style. "Its translation guidelines favor the translation approach of literal/formal equivalence, often implemented as a

---

42. Magas, "Issues in Eucharistic Praying," 496.

word-for-word translation, which 'strives to retain from the source text as much as possible of the syntax (e.g., relative and subordinate clauses, word order, vocabulary, and even capitalization).'"[43]

Over the next decade, the Roman Missal was retranslated according to the new principles outlined in *LA*, and the third typical edition was approved in 2010 (implemented in 2011). The English translation of the Roman Canon received significant reworking in this new edition. The more literal translation of the Latin text produced the multiplication of adjectives, longer and more complex sentences, and the addition of phrases imported into the English language. While this stylistic choice was intended to approximate a sacred or elevated language, many believe that the changes made the Canon sound archaic and increasingly incomprehensible when read aloud. Others have made critiques about the lack of nuance and ambiguity in the word-for-word translation of the Canon.[44] It is often said that the most recent edition does not take into account contemporary liturgical, sacramental, and historical scholarship, as well as the ecclesiology important to Vatican II. For example, the literal translation of the *Communicantes* leaves out the connection between the venerated saints (with Mary) and the whole church with whom they are in communion. The earlier translations added the phrase *with the whole Church* to the communion of saints because it served to highlight the ecclesial reality of the church in heaven and on earth, united in the eucharistic celebration. Another issue that critics have raised is the translation of *hostia* as *victim* in the *Unde et memores*. This word (post-consecration) refers to the "holy bread" and "chalice of everlasting salvation," which are offered to the Lord. Many have suggested that the earlier translations rendered the subject of this offering more clear—that is, a perfect *sacrifice* (as opposed to victim, which is so readily associated with Christ himself as the Victim).[45]

Similarly, the previous translations had been careful in their interpretation of a confusing phrase in the *Memento domine*. The new literal translation reads, "For them [N. and N.], we offer you this sacrifice of

---

43. Ibid., 489.
44. This section pulls heavily from ibid., 500–505.
45. See Mazza, *Eucharistic Prayers of the Roman Rite*, 77–78; and Maxwell E. Johnson, "Recent Thoughts on the Roman Anaphora: Sacrifice in the *Canon Missae*," below, 287–318.

praise *or* they offer it for themselves and all who are dear to them." Enrico Mazza points out that this phrase was historically situated in the practices of offering Masses for others (or self) through a stipend. In this case, the Mass was offered for a patron *with or without* their physical presence. "The word 'or' (*vel*) is rubrical, that is, it points to an alternative: either the offerors themselves are present, or they are absent, in which case the celebrant offers the sacrifice of praise in their stead."[46] The earlier translations interpreted this phrase in light of the *presence* of those who were worshiping, and took out the confusing either-or phrasing: "we offer you this sacrifice of praise for ourselves and those who are dear to us."

Scholars have also noted that a literal translation of "sign of faith" (*signum fidei*) in the *Memento etiam* neglects the baptismal undertones of the prayer. The 2010 translation reads: "who have gone before us with the sign of faith." The earlier translation added explicit emphasis to the *mark* imprinted on the soul in the sacrament of baptism in its translation, "and have gone before us *marked* with the sign of faith." The strict literal translation does not allow for this kind of sacramental nuance. This brief examination of critiques of the implementation of the *LA* in the current translation of the Roman Canon is not exhaustive. Suffice to say, many scholars conclude that a reliance on formal equivalence in the translation of text does not render the most rich and readable prayer, and serves to inhibit the communication of the venerable text of the Roman Canon to the faithful. On the opposite side of this argument, many in the Church have claimed that the new translation allows for a more hieratic and supplicative language. This contingent held that a certain sense of mystery, veiling, and reverence was missing from the previous English translations, qualities that were loved and cherished in the Tridentine Mass. These competing factions have not as of yet found a middle ground.

Conclusion

The complicated history of the translation of the Roman Canon has only been touched on here in the briefest of manners. My aim in this essay was to highlight the basic movements of translation that produced the text of the prayer that the Catholic Church uses as Eucharistic Prayer

---

46. Mazza, *Eucharistic Prayers of the Roman Rite*, 64–65.

I today. The language of the Roman liturgy, its translation, and various reforms are all still very contentious issues, as most recently shown by Pope Francis's Apostolic Letter issued *motu proprio*, *Traditionis custodes*. By way of conclusion, I offer a reflection on the discussion that I have begun to engage.

Sacrosanctum Concilium called for full, conscious, and active participation in the liturgy. From the beginning, the conversation assumed that this active participation was synonymous with cognitive understanding. It is clear from tracing the history of the translation of the Roman Canon that two values were constantly being balanced—the revered tradition of the Roman Canon and the comprehension of its words by the faithful. In reference to the latter value, I wonder if the more appropriate articulation should be the "participation of the faithful in the eucharistic liturgy" rather than "the faithful's comprehension of the words of the Canon." Sacramental participation in the life of the Trinity through the mysteries of liturgical worship is a broader and more comprehensive human experience than the cognitive comprehension of the words of the eucharistic prayer (to say nothing of the participation of those who possess less cognitive ability than is expected of the "average" adult). I bring up this point not to lessen the importance of producing comprehensible translations of the Roman Canon, but only to suggest that the conversation on translation could be aided by a broader definition of participation. Perhaps if "the psychological mechanism which we call the 'sense of the sacred,'"[47] as Mazza defines it, were taken more seriously as an additional means for communicating God's presence and the laity's participation in the sacramental economy, then there might be room in the translation of the Roman Canon for a happier medium of sacred and familiar language. At the very least, the discussion could include a more robust vocabulary for identifying the effectiveness of language as *one* sign within the sacramental encounter.

---

47. Mazza, *Eucharistic Prayers of the Roman Rite*, 53–54.

IX

Igbo Translations of the Roman Canon

Inculturation, the Battle for the Soul of Latin, or . . . ?

Joachim Chukwuebuka Ozonze

The Roman Canon has always commanded a high degree of reverence and admiration.[1] In fact, as Neil J. Roy remarks, when, in the 1960s, liturgists and other specialists approached Paul VI for permission to update and reform the Canon, the pope altogether forbade any tampering with the prayer. Instead, Cipriano Vagaggini was allowed to compile an alternative to the Roman Canon that might be used, for instance, on weekdays (known today as Eucharistic Prayer III).[2] However, the resolution of the Second Vatican Council to translate liturgical texts into the vernacular, "with the purpose of bringing about in the most diligent way

---

1. Matthieu Smyth speaks of "the only and unique tradition of the Roman Canon, with its structure and its distinctive speech." Matthieu Smyth, "The Anaphora of the So-called 'Apostolic Tradition' and the Roman Eucharistic Prayer," in *Issues in Eucharistic Praying in East and West: Essays in Liturgical and Theological Analysis*, ed. Maxwell E. Johnson (Collegeville, MN: Liturgical Press, 2010), 74.
2. Neil J. Roy, "The Mother of God, the Forerunner, and the Saints of the Roman Canon: A Euchological *Deësis*," in Johnson, *Issues in Eucharistic Praying in East and West*, 327.

that renewal of the sacred Liturgy,"[3] meant that the *Great Roman Canon* itself was going to exist in a garb other than its Latin regalia. What would that garb look like?

The present essay has its origins as an attempt to trace closely the translation of the Roman Canon into the vernacular. It began with a study of the origins and formation of the Roman Canon from the end of the fourth century to the beginning of the seventh century,[4] including its relationship with Ambrose's *De Sacramentis* and other eucharistic prayers like the Alexandrian Anaphora of St. Mark[5] or the East Syrian Anaphora of Mar Theodore.[6] This was followed by a comparative study of the Canon in the 1570 Roman Missal of Pope Pius V and the 1970 Missal of Pope Paul VI (the current *editio typica*), and a comparative study of the various English translations—approved and unapproved—of the *editio typica*, noting the commonalities and differences in translations, the raison d'être of the translations, the decisions of the translators, and the politics of approval and disapproval. These studies formed the background to an exploration of the translation of the Roman Canon into the Igbo language.

This essay, therefore, focuses principally on the two translation texts of the Roman Canon into Igbo. It unpacks the assumptions and principles that undergird both translations, and raises deeper questions about the meaning and intention of the translation project, when such translations involve living texts and real liturgical communities.

---

3. Congregation for Divine Worship and the Discipline of the Sacraments, Fifth Instruction "For the Right Implementation of the Sacred Liturgy of the Second Vatican Council" (*Sacrosanctum Concilium* 36), *Liturgiam authenticam*, On the Use of Vernacular Languages in the Publication of the Books of the Roman Liturgy, no. 2.

4. Enrico Mazza, *The Eucharistic Prayers of the Roman Rite*, trans. Matthew J. O'Connell (Collegeville, MN: Liturgical Press, 1986); Allan Bouley, *From Freedom to Formula: The Evolution of the Eucharistic Prayer from Oral Improvisation to Written Texts*, Studies in Christian Antiquity 21 (Washington, DC: Catholic University of America Press, 1981), 200–216; Johnson, *Issues in Eucharistic Praying in East and West*, 224.

5. Enrico Mazza, *The Origins of the Eucharistic Prayer*, trans. Ronald E. Lane (Collegeville, MN: Liturgical Press, 1995), 240–86.

6. Matthew S. C. Oliver, "Connections between the Roman *Canon Missae* and the East Syrian Anaphora of Mar Theodore," *Questions Liturgiques* 101 (2021): 276–304.

The Igbo Missal

Since the Second Vatican Council, there have been two officially approved Igbo translations of the Roman Missal. The first one, *Usoro Emume Nke Missa,* was approved *ad experimentum* on July 17, 1971, by the Sacred Congregation for Divine Worship, and began to be used in 1973. The second translation, *Usoro Emume Missa,* received full approval from the same congregation, then renamed Congregation for Divine Worship and Discipline of the Sacraments (CDWDS), on February 24, 2017. Like the older Missal, it became available for use two years later on Pentecost Sunday, June 9, 2019.[7]

Following the official approval and use of the 2017 Igbo Missal, there has been a number of symposiums and essays trying to make sense of this new translation. In response to the "great controversy" and "mixed feelings" with which the missal was received, Emmanuel Chinedu Anagwo, the Nigerian professor of liturgy at the Catholic Institute of West Africa in Port Harcourt, undertook the project of explaining the liturgical, theological, and doctrinal bases of the "salient changes" that characterize the new translation.[8] In his essay, "Understanding the New Translation of the Roman Missal in Igbo Language," Anagwo notes that while "especially the conservatives are worried that it [the new translation] will distort, confuse and upset the nature and spirit of the liturgy . . . the progressives in particular, see the new translation as a development that will affirm the Latin expression: *liturgia semper reformanda est.*"[9] While this is an interesting remark in itself, it is not clear who or what is meant by "conservatives" and "progressives." Perhaps more importantly, I wonder whether these terminologies do not introduce mostly-Western binaries that, for whatever gains, have proved to constitute unhealthy polarizing epistemic categories that need not be imposed on other parts of the world. All the same, Anagwo sees the new translation as a rich development

---

7. As Anagwo explains, the 2017 Igbo Missal was initially planned to begin use on December 2, 2018, but for multiple reasons, especially the late arrival of the liturgical book, which was printed outside the country, it effectively started to be used on June 9, 2019. Emmanuel Chinedu Anagwo, "Understanding the New Translation of the Roman Missal in Igbo Language," *Journal of the Institute of Theology* 18, no. 1 (2021): 35.

8. Anagwo, "Understanding the New Translation," 57.

9. Ibid., 35.

that makes the Igbo translation closer to the Latin original. Hence, he charges the leaders of the Church to take on the duty of educating the faithful on these salient changes.[10]

While Anagwo offers the theological and doctrinal bases for the translation, Chidoo Ezika treats the new translation within the framework of Newmark's semantic and communicative theory of translation. He identifies the old translation as communicative translation and the newer one as a semantic translation that "focuses on the source text language *as requested by the authority of the Church*."[11] Although Ezika submits that his "study shows that many have accepted the translation while few are of the opinion that the new translation is not suitable,"[12] one would wish to see what this "study" consists of and how it was done, including the meaning and nature of this "acceptance," and who or what constitutes the "many" or the "few."

Whereas it may be hard to ignore the confirmation bias of Ezika's treatment, J. Obi Oguejiofor's approach features a more balanced treatment of the question. In his *"Nonyekwara Mmuo Gi*: Reviewing the New Igbo Translation of the Order of Mass," Oguejiofor highlights the strengths and weaknesses of the new translation using a tripartite framework of "necessary changes," "unnecessary changes," and "questionable or wrong translations." He concludes that the 2017 Missal is "usable," having been approved both by the CBCN and the CDWDS.[13] Remarkably, Oguejiofor treats the project of translation within a hermeneutic of perfection (even if comparing the missal to pizza can be somewhat unsettling),[14] and in this way opens the project to deeper questions about the meaning and possibilities of perfection in liturgical translation. Even if he does not explicitly discuss what this ideal of perfection is, it is not difficult to see that, following his analysis, perfection here entails a correct rendering of the Latin of the *editio typica* into the Igbo language. But, ought this be the ideal of perfection for liturgical translation? Calling to

---

10. Ibid., 57.
11. Chidoo Ezika, "On the Retranslation of the Igbo Missal," *Theory and Practice in Language Studies* 11, no. 3 (2021): 286.
12. Ezika, "On the Retranslation of the Igbo Missal," 286. Italics mine.
13. J. Obi Oguejiofor, "*Nonyekwara Mmuo Gi:* Reviewing the New Igbo Translation of the Order of Mass," *Bigard Theological Studies* 41, no. 2 (2021): 96.
14. "This version is usable. As with pizza, it does not have to be perfect to be good" (Oguejiofor, "*Nonyekwara Mmuo Gi*," 96).

mind Paul Ricœur's famous caution to "give up the ideal of the perfect translation,"[15] one may additionally ask whether and to what extent liturgical translation should be guided by the hermeneutic of perfection? Or, as David A. Stosur suggests, is perfection rather to be mourned and renounced even as translation happens?[16] What if, beyond a hermeneutic of perfection so construed, we talked more of a hermeneutic of encounter between liturgical communities across space, time, and culture?

If Oguejiofor locates the project of translation as an ongoing search for perfection, Michael Muonwe frames the project within the larger process of inculturation that requires faithfulness to the Latin *editio typica,* to the local culture, and a third fidelity to the official document that inspires the translation. Basing his paper on two different translations of the Latin expressions, *"Et cum spiritu tuo"* and *"fratres"* in the Igbo Missals, Muonwe concludes that the 2017 Missal is more inculturated than the 1971. However, he submits that a more detailed study of the two texts "may yield a different and more revealing conclusion" than two "isolated examples."[17]

This essay can be read as a response to this urgent call for "a more detailed study." Underlining how fidelity to the official document has both given rise to and shaped each translation, it goes beyond the analysis of isolated words and phrases, characteristic of most studies on the project of translation. Rather, the essay focuses on an entire *liturgical text* as a historical and living tradition of a praying community, recognizing that

---

15. Paul Ricœur, *On Translation,* trans. Eileen Brennan (New York: Routledge, 2006), 8. Here, Ricœur likens the task of translation to the work of mourning where the acceptance of loss (lament, if you like) offers an invaluable corrective to the project of translation and demands a renunciation of the ideal of the perfect translation.

16. David A. Stosur's remarks are worth citing at length: "It is an idealized perfection that must be mourned or renounced, even as translation happens. What is mourned is what no longer can be in the new context as it unfolds; but faithfulness to what is remembered in the text is also faithfulness to what is becoming, what emerges under present conditions: it is faithfulness to the living tradition. . . . [What is mourned is] an ideal of perfection that hinders the authentic liturgy of real persons and real communities in relationship with the One who makes all things new." David A. Stosur, "A Tale of Two Translations: Rhetorical Style and the Post-Conciliar English Translations of the Mass," *Theological Studies* 79, no. 4 (2018): 780–81.

17. Michael Muonwe, "Translation of Liturgical/Religious Texts (Catholic Igbo Missal): Transfer or Betrayal of Meaning in the Process of Inculturation," *Ministerium* 5 (2019): 46.

liturgical translation is not simply the rendition of words, phrases, and constructs from one language to another, but an encounter of real, historical persons and communities in relationship with the One who makes all things new.[18] In this methodological approach, to focus on the *text* as living text means to be shaped and guided by the history and culture of the liturgical communities, not in order "to recover the past (which is impossible), much less to imitate it (which would be fatuous), but to understand liturgy which, because it has a history, can only be understood in motion, just as the way to understand a top is to spin it."[19]

Consistent with this method, the essay focuses on the Roman Canon as a living liturgical text and as the unit of its reflection on translation.

The Roman Canon

There is something venerable about this "ancient piece of Milanese, Mozarabic, and Roman euchology," as Maxwell Johnson calls it.[20] Whatever that may be—its antiquity, its ability to evoke a sense of the sacred,[21] its oration of names, and so on—the Roman Canon stands across time as the prided eucharistic prayer of the Latin West. However, a study of the formation of this text reveals varying degrees of similarities, connections, and differences with anaphoras from different liturgical communities like the Alexandrian Anaphora of St. Mark or the Strasbourg Papyrus,[22] and even the East Syrian Anaphora of Mar Theodore.[23] Thus, the Roman Canon is reputed as "one of the most notable examples of liturgical inculturation in the history of Christian worship,"[24] and is therefore fitting as a case study for a reflection on liturgical translation.

---

18. Stosur, "Tale of Two Translations," 781. In his Apostolic Letter, *Spiritus et Sponsa* (3), John Paul II describes the liturgy as "the voice of the Holy Spirit and of the Bride, holy Church, crying in unison to the Lord Jesus: 'Come.'"

19. Robert Taft, *Beyond East and West: Problems in Liturgical Understanding*, 2nd ed. (Rome: Pontifical Oriental Institute, 1997), 192.

20. Maxwell E. Johnson, "Recent Thoughts on the Roman Anaphora: Sacrifice in the *Canon Missae*," *Ecclesia Orans* 35 (2018): 218.

21. Johnson, "Recent Thoughts on the Roman Anaphora," 219.

22. Walter Ray, "Rome and Alexandria: Two Cities, One Anaphoral Tradition," in Johnson, *Issues in Eucharistic Praying in East and West*, 99–127.

23. Olver, "Connections between the Roman *Canon Missae*," 276–304.

24. Mark R. Francis, *Local Worship, Global Church: Popular Religion and the Liturgy* (Collegeville, MN: Liturgical Press, 2014), 57.

However, before venturing into the translations of the Roman Canon into Igbo, this *text*ual study will be preceded by a presentation, in summary form, of the documents that gave rise to the translations. These documents provide the context for understanding these translation texts and for making sense of our comparative study.

Pax Romana and the Art of Translating

To guide the implementation of the liturgical reform called for by the Council, Paul VI, on January 25, 1964 established the *Consilium*. On exactly the same day four years later, (January 25, 1969, the Feast of the Apostle to the Gentiles), the *Consilium* issued the document, *Comme le prévoit* ("As is foreseen")[25] to guide the official translation of liturgical texts into the vernacular. This document, which gave rise to the 1971 Igbo Missal, offered "important theoretical and practical principles for the guidance of all who are called upon to prepare, to approve, or to confirm liturgical translations."[26]

Comme le prévoit

Consistent with the desire of the Council to encourage and facilitate the full, active, and conscious participation of the faithful in the liturgy,[27] *Comme le prévoit* emphasized the need for the translated text to come alive to the present community of the faithful. Thus, "it is not sufficient that a liturgical translation merely reproduce the expressions and ideas of the original text. Rather it must faithfully communicate to a given

---

25. *Comme le prévoit* appeared in French along with five other major receptor languages into which the Latin liturgical texts were being translated. The document is known in English as "The 1969 Instruction on the Translation of Liturgical Texts." The document emerged from a conference on translation in Rome (November 9–13, 1965) attended by 249 representatives and experts already working on translations around the world. See Gerald O'Collins with John Wilkins, *Lost in Translation: The English Language and the Catholic Mass* (Collegeville, MN: Liturgical Press Academic, 2017), 23.

26. *Comme le prévoit*, 4. Hereafter, CLP.

27. Second Vatican Council, Constitution on the Sacred Liturgy, *Sacrosanctum Concilium* 14. It is important to note that the council considered this as the preeminent criterion—the *prima et suprema lex*, if you like—of the liturgical reform. Thus, "In the restoration and promotion of the sacred liturgy, this full and active participation by all the people is the aim to be considered before all else; for it is the primary and indispensable source from which the faithful are to derive the true Christian spirit" (SC 14).

people, and in their own language, that which the Church by means of this given text originally intended to communicate to another people in another time."[28] Thus, translation must take cognizance of "the literary form proper to the respective language" rather than a word-for-word or phrase-for-phrase translation that "obscures or weakens the meaning of the whole." *Comme le prévoit* insists that "the 'unit of meaning' is not the individual word but the whole passage."[29] Very importantly, the document emphasizes that the translated texts should be so accessible and intelligible that "the greater number of the faithful . . . even children and persons of small education"[30] should be able to "find and express himself or herself."[31] In fact, intelligibility of prayers when said aloud may take precedence over verbal fidelity.[32] Finally, *Comme le prévoit* states that a sufficient interim period such be allowed before the text is properly approved by the liturgical commission of the conference of bishops.[33]

While this document shows a deep sympathy for the "present community of the faithful," it can seem that this community is simply a recipient of that which the church communicates to her, even if in her language. On this reading, liturgical translation becomes a faithful communication of a text to another community in their language. This is hardly a hermeneutic of encounter that recognizes the multilateral dimensions of the movement of the Spirit. In this light, I consider these lines of *CLP* remarkable:

> The prayer of the church is always the prayer of some actual community, assembled here and now. It is not sufficient that a formula handed down from some other time or region be translated verbatim, even if accurately, for liturgical use. The formula translated must become the genuine prayer of the congregation and in it each of its members should be able to find and express himself or herself.[34]

After *Comme le prévoit*, three other documents were issued on implementing the liturgical reforms: *Liturgicae instaurationes* (September 5,

---

28. CLP, 6.
29. CLP, 12.
30. CLP, 15.
31. CLP, 20.
32. CLP, 29.
33. CLP, 39.
34. CLP, 20c.

1970), *Varietates legitimate* (January 25, 1994), and *Liturgiam authenticam* (March 28, 2001). Of these three, it was *Liturgiam authenticam*, issued three decades later, that dealt directly with translation of liturgical texts into vernacular, and it was clearly a reaction to *Comme le prévoit*.

Liturgiam authenticam

Issued by the CDWDS as the fifth instruction for the right implementation of the Constitution on the Sacred Liturgy of the Second Vatican Council,[35] *Liturgiam authenticam* (LA) was a cautionary response to what was perceived as a manifest infidelity to the faith and derailment from the faithful rendering of the original Latin. Although beyond the scope of this essay, a history of, for example, the face-off between the ICEL and CDWDS offers an important lens for understanding the tone of the document.[36]

While LA, like CLP, wants translations to be characterized by a kind of language that is easily understandable,[37] it is clear that the priority of the document is to preserve the "dignity, beauty, and doctrinal precision" of the original Latin text. Therefore, any adaptation to the characteristics or nature of the various vernacular languages has to be sober and discreet.[38] For LA, translations of liturgical books must be "marked by sound doctrine, which are *exact in wording, free from all ideological influence*, and otherwise endowed with those qualities by which the sacred mysteries of salvation and the indefectible faith of the Church are *efficaciously transmitted* by means of human language to prayer, and worthy worship is offered to God

---

35. The first was *Inter oecumenici*, Instruction on Implementing Liturgical Norms, issued by the Consilium of the Sacred Congregation of Rites on September 26, 1964. *Tres abhinc annos*, the Second Instruction on the orderly carrying out of the Constitution on the Liturgy, was given three years later, on May 4, 1967, by the same Sacred Congregation of Rites. The third, *Liturgicae instaurationes*, was given by the Sacred Congregation for Divine Worship on September 5, 1970, while the fourth instruction for the right application of the conciliar Constitution on the Liturgy (nos. 37–40), *Varietates legitimate*, was given on March 29, 1994, by the Congregation for Divine Worship and the Discipline of the Sacraments. It is noteworthy that LA claims to substitute all these other instructions with the exception of *Varietates legitimate*.

36. For a detailed treatment of this history see John Wilkins, "Lost in Translation: The Bishops, the Vatican, and English Liturgy," *Commonweal* (November 28, 2005).

37. LA, 25.

38. LA, 20.

the Most High."[39] Thus, while CLP pays greater attention to the receptor language and community, LA focuses more on preserving the integrity of the original texts. In fact, LA states clearly that "the original text, insofar as possible, must be translated integrally and in the most exact manner, without omissions or additions in terms of their content, and without paraphrases or glosses."[40]

Very importantly, LA not only claimed to abrogate whatever instruction came before it (with the exception of *Varietates legitimate*),[41] it also understood itself as setting forth "anew, and in the light of the maturing of experience, the principles of translation to be followed in future translations" if vernacular translations are still be considered "authentic voice of the Church of God."[42] As such, the document called for "the making of emendations or for undertaking anew" translations that do not follow its instructions.[43] In fact, the CDWDS gave episcopal conferences and religious institutes a five-year ultimatum to submit ("bound to present") a compliant vernacular text to the Congregation. It was this instruction that gave rise to the 2017 Igbo Missal.

The Rationale of the 2017 Missal Translation Project

The 2017 Igbo Missal was driven by LA's idea of authentic translation as "rendering the original texts faithfully and accurately into the vernacular language."[44] Given that in most Igbo liturgical communities, the liturgy was celebrated in Igbo and (sometimes) English, the urge to retranslate the 1971 Igbo Missal to match the 2010 English Missal is understandable. Thus, while the 1971 Missal used the *editio typica* and the 1971 English translation as source texts, the source texts for the 2017 Igbo Missal were both the *editio typica* and the 2010 English Roman Missal. The goal of this translation project was the exact rendition of the Latin *editio typica* into Igbo. Anagwo describes this aptly:

---

39. LA, 3 (emphases mine).
40. LA, 20.
41. LA, 7.
42. LA, 7.
43. LA, 131.
44. LA, 20.

The reasons are anchored on the same understandings that informed the promulgation of the new English translation of the Roman Missal. . . . More importantly, this translation is on a restoration mission, to return more to the original Latin, using the principle of formal correspondence. The shortcoming of the previous translation was the levity in using more dynamic equivalence principle of translation, one that was free with the structure and content of the Latin sentences. The result is that some texts of the original Latin were sacrificed in order to bring out the idiomatic expressions. The guiding principle of the new translation expresses more grandly what the Latin says in the texts of the Mass through a more direct, literal and faithful translation of the original through an analysis of specific words and syntax.[45]

The presupposition here is that an accurate and faithful rendering of the Latin text in Igbo will give rise to theological accuracy, liturgical renewal, and a better worship of God in a dignified, devout, and attentive manner.[46] But how much does this presupposition hold true? How did this desired outcome play out in the translation process? A synoptic presentation of the 1971 and 2017 Missal will help to make this clear.

Synoptic Presentation of the 1971 and 2017 Igbo Missal

1971 IGBO MISSAL	2017 IGBO MISSAL
EKPERE NKE INYE EKEKE I	**EKPERE YUKARỊSTỊA 1**
Te Igitur	
Ụkọchukwu ga agbasa aka ya, were sị: Ya mere anyị ji si na aka Jesu Kristi, Nwa Gị, na-ariọ Gị, O Nna kacha ebere	Ụkọchukwu ga-agbasa aka ya, sị: Ya mere anyị ji si n'aka Jesu Kristi Nwa Gị bụ Dinwenụ anyị were umeala na-ekpe, na-ariọkwa Gị, O Nna kacha ebere.
Ọ ga ejikọ aka ya sị:	O jikọọ aka ya, sị:
ka Ị nara onyinye ndị a anyị ji achunyere Gị aja,	Ka Ị nabata,

---

45. Anagwo, "Understanding the New Translation," 37.
46. Ibid., 58.

	O mee akara nke obe n'elu achịcha na ikonsọ otu mgbe na-asị:
O mee akara nke obe n'elu iko sị:	
†Gọzie.	Ma gọzie † onyinye ndị a, ihenhunye ndị a, na aja ndị a dị nsọ na-enweghị ntụpọ.
bịa gbasaa aka ya	Ụkọchukwu ga agbasa aka, gụrụ na-aga:
Anyị na-ehunyere Gị ha maka Nzukọ Gị dị nsọ bụ Katọlik. Biko, nye ya udo, chekwawa ya, na-edu ya; mee ka ọdigide n'otu gazuo ụwa niile. Anyị na-ehunyekwa ha maka nwodibo Gị, bụ Nna anyị, Pope na Bishop anyị bụ (*) . . . na ndị nile kwerenụ, na-agbasa ezi okwukwe nke Nzụkọ Katọlik nke si n'aka ndị Apọstul bịa.	Na mbụ, anyị na-ehunyere Gị ha, maka Nzukọ Gị dị nsọ bụ Katọliki; biko ka ọ masị Gị inye ya udo, Ichekwaba ya, ijikọta ya na ịchị ya, gazuo ụwa niile: ya na nwaodibo Gị bụ Nna anyị Poopu . . . . na Bishọpụ anyị bụ (*) . . . na kwa ndị na-echekwa ezi okwukwe nke Nzukọ Katọliki nke si n'aka Ndịapọstụl bịa. (*) N'ebe a, e nwere ike kpọọ aha ndị Bishọpụ: Bishọpụ onye enyemaka pụrụ iche ma ọ bụ Bishọpụ ndị inye aka, dịka o siri dị na G.I.
Memento, Domine	
Ncheta ndị dị ndụ Cheta kwa ndị nke Gị, O Osebrụwa, ndị anyị bu n'uche ugbu a . . . . . . , Ebe a ọ ga ejikọ aka ya, kpere ndị o chere ekpere; bịa gbasa kwa ọzọ, were sị: na ndị nile ji okwukwe na ịhụnanya gbakọwa n'ihu Gị n'ebe a. Anyị na-ehunyere Gị aja otito nke a maka onwe anyị na ndị dị anyị n'obi, na-arịọ Gị, bụ ezi Chineke dị ndụ, ka Ị nye anyị mgbapụta nke mkpụrụobi na ọdịmma nke ahụ.	Ncheta ndị dị ndụ. Cheta ụmụodibo gị ndị nwoke na ndị nwanyị (Aha) . . . . O Osebụrụwa, O jikọọ aka ya kpeere ndị o bu n'uche epkere nwantịti oge. Ọ ga agbasakwa aka ya, kperekwa gawa na-asị: Chetakwa ndị niile gbara ebe a okirikiri ndị Ị maara okwukwe na mmụọ ofufe ha. Ọ bụ n'ihi ha ka anyị na-achụnyere Gị aja otito nke a, maọbụ ha onwe ha na-achụnyere Gị ya maka onwe ha na ndị niile dị ha n'obi:

Igbo Translations of the Roman Canon 267

	maka mgbapụta nke mkpụrụobi, olileanya nzọputa na ọdịmma nke ahụ ha. Ha na ehunyere Gị ekpere ha, Chineke dị ọkpụ, onye dị ndụ bụrụkwa ezie.
Communicantes	
Ncheta Ndị nsọ nọ n'eluigwe Anyị ewere nsọpụrụ na-echeta Ndị nsọ anyị na ha na emekọrịta; Onye mbụ bụ Maria, Vejin ọkpụ dị otito, Nne Dinwenụ anyị Jesu Kristi, Onye bụ Chukwu, † na Joseph dị nsọ bụ di ya. Ndị ọzọ bụ ndị Apostul, na ndị egburu egbu n'ihi okwukwe: Peter na Paul, Andrew, (James, John, Thomas, James, Philip, Bartholomew, Mathew, Simon na Thaddeus; Linus, Cletus, Clement, Sixtus, Cornelius, Cyprian, Lawrence, Chrysogonus, John na Paul, Cosmas na Damian) na ndị nsọ Gị nile. Mee ka anyị si na-arịrịọ ha, na ụgwọ dịrị ezi omume ha, kwusie ike na nchedo Gị n'ihe nile. (Site n'otu Kristi ahụ, Onyenweanyị. Amen)	Lekwaa anya n'okpuru! Na mmekọrịta anyị, na ndị anyị ji nsọpụrụ na-echeta: na mbụ, Marịa Vejin ọkpụ dị otito, Nne nke Chukwu na Dinwenụ anyị, Jesu Kristi, † Nakwa Josef dị ngọzi bụ di ya, Ndịapọstul Gị dị ngọzi, na ndị nke Gị e gburu egbu maka okwukwe: Pita na Pọl, Andru, (Jemis, Jọn, Tọmọs, Jemis, Filip, Batolomi, Matiu, Saịmọn, na Tadeus, Laịnus, Kletus, Klementi, Sistus, Kọnelus, Siprẹn, Lọrensị, Krisọgọnus, Jọn na Pọl, Kọsmas na Demịọn) na ndị nso Gị niile: Mee ka anyị si n'ụgwọ dịịrị ezi omume na arịrịọ ha nweta nchedo n'ihe niile site n'enyemaka nchekwa Gị (Site na Kristi Dinwenụ anyị Amen.)
Hanc Igitur	
Ụkọchukwu agbasaa aka ya sị: Biko, Nna, nara onyinye nke a n'aka ndị Ụkọchukwu Gị na ndị ezinaụlọ Gị. Mee ka udo Gị dị na ndụ anyị nke a; zọpụta anyị na ndafu ebebe, gụnye kwa anyị n'otu ndị Ị họọrọ	Ọ ga-agbasa aka ya, kpere na-aga: Ya bụ, Dinwenụ, anyị na-arịọ ka ọ masị Gị ịnara aja ofufe anyị, ya na nke ezinaụlọ Gị niile. Hazie ụbọchị anyị niile n'udo Gị. nye iwu ka a zọpụta anyị na ndafu ebighịebi

268 *Further Issues in Eucharistic Praying in East and West*

	ka a gụnyekwa anyị n'igwe atụrụ Ị họọrọ Ọ jikọọ aka ya
(Site na Kristi Onyenweanyị. Amen.)	(Site na Kristi Dinwenụ anyị. Amen.)
Quam Oblationem	
O kpukwasa aka ya n'elu ihe-aja were sị Anyị na-arịọ Gị O Chineke, ka Ị gọzie onyinye nke a, mee ka o si na mụọ anyị pụta, ka okwesị na Ị ga-anara ya, ka o wee ghọọrọ anyị Ahụ na Ọbara Nwa Gị, Ị hụrụ na anya nke Ukwu, bụ Onyenweanyị, Jesu Kristi	Ọ ga esetịpụ aka ya abụọ n'elu iheaja, na-ekwu sị; Anyị na-arịọ Gị O Chukwu ka ọ masị Gị ịme ka aja nke a bụrụ ihe a gọziri agọzi, ihe a nabatara, ihe bu ezie, si na mmụọ, kwesikwa na a ga-anara, n'ụzọ niile, ka o wee bụụrụ anyị Ahụ na Ọbara Nwa Gị Ị hụrụ n'anya nke ukwuu, Dinwenụ anyị Jesu Kristi.
Qui Pridie	
Ọ bịa jikọọ aka ya, Onye bịara n'ubọchị bọrọ mbọsị Ọ tara ahụhụ, O welite achịcha nwantịtị were achịcha n'aka Ya dị nsọ, Welite anya n'eligwe, lee Gị bụ Chineke Nna Ya ji ike nile anya, nye Gị ekele na otito, nyawaa ya, nye ya ụmụazụ Ya, sị: O hulata ntakịrị were nwayọ kpọpụta okwu ndị a nke ọma:	O jikọọ aka ya N'okwu ndị na-esonụ, a ga-ekwupụta mkpụrụokwu nke Dinwenụ n'ụzọ chawapụrụ achawapụ, doro anya, dịka ụdị okwu ndị ahụ kwesịrị Onye bịara n'ụbọchị bọrọ ụbọchị Ọ tara ahụhụọnwụ, O were achịcha, welite ya elu nwantịntị n'elu ekwuaja, kwuru gawa: Weere achịcha n'aka Ya dị nsọ dịkwa ebube, O welite anya welite anya n'eluigwe chee Gị bụ Chineke Nna Ya ji ike niile ihu,

Igbo Translations of the Roman Canon

NARANỤ NKE A, RIENỤ YA, ỤNỤ NIILE NKE A BỤ AHỤ M, NKE A GA-EBURU NYE MAKA ỤNỤ. Ugbu a O gosi ndị mmadụ Oriri Nsọ, bịa gbuo ikpere n'ala sekpuoro ya Otu ahụ kwa ka O si mee mgbe ha richara nri-anyasị, O bulu iko na aka ya, bulie ya elu ntakiri O bulu iko mmanya na aka Ya dị nsọ, nye Gị ekele na otito, bunye ya ụmụazụ Ya sị: O hulata ntakiri were nwayọ kpọpụta okwu ndị a nke ọma: NARANỤ NKE A, ÑỤỌNỤ YA, ỤNỤ NIILE: NKE A BỤ IKO NKE ỌBARA M NKE ỌGBỤGBANDỤ ỌHỤRỤ DỊ EBEBE: A GA-AGBA YA N'IHI ỤNỤ, NA N'IHI MMADỤ NILE KA E WERE GBAGHARA NJỌ. NA-EMENU NKE A NA NCHETA NKE M. Ugbu a O gosi ndị mmadụ iko-nsọ, bịa gbuo ikpere n'ala sekpuoro Ya.	ka Ọ na-enye Gị ekele, Ọ gọzie, nyawaa, nyekwa ya ndị ụmụazụ Ya, na-asị: O hulata nwantịtị NARA NỤ NKE A, RIE NỤ YA ỤNỤ NIILE: NKE A BỤ AHỤ M, NKE A GA-EDURU NYE MAKA ỤNỤ. Ọ ga-egosi ndị mmadụ achịcha e doro nsọ, weghachikwa ya n'efereaja gbuokwa ikpere sekpuo. Mgbe o mechara nke a, o kwuru na-aga: Otu a kwa ka O siri mee, mgbe e richara nri anyasị Ọ ga-eburu ikonsọ, welite ya elu nwantịtị n'elu ekwuaja kwuru na-aga: O buuru ikonsọ a tosịrị nsọpụrụ n'aka Ya dị nsọ dịkwa ebube ka Ọ na-enyekwa Gị ekele, Ọ gọzie ya, bunyekwa ya ụmụazụ Ya, na-asị: O hulata nwantịtị NARA NỤ NKE A, ÑỤỌ NỤ YA ỤNỤ NIILE: NKE A BỤ IKONSỌ NKE ỌBARA M, NKE ỌGBỤGBANDỤ ỌHỤRỤ DỊ EBIGHỊEBI, A GA-AGBA YA N'IHI ỤNỤ, NA N'IHI IMERIME MMADỤ KA E WERE GBAGHARA NJỌ GA, NA-EME NỤ NKE A NA NCHETA NKE M.

	Ọ gosi ndị mmadụ ikonsọ dowe ya n'elu akwandosa Ahụ Kristi, gbuokwa ikpere, sekpuo.
O welite olu kwuo:	Ọ ga-ekwuzi sị:
Ka anyị kwupụtanụ ihe omimi nke okwukwe anyị na-eme ugbu a:	Iheomimi nke okwukwe
Ndị mmadụ azasie ike sị:	Ndị agaa n'ihu na-ekwuwapụta:
1. Anyị na-ekwupụta ọnwụ Gị, Na-egosi kwa mbilite n'ọnwụ Gị, O Kristi, Wee lue mgbe Ị ga-abia ọzọ.	Anyị na-ekwusa ọnwụ Gị na-ekwupụtakwa mbilitenọnwụ Gị, O Dinwenụ, wee ruo mgbe Ị ga abịa.
Ihe ndị ọzọ ndị mmadụ nwere ike iza, ma achọọ 2. Site n'ọnwụ Gị iwepugoro anyị ọnwụ, Site na mbilite n'ọnwụ Gị Ị nyechigo anyị ndụ, Dinwenu Jesu were otito bịa.	
3. Oge ọbụla anyị riri achịcha nke a, ñụọ iko nke a, anyị na-egosi ọnwụ Gị, O Dinwenu, ruo mgbe Ị ga-abịa ọzọ.	Maọbụ Oge ọbụla anyị na-eri achịcha nke a, na-añụ ikonsọ nke a, anyị na-ekwusa ọnwụ Gị, O Dinwenụ, wee ruo mgbe Ị ga abịa.
4. Ọ bụ site n'obe Gị na mbilite n'ọnwụ Gị ka anyị ji nwere onwe anyị, O Kristi, Onye Nzọpụta nke ụwa.	Maọbụ: Onyenzọpụta nke ụwa, biko zọpụta anyị: Gị bụ Onye sitere n'obe na na mbilitenọnwụ Gị tọhapụ anyị.
Unde et Memores	
Ụkọchukwu agbasaa aka ya sị: O Chineke Nna; ndị ofufe olta Gị, na ndị nke Gị nile e doro nsọ, nọ n'ebe a, na-edowe ncheta nke Kristi Nwa Gị, Onyenweanyị. Anyị na-echeta ahụhụ Ya dị ngọzị, Mbilite n'ọnwụ Ya, na nrọgoro n'eligwe Ya dị otito. Anyị esị n'onyinye nile Ị nyere anyị, chunyere Gị.	Nke a gachaa, ụkọchukwu agbasaa aka ya sị: N'ihi nke a, O Dinwenụ, ebe anyị bụ ụmụodibo Gị, na ndị nke Gị dị nsọ na-echeta ahụhụ na ọnwụ dị ngọzi nke Kristi Nwa Gị bụ Dinwenụ anyị, na mbilitenọnwụ Ya site na ndị nwụrụ anwụ, na kwa nrọgoro n'eluigwe Ya dị otito, anyị na-esite n'onyinye Gị Ị nyegara anyị

Igbo Translations of the Roman Canon 271

O Chukwu dị ebube, aja nke a dị nsọ, aja nke na-enweghị atụtụ, achịcha dị ngọzị nke ndụ, na iko nke nzọpụta ebebe.	na-ehunyere ebubeeze Gị dị ukwu, aja nke a dị sam, aja dị nsọ, aja na-enweghị ntụpọ achịcha dị nsọ, nke ndụ ọkpụ na ikonsọ nzọpụta ebighịebi.
Supra Quae	
Biko, were ihu ọma nara ya, dịka Ị si nara onyinye nwa odibo Gị dị nsọ bụ Abel, na aja nke Nna anyị Abraham chụrụ, na aja dị nsọ, aja na-enweghị atụtụ nke Melchisedech, nnukwu Ụkọchukwu Gị chụnyere Gị.	Biko were ihu ọma na obi ebere lekwasị ha anya, narakwa ha dịka o si masị Gị ịnara onyinye nke nwaodibo Gị bụ Ebel, onye ezi omume na aja nke nna anyị Ebraham, na kwa aja dị nsọ, aja na-enweghị atụtụ nke Melkizedek, nnukwu Ụkọchukwu Gị chụnyeere Gị.
Supplices Te	
O hulata, jikọọ aka ya	O hulata jikọọ aka ya kwuru na-aga:
Chineke ji ike nile, anyị ji umeala arịọ Gị, Ka Ị zite Mụọ ozi Gị, ka o were aka ya buru onyinye ndị a, burute n'alta Gị dị n'elu, n'ihu ebube eze Gị. Mee ka ndị nile siri n'alta nke a nata Ahụ na Ọbara dị nsọ nke Nwa Gị rie	Anyị ji obi umeala na-arịọ Gị, O Chukwu pụrụ ime ihe niile, nye iwu ka Mmụọọma Gị dị nsọ were aka Ya buru ihe ndị a rute n'ekwuaja Gị dị elu, n'ihu ebube eze Gị bụ Chukwu, ka anyị niile sitere n'isonye na-mmemme ekwuaja nke a nata Ahụ na Ọbara kasị nsọ nke Nwa Gị,
O kulie, mee akara nke obe	O kulie dụọ akara nke obe na-asị:
jupụta na grasia na ngọzị nile nke eligwe.	jupụta na ngozi niile nke eluigwe na n'amara
O jikọọ aka ya. (Site na otu Kristi ahụ, Onyenweanyị. Amen)	O jikọọ aka ya (site na Kristi Dinwenụ anyị. Amen.)
Memento Etiam	
Ncheta Ndị Nwụrụ Anwụ:	Ncheta ndị nwụrụ anwụ
Ụkọchukwu agbasaa aka ya, were sị: Cheta, O Osebrụwa,	Ọ gbasaa aka ya sị: Chetakwuazi, O Osebrụrụwa,

ndị nke Gị hapụworo ụwa nke a, ndị ji okwukwe buru anyị ụzọ gawa, na-arahụ ụra nke udo.	ụmụodibo Gị ndị nwoke na ndị nwaanyị (Aha) . . . , ndị ji akara nke okwukwe, buru anyị ụzọ na-arahụ ụra nke udo.
O ga ejikọ aka ya, kpeere ndị nwụrụ anwụ o bu n'uche ekpere. Ọ gbasa kwa aka ya ọzọ, were sị:	O jikọọ aka ya kpeere ekpere nwantịtị oge maka ndị nwụrụ anwụ o bu n'uche. Nke a gachaa, ọ gbasakwaa aka ya kperekwa na-aga:
Biko, Nna, kpọbata ha, na ndị nile na-ezuru ike na Kristi, ebe ha ga-anọ nweta ihe, anụrị, na udo.	Biko Dinwenụ, anyị na-arịọ ka Ị nye ha na ndị niile na-ezuru ike na Kristi, ọnọdụ ezumike, ihe na udo
O jikọọ aka ya (Site na otu Kristi ahụ, Onyenweanyị. Amen)	O jikọọ aka ya (Site na Kristi Dinwenụ anyị. Amen.)

Nobis Quoque

O were aka nri suo n'obi ya, sị; Anyịnwa bụ ndị njọ. Ọ gbasaa aka ya Ndị chekwubere na ebere Gị, na-arịọ ka Ị nye anyị ọnọdụ n'etiti ndị Apostle na ndị nke Gị egburu maka okwukwe: John, Stephen, Mathias, Barnabas, (Ignatus, Alexaner, Marcelinus, Peter, Felicitas, Perpetua, Agatha, Lucy, Agnes, Cecilia na Anastasia) na ndị nsọ Gị nile. Ejela nyochawa ka ihe ọma anyị metara ha, ma were ihi ebere na obiọma Gị gunye anyị na otu ha, Ọ bia jikọọ aka ya (site na Kristi, Onyenweanyị.)	O were aka nri suo n'obi ya sị: Biko, nyekwuazi anyị onwe anyị bụ ụmụodibo Gị, Ndị njọ, Ọ gbasakwa aka ya kperekwa na-aga ndị chekwubere n'ụbara ebere Gị, oke na ọnọdụ n'etiti ndị Apọstul Gị dị nsọ na ndị egburu maka okwukwe: Jọn, Stivin, Matayas, Banabas, (Igneshọs, Elezanda, Masilinus, Pita, Felisitas, Pepechụa, Agata, Lusi, Agnes, Sisilịa, Anastesịa) na Ndịnsọ Gị niile. Anyị na-arịọ, ejela nyochawa ka ihe ọma anyị metara ha, ma were ihi ebere na obiọma gụnye anyị n'otu ha. O jikọọ aka ya sị: (Site na Kristi Dinwenụ anyị.)

	O kperekwa gawa:
Onye, I na-esite na Ya, oge nile, O Osebrụwa, eke ihe ọma nile ndị a, edo ha nsọ, tinye ha ndụ, gọzie ha, were ha nye anyị.	Onye I na-esite na ya mgbe niile, O Osebụrụwa eke iheọma niile ndị a, edo ha nsọ, enye ha ndụ, na-agọzi ha na-enyekwa anyị ha.
Per Ipsum	
O bulie, ma iko, ma efere nsọ Oriri-nsọ dị ime ya, welite olu kwuo: Ihe niile ekere eke na-eso Ya bụ Kristi na-esi kwa n'ịme Ya na n'aka Ya n'idikọ n'otu nke Mụọ Nsọ, Na-enye Gị bụ Chukwu Nna, ji ike nile, nsọpụrụ na otito nile, site n'ụwatụwa nile.	O were efereraja iheaja dị n'ime ya na ikonsọ bulite ha elu kwuo sị: Site na Ya bụ Kristi na n'isonye Ya na kwa n'ime Ya na n'ịdịkọ n'otu nke Mmụọ Nsọ ka nsọpụrụ na otito niile si adịrị Gị Chukwu Nna ji ike niile site n'ụwatụwa niile.
Ndi mmadụ ewelite olu, zaa: Amen.	Ndị mmadụ anakwee: Amen.

"I Belong to Paul; I Belong to Cephas": Two Documents, Two Translations

True to LA, the 2017 Missal is generally closer in formal equivalence to the Latin original than the 1971 Igbo Missal, even if Oguejifor highlights different instances where the 2017 Missal wrongly translates the Latin.[47] While the 1971 Missal takes some liberties in its translation of the original text, the 2017 text painstakingly tries to render the Igbo as closely as possible to the Latin text. However, in this desire for grammatical perfection, the 2017 Missal is replete with expressions that sound awkward, clumsy, and somewhat distracting. For example, in the *Te Igitur*, in place of "mee ka ọdigide n'otu gazuo ụwa niile" (grant that she may be united to the ends of the world), the new missal reads "Ichekwaba ya, ijikọta ya na ịchị ya, gazuo ụwa niile" (to govern her, to unite her and to govern her, reaching the whole world). Except for the purpose of a frantic attempt to render the Latin as closely as possible,

---

47. Oguejiofor, "*Nonyekwara Mmuo Gi*," 92–96.

this phrase sounds clumsy and unnatural to the native Igbo speaker in the context where it appears.

This clumsiness and awkwardness also show up in the *Communicantes*. The 1971 Missal begins the *Communicantes* thus: "Anyị ewere nsọpụrụ na-echeta Ndị nsọ anyị na ha na emekọrịta" (We reverently remember the saints with whom we have communion). The newer translation, however, renders the same expression as "Na mmekọrịta anyị, na ndị anyị ji nsọpụrụ na-echeta" (In our communion, and those we reverently remember). While the earlier translation is straightforward and free flowing, it still renders the meaning of the *Communicantes* well. The latter translation, on the other hand, in a bid for a word-for-word rendering of the *Communicantes,* sounds rather eccentric to the Igbo ear.

This clumsiness manifests even more in those attempts to ape the accretion of adjectives and verbs in the Latin text. *Comme le prévoit* noted that "the piling up of *ratam, rationabilem, acceptabilem* may increase the sense of invocation" in the Latin language, but, on the contrary, this "succession of adjectives may actually weaken the force of prayer" in other languages.[48] This is especially true when comparing these translations. In the *Te Igitur*, for example, where the 1971 Missal simply says "onyinye ndị a" (these gifts), the 2017 Missal says, "onyinye ndị a, ihenhunye ndị a, na aja ndị a dị nsọ na-enweghị ntụpọ" (these gifts, these offerings, and these holy and unblemished sacrifices). What is expected to be an increase of intensity becomes, in this context, a somewhat distracting repetition that lacks the rhetorical resonance and metric style that could have created the intended sense of intensification. In fact, the 2017 Igbo Missal is reputed for its difficulty to be put into music.

In addition, the 2017 Missal is unsurprisingly punctuated by the imperial language of the Roman Canon. For example, in the *Hanc Igitur*, the older translation says "Mee ka udo Gị dị na ndụ anyị nke a; zọpụta anyị na ndafu ebebe, gụnye kwa anyị n'otu ndị Ị họọrọ" (Grant that your peace may be in our present lives; save us from eternal damnation, and count us among your elect). The new translation, however, reads "Hazie ụbọchị anyị niile n'udo Gị. Nye iwu ka a zọpụta anyị na ndafu ebighịebi ka a gụnyekwa anyị n'igwe atụrụ Ị họọrọ" (Arrange all our days in your peace. Command that we be saved from eternal damnation, so that we

---

48. CLP, 12.

may also be counted among the sheep you have chosen). This language of command also appears in the *Supplices Te*, where the newer translation asks God to command ("send" in the older missal) his angel to carry these gifts to God's altar in heaven.

CLP admits that "many of the phrases of approach to the Almighty in the Latin text were originally adapted from Byzantium and Roman imperial court ceremonials."[49] For this reason, the document calls on translators to "study how far an attempt should be made to offer equivalents" in the vernacular for such Latin words (like *quaesumus, dignare, clementissime, maiestas*) that smacks of this imperial tradition. Might this not be an invitation to read again the message of the Council of Jerusalem and to reimagine what it would mean in this context "to not burden the Gentiles" (Acts 15:19)? As such, rather than a forced attempt to translate (if not impose) this imperial worldview, might this be an opportunity to offer to the Church something from the hearth of the Igbo praying community? For example, in his theological reflection on the commonalities between the world of the ancient Near East and contemporary northern Uganda and South Sudan, Todd Whitmore sees an opportunity of the latter not only to serve as "bridge cultures" for understanding the former, but also "as a theological corrective for the distortions of modern biblical scholarship,"[50] which are so far removed from the culture and worldview of the ancient Near East.

Along this line, remarkably, the 1971 Missal, in contrast to the 2017 Missal, is strikingly familial. For example, in the *Hanc Igitur*, while the 2017 Missal addresses God thus: "Ya bụ, Dinwenụ, anyị na-ariọ, ka ọ masị Gị ịnara aja ofufe anyị" (Therefore, Lord, we plead that it may please you to receive our sacrifice of worship), the 1971 missal prays, "Biko, Nna, nara onyinye nke a" (Please, Father, receive our gifts). In the *Memento Domine*, for example, while the new translation says "ụmụodibo gị ndị nwoke na ndị nwanyị" (your male and female servants), the 1971 Missal uses "ndi nke Gi" (your own people)—an expression that has the added meaning of dearness and friendship in the Igbo language.[51]

---

49. CLP, 13.

50. Todd D. Whitmore, *Imitating Christ in Magwi: An Anthropological Theology* (New York: T&T Clark, 2019), 9.

51. In the Igbo language, to call a person "Onye nke m" shows a certain marking out of that person as "yours," as "someone dear to you," someone you trust, someone you share trust with.

As John Paul II rightly remarks in *Ecclesia in Africa,* this familial experience is an important gift that Africa offers the family of God.[52] This is not some form of antiquarianism or exoticization of culture. Rather, it is a recognition that the way we address God matters, and that liturgy can and ought to transform, or at least challenge, everyday life, including forms of imperialism that oppose the flourishing of the family of God.

Furthermore, in its drive towards a neat translation of the Latin, the 2017 Missal carries over what is arguably an error in the *Missale Romanum* of Paul VI. As Enrico Mazza points out, in earlier texts of the Roman Canon, like the 1570 Missal, the *"vel"* of the *Memento, Domine* is rubrical and points to an alternative: "either the offerers are themselves present, or they are absent, in which case the celebrant offers the sacrifice of praise in their stead."[53] In the *Missale Romanum,* however, the *"vel"* becomes part and parcel of the text so that the *Memento, Domine* reads thus: *"pro quibus tibi offerimus: vel qui tibi offerunt hoc sacrificium laudis, pro se, suisque omnibus."*

Notably, this error is avoided by the 1971 Igbo Missal, which renders the prayer as "Anyị na-ehunyere Gị aja otito nke a maka onwe anyị na ndị dị anyị n'obi" (We are offering you this sacrifice of worship for ourselves and for those in our hearts). It is straightforward, clear, and beautiful. On the contrary, the new missal, strictly following the *Missale Romanum* and the 2010 English translation of the Roman Missal, prays thus: "Ọ bụ n'ihi ha ka anyị na-achụnyere Gị aja otito nke a, maọbụ ha onwe ha na-achụnyere Gị ya maka onwe ha na ndị niile dị ha n'obi" (It is for them that we are offering you this sacrifice of thanksgiving, or they themselves are offering it to you for themselves and for those who are in their hearts).

This carry-over is, perhaps, most notable in the *Qui Pridie,* where the 2017 Missal translates the cup as "ikonsọ a tosịrị nsọpụrụ" (this holy cup worthy of reverence) following the 2010 English Missal's rendition of "calicem" as "chalice" (as against "cup" in the 1967 English Missal). However, this translation of "calicem" in the 2017 Missal is sadly inaccurate and anachronistic.[54] As Gerald O'Collins explains, in

---

52. John Paul II, Post-Synodal Apostolic Exhortation *Ecclesia in Africa,* September 14, 1995.

53. Mazza, *Eucharistic Prayers of the Roman Rite,* 65.

54. Oguejiofor, "*Nonyekwara Mmuo Gi,*" 94–95.

the translation of the accounts of the institution narrative from Greek to Latin, the Vulgate renders "potērion" as "calix," a word that, at the time, simply meant "'cup' (especially for holding wine) or 'drinking vessel' . . . and not 'chalice' as used in later, ecclesiastical Latin to denote an ornamented drinking vessel reserved for use in the eucharistic liturgy."[55] The fourth-century framers of the Roman Canon, Baldovin clarifies, intended *calix* to mean "cup."[56] I wonder whether this attempt to translate *calix* as "ikonso" (holy cup) may not miss or at least conceal an important theological point: the ordinariness of the salvific work of Christ?

Considering the place of the Words of Consecration in the Roman Rite, the very important change from *"N'IHI MMADỤ NILE"* (FOR ALL) to *"N'IHI IMERIME MMADỤ"* (FOR MANY) ought not be ignored. While I do not wish to reproduce here the debate on "for all" versus "for many,"[57] I find stunning the addition of the suffix, "GA," to *NJỌ* (sin). This addition, which is done to translate *"peccatorum,"* has an interesting history that Bishop Dennis Isizoh, the liaison bishop in charge of the translation, narrates in his pastoral journal:

> I worked with the Vatican offices involved in the approval of Liturgical texts: Congregation for Divine Worship and the Discipline of the Sacraments and the Congregation for the Doctrine of Faith. This latter office discovered that we did not accurately translate *"peccatorum"* in the prayer for the consecration of wine. This influenced that new formular with "njo ga."[58]

While one would wish to know the process of this "discovery," it may be enough to mention that the use of "GA" in this context sounds unnecessary at best, since "NJỌ," the Igbo word for "sin," can rightly function here as a collective signifying both the singular and the plural.[59]

---

55. O'Collins, *Lost in Translation*, 69.

56. John F. Baldovin, *Reforming the Liturgy: A Response to the Critics* (Collegeville, MN: Liturgical Press, 2008), 123.

57. For a synoptic treatment of this debate, see O'Collins, *Lost in Translation*, 44–50. It is remarkable that the current Italian Missal (approved in 2018), which the pope uses, has the "per tutti"—for all.

58. https://totusdei.net/daily-pastoral-journal.html, accessed December 8, 2021.

59. Its clumsiness is all the more felt in the *Agnus Dei*, where instead of the "Nwaturu nke Chukwu, onye na-ekpochapu njo nke uwa," which the people have said for decades,

But were not the translators native Igbo speakers? How then can this be explained? Or is the submission of this essay grossly unfounded?

Firstly, it is significant that the draft that was sent to the CDWDS did not have the "GA" suffix, which was added after CDF "discovered" the "error." Even in the absence of a knowledge of the process of this "discovery," this suffixation might make sense within the context of a drive for formal equivalence and the desire to construct a sacral vernacular different from the ordinary usage of a language and befitting of divine worship. Yet, despite LA's penchant for an elevated sacral style and sacral vernacular as the authentic liturgical expression, it is important to ask whether and to what extent this style is true to scripture, especially the gospels. What does Jesus say about prayer? Would the Our Father fit this elevated sacral style? As Gerald O'Collins rightly notes, "It is the straightforward and not particularly 'sacral' style of the psalms that fed Jesus' own prayer and made them enduringly effective as prayers for Jews and Christians alike. Their language is simple and powerfully direct and does not keep intelligibility at bay. . . . A sacral style was not the style that inspired either Jesus or the psalmists."[60] In prioritizing the so-called sacral style over the simplicity of scripture, are we setting up our own traditions in place of and in opposition to God's design?

There is, of course, the possibility of seeing the discourse of a sacral vernacular as an opportunity to "rediscover and rethink the evangelical potential of Catholic worship in a sacral idiom,"[61] as Clinton Allen Brand puts it. But an important question to ask is whether a sacral vernacular

---

the people are made to say, "Nwa aturu nke Chukwu, onye na-ekpochapu njo**ga** nke uwa." For the native Igbo speaker, this can sound funny and rough. What makes this all the more striking is that the "*peccata*" of the Roman Missal is not a literal translation of either the Greek New Testament (ἁμαρτίαν) or the Latin Vulgate (*peccatum*). Mark Francis notes that one remarkable difference between Greek prayer and Roman prayer is that while the former appears to be much more dependent on direct quotations from Scripture, the latter rarely cites Scripture directly. "Even when the Bible was the source or inspiration for a liturgical text in the Canon of the Mass, it was restyled by the redactors of the Latin text to reflect this hieratic balanced mode of expression" (Francis, *Local Worship, Global Church*, 64).

60. O'Collins, *Lost in Translation*, 34.

61. Clinton Allen Brand, "Very Members Incorporate: Reflections on the Sacral Language of Divine Worship," *Antiphon* 19, no. 2 (2015): 139.

must be arrived at precisely through a Latinization of the vernacular. Perhaps, more importantly, what does this language *do*? What sort of liturgical reality and community does it give rise to, nourish, and legitimize? Going back to the Roman Canon as a historical and living document may help us to begin to answer these questions.

Historicizing the Roman Canon

Historical studies on the Roman Canon reveal a gap in intelligibility between the liturgical language and the ordinary language spoken by the people of the time. However, to use this as an argument for "a sacral vernacular, characterized by a vocabulary, syntax and grammar that are proper to divine worship,"[62] may amount to stretching this history too far. For the so-called sacral language of the Roman Canon/Rite can be traced back to the history of the Latinization of worship in the fourth century[63] and the conscious attempt to make liturgical Latin up to par with the juridical, technical, and abstract character of the pagan sacrificial prayers that Christian liturgy intended to replace or at least effectively counteract.[64] With the movement of Christian worship from the margins to the center of the empire, as the *cultus publicus*, Christian liturgical prayer was modelled in a language distinct both from the *sermo utilis* of everyday commerce and the *sermo vulgaris* of the illiterate.[65] Rather, as Francis remarks, the Roman Canon was "modelled after the archaic and legalistic Latin prescribed by the old *ius divinum* in which the pagan sacrificial prayers had been composed."[66] "Even for educated Romans," Francis explains further, "these texts were difficult to understand. But understanding or accessibility was not the point. The use of this traditional language—however archaic—was meant to promote 'mystery,' a sense

---

62. LA, 47.
63. While Greek was the liturgical language of the first Roman Christians, the major shift to Latin in the Roman liturgy took place during the long pontificate of Damascus (366–84). Francis, *Local Worship, Global Church*, 62.
64. Francis, *Local Worship, Global Church*, 62–65.
65. Christine Mohrmann, *Liturgical Latin: Its Origins and Character* (Washington, DC: Catholic University of America Press, 1957).
66. Francis, *Local Worship, Global Church*, 63.

of religious awe."[67] Thus, we see here that the intention was "to offer a culturally resonant, sophisticated style of prayer in keeping with Roman pagan tradition"[68] so that the Christian liturgy might effectively replace the pagan *ius divinum* as the new *cultus publicus*.

In this light, therefore, it is realistic that the Roman Canon/Rite is seen as a classic example of liturgical inculturation, as LA calls it,[69] and "one of the most notable examples of liturgical inculturation in the history of Christian worship,"[70] for it was a vivid product of the attempt in the fourth century to inculturate worship into Latin religious culture. However, when this point is taken to mean that the Roman Rite leaves little or no room for further inculturation, since it has become transcultural,[71] then the Roman Missal becomes an obstacle to inculturation and an imposition of Latin culture. Consistent with the history of the Roman Rite, the Roman Canon, while maintaining its venerability, ought to be an impetus rather than a barrier to inculturation.

Furthermore, this historical lens also allows us to glean whether and how this penchant for a sacral vernacular can give rise to and nurture a sort of liturgical elitism—one that will necessitate the reform of Gregory the Great (604), who tried to bridge the growing gulf between the liturgy and the faithful.[72] Thus, it is important to ask whether this Igbo translation process, driven by LA's ideal of a sacral vernacular, does not engender forms of liturgical elitism.

Perhaps a sign of this elitism can be an attitude that assumes that liturgical texts need not be easily intelligible to everyone. In his address to the clergy of Rome in 2013, Pope Benedict XVI noted that "Intelligibility does not mean banality, because the great texts of the liturgy—even when, thanks be to God, they are spoken in our mother

---

67. Ibid.
68. Ibid., 64.
69. LA, 5.
70. Francis, *Local Worship, Global Church*, 57.
71. LA (5) seems to give this impression: "Indeed, it may be affirmed that the Roman Rite is itself a precious example and an instrument of true inculturation. For the Roman Rite is marked by a signal capacity for assimilating into itself spoken and sung texts, gestures and rites derived from the customs and the genius of diverse nations and particular Churches—both Eastern and Western—into a harmonious unity that transcends the boundaries of any single region."
72. Francis, *Local Worship, Global Church*, 70.

tongue—are not easily intelligible, they demand ongoing formation on the part of the Christian, if he is to grow and enter ever more deeply into the mystery and so arrive at understanding."[73] Remarkably, *Comme le prévoit* emphasizes that liturgical texts be readily accessible and easily intelligible to even children and persons of small education.[74] But even more, while recognizing the significance of liturgical formation, are intelligibility and ongoing formation mutually exclusive? Does intelligibility prevent ongoing formation, or does the latter require that a text not be easily intelligible?

Perhaps most importantly, how might the project of translation diminish liturgical elitism and engender true liturgical renewal of the whole people of God? Guided by the important need to critically evaluate the operational principle of translation of a liturgical text and unveiling its presuppositions, it is important to seriously consider the members of the translation commission. Anagwo notes that the translation was prepared by the Igbo speaking bishops of Southeastern Nigeria, consisting of Onitsha and Owerri ecclesiastical provinces. Thankfully, Bishop Isizoh, the liaison bishop of the commission, lists the names of the members of the commission in his pastoral journal:[75]

1. ANYANWU, Rev. Fr. Gerald (PhD Christian and Classical Literature, Salesian University, Rome)

2. CHINAGOROM, Rev. Fr. Longinus (PhD [Nigeria] in Linguistics/Igbo, MA in Igbo, BA Linguistics/Igbo)

3. EZENDUKA, Msgr. Cyril (Masters in Sacred Music, Catholic University of America, Washington, DC)[76]

4. EZEOMEKE, Mr. Simon Odili (MA Igbo, BA Igbo)

---

73. Benedict XVI, Address of His Holiness Pope Benedict XVI, Meeting with the Parish Priests and the Clergy of Rome, Thursday, February 14, 2013, https://www.vatican.va/content/benedict-xvi/en/speeches/2013/february/documents/hf_ben-xvi_spe_20130214_clero-roma.html.

74. CLP, 15. Also, *Varietatis legitimae* 34 submits that "Rites also need 'to be adapted to the capacity of the faithful and that there should not be a need for numerous explanations for them to be understood.'"

75. https://totusdei.net/daily-pastoral-journal.html.

76. Msgr. Ezenduka died on April 21, 2012.

5. MADUBUKO, Msgr. Lawrence (Laurea in Sacred Liturgy, San Anselmo, Rome)

6. MADUEKE, Msgr. Jerome (Laurea in Dogmatic Theology, Urban University, Rome)

7. NGOESI, Mr. Michael (Masters in Igbo Language)

8. ODAJIRI Rev. Fr. Samuel (HND Mass Communications, MA Education and Administration)

9. OGUDO, Msgr. Donatus Emeka (Laurea in Sacred Liturgy, San Anselmo, Rome)

10. UBA, Rev. Fr. Bartholomew (Masters in Christian and Classical Literature, Salesian University, Rome)

Remarkably, in this list are represented experts in Christian and classical literature, Igbo language, sacred liturgy, dogmatic theology, and mass communication.[77] However, recognizing the enormous amount of work that these experts have done, one wonders whether the translation project would not have been further enriched by the participation of experts from several liturgical and theological schools in addition to Rome.

But also, there is only one layman (with a master's degree in Igbo) and, surprisingly, no women, lay or professed. This relative absence of the lay faithful is further heightened by the absence of an *experimental* period. Such an interim period, if well observed, can be a medicine to liturgical elitism and an opportunity to listen to the faithful. To be beneficial, this period could feature, among other things, a detailed and well planned out ethnographic study of the appreciation of the Missal by the faithful: lay and ordained of all ranks and file. Such an endeavor would be marked by a desire to take seriously the experience of those who do not have the leisure of spending hours in liturgy and theology classes. In this way, liturgical translation will take seriously an important aspect of the Christian faith: the *sensus fidelium*. Unsurprisingly, this aspect of the faith hardly surfaces in a translation process that is understood as transmitting to a recipient community a sacral monument that would impress on her the status of true worship. But as Mark R. Francis remarks, "What

---

77. LA, 70.

would the history of worship look like if we paid more attention to the experience of the 'people in the pews'—viewing the liturgy through what we know about their popular piety. . . . How can more sensitivity to the 'faith of the people' as expressed in their popular piety aid us in the task of liturgical inculturation?"[78] Although this remark is made to contest the binary between popular piety and liturgy, Francis's question also speaks to our present reflection. Thus, in the light of LA's cautionary tone, what if caution means trusting the *sensus fidei fidelium*? Trusting the faithful to be part of the process of translation? As LA puts it beautifully, "The translation of liturgical texts requires not only a rare degree of expertise, but also a spirit of prayer and of trust in the divine assistance granted not only to the translators, but to the Church herself, throughout the whole process leading to the definitive approbation of the texts."[79]

Yet, it seems that all of the above hinge on the meaning and purpose of translation; on whether the translation of the Latin texts into the vernacular amounts to an unfortunate concession to a subordinate culture, an instance of cultural hegemony, a deference to a superior liturgical expression, or a sincere and Spirit-led desire to foster local expressions of faith and piety.[80]

As earlier noted, the new Igbo translation hinges on the understanding, using the *lex orandi lex credendi* maxim, that a literal rendering of the Latin text in the Igbo language will amount to theological accuracy and liturgical renewal.[81] Yet, it is not hard to see how this presupposition hinges on shaky foundations. Firstly, while theological truths are expressed and celebrated in liturgical actions, such a stance risks reducing the rule of faith to the formulations of liturgical prayer, diminishing the multivocality of the liturgy as a symbolic action, and missing the reciprocal relationship between the *orandi* and *credendi*. Secondly, as Kenneth Amadi puts it, "Is the *Lex Orandi* of the church understood as a scripted, never changing reality? Or is it not in fact how the church prays through all times and peoples and cultures rather than simply how the church prayed within a

---

78. Francis, *Local Worship, Global Church*, 5–6.
79. LA, 75.
80. Rita Ferrone, "Notes on the Committee to Revise *Liturgiam authenticam*," *Pray Tell Blog*, March 16, 2017, https://www.praytellblog.com/index.php/2017/03/16/notes-on-the-committee-to-revise-liturgiam-authenticam/.
81. Anagwo, "Understanding the New Translation," 56–58.

particular time and place?"[82] Neglecting the historical context of the *lex orandi, lex credendi* axiom and applying it sweepingly as an *a priori* liturgical maxim, as Maxwell Johnson has shown, both misses Prosper's use of this statement and constructs liturgical prayer as a "proof text" rather than as "a source that is continually experienced over and over again by the members of the church in their liturgical convocations."[83] The Roman Canon is an expression of the church's *lex orandi* whose appropriation by the Universal Church is geared towards the enrichment, not stifling, of that *orandi* as manifested in particular cultures, places, and peoples.

Thus, while "renewal" has become a buzzword in liturgical circles especially following Vatican II, liturgical renewal ought not be founded on cultural hegemony or liturgical imperialism, or even on a frantic attempt by liturgists to communicate theological truths to the lay faithful.[84] Rather, authentic liturgical renewal is the fruit of a genuine loving encounter between praying communities and the Lord; an encounter that arises from a recognition that no one—tribe, tongue, people, nation—has earned a place at that Supper, but that all—equally and without exception—are invited to the supper of the Lamb.[85]

Hence, if the fruit of liturgical renewal is to be like the One I/We encounter, then, perhaps, a different question may be asked of the translation process: What does the project of translation do? What kind of

---

82. Kenneth Onyema Amadi, "*Lex Orandi, Lex Credendi:* Overcoming the Impasse. Comparative Insights from Martin Riesebrodt's Theory of Religion," unpublished paper, 2020.

83. Maxwell E. Johnson, *Praying and Believing in Early Christianity* (Collegeville, MN: Liturgical Press, 2010), 23.

84. Pope Francis emphasizes that the liturgy is not about the acquisition of mental concepts but the entering into an experience: "From all that we have said about the nature of the Liturgy it becomes clear that knowledge of the mystery of Christ, the decisive question for our lives, does not consist in a mental assimilation of some idea but in real existential engagement with his person. In this sense, Liturgy is not about 'knowledge,' and its scope is not primarily pedagogical, even though it does have great pedagogical value. (Cf. Sacrosanctum Concilium, n. 33) Rather, Liturgy is about praise, about rendering thanks for the Passover of the Son whose power reaches our lives. The celebration concerns the reality of our being docile to the action of the Spirit who operates through it until Christ be formed in us. (Cf. Gal 4:19)." Francis, Apostolic Letter On the Liturgical Formation of the People of God (*Desiderio desideravi*) 41, June 29, 2022.

85. Francis, *Desiderio desideravi* 4.

liturgical community does it engender? What ecclesial imagination does it inscribe? Translation, this essay suggests, is not merely the transfer of words from one language to another, or simply a matter of correct rendering of words and constructs, as important as this may be. Beyond these, liturgical translation, this encounter of living texts and communities with God, has deep implications for the meaning of liturgy and what it means to be church. For all of its good intentions and laudable efforts, the project of translation of the 2017 Missal risks engendering and nurturing liturgical elitism, diminishing liturgical renewal, and constituting a Latinization of the Igbo church.

Conclusion: *Magnum principium* and Reimagining Translation

On September 9, 2017, Pope Francis issued *Magnum prinicipium*. In this apostolic letter *motu proprio*, the pope highlighted the need for vernacular translations that are accessible to the people and expressive of their language, while taking care that they be "congruent with sound doctrine." Echoing *Comme le prevoit*, Francis restates that "fidelity cannot always be judged by individual words but must be sought in the context of the whole communicative act and according to its literary genre" (7). What is, perhaps, most striking is that the Holy Father points out that the purpose and *telos* of translation is not that the Latin texts wear the garb of other languages, but rather that the vernacular languages can themselves become liturgical languages, "standing out in a not dissimilar way to liturgical Latin for their elegance of style and the profundity of their concepts with the aim of nourishing the faith" (3).[86] The veracity and urgency of these words cannot be overemphasized if liturgical communities are not to become perpetual translators. But also,

---

86. The drama surrounding this *motu proprio* is remarkable. In the wake of the *motu proprio*, Cardinal Sarah, prefect of the CDWDS, published a commentary on *Magnum principium* in the French Catholic publication *L'Homme Nouveau*, stating that LA remains "the authoritative text concerning liturgical translations." Pope Francis, in a gentle but public rebuke, clearly restated that some of LA's provisions, particularly those dealing with the *recognition* (79–84), have been abrogated or reformulated according to his *motu proprio*. See "The Relationship between *Magnum Principium* and *Liturgicam Authenticam*," *Pray Tell Blog*, December 23, 2017.

in these words may be found an authentic expression of the purpose of liturgical inculturation and the marker of a translation that is driven by a hermeneutic of encounter. It is my hope that this vision will inspire subsequent translations of liturgical texts into the Igbo language. As Bishop Isizoh notes in his pastoral journal,

> The next stage of the work, which the Translation Committee has started, is the translation of the Prayers (Collect, Prayer of the offerings, After Communion Prayer). . . . When the Translation Committee finishes working on the Missal, the next task will be updating the prayers for Funeral and Marriage. . . . The Bishops in Igboland are also working on the Daily Igbo Lectionary.[87]

This is a welcome development, a *Kairos* moment for the Igbo church, and while this article does not discuss liturgical gestures, it recognizes that this oft-neglected yet important aspect of worship is an area where the Igbo church has so much to offer the world. Inspired by the Holy Spirit, may the Igbo church gift to the universal church an authentic Igbo liturgical expression.

May the Holy Spirit, true agent of inculturation, come!

---

87. https://totusdei.net/daily-pastoral-journal.html.

Recent Thoughts on the Roman Anaphora

Sacrifice in the Canon Missae

Maxwell E. Johnson

In a 2017 *Worship* article, Lutheran liturgical scholar Gordon Lathrop[1] includes himself among those contemporary Lutherans referred to in the 2015 Lutheran-Roman Catholic *Declaration on the Way*, who "continue to regard the language of sacrifice found in Catholic theology and the Catholic Eucharistic rite to be a potential stumbling block to unity."[2] Along with stating that it is possible to give a more "evangelical interpretation" to sacrificial or offering language "in the other (official) and (more frequently used) Roman Eucharistic prayers,"[3] Lathrop's primary target of critique, together with the *Orate fratres* dialogue, is the Roman *Canon Missae*, especially in light of its most recent 2010 English translation. Here, in contrast to the previous version, phrases like "these gifts" have become, in fidelity to Latin syntax, grammar, punctuation, rhythm, and repetitive rhetorical flourish, "these gifts, these offerings, these holy

---

1. Gordon Lathrop, "Sacrifice as a Word That Cracks: One Liturgical 'Consideration Moving Forward,'" *Worship* 91 (November 2017): 500–517.

2. Committee on Ecumenical and Interreligious Affairs, United States Conference of Catholic Bishops, and Evangelical Lutheran Church in America, *Declaration on the Way: Church, Ministry, and Eucharist* (Minneapolis: Fortress Press, 2015), 111.

3. Lathrop, "Sacrifice as a Word," 506.

and unblemished sacrifices," and, following the narrative of institution "this holy and perfect sacrifice, the bread of life and the cup of eternal salvation," has become "this pure victim, this holy victim, this spotless victim, the holy Bread of eternal life and the Chalice of salvation."[4] Lathrop concludes with the hope that the *Orate fratres* dialogue might ultimately be suppressed in Roman Catholic worship and that the Roman *Canon Missae* itself "be used less often [and] . . . always be interpreted when used."[5] While the *Orate fratres* dialogue will probably not go away any time soon, infrequent use of the Roman Canon—except among some priests for whom it is a new badge of orthodoxy—may well be almost guaranteed, due to its current unfortunate English translation and to the popularity of the other (shorter) Eucharistic Prayers II and III.

This essay is not intended as a response to Lathrop's article, which should come from a Roman Catholic, since Lathrop's comments are directed primarily toward eliciting Roman Catholic responses. Rather, his article is more of a catalyst for my own reflections here, since there is no question but that he has drawn attention to an absolutely crucial issue with which I would suspect there would be very wide Lutheran–Catholic agreement.

> I know that there are Roman Catholic theologians who are as critical of the theology of the Roman Canon, Roman Eucharistic Prayer I, as I am, perhaps more. I also know what the dialogues have said about Christ's one sacrifice and ours. And I know the idea of the priest confecting and then offering is a medieval caricature. Still, the plain sense of the words is before me, even when the Roman Canon is not used, certainly in the *Orate fratres* invitation and response and even in the other . . . Roman Eucharistic prayers, though more subtly there.[6]

---

4. Texts from the Roman Canon are from *The Roman Missal* (Collegeville, MN: Liturgical Press, 2011), 635–43. Texts from the earlier translation are from *The Sacramentary of the Roman Missal* (Collegeville, MN: Liturgical Press, 1985), 502–8. For an excellent critique of the 2010 English translation see Gerald O'Collins with John Wilkins, *Lost in Translation: The English Language and the Catholic Mass* (Collegeville, MN: Liturgical Press Academic, 2017).

5. Lathrop, "Sacrifice as a Word," 515.

6. Ibid.

Lathrop may be overly generous here when he refers to the idea of confecting and then offering as but a "medieval caricature" of eucharistic offering. Indeed, such "caricature" remains alive and well pastorally. For example, in a recent catechetical pamphlet, *My Sacrifice and Yours,* published with both *nihil obstat* and *imprimatur*, the eucharistic sacrifice is interpreted in a way highly reminiscent of Gabriel Biel's *Expositiones Missae,* and lends credence to Luther's (and Lutheran) fears about what was and is understood to be going on in the Roman Mass:

> At every Mass, shortly after the Consecration, you hear the priest say the words, "we offer." For example, in Eucharistic Prayer III, he says, "we offer you in thanksgiving / this holy and living sacrifice," and in Eucharistic Prayer IV, "we offer you his Body and Blood, / the sacrifice acceptable to you." This is the oblation. When we speak of "the sacrifice of the Mass," we are speaking specifically of this part. You, a member of the common priesthood, participate in the priestly action of Jesus Christ, who offered himself on the Cross. You join him by offering to God what he offers—his very Body and Blood. Eucharistic Prayer I calls this offering "this pure victim, / this holy victim, / this spotless victim, / the holy Bread of eternal life / and the Chalice of everlasting salvation."
> . . . At every Mass you put yourself on the altar together with the bread and wine. Once they have been transformed into the Body and Blood of Christ, we offer them to the Father together with ourselves.[7]

Exactly what influence, if any, contemporary Roman Catholic theologies of the eucharistic sacrifice or the Lutheran–Roman Catholic dialogues have had for this remains to be seen.[8] Similarly, by continuing the use of the term "consecration" to refer to the recitation of the narrative of institution, it is difficult, indeed, to see the sense of the entire eucharistic prayer as consecratory, an insight that has been a characteristic of modern liturgical renewal in general.[9]

---

7. Paul Turner, *My Sacrifice and Yours: Our Participation in the Eucharist* (Chicago: Liturgy Training Publications, 2013), 15–16.
  8. On this, see below, Lutherans and Catholics on the Eucharistic Sacrifice.
  9. The best example of this may well be the ancient Anaphora of Addai and Mari, which did not even contain an institution narrative. On this, see Robert Taft, "Mass Without Consecration? The Historic Agreement on the Eucharist between the Catholic Church and the Assyrian Church of the East Promulgated 26 October 2001," *Worship*

The Roman Canon and Its Orality

My purpose in this essay is much more modest than responding to Lathrop or even to revisiting again the overall theology and development of eucharistic sacrifice, or whether sacrifice is even the appropriate metaphor to use in describing either the cross or the Eucharist. My approach here—building, in some ways, upon Lathrop's article—is a brief, even cursory, investigation of the theology of eucharistic sacrifice, specifically in the text of the *Canon Missae*, and to ask whether or not this theology might be viewed with a generous "evangelical [Lutheran] interpretation" as well.

Let me begin autobiographically. In what may seem surprising for a Lutheran liturgical scholar to confess, I often say that I am a student and teacher of liturgy in large part *because* of the text and orality of the Roman *Canon Missae*. I heard this ancient piece of Milanese, Mozarabic, and Roman euchology frequently in my youth, according to its excellent 1967 ICEL translation,[10] having been privileged to worship with some degree of regularity, usually at Saturday night Vigil Masses, with high school friends at St. Bridget's Church in DeGraff, Minnesota, and at St. Francis Xavier Church in Benson, Minnesota, where I lived. Hearing but once a month at Trinity Lutheran Church a somewhat truncated version of the Service of Holy Communion from the 1958 "Red Book," the *Service Book and Hymnal* (SBH),[11] wherein after preface and *Sanctus*, the *Verba* alone, and never the excellent Strodach-Reed Eucharistic Prayer,[12]

77, no. 6 (2003): 482–509; and Nicholas Russo, "The Validity of the Anaphora of *Addai and Mari*: Critique of the Critiques," in *Issues in Eucharistic Praying in East and West: Essays in Liturgical and Theological Analysis*, ed. Maxwell E. Johnson (Collegeville, MN: Liturgical Press, 2010), 21–62.

10. See Jeffrey N. Kemper's *Behind the Text: A Study of the Principles and Procedures of Translation, Adaptation, and Composition of Original Texts by the International Commission on English in the Liturgy*, PhD diss. (Notre Dame: University of Notre Dame, 1992). The publication of Kemper's study might have had great influence on the current translation fiasco of the Roman liturgy. See also Kevin Magas, "Issues in Eucharistic Praying: Translating the Roman Canon," *Worship* 89 (2015): 482–505.

11. *Service Book and Hymnal* (Philadelphia: Fortress Press, 1958), 11. On the origins and development of this prayer see Luther D. Reed, *The Lutheran Liturgy* (Philadelphia: Fortress Press, 1947), 356–63.

12. A version of this prayer was the third option in the 1978 *Lutheran Book of Worship* and now, revised further, appears as the first option in the current *Evangelical Lutheran Worship*.

were recited, the prayerful proclamation of the *Canon Missae* spoke to me on a profound, if unconscious, level. Undoubtedly, this was because it regularly evoked the church in heaven in communion with the Virgin Mary, Joseph, all of the apostles, the early bishops of Rome (Linus, Cletus, Clement, Sixtus II, etc.), and others venerated in the stational-titular churches of Rome (in the *Communicantes*), all those early North African and Roman martyrs, especially the women (Felicity, Perpetua, Agatha, Lucy, Agnes, Cecilia, and Anastasia), whose names I had never heard before in Lutheran Sunday School or confirmation (in the *Nobis quoque peccatoribus*), the great biblical figures of Abraham, Abel, and the high priest of Salem, Melchizedek, who offered bread and wine. Together with this listing of so many in the communion of saints and from Old Testament salvation history, along with reference to the angel and the "altar in heaven" from which the assembly was to share Christ's Body and Blood, the Canon was wedded to powerful performative gestures like the signing of the bread and cup during the *Te igitur*, the extension of the priest's hands over the bread and cup at the *Quam oblationem*, the genuflections and ringing of bells at the "consecration," the signing of the cross over oneself during the *Supplices te rogamus*, and the slight striking of the breast at the *Nobis quoque peccatoribus*. All of this made and continued to make a strong and lasting impression on this West Central Minnesota Lutheran kid, who used to frequent Catholic rectories with numerous questions for kind and patient Catholic priests. My appetite for the study of early Christianity and liturgical history and theology was clearly being whetted as the *lex orandi* was forming and informing me in ways I did not yet know. While I did not then have the language to express it, I was surely experiencing what Enrico Mazza describes as the Roman Canon's ability to evoke the "sense of the sacred." He writes:

> When we begin to speak of the Roman Canon, we feel a need to praise this venerable document of our tradition. And, indeed, it is deserving of respect both as a constant factor in the history of the Roman Church and because of its unchanging identity. The text as we have it today acquired its form between the end of the fourth century and the seventh century, and has not been changed significantly since the days of Pope Gregory the Great (d. 604). . . . It is also deserving of veneration because of its widespread use. . . . It is venerable because it was for so long the only eucharistic prayer of the Roman Church; until quite recently, no one

thought that there might be an alternative to the Roman Canon. . . . It is venerable because of the impression its archaic and unusual language has made. *It is full of words and phrases that are hard to understand and therefore evoke rather than communicate, suggest rather than say outright. It awakens a sense of the ineffable and undefinable or, in other words, a sense of mystery.* . . . Once this sense of mystery is roused, the rationalizing unconscious forms the attitude, or, more accurately, the psychological mechanism which we call the "sense of the sacred." In fact, all the characteristics listed as making the Roman Canon venerable can be summed up in its sacredness. Moreover, since immutability and untouchableness are two factors that constitute the sacredness, it can be said that Canon Law and Roman practice gave this sacredness a theological status.[13]

So enamored was I with this "venerable document," in fact, that when the final version of the translation came out in the early 1970s for the Missal of Paul VI, and most of the saints both in the *Communicantes* and the *Nobis quoque peccatoribus* were relegated now to parentheses and so made optional, I was deeply disappointed.[14] The Roman Canon no longer *sounded* right to me, which is a similar complaint I would make of the 2010 translation, although for other reasons. Of course, little did I reflect then that what was happening, especially with regard to the martyrs in the *Nobis quoque peccatoribus*, was that it was the *women* saints who were now being regularly excluded. Several years ago, Benedictine sister Mary Collins drew attention to this, writing:

> How ironic it is . . . that this postconciliar generation, which thinks of itself as having heightened sensitivity to women in the liturgical assembly, is the first generation of Roman Catholics for whom the names of the women in the ancient Roman canon are not being sounded! How seldom we hear proclaimed on Sunday the names of "Felicity, Perpetua, Agatha, Lucy, Agnes, Cecilia, and Anastasia" as those in whose company we make Eucharist! The rubric that allows for the abbreviation of

---

13. Enrico Mazza, *The Eucharistic Prayers of the Roman Rite*, trans. Matthew J. O'Connell (Collegeville, MN: Liturgical Press, 1986), 53–54; emphasis added.

14. Of course I was also disappointed in the new form of the *Confiteor* and the embolism after the Our Father for the same reason. Just where did Mary, Michael the Archangel, John the Baptist, Peter and Paul, and (in the embolism only) Andrew go?

the commemorations for pastoral reasons brackets out some of the men but all of the women, and many presiders consistently use the option to abbreviate, oblivious to what is going unsaid.[15]

The issues I have noted above with regard to saints (probably later insertions anyway), gestures, and the sense of the sacred evoked by the *Canon Missae* are somewhat peripheral, of course, to what has been *the* issue between Lutherans and Roman Catholics at least from the time of Luther to the present day—that is, the preponderance of sacrificial terminology in this prayer. In his *Formula Missae* of 1523, in which Luther omitted the offertory and the Canon and attached the *Verba* to the preface culminating in the *Sanctus*, he provided this rationale:

> That utter abomination follows which forces all that precedes in the Mass into its service and is, therefore, called the offertory. From here on almost everything smacks and savors of sacrifice. And the words of life and salvation (the Words of Institution) are imbedded in the midst of it all, just as the ark of the Lord once stood in the idol's temple next to Dagon. And there was no Israelite who could approach or bring back the ark until it "smote his enemies in the hinder parts, putting them to a perpetual reproach," and forced them to return it—which is a parable of the present time. Let us, therefore, repudiate everything that smacks of sacrifice, together with the entire canon, and retain only that which is pure and holy, and so order our mass.[16]

Indeed, given this biting critique, how might a Lutheran even dare to attempt a positive evaluation of this ancient and venerable prayer without being accused of entering again into the temple of Dagon and abandoning all Lutheran liturgical purity and holiness? Is all, then, lost with regard to the *Canon Missae*, and does Lutheran–Catholic agreement eventually founder on this early Christian prayer? I think not, as I explore in what follows.

---

15. Mary Collins, OSB, *Contemplative Participation:* Sacrosanctum Concilium *Twenty-Five Years Later* (Collegeville, MN: Liturgical Press, 1990), 31.
16. Martin Luther, "An Order of Mass and Communion for the Church at Wittenberg, 1523," *Luther's Works*, vol. 53: *Liturgy and Hymns* (Philadelphia: Fortress Press, 1965), 26.

Sacrifice and Offering in the Text of the Roman Canon

There is no question but that the Roman Canon has received a bad rap in contemporary liturgical renewal, not only from Lutherans (from whom it might be expected), but from Roman Catholic liturgical scholars as well. While the reasons for this are numerous (e.g., an overemphasis on supplication and offering, the lack of a strong articulation of salvation history culminating in Christ, and what has been decried as a serious lack of pneumatology), the *Canon Missae* has also been the victim of a widely held liturgical scholarly position that favored and favors what is often called the "Antiochene" or "Syro-Byzantine" structure of the eucharistic prayer, with its tripartite trinitarian form, based, presumably, on the Jewish *Birhat ha-mazon*, allegedly used by Jesus himself at the Last Supper. Among previous liturgical scholars, only Louis Bouyer challenged the priority of this model underscoring its highly developed trinitarian-creedal form, while favoring the Canon itself.[17] The Alexandrian pattern, as known by a vast number of Egyptian sources, including the Anaphora of St. Mark, has not been viewed in the same authoritative manner by scholars, although the Roman Canon shares a general overall structure with it, as do all the other current Roman eucharistic prayers, with a "consecratory" epiclesis of the Holy Spirit placed before the narrative of institution at the location of the Roman Canon's *Quam oblationem* and a "communion" epiclesis at the location of the *Supplices te rogamus* in the Canon. In fact, more recent scholarship on the Roman Canon has underscored its relationship to early Egyptian liturgical documents like the *Strasbourg Papyrus*, and claimed that Alexandria and Rome are "two cities with one anaphoral tradition," which developed in distinct ways.[18] Indeed, for Walter Ray, both halves of the Roman Canon, separated by the narrative of institution, are explainable by what he considers to have been a doubling of the tripartite structure of the *Strasbourg Papyrus*, twice repeating a pattern of thanksgiving (praise), offering, and supplication.[19]

Further, the ecumenical-liturgical hegemony of the anaphora from *Apostolic Tradition* 4 (Eucharistic Prayer II in the *Roman Missal* and Eucha-

---

17. Louis Bouyer, *Eucharist: Theology and Spirituality of the Eucharistic Prayer* (Notre Dame: University of Notre Dame Press, 1968), 244ff.

18. See Walter Ray, "Rome and Alexandria: Two Cities, One Anaphoral Tradition," in *Issues in Eucharistic Praying in East and West*, ed. Johnson, 99–127.

19. Ibid.

ristic Prayer XI in *Evangelical Lutheran Worship*, ELW), earlier viewed as authored by St. Hippolytus at Rome in the early third century, thanks to scholars like Joseph Jungmann,[20] Gregory Dix,[21] Bernard Botte,[22] and Cyprian Vaggagini,[23] focused scholarly and liturgical attention away from a prayer like the Roman Canon toward what we were then certain was the *earliest* evidence of authentically Roman, if not even *apostolic*, liturgy.[24] But it must be acknowledged here that the Roman *Canon Missae* is itself a *patristic* document, first witnessed to and used by none other than Ambrose of Milan.[25] As Aidan Kavanagh has been quoted as saying: "The Roman Canon spends most of its time hunkered down effacing itself . . . it was not composed by wild-eyed medieval bishops."[26] Even its lack of pneumatology, Robert Taft has noted on numerous occasions, is a sign of its antiquity and, given the presence of an invocation of the Holy Spirit in the anaphora of *Apostolic Tradition* IV, suggests that the Canon, apart from what we know are later insertions, is earlier than the final mid-fourth-century shape of that text. Taft has said it this way: "The Roman Canon is like the disciples of John the Baptist in Acts 19, who had received only the baptism of John, and told St. Paul, 'we have not even heard that there is a Holy Spirit' (Acts 19:2)."[27]

20. Josef A. Jungmann, SJ, *The Mass: A Historical, Theological, and Pastoral Survey* (Collegeville, MN: Liturgical Press, 1976), 33.

21. Gregory Dix, *The Apostolic Tradition of St. Hippolytus* (London: Morehouse Press, 1937; 2nd ed., 1968).

22. Bernard Botte, *La Tradition Apostolique de Saint Hippolyte*, 5th ed., LQF 39 (Münster: 1963, 1989).

23. Cyprian Vaggagini, *The Canon of the Mass and Liturgical Reform* (London: Geoffrey Chapman, 1967), 25.

24. For a contemporary view of the *Apostolic Tradition*, see Paul F. Bradshaw, Maxwell E. Johnson, and L. Edward Phillips, *The Apostolic Tradition: A Commentary*, Hermeneia—A Critical and Historical Commentary on the Bible (Minneapolis: Fortress Press, 2002); and Maxwell E. Johnson, "Imagining Early Christian Liturgy: The *Traditio Apostolica*—A Case Study," in *Liturgy's Imagined Past/s: Methodologies and Materials in the Writing of Liturgical History Today*, ed. Teresa Berger and Bryan D. Spinks (Collegeville, MN: Liturgical Press, 2016), 93–120.

25. See Ambrose of Milan, *De Sacramentis*, Bk. IV.

26. Aidan Kavanagh, transcribed by students from a lecture at Yale Divinity School, February 26, 1987.

27. "Paul as as Liturgical Theologian," unpublished lecture, Notre Dame Center for Liturgy, University of Notre Dame, June 2009.

Now if we understand the Roman Canon as primarily a patristic liturgical document, being relatively established by the end of the fourth century and coming into its final form by the beginning of the seventh,[28] then this makes its rejection by the sixteenth-century Reformers even more radical than often appears. That is, it is not some medieval textual aberration of eucharistic praying that is rejected. It is an ancient, daily prayer that has governed the eucharistic action (the *canon actionis*) at Rome, Milan, and elsewhere in some close to finished form, from the end of the fourth century until the additional Roman eucharistic prayers appeared in 1967. To reject the *Canon Missae* outright, therefore, is to reject a significant prayer of the early Western liturgical tradition! Hence, it is necessary to view its theology of sacrifice in an overall *patristic*, rather than late-medieval, Reformation, or post-Reformation theological context. As Frank Senn notes in his *Christian Liturgy: Evangelical and Catholic*:

> There is no question that in the Roman canon we are dealing with a patristic rather than a medieval text, even though no text of the canon exists before the eighth-century sacramentary manuscript. This means that it is also possible to interpret the language of oblation in the Roman canon according to patristic rather than medieval concepts of eucharistic sacrifice.[29]

Nathan Mitchell has noted that "medieval Latin theology's preoccupation with the sacrificial aspects of Eucharist developed in part from a tendency to separate 'sacrifice' from 'sacrament,' and 'consecration' from the church's 'offering' and communion."[30] And, of course, it has been a classic Lutheran position that "sacrament" and "sacrifice" *must* be separated and never confused! But the text of the Roman Canon long

---

28. In addition to the work of Mazza cited above, see Allan Bouley, *From Freedom to Formula: The Evolution of the Eucharistic Prayer from Oral Improvisation to Written Texts*, Studies in Christian Antiquity 21 (Washington, DC: Catholic University of America Press, 1981), 200–216.

29. Frank Senn, *Christian Liturgy: Evangelical and Catholic* (Minneapolis: Fortress Press, 1997), 142.

30. Nathan Mitchell, "Eucharistic Theologies," in *The New Westminster Dictionary of Liturgy and Worship*, ed. Paul F. Bradshaw (Louisville: Westminster John Knox Press, 2002), 200.

predates this preoccupation of medieval Latin theology and its later rejection by Luther. Taft has shown in the Eastern liturgical traditions, with particular reference to the anaphoral oblation in the Byzantine Rite, that an earlier theological approach remains in which separation and compartmentalization of the Eucharist simply does not take place:

> There is one single offering of the Church within which several things happen. These things are expressed in various ways and moments according to the several pre-reformation traditions of East and West, all of which agree on the basic ritual elements of their traditions. These classical anaphoras express that the Eucharist is a sacrifice, the sacramental memorial of Christ's own sacrifice on the cross, in which the Church, repeating what Jesus did at the Last Supper, invokes God's blessing on bread and wine so that it might become Jesus' body and blood, our spiritual food and drink. . . . All attempts to squeeze more out of the words of the prayer . . . is an inference that can only be made by imposing on the text the results of later theological reflection and/or polemics. . . . So the most one can say is that the "offering" expressions that fall between institution and epiclesis in BAS and CHR neither confirm nor exclude any particular theological thesis of when or by what particular part of the anaphoral prayer the consecration is effected, or just *what*, beyond the Eucharistic service in its most general sense of the Church's offering of the memorial Jesus is believed to have commanded the Church to repeat, is offered: bread and wine, body and blood, the "reasonable and unbloody sacrifice" of the Church, the sacrifice of Christ represented in its sacrament. . . . My own view is that later precisions, in the sense in which they are sometimes posed today as the result of confessional disputes are sterile and pointless. . . . I would prefer that the earlier liturgical language, which is metaphorical and evocative, not philosophical and ontological, includes *all these "offerings,"* if implicitly and not self-consciously.[31]

Or, as he says elsewhere in this same chapter: what is "offered" *in* the Eucharist, then, "is what the New Testament has Jesus order us to offer:

---

31. Robert Taft, "Understanding the Byzantine Anaphoral Oblation," in *Rule of Prayer, Rule of Faith: Essays in Honor of Aidan Kavanagh, O.S.B.*, ed. Nathan D. Mitchell and John F. Baldovin (Collegeville, MN: Liturgical Press, 1996), 32–55, here at 53–54.

the memorial of his own self offering," that is, the liturgical *doing* of the Eucharist in obedience to his command.[32]

Reference to the Christian East and its eucharistic prayer traditions here is most helpful, as we shall see. Luther's words on eucharistic sacrifice do not constitute, of course, the only or final word for Lutheran theology and liturgical practice. To this end, I have always found it fascinating that Philip Melanchthon, in Article XXIV of his *Apology of the Augsburg Confession*, speaks approvingly of offering in what he calls the "Greek canon," that is, the Anaphoras of St. John Chrysostom and St. Basil:

> The Greek canon says a lot about an offering but it clearly shows that it is not talking about the Body and Blood of the Lord in particular, but about the entire service, about the prayers and thanksgiving. This is what it says: "And make us worthy to come to offer you entreaties and supplications and bloodless sacrifices for all the people." Properly understood, this is not offensive. It prays that we might be made worthy to offer prayers and supplications and bloodless sacrifices for the people. It even calls prayers "bloodless sacrifices." It also says this a little later: "we offer you this reasonable and bloodless service." It is a misinterpretation to translate this as a "reasonable victim" and to apply it to the body of Christ itself. For the canon is talking about the entire service; and by "reasonable service" [Rom 12:1] Paul meant the service of the mind, fear, faith, prayer, thanksgiving, and the like, in opposition to a theory of *ex opere operato*.[33]

Melanchthon fails to address here the offering language of the anamnesis in the Byzantine anaphoras, namely, "Your own of your own, we offer unto You," which actually provides a key parallel to the anamnesis in the Canon. Nevertheless, elsewhere in his *Apology* he makes a contrast between the once-for-all atoning sacrifice of Christ and what he calls, in language seldom used by contemporary Lutherans, the "eucharistic sacrifice"!

---

32. Ibid., 45.

33. Philip Melanchthon, *Apology of the Augsburg Confession: Article XXIV*, in *The Book of Concord: The Confessions of the Evangelical Lutheran Church*, ed. Robert Kolb and Timothy J. Wengert (Minneapolis: Fortress Press, 2000), 274. On the importance of the prayers of the Christian East in relationship to those of the West, see Kenneth Stevenson, *Eucharist and Offering* (New York: Pueblo, 1986), 38–101.

Now the rest are eucharistic sacrifices, which are called "sacrifices of praise," namely, the preaching of the gospel, faith, prayer, thanksgiving, confession, the afflictions of the saints, and, indeed, all the good works of the saints. These sacrifices are not satisfactions for those who offer them, nor can they be applied to others so as to merit the forgiveness of sins or reconciliation for others *ex opere operato*. They are performed by those who are already reconciled. . . . These are the sacrifices of the New Testament, as Peter teaches [1 Pet 2:3], "a holy priesthood, to offer spiritual sacrifices." Spiritual sacrifices, however, are contrasted not only with animal sacrifices but also with human works offered *ex opere operato*, because "spiritual" refers to the work of the Holy Spirit within us. Paul teaches the same thing in Romans 12[:1]: "Present your bodies as a living sacrifice, holy and acceptable to God, which is your spiritual worship." "Spiritual worship" refers to worship where God is recognized and grasped by the mind, as happens when it fears and trusts God. Therefore, it is contrasted not only to Levitical worship, in which animals were slain, but with any worship in which people imagine they are offering God a work *ex opere operato*. The Epistle to the Hebrews, chapter 13[:15], teaches the same thing, "Through him, then, let us continually offer a sacrifice of praise to God," and it adds an interpretation, "that is, the fruit of lips that confess his name." He commands us to offer praises, that is, prayer, thanksgiving, confession, and the like. These avail not *ex opere operato* but on account of faith. This is stressed by the phrase, "through him let us offer," that is, by faith in Christ.[34]

Might Melanchthon's positive assessment of the "Greek canon" and his use of both "eucharistic sacrifice" and "sacrifice of praise" in his theological interpretation of sacrifice be of assistance for an interpretation of sacrifice in the Roman *Canon Missae* for a *patristic* interpretation of its sacrificial elements? I think so. Mindful of what Mark Francis has called the "hieratic and technical" language of Latin liturgy at Rome, which characteristically expressed itself by piling up "synonymous adjectives of a sacral or juridical nature" as it sought to replace the Roman pagan *ius divinum* with a new Christian *cultus publicus*,[35] what lies behind this sacrality in terms of eucharistic sacrifice is actually quite simple. In the

---

34. Ibid.
35. Mark R. Francis, *Local Worship, Global Church: Popular Religion and the Liturgy* (Collegeville, MN: Liturgical Press, 2014), 62–63.

first section of the Roman Canon leading up to the *Qui pridie* of the narrative of institution, the sacrifice is referred to explicitly as "*sacrificium laudis*," a "sacrifice of praise," which, as in the ancient *Strasbourg Papyrus* ("over this sacrifice and offering we pray and beseech you . . .") is directly connected to intercessions for the church and the living.[36] In fact, it appears quite likely that the threefold "these gifts, these offerings, these holy and unblemished sacrifices" in the *Te igitur* correspond originally to the three offerings referred to in the Anaphora of St. Mark ("those who offer you sacrifices [*thysias*], offerings [*prosphoras*] and gifts [*eucharisteria*])," the third of which refers to the bread and wine to be used in the Eucharist itself. In addition, the statement that they are "holy and unblemished" relates as much to those bringing the offerings as it does to the offerings themselves. Here, notes Mazza, "sacrifice is symbolic of human beings, not a substitute for them; the 'spotlessness' of the act of worship or the offering cannot replace the 'spotlessness' of the offerer but rather calls for it and makes it necessary."[37] While the *Quam oblationem* makes it perfectly clear that this sacrifice has become embodied in the bread and wine, even there the request that the offering be made "spiritual and acceptable" (or, as in the previous translation, "an offering in spirit and truth"), is biblical language evoking both Romans 12:1 and John 4:23 with regard again to the worshippers themselves. Sacrifice here, then, can easily be interpreted also as prayer and worship even as that becomes embodied in the bread and wine, an embodiment that Enrico Mazza notes,[38] is reminiscent of the anti-Gnostic eucharistic emphasis of Irenaeus of Lyons, who writes in *Adversus Haereses* 4.17.5:

> The Lord gave directions to his disciples to offer first-fruits to God from God's own creatures, not as though God stood in need of them, but that they themselves may be neither unfruitful nor ungrateful. Thus, he took the bread, which comes from creation, and he gave thanks, saying, "This is my body." He did likewise with the cup, which is part of the creation to which we ourselves belong, declaring it to be his blood, and [so] he taught the new offering of the new covenant. This is the offering which the church received from the apostles, and which it offers throughout the whole world, to God who provides us with nourishment, the first-fruits of

---

36. See Ray, "Rome and Alexandria," 115–16.
37. Ibid, 60.
38. Mazza, *Eucharistic Prayers of the Roman Rite*, 77–78.

divine gifts in this new covenant. Of this offering, among the prophets, Malachi had spoken beforehand in these terms: "I have no pleasure in you, says the Lord almighty, and I will not accept sacrifice from your hands. For from the rising of the sun even to its setting my name is glorified among the nations, and in every place incense is offered to my name, and a pure sacrifice; for my name is great among the nations, says the Lord almighty" [Mal 1:10–11]. By these words, he shows in the plainest manner that the former people [the Jews] shall cease to make offering to God, but that in every place sacrifice shall be offered to God, one that is pure, and that God's name is glorified among the nations.[39]

With regard to the first half of the Roman Canon, then, it should be possible to give an "evangelical interpretation." The "sacrifices" referred to are consistent with what is known of sacrificial vocabulary and theology in ante-Nicene liturgical sources and texts with regard to prayer in general and the Eucharist in particular.[40]

What, however, of the second half, after the narrative of institution, especially in the *Unde et memores*, or anamnesis? The current official English translation would seem to make this rather problematic:

> Therefore, O Lord, as we celebrate the memorial of the blessed Passion, the Resurrection from the dead, and the glorious Ascension into heaven of Christ, your Son, our Lord, we your servants and your holy people, offer to your glorious majesty from the gifts you have given us, *this pure victim, this holy victim, this spotless victim*, the holy Bread of eternal life and the Chalice of everlasting salvation.

Contrast this with the previous (and 1998) translation:

> Father [1998: And so, Lord God], we celebrate the memory of Christ, your Son. We, your people and ministers, recall his passion, his resurrection

---

39. ET from David N. Power, *Irenaeus of Lyons on Baptism and Eucharist*, Joint Liturgical Study 18 (Nottingham: Grove Books, 1991), 15–16.

40. The best studies of sacrifice in relationship to the Eucharist in early Christianity remain those of Robert Daly, *Christian Sacrifice: The Judaeo-Christian Background before Origen*, Studies in Christian Antiquity 18 (Washington, DC: Catholic University of America Press, 1978); *The Origins of the Christian Doctrine of Sacrifice* (Philadelphia: Fortress Press, 1978), especially 84–134; and *Sacrifice Unveiled: The True Meaning of Christian Sacrifice* (London: Continuum, 2009).

from the dead, and his ascension into glory; and from the many gifts you have given us we offer to you, God of glory and majesty, this holy and perfect sacrifice: the bread of life and the cup of eternal salvation.[41]

The language of the current translation with the repetition of "victim" to translate *"hostia,"* although not capitalized (!), rather than "sacrifice" or even "worship," can suggest that what is being offered here now, in contrast to the first half of the Canon, is the Body and Blood of Christ himself, the "Victim" sacrificed for us on the cross, since in late medieval and current usage the narrative of institution has just confected that Body and Blood. But is this a correct inference or interpretation? John Baldovin has suggested another approach, an approach that, again like Melanchthon, directs us to the eucharistic prayer traditions of the Christian East:

> Luther was correct in his suspicion that late medieval theology and practice of offering *could* and often was understood as moving God to do something but the Roman theological and liturgical tradition need not be read in this way. [Note] the Roman Canon's *anamnesis* formula: "and from the many gifts you have given us (*de tuis donis ac datis*) we offer to you God of glory and majesty, this holy and perfect sacrifice." *Here the Western tradition coincides nicely with the Byzantine Anaphoras of John Chrysostom and Basil,* which *employ at this same point: "We offer you your own from your own* ('ta sa ek ton son')." But this is precisely where we recognize that we can only offer back what was given to us by God in the first place.[42]

But, while Baldovin is using the previous English translation to make his point, what about the repetitive use of "victim" to translate *hostia* in the current (2010) translation? Already in 1986 (actually 1984 in Italian), Enrico Mazza argued convincingly, like Melanchthon did centuries before, that "victim," used in the Italian translation of this in the *Mes-*

---

41. *The Sacrament of the Roman Missal* (Collegeville, MN: Liturgical Press, 1985), 506, emphasis added. The 1998 version is from *The Roman Missal*, vol. 1, part 2 (Washington, DC: International Commission on English in the Liturgy, 1998), 595.

42. John F. Baldovin, "The Twentieth Century Reform of the Liturgy: Outcomes and Prospects (2017)," *Institute of Liturgical Studies Occasional Papers* 126, http://scholar.valpo.edu/ils_papers/126; emphases added.

sale Romano, should *not* have been used to translate "hostia," precisely because it is so easily misinterpreted!

> This "victim," after all, is immediately described as the "sacred bread of everlasting life and the chalice of eternal salvation." In everyday speech, even for a person with some education, it is difficult to understand how bread and chalice are a "victim" or of what they are a victim? It would be preferable, therefore, to translate *hostia* as "sacrifice" or even "worship and sacrifice," or something similar. . . . When you read or hear the term "victim" applied to the bread and wine, your thoughts move in a different direction: you think of the bread and wine as consecrated and therefore as the body and blood of the Lord. "Victim" certainly applies to the dead Lord on the cross. . . . We can, of course, always say that Christ is the victim who brings salvation; we cannot, however, say that the sacrament of his body and blood is a sacrificed victim.[43]

Further, as long ago as Tertullian in third-century North Africa, "*hostiam spiritalis*" or "spiritual sacrifice," not a spiritual "victim," was what Christians offered to God by means of prayer at the altar.[44] And it is interesting to note here that in contrast to the current English translation, the 2018 Spanish *Misal Romano,* for use in the dioceses of the United States, uses "*sacrificio puro, inmaculado y santo*," rather than "victim" at this point.[45]

What must be made clear theologically, pastorally, and catechetically, therefore, is that this "holy and perfect sacrifice," "this pure victim, this holy victim, this spotless victim," in the Roman *Canon Missae* is *not* Christ, *not* Christ's Body and Blood, *not* the sacrament of his Body and Blood, *not* the meal somehow being offered to God. In other words, the notion of sacrifice even in the anamnesis of the Roman *Canon Missae* is very little different from that in the first part of the Canon, and is consistent with the anaphoral anamneses in the Byzantine East. That is, it is still primarily a *sacrificum laudis*, a sacrifice of prayer, praise, and thanksgiving embodied in the bread and cup, an interpretation still evocative of the "pure sacrifice" or "offering" of Malachi 1:10-11 and the theology of Irenaeus of Lyons here as well ("we offer to God those

---

43. Mazza, *Eucharistic Prayers of the Roman Rite*, 79.
44. Tertullian, *De Oratione* 28, 3.4. See Stevenson, *Eucharist and Offering*, 19.
45. *Misal Romano* (Collegeville, MN: Liturgical Press, 2018), 665.

things which belong to God, proclaiming fittingly the communion and unity of the flesh and the spirit").[46]

Mazza is certainly correct to suggest that even "worship" might be the best way to translate *hostia* at this point. Similarly, when in the *Supplices te rogamus*, God is asked to command the angel to take these "gifts" (or "sacrifice" in the previous translation) to the altar in heaven so that in receiving Christ's Body and Blood the communicants "may be filled with every grace and heavenly blessing," the angel is not being commanded to take Christ's Body and Blood or even the bread and cup to heaven. Here and throughout the *Canon Missae* it is clear that the dynamic remains: bread and cup, other offerings, prayer, praise and thanksgiving, the worshippers themselves are *offered*; Body and Blood are *received*. This is the same dynamic in the current Roman Eucharistic Prayer II ("we offer you, Lord, the Bread of life and the Chalice of salvation . . . partaking of the Body and Blood of Christ") and III ("we offer you in thanksgiving this holy and living sacrifice . . . grant that we who are nourished by the Body and Blood of your Son"). It appears also in the four additional Eucharistic Prayers for Various Needs in the Appendix to the Roman Missal ("we offer you the Bread of life and the Chalice of salvation . . . in whose Body and Blood we have communion"). Hence, if it is possible to give an "evangelical interpretation" to the sacrificial terminology in *these* prayers, it should be possible to do the same with the Roman Canon, since in spite of the preponderance of offering and what amounts to a seriously flawed English translation, the theology of Eucharistic sacrifice is the same.

Such is not the case, however, with Eucharistic Prayer IV, based presumably on the early Egyptian version of the Anaphora of St. Basil, although the structure is decidedly "Antiochene" or "Syro-Byzantine." While incredibly rich in biblical imagery (especially Johannine), salvation history, and language, the composers of this prayer actually inverted the dynamic in Basil and as a result, raised all kinds of ecumenical red flags. The anamnesis in this prayer reads:

---

46. Irenaeus, *Adversus Haereses* 4.18.5; ET from Power, *Irenaeus of Lyons*, 21. This was also the understanding expressed by Joseph Jungmann in his classic study, *The Eucharistic Prayer: A Study of the* Canon Missae (Notre Dame: Fides Publishers, 1956), 18ff.

. . . as we await his coming in glory, *we offer you his Body and Blood, the sacrifice acceptable* to you which brings salvation to the whole world.

Look, O Lord upon the Sacrifice (*Hostiam*) which you yourself have provided for your Church, and grant in your loving kindness to all who partake of this *one Bread and one Chalice* that, gathered into one body by the Holy Spirit, they may truly become a living sacrifice (*hostia viva*) in Christ to the praise of your glory.

Neither the previous nor the 1998 translation can fix this, since the problem is the Latin text itself, with the result that the text is a drastic revision of Egyptian Basil and is decidedly unique in comparison with the other Roman eucharistic prayers. Although *hostia* is not translated as "victim" and evokes Romans 21:1 ("living sacrifice") as one of the fruits of communion, it is now Body and Blood, rather than Bread and Cup, which are offered, and Bread and Cup that are received although, to be fair, the reception of bread and cup appears in Egyptian Basil at this point as well, but only after the epiclesis has already invoked the Holy Spirit to sanctify them as Christ's Body and Blood. As early as 1977, Ralph Keifer drew critical attention to this shift in Roman Eucharistic euchology, writing:

> Prayer IV uses the expression, "We offer you his body and blood, the acceptable sacrifice which brings salvation to the whole world" (*offerimus tibi eius Corpus et Sanguinem, sacrificium tibi acceptabile et toti mundo salutare*). Such literalistic expression is unknown to the Roman Canon, which speaks instead of offered *gifts*, as do the various texts of the Anaphora of St. Basil which is the basis of Prayer IV. Traditional Eucharistic prayers have been careful to respect the character of the offered gifts as signs, a respect that is not observed in these new prayers. In addition to departing from Roman Catholic liturgical tradition, such expressions are also an ecumenical offense. Dialogue had made it clear that a language of "offering Christ" is anything but clear and is in fact misleading. The "correction" of the Anaphora of Saint Basil represented by Prayer IV presents a further problem because that anaphora is still used by the Orthodox and Coptic Churches. The offense is compounded by the addition of an invocation before the institution narrative to set the narrative off most emphatically as the moment of consecration, a direct assault on Eastern understanding of the Eucharist. It is not a happy

gesture to take the prayers of other churches and "correct" them without consultation before they are esteemed fit for use.[47]

This text is simply *not* reflective of what Taft refers to above as "earlier liturgical language, which is metaphorical and evocative, not philosophical and ontological, [and] includes *all these 'offerings,'* if implicitly and not self-consciously."[48] The language here is precisely explicit and self-conscious, something that appears to have been "made by imposing . . . the results of later theological reflection and/or polemics" into the creation of a modern text. The change in dynamics, in inverting Bread and Cup, Body and Blood, was not an accident, but deliberate, it seems. It is hard to read it any other way.

The greatest problem here, however, is whether this explicit theology of the anamnesis of Eucharistic Prayer IV is now to govern the interpretation of the offering language in all of the other Roman eucharistic prayers. If so, then the Reformation critique remains as important today as in the past, and the Roman Canon's offering of "this pure victim, this holy victim, this spotless victim, the holy Bread of eternal life and the Chalice of salvation," along with the offering in Eucharistic Prayers II ("we offer you, Lord, the Bread of life and the Chalice of salvation") and III ("we offer you in thanksgiving this holy and living sacrifice") are to be interpreted precisely as referring to Christ's Body and Blood, to the Victim sacrificed on the cross. If so, while Lathrop hopes that the Roman Canon might be used only infrequently, my hope would be that Eucharistic Prayer IV not be used *at all* until this liturgical-theological problem is fixed, first, at the level of the authoritative Latin text, and, second, in all vernacular translations. Indeed, if there are some Lutherans who "continue to regard the language of sacrifice found in Catholic theology and the Catholic Eucharistic rite to be a potential stumbling block to unity," it is the anamnesis of Eucharistic Prayer IV, and not really the Roman *Canon Missae*, to which we should look as constituting that potential stumbling block.

---

47. Ralph Keifer, "Liturgical Text as Primary Source for Liturgical Theology," *Worship* 51, no. 3 (1977): 189.

48. See above, n. 30.

Far superior, and adapted by a group of Episcopalian, Lutheran, and Roman Catholic liturgical scholars in 1974,[49] under the leadership of Marion J. Hatchett, is the Eucharistic Prayer known as "A Common Eucharistic Prayer," and appearing in the liturgical books of Episcopalians,[50] Presbyterians,[51] and others. While offered for trial use among Lutherans in the late 1970s, unfortunately, in the words of Gail Ramshaw, "neither its profuse praise nor its ecumenical implications caught on among Lutherans,"[52] and it was not included in the 1978 *Lutheran Book of Worship*. With a total of *eleven* eucharistic prayers in the 2006 *Evangelical Lutheran Worship*, however, it remains a mystery to me as to why this great text was not included somewhere as an option among the several options that are there. In any event, unlike Eucharistic Prayer IV in the Roman Rite, the text of this prayer is faithful to Basil:

> Recalling Christ's death and his descent among the dead, proclaiming his resurrection and ascension to your right hand, awaiting his coming in glory; *and offering to you, from the gifts you have given us, this bread and this cup*, we praise you and we bless you. . . .
>
> Lord, we pray that in your goodness and mercy your Holy Spirit may descend upon us, and upon these gifts, sanctifying them and showing them to be holy gifts for your holy people, the bread of life and the cup of salvation, the Body and Blood of your Son Jesus Christ. Grant that all who share this bread and cup may become one body and one spirit, a living sacrifice in Christ, to the praise of your Name.[53]

---

49. The "authors" of this prayer constitute a kind of "who's who" of ecumenical liturgical scholars in the early 1970s: Ralph Keifer, Aidan Kavanagh, Eugene Brand, Ross Mackenzie, Marion J. Hatchett, Howard Galley, and Don Saliers. For a brief description, see Marion J. Hatchett, *Commentary on the American Prayer Book* (New York: Seabury Press, 1981), 377–78.

50. *The Book of Common Prayer* (New York: Church Hymnal Corporation, 1979), 372–75.

51. *Book of Common Worship* (Louisville: Westminster John Knox Press, 1993), 146ff.

52. Gail Ramshaw, "Toward Lutheran Eucharistic Prayers," in *New Eucharistic Prayers*, ed. Frank Senn (New York: Paulist Press, 1987), 76. This has not stopped certain Lutherans, like me, from using it in Lutheran contexts, especially on Maundy Thursday and at the Easter Vigil.

53. *Book of Common Prayer* (1979), 374–75. On a related note, in 1985 the International Commission on English in the Liturgy (ICEL) prepared for consultation a

Lutherans and Catholics on the Eucharistic Sacrifice

Was not the question of Eucharist and sacrifice for Lutherans and Roman Catholics, including even the language of "offering Christ" to the Father, resolved in the United States dialogues, at least, as long ago as 1967 in *Lutherans and Catholics in Dialogue III: The Eucharist as Sacrifice*, at a time when *only* the Roman *Canon Missae* was still being used regularly (officially, at least) and the newer Roman anaphoras were only beginning to appear? In the joint statement resulting from this dialogue, "The Eucharist: A Lutheran–Roman Catholic Statement," the following interpretation of eucharistic sacrifice is jointly presented:

> Lutherans and Roman Catholics alike acknowledge that in the Lord's supper "Christ is present as the Crucified who died for our sins and who rose again for our justification, as the once-for-all sacrifice for the sins of the world" . . . .
>
> The confessional documents of both traditions agree that the celebration of the eucharist is the church's sacrifice of praise and self-offering or oblation . . . .
>
> Historically, our controversies have revolved around the question whether the worshiping assembly "offers Christ" in the sacrifice of the mass. In general, Lutherans have replied in the negative, because they believed that only thus could they preserve the once-for-all character and the full sufficiency of the sacrifice of the cross and keep the eucharist from becoming a human supplement to God's saving work, a matter of "works-righteousness" . . . .
>
> Catholics as well as Lutherans, affirm the unrepeatable character of the sacrifice of the cross. . . . We recognize our agreement in the assertion

---

translation of the *Eucharistic Prayer of Saint Basil*, which actually corrected the offering problem in Eucharistic Prayer IV by saying: "and so, from the many gifts you have given us we offer you what is yours, in the name of every creature and for the sake of all the world," without even any reference to the bread and cup or Body and Blood, until the single epiclesis appearing in its classic Syro-Antiochene position. Unfortunately, this prayer was never approved for Roman Catholic liturgical use. See *Eucharistic Prayer of Saint Basil*, Text for Consultation (Washington, DC: International Commission on English in the Liturgy, 1985).

that "What God did in the incarnation, life, death, resurrection and ascension of Christ, he does not do again. The events are unique; they cannot be repeated, or extended or continued. Yet in this memorial we do not only recall past events: God makes them present through the Holy Spirit, thus making us participants in Christ (1 Cor 1:9) . . . ."

The members of the body of Christ are united through Christ with God and with one another in such a way that they become participants in his worship, his self-offering, his sacrifice to the Father. Through this union between Christ and Christians the eucharistic assembly "offers Christ" by consenting in the power of the Holy Spirit to be offered by him to the Father. Apart from Christ we have no gifts, no worship, no sacrifice of our own to offer to God: All we can plead is Christ, *the sacrificial* lamb and *victim* whom the Father himself has given us.[54]

And with regard to this, one of the Lutheran dialogue participants, Kent Knutson, stated the following helpful interpretation:

Roman Catholics have called the Mass a sacrifice. They mean by this that the Eucharist is a gracious act in which God makes present this propitiatory sacrifice for [humanity]. This is not a new, or different sacrifice but the same sacrifice of Calvary. The Mass is properly, and necessarily, called sacrifice because the Christ who is the sacrifice is present in the Supper. . . . Lutheran[s] have often understood Roman Catholics to say that the Mass adds to Calvary, is a "re-doing" of Calvary and by this have implied that the one sacrifice of Christ is defective and incomplete. . . . Now we can agree that this is not what Roman Catholics intend to say. The sacrifice of Christ is complete and unalterable and cannot be supplemented or completed by any subsequent action. Rather, that sacrifice, complete in itself, is made present, made effective and the benefits communicated in the Eucharist. . . . Catholics have used the word "re-presentation," not in the sense of doing again, but in the sense of "presenting again." Lutherans can agree wholeheartedly. Lutherans have sometimes used the term "actualize" to communicate the same understanding. . . . It was agreed that that the unrepeatable sacrifice which was, now is in the Eucharist. There is therefore a continuing

---

54. "The Eucharist: A Lutheran–Roman Catholic Statement," in *The Eucharist as Sacrifice*, ed. Paul Empie and T. Austin Murphy, *Lutherans and Catholics in Dialogue, III* (Minneapolis: Augsburg, 1967), 188–90; emphases added.

work of Christ in the sense that he continues to plead before the Father and continues to communicate to [humanity] his work of redemption.[55]

Recent international Lutheran–Roman Catholic dialogue statements have continued to reflect this same level of ecumenical agreement. Based on earlier international dialogues, like *The Eucharist: Final Report of the Joint Roman Catholic-Lutheran Commission* (1978),[56] the 2013 document of the Lutheran World Federation and the Pontifical Council for Promoting Christian Unity, *From Conflict to Communion: Lutheran-Catholic Common Commemoration of the Reformation, 2017*, made this bold declaration:

> The decisive achievement was to overcome the separation of *sacrificium* (the sacrifice of Jesus Christ) from *sacramentum* (the sacrament). If Jesus Christ is really present in the Lord's Supper, then his life, suffering, death, and resurrection are also truly present together with his body, so that the Lord's Supper is "the true making present of the event on the cross." Not only the effect of the event on the cross but also the event itself is present in the Lord's Supper without the meal being a repetition or completion of the cross event. The one event is present in a sacramental modality. The liturgical form of the holy meal must, however, exclude everything that could give the impression of repetition or completion of the sacrifice on the cross. If the understanding of the Lord's Supper as a real remembrance is consistently taken seriously, the differences in understanding the eucharistic sacrifice are tolerable for Catholics and Lutherans.[57]

The recent declaration, *Communion in Growth: Declaration on the Church, Eucharist, and Ministry* of the Evangelical Lutheran Church of Finland and the Catholic Church of Finland (2017), asserts even that, as a result of dialogue, the Lutheran–Catholic mutual sixteenth-century

---

55. Kent S. Knutson, "Eucharist as Sacrifice: Roman Catholic—Lutheran Dialogue," in ibid., 12–13.

56. The text is available at http://www.prounione.urbe.it/dia-int/l-rc/doc/e_l-rc_eucharist.html.

57. Lutheran World Federation and the Pontifical Council for Promoting Christian Unity, *From Conflict to Communion: Lutheran-Catholic Common Commemoration of the Reformation, 2017* (Leipzig: Evangelische Verlagsanstalt GmbH; and Paderborn: Bonifatius GmbH Druck—Buch—Verlag, 2013), 59–60.

condemnations on eucharistic sacrifice may be seen as no longer applying to the current situation:

> We agree that the sacrifice of the Mass is based on the sacrifice of Jesus Christ on the cross. The unique sacrifice of Jesus Christ is made sacramentally present in the Eucharist. Through the anamnesis (*memoria*), which breaks the boundaries of time and place, his offer is present (*repraesentatio*) and actualised in the Mass. The second person of the Triune God is really present in the Eucharist as a reconciling and redemptive sacrifice to God. The priest acts in the person of Christ (*in persona Christi*) when he consecrates the elements of bread and wine and invokes the Holy Spirit (*epiclesis*), administers the consecrated elements, the body and blood of Christ, to the communicants (*applicatio*), and leads the thanksgiving prayer.
>
> We agree that there is an intimate and constitutive connection between Christ's sacrifice, the Eucharist, and the Church. The Church "draws her life from the Eucharist" [John Paul II, *Ecclesia de Eucharistia*, n. 1] since the Eucharist makes present Christ's redeeming sacrifice. The Eucharist is Christ, who gives himself to us and continually builds us up as his body. The memorial of Christ is "the supreme sacramental manifestation of communion in the Church" [John Paul II, *Redemptor hominis*, 4.3.1979, n. 20].
>
> In the light of this consensus on the basic truths of the Eucharist as sacrifice, grounded in the formulation of the living presence of the unique sacrifice of Christ in the Mass, we can say that the condemnations in the Lutheran confessional writings as well as those in Trent are not applicable.[58]

If Lutherans and Roman Catholics are in agreement on this once church-dividing issue—and have been in the United States since even *before* the appearance of the 1969 *Missale Romanum* of Pope Paul VI—what really *is* the issue any longer in terms of eucharistic sacrifice and offering? Interestingly enough, against the characteristic charge that

---

58. Evangelical Lutheran Church of Finland and the Catholic Church of Finland, *Communion in Growth: Declaration on the Church, Eucharist, and Ministry* (Helsinki: Grano, 2017), 52–53.

eucharistic sacrifice, especially in the offertory and Roman Canon, constitutes a Pelagian or semi-Pelagian "human supplement to God's saving work, a matter of 'works-righteousness,' " British Methodist liturgical theologian Geoffrey Wainwright has written that attention to the concept and liturgical expression of eucharistic sacrifice might well underscore an "anti-Pelagian" affirmation of grace:

> Could not the contentious notion "we offer Christ" paradoxically be seen as anti-Pelagian? It could be an acknowledgement that we have nothing else to offer. . . . To say "we offer Christ" may then become a bold way of acknowledging the transforming presence and work of Christ within us. Again, paradoxically, it could thus be the very opposite of Pelagianism.[59]

This anti-Pelagian emphasis appears also at the conclusion to the *Nobis quoque peccatoribus*, where in the current translation it is asked: "admit us, we beseech you into their [the saints'] company, not weighing our merits but granting us your pardon." Here in the Roman Canon is the evangelical corrective to what might easily be interpreted as a Pelagian request in Eucharistic Prayer II: "Have mercy on us all, we pray, that with the Blessed Virgin Mary, Mother of God, with the blessed Apostles, and all the Saints who have pleased you throughout the ages, we *may merit* to be coheirs to eternal life . . ." The previous and 1998 translations here reflected more clearly the Augustinian sense of the meaning of "*aeternae vitae mereamur esse consortes*" with "make us worthy to share eternal life."[60]

Let me say here that I am one of those Lutherans who does not *necessarily* "continue to regard the language of sacrifice found in the Catholic Eucharistic rite to be a potential stumbling block to unity." Properly understood, even the Roman *Canon Missae* need not be interpreted in any way different from the way in which Melanchthon interpreted the "Greek canon" of St. John Chrysostom or St. Basil. The problem that remains for us today—but not for our early Christian ancestors from

---

59. Geoffrey Wainwright, *Doxology: The Praise of God in Worship, Doctrine, and Life: A Systematic Theology* (Oxford and New York: Oxford University Press, 1980), 272–73.

60. On the use of merit in general in the current translation see O'Collins, *Lost in Translation*, 73–74.

whom this prayer comes—is the relationship of the anaphoral location of sacrifice language to the narrative of institution and to questions of the precise "moment" of either consecration or offering. Here I am with Taft wholeheartedly when he says above that:

> All attempts to squeeze more out of the words of the prayer . . . is an inference that can only be made by imposing on the text the results of later theological reflection and/or polemics. . . . So the most one can say is that the "offering" expressions that fall between institution and epiclesis in BAS and CHR neither confirm nor exclude any particular theological thesis of when or by what particular part of the anaphoral prayer the consecration is effected, or just *what*, beyond the Eucharistic service in its most general sense of the Church's offering of the memorial Jesus is believed to have commanded the Church to repeat, is offered.

If this is an accurate assessment for the anaphoras of Chrysostom and Basil in the East, is it not also accurate for the Roman Canon in the West? We simply have to get back to the point where we see not words and/or formulas as "consecratory" but the whole Great Thanksgiving from preface dialogue through concluding doxology, with language of prayer, praise, the recital of salvation history, invocation, remembrance, offering, intercession, doxology, and praise as "consecrating" the bread and cup as Christ's Body and Blood for the purposes of communion. And this remains a challenge for Roman Catholics and Lutherans alike.

Related to all this is a particular challenge I would make to Lutherans. Indeed, the Lutheran allergy to the use of offering metaphors in the construction of Eucharistic praying is even more pronounced today than when the 1978 *Lutheran Book of Worship* (LBW) was being produced. Contrary to the language in the variable prefaces in LBW, it is no longer "indeed right and salutary that we should at all times and in all places *offer* thanks and praise,"[61] which had been common Lutheran language from SBH through LBW. Now Lutherans cannot even *offer* thanks and praise and doing so is no longer "salutary," for now "it is indeed right, our duty and our joy, that we should at all times and in all places *give* thanks

---

61. To be fair, the Latin of the traditional preface does not contain an offering verb; *nos tibi semper et ubique gratias agere*—"that we should at all times and in all places give thanks to you."

and praise to you . . ." Such may not seem all that significant until we compare the similar shift in the language of the anamnesis in the eucharistic prayer taken from *Apostolic Tradition* IV, which appears in ELW as Eucharistic Prayer XI, and which appeared in LBW, but *only* in the altar edition, as Eucharistic Prayer IV. The anamnesis of this version reads:

> Remembering, then, his death and resurrection, *we lift this bread and cup* before you (*offerimus tibi panem et calicem*), giving you thanks that you have made us worthy to stand before you and to serve you as your priestly people.[62]

The *Declaration on the Way* refers to the distinction often made between what it calls a "traditional contrast" in the Eucharist between *ad Patrem* (to the Father) as the Roman Catholic approach and *ad populum* (to the people) as the Lutheran emphasis.[63] But LBW Eucharistic Prayer IV in the anamnesis is clearly *ad Patrem*, in spite of the fact that the offering verb (*offerimus*) is changed to "we lift," giving rise in some contexts even to rubrical suggestions that the Bread and Cup were actually to be lifted up here at the anamnesis rather than during the concluding doxology. The change from the original Latin's "we offer" to "we lift" was criticized strongly by Paul Marshall in 1980:

> The least satisfying aspect of this translation is the treatment of the anamnesis-oblation. The textual evidence is unanimous for *Offerimus tibi panem et calicem* here rendered "we lift this bread and cup before you." . . . This apparent avoidance of directly sacrificial language raises the question of just what the LBW drafters would consider appropriate language of sacrifice. . . . The alteration of an historic text may be the occasion for those responsible for LBW to ask themselves whether they are not indicating their own difference from the classic tradition.[64]

But if this raised a question about "appropriate language of sacrifice" for the LBW drafters, the more radical revision of this anamnesis in ELW clearly represents a further departure from the classic tradition. If

---

62. LBW, Minister's Edition, 226.
63. *Declaration on the Way*, 63.
64. Paul V. Marshall, "The Eucharistic Rite of the Lutheran Book of Worship," *Worship* 54, no. 3 (1980): 246–56, here at 255–56.

the LBW version could, at least, be considered ambiguous and kept the *ad Patrem* orientation, ELW is squarely in the tradition of *ad populum*:

> Remembering, then, his death and resurrection, *we take this bread and cup,* giving you thanks that you have made us worthy to stand before you and to serve you as your priestly people.[65]

The traditional Lutheran reluctance to speak any eucharistic offering verb characterizes ELW, which has moved further away from all offering language whatsoever except for the rite still called "Offering" before the eucharistic prayer, something that the Roman Rite since 1969 has called the "Preparation of the Gifts," *not* the offering or offertory. Here I can only direct the attention of Lutherans back to a statement made by Gail Ramshaw at the conclusion of her survey of the Eucharistic Prayers in LBW several years ago:

> One criticism must be directed especially at Lutherans. Granting the agreements reached in the Lutheran–Roman Catholic dialogues on the eucharist, and granting current scholarship on the metaphoric use of the word "sacrifice" in the Christian tradition, it is no longer defensible for Lutherans to continue their eccentric refusal to speak the language of offering and sacrifice in the eucharist. Merely repeating late medieval quarrels, which surfaced in a far different situation than our own and were carried on in Latin and European languages, keeps Lutheranism in a linguistic warp and turns the Lutheran movement in the church catholic into an anachronistic sect. Such fundamentalistic interpretation of religious language does not commend the descendants of Luther, who ought to know a good deal about the riches of Christological metaphor.[66]

Conclusion

My argument in the foregoing has been rather simple. While some Lutherans today may indeed "continue to regard the language of sacrifice found in Catholic theology and the Catholic Eucharistic rite to be a potential stumbling block to unity," my thesis is that, properly understood, the

---

65. ELW, Leader's Edition, 293.
66. Ramshaw, "Toward Lutheran Eucharistic Prayers," in *New Eucharistic Prayers*, ed. Senn, 77–78.

Roman *Canon missae* should not be seen as constituting this stumbling block. The sacrificial-offering language of the Roman Canon is patristic, even ante-Nicene, in its emphasis, evoking the language of Malachi, the *Strasbourg Papyrus*, Tertullian, and Irenaeus of Lyons, and, if the language of offering in the "Greek canon" is acceptable, then the Roman Canon should be deemed acceptable as well. They both belong to a similar world of thought, though the Greek canon is more Antiochene in structure and theology and the Roman Canon is more Alexandrian.

Please note, I am not advocating for the use of the Roman *Canon Missae* among Roman Catholics, Anglo-Catholics, or anyone else. I am not even saying that it is a *good* or model eucharistic prayer for the church today, since several elements we would want to see included in eucharistic praying are missing (e.g., a more pronounced sense of thanksgiving, epiclesis, and eschatology), elements that are present in other available prayers. And I would never advocate for the current translation. Nor am I saying that "sacrifice" is even the best metaphor to use in describing the Eucharist or redemption in Christ, though it is clearly a word belonging to the Scriptures and the classic Christian tradition. All I am saying is that on this *one* issue there is no need to reject the Roman *Canon Missae* outright. Whatever theologies of eucharistic sacrifice may have been or continue to be imposed on that text is a different issue. But at the level of the liturgical text itself, one must be very cautious. Equally problematic here, as I have argued above, is the theology of consecration also imposed on the liturgical text from elsewhere, centered on the narrative of institution as the "moment" of that consecration, which then suggests that whatever happens after that "consecration" takes place with Christ's Body and Blood. But since similar offering language follows that narrative also in the "Greek canon," why is one tradition acceptable to the Lutheran tradition (the Greek) and the other not (Roman), even when the Byzantine version of St. Basil has no qualms in referring to the bread and cup having been offered or set before God (aorist tense) as "antitypes" or "likenesses" of Christ's Body and Blood?[67]

Finally, eucharistic sacrifice may remain an ecumenical issue for Lutherans and Roman Catholics, perhaps even a stumbling block. But I

---

67. Paul Bradshaw and Maxwell Johnson, eds., *Prayers of the Eucharist: Early and Reformed*, 4th ed. (Collegeville, MN: Liturgical Press, 2019), 119.

would like to suggest that with a classic patristic text like the Roman *Canon Missae*, older even than the "Greek canon," this is not an issue at the level of liturgical language, which, as Taft says, "is metaphorical and evocative, not philosophical and ontological." What makes it an issue has been our now overcome medieval inheritance of separating, in the words of Nathan Mitchell, "'sacrifice' from 'sacrament,'" and "'consecration' from the church's 'offering' and communion." Long before *From Conflict to Communion*, Regin Prenter from within the Danish Lutheran tradition underscored the unity of "consecration," sacrifice, and communion, arguing that for Lutherans the liturgical recovery of the language of eucharistic sacrifice would actually affirm both salvation by "grace alone" and through "faith alone."

> In the Holy Eucharist Christ is present as our High Priest in a peculiar manner. He is present . . . bodily, in his sacrificed body and blood, sacramentally present under bread and wine. Through the real sacramental presence . . . he unites us with himself as the Priest and victim. He takes us into his own sacrifice. Sitting at his table and receiving his body and blood we are, so to speak, not only behind him, when he enters the heavenly sanctuary with our prayers and thanksgivings, but we are with him, nay in him, because [he] is with us. Thus we offer Christ to God, imploring him, giving him occasion and moving him to offer himself for us and us with himself in the Eucharistic meal, while he through his body and blood under bread and wine communicates with us.[68]

And:

> Through this sacrifice of thanksgiving we plead His one perfect atoning sacrifice in order to assert our right to appear before God. In so doing we offer bread and wine to God in remembrance of Christ. If we thank God for the sacrifice, offered by Christ on Calvary for our sins, we thereby confess that we have no right whatsoever to appear before God in our own righteousness, but only in the righteousness of Jesus Christ, our only high priest and mediator. Thus our self-sacrifice in Jesus Christ implies that we abandon any righteousness of our own. . . . The Eucharistic sacrifice . . . then, is the liturgical expression of the "sola fide"

---

68. Regin Prenter, "Eucharistic Sacrifice according to the Lutheran Tradition," *Theology* 67, no. 529 (1964): 286–95, here at 290.

corresponding to the Eucharistic sacrament as the liturgical expression of the "sola gratia."[69]

Lutherans need no longer be allergic to eucharistic sacrifice and offering language in the Roman *Canon Missae*. In fact, the challenge remains for contemporary Lutherans as to whether they are able to embrace the classic catholic liturgical tradition of both East and West and cease living in what Gail Ramshaw referred to as "a linguistic warp [that] turns the Lutheran movement in the church catholic into an anachronistic sect." In spite of many good liturgical developments, we Lutherans have not been able to do that so far. And it is not without significance in this context that in the evolution of eucharistic praying our earliest anaphoral sources (e.g., *Didache*, *Strasbourg Papyrus*, Addai and Mari, and the prayer of Polycarp) contain offering and sacrificial language but no narrative of institution.[70] The offering of the eucharistic sacrifice, however that sacrifice may be conceived or interpreted, along with praise and intercession, appears, then, as a constituent element in the eucharistic praying of the church from its earliest days. As such, the burden of proof, as I heard Jaroslav Pelikan once say, is always on those who deny or reject it.

---

69. Regin Prenter, "A Lutheran Doctrine of Eucharistic Sacrifice?," *Studia Theologica* 19 (1965): 189–99, here at 195–97.

70. See my "Martyrs and the Mass: The Interpolation of the Narrative of Institution into the Anaphora," *Worship* 87, no. 1 (2013): 2–22.

Acknowledgments

Thanks are due to the following for permission to include copyrighted materials in this volume:

The editors of *Ex Fontes* for select portions of "The Barcelona Papyrus and the Opening Dialogue of the Christian Anaphora: Resituating Egyptian Scribal Practices Amid Scholarly Anaphoral Reconstructions," in *Ex Fonte–Journal of Ecumenical Studies in Liturgy* 1 (2022): 129–68.

The editors of *Ecclesia Orans* for reprinting Maxwell E. Johnson, "Recent Thoughts on the Roman Anaphora: Sacrifice in the *Canon Missae*," *Ecclesia Orans* 35 (2018): 217–51.

Liturgical Press for permission to reproduce eucharistic prayer texts in English translation from R. C. D. Jasper and G. J. Cuming, *Prayers of the Eucharist: Early and Reformed*, 4th edition, ed. Paul F. Bradshaw and Maxwell E. Johnson, Alcuin Club Collections 94 (Collegeville, MN: Liturgical Press, 2019).

Contributors

Julia Canonico, a Roman Catholic, holds a master of theological studies (liturgy) from the University of Notre Dame, Notre Dame, IN, where she is a doctoral candidate in liturgical studies.

Nathan P. Chase, a Roman Catholic, is assistant professor of liturgical and sacramental theology at Aquinas Institute of Theology, St. Louis, MO, and holds a PhD in liturgical studies from the University of Notre Dame, Notre Dame, IN.

Lucas Lynn Christensen, a priest of the Greek Orthodox Archdiocese of America (Ecumenical Patriarchate), is a doctoral candidate in liturgical studies, department of theology, University of Notre Dame, Notre Dame, IN.

Megan Effron, a Roman Catholic, holds a master of divinity from the department of theology, University of Notre Dame, Notre Dame, IN, where she is a doctoral student in systematic theology.

Paul J. Elhallal, a Maronite Catholic, holds a master of theological studies (liturgy) from the department of theology, University of Notre Dame, Notre Dame, IN, where he is a doctoral student in liturgical studies.

Andrij Hlabse, SJ, a Ukrainian Greek-Catholic priest, holds a licentiate from the Pontifical Oriental Institute, Rome, Italy, and is a doctoral student in the department of theology, University of Notre Dame, Notre Dame, IN, specializing in patristics and East-West church relations.

Maxwell E. Johnson is professor emeritus of theology (liturgical studies) in the department of theology, University of Notre Dame, Notre Dame, IN, from which he holds a PhD in liturgical studies.

Joachim Chukwuebuka Ozonze, a Roman Catholic priest of the Diocese of Nnewi, Nigeria, holds a master of theological studies (liturgy) from the University of Notre Dame, Notre Dame, IN, where he is a doctoral student in liturgical studies and peace studies.

Arsany Paul, a monk of St. Paul's Coptic Orthodox Abbey, Murrieta, CA, holds a master of theological studies (liturgy) from the department of theology, University of Notre Dame, Notre Dame, IN, where he is a doctoral student in liturgical studies.

Index

A

Addai and Mari, Anaphora of (A&M), ix, 25, 85, 91, 103, 109, 113, 140, 142, 175, 193, 289

Aksumite, xiii, 40, 43, 47, 172, 176–179, 181–83, 185–86, 188, 190, 193, 199

Alexandria(n), xii, xiii, 62, 136, 147, 151, 176, 179, 180, 181, 182, 184, 188–90, 195, 197, 199, 256, 260, 294

Ambrose of Milan, 25, 39, 256, 295

Anamnesis, 7, 9, 23, 41, 58, 60, 69, 88, 90, 94–96, 109, 121–30, 135, 138, 143, 149, 194, 213, 237, 298, 301

Antony, Monastery of, 81

Apostles, Anaphora of the Twelve (AP), xiii, 50, 150, 172, 178

Apostles (Ethiopian), Anaphora of the (EAA), ix, xiii, 43, 171, 176, 179, 181, 194, 201

Apostolic Constitutions (AC), 99, 174

Apostolic Tradition (ApTrad, AT), xii, xiii, 24, 26, 27, 30, 35, 37, 45, 50, 140, 142, 171, 173, 181, 197, 295

Armenian, 42, 131, 162

Arsenius, St., 81

Assyrian Church of the East, 99

Athanasius, 36, 169, 195

B

Barcelona papyrus (BARC), ix, x, xi, 26, 37, 39, 43, 47, 58, 61, 64, 65, 72, 76, 81, 83, 140, 144, 145, 146, 147, 148, 151

Basil (the Great) of Caesarea, Anaphora(s) of (BAS), ix, xii, xiv, 49, 62, 82, 131, 138, 148, 151, 154, 161, 167, 204, 298, 302

Benedictus (qui venit), 137, 189

Birkat ha-mazon, 86, 87, 89, 90, 97, 98, 100, 102, 104, 106, 109, 110, 128, 175

Bloodless, 40, 133, 138, 142–43, 145, 149–50, 163–64, 298

Bouley, Allan, xv, 138

Bradshaw, Paul, ix, xii, 32, 34, 51, 57, 86, 173, 174, 178, 180, 181, 184, 192, 198

British Museum Tablet, 58, 180

Brock, Sebastian, 42

Budde, Achim, 47

Byzantine, xii, 151, 153, 155, 297

C

Canon missae, xiii, xiv, 231, 287, 290, 293, 296, 299

Canons of Hippolytus (CH), 143, 174

Chrysostom, John, Anaphora/Liturgy of St., xiv, 50, 137, 144, 150, 298

Church of the East, 99
Consecration, 97, 222, 228, 239, 252, 277, 289, 291, 296, 297
Constantinople, 150, 153, 197
Coptic, 41, 65, 79, 80, 82, 136, 143, 145, 149
Corinthians, First, x, 8, 9, 11, 13, 17, 19, 73
Cuming, Geoffrey, 44, 48, 50, 51, 137, 138, 141, 144, 147, 148
Cyril, Anaphora of St., 41, 136, 138, 145, 146, 147
Cyril of Jerusalem, ix, xii, 25, 131, 135, 136, 138, 141, 144, 150

D

Day, Juliette, 51, 52, 53, 135, 139, 141, 143, 144
De sacramentis, 256, 295
Deir Balyzeh Papyrus (DB), 46, 144
Didache, x, 8, 13, 15, 20, 27, 29, 46, 87, 90, 97, 98, 102, 103, 105, 110, 112, 128, 140, 175
Didascalia Apostolorum, 30
Dix, Gregory, 135, 136, 137, 141, 148, 295

E

East Syria(n), ix, xi, xii, 26, 33, 36, 85, 95, 96, 99, 121, 125, 128, 256, 260
Egypt(ian), xi, xii, 25, 34, 39, 41, 45–46, 47, 62, 64, 72, 77, 79–80, 82, 131, 136–37, 141, 143–44, 147, 150–51, 171, 174, 177, 195, 198, 294
Engberding, Hieronymus, 96, 108, 127
Epiclesis/epiclesis, x, 23, 26–27, 38–42, 44, 48, 56, 60, 63, 87, 94–97, 100, 121, 125, 127, 129, 132, 135, 137, 138, 142, 144, 146, 149–50, 180–81, 194, 196, 214, 221, 294, 297
Ethiopia(n), 40, 47, 172–73, 176–77, 179, 182, 188, 192–93, 197, 198, 201
Eucholog(y/ion), 47, 65, 99, 155, 178, 181, 260, 290

F

Fenwick, John R.K., 131, 141–43, 147–49
Fritsch, Emmanuel, xiii, 176–78, 181, 183, 188, 192, 195, 197, 199

G

Gehanta, 86, 110, 112, 127
Gelston, Anthony, 85, 86, 87, 95, 108, 110, 112, 127
Gregory the Great, 218, 280, 291

H

Heaven, 19, 39, 40–41, 58, 67–68, 76, 91–93, 113–15, 119, 125, 127, 132, 142, 145–46, 180, 184, 186, 188, 189, 194, 202, 204–9, 211, 222, 244, 246–48, 252, 275, 291, 301
Hippolytus, 171, 173, 174, 175, 295

I

Institution Narrative, x, 11, 13, 19, 21, 23, 25, 26, 38, 41, 49, 55, 57–58, 60, 68, 90, 94, 96, 121–30, 135–43, 146, 148–50, 181, 186, 189, 192, 198, 222, 277, 288–89, 294, 301–2
Intercession(s), 23, 26, 40, 41, 43, 55, 81, 95, 96, 117, 127, 129, 133,

134, 135, 138, 142, 143, 145, 147, 150, 180, 181, 184, 185, 186, 187, 192, 198, 202, 221, 300
Irenaeus of Lyons, 39, 175, 300
Isho'yahb I, 99, 112, 128

J

James, Anaphora/Liturgy of St. (JAS), xi, 44, 49, 131, 132, 135, 138, 139, 140, 141, 142, 148, 150, 151, 203, 232, 242, 267
Jerusalem, xii, 45, 99, 101, 111, 136, 137, 138, 139, 142, 147, 150, 151, 155, 203, 275
John, Gospel of, 11, 94, 121, 122, 166
Johnson, Maxwell E., 32, 44, 174, 180, 181, 260, 284, 300
Justin Martyr, 31, 39, 56, 175

K

Kretschmar, Georg, 136

L

Last Supper, 1, 8, 10, 12, 14, 16, 18, 19, 21, 27, 35, 58, 68, 136, 158, 191, 192, 193, 194, 223, 244, 284, 294, 297
Leaven, 159
Louvain Coptic Papyrus, 65, 144, 149
Luke, Gospel of, 12, 158, 203

M

Mark, Gospel of, 10, 12, 19
Mark, Anaphora of St., xiii, 24, 39, 40, 41, 44, 45, 47, 48, 50, 58, 136, 138, 143, 145, 172, 179, 181–84, 186–90, 192–99, 256, 260, 300; see also Cyril, Anaphora of St.

Maronite, ix, xi, 85, 88, 97, 128, 130
Martyr(s), martyrdom, 54, 55, 60, 93, 101, 104, 134, 203, 242, 291
Mazza, Enrico, 175, 219, 253, 254, 276, 291, 300, 302
McGowan, Andrew, 31
Meßner, Richard, 33
Mystagogical Catecheses (MC), ix, xii, 25, 39, 40, 44, 45, 49, 131–52
Mystery, 22, 93, 95, 126, 219, 222, 227, 233, 245, 279, 281, 284, 292

N

Nestorius, Anaphora of, 95, 96, 121, 128, 129

O

Oblation, xii, 68, 93, 117, 118, 119, 122, 124–25, 129–30, 138, 142–45, 149, 155, 164, 166, 167–69, 194–95, 199–201, 221, 233, 243, 268, 289, 291, 294, 296, 297, 300
Offering, xii, 13, 16–17, 40–41, 62, 89, 91, 113, 121, 132, 134, 138, 144–50, 155–58, 160, 162–69, 183, 191, 194–95, 198, 221, 231, 233–34, 237, 240, 243, 246, 252–53, 274, 276, 286–89, 294, 296–302
Origen of Alexandria, 136

P

Paul, St., x, 4, 8, 9, 10, 11, 13, 14, 15, 17, 163–64, 169, 242, 267, 273, 295, 298–99
Pneumatological (Holy Spirit), 27, 40, 41, 56, 69, 93, 145–46, 149, 169, 180, 184, 192–97, 204, 222, 223, 294, 295, 299

Post-*sanctus*, 41, 56, 68, 142–45, 180, 181, 186–87, 192, 198
Praise, 14, 16, 67, 91–93, 101, 103–4, 106, 108–10, 113, 132, 135, 142, 147, 156, 159, 162, 168, 189, 195–97, 209, 214, 232–33, 236, 240–41, 244, 253, 276, 294, 299–300
Pre-*sanctus*, 40, 67, 142–143, 181, 188
Preface, 38–41, 56, 67, 94, 132, 142–143, 147–48, 150, 180–81, 218, 223, 290, 293
Prosphora, 300

R
Ray, Walter D., xi, 89–91, 93–94, 96, 98, 106, 121, 126
Roca-Puig, R., 62, 72–73
Roman Canon (RC), ix, xiii, xiv, 25, 217–24, 228, 230, 236, 240, 249, 252–54, 255–56, 260, 274, 276, 279–80, 284, 287–88, 290–92, 294–96, 299–302
Rome, 15, 34, 171, 174, 280–82, 291, 294, 295, 299

S
Sacred, 7, 71, 78, 163, 217–19, 228, 234, 236, 238, 244, 247, 252, 254, 256, 257, 260, 261, 291–93
Sacrifice, xii, xiv, 1, 14, 16, 55, 57, 133–34, 137–38, 142–43, 145, 149, 153–69, 192–93, 219, 221, 232, 234, 237, 240–41, 246–47, 252–53, 265, 274–76, 287–90, 293–94, 296, 297–302
Saint, 55, 81, 119, 180, 203, 210, 223, 228, 232, 235, 237, 239, 242–43, 248, 252, 274, 291–93, 299
Sanctus, x, 23, 24, 27, 38–39, 42, 48–49, 68, 87, 94, 96–97, 110, 129, 132, 135, 136, 137, 138, 142–44, 147–50, 176, 181, 184, 187–92, 198, 208, 221, 229, 290, 293
Sarapion of Thmuis (SAR), 46–47, 51, 136, 140, 142–43, 145–47, 149, 151, 180, 189, 195
Sharar, ix, xi, xii, 49, 85, 87–90, 98, 112, 121–30
Spinks, Bryan D., 44, 86, 126–27, 136, 144, 148
Strasbourg Papyrus, 48, 138, 140, 144, 175, 260, 294, 300
Suryān, Monastery of, 80
Syria(c/n), ix, xi, xii, 31, 39, 42, 50, 111, 126, 139, 147, 150–51, 154, 189

T
Taft, Robert F., 57, 87, 142, 150, 167, 168, 295, 297
Testamentum Domini (TD), 24, 26, 45, 174
Thanksgiving, x, 7, 13–15, 18, 66, 67, 70, 74, 93–94, 101–4, 106, 108, 124, 138, 149, 159, 175, 181, 183–84, 186, 192–93, 197–98, 202, 231, 240, 276, 289, 294, 298–99
Theodore of Mopsuestia, Anaphora of, 25, 39, 121, 137, 256, 260

W
West Syrian, 130

Winkler, Gabriele, 131, 140, 141, 189
Worship, x, 2–3, 7–8, 40, 52, 54, 87, 113, 117, 133, 138, 145, 150, 154–56, 160–61, 164, 165, 167–68, 198, 225, 231, 238, 251, 253–54, 257, 260, 263, 265, 275–80, 283, 286, 288, 290, 295, 299, 300, 302

Z

Zheltov, Michael, xi, 62, 66, 72–74, 147–48

Milton Keynes UK
Ingram Content Group UK Ltd.
UKHW020637300424
441953UK00010B/131